Dialogue Interpreting

C000109060

Routledge Interpreting Guides cover the key settings or domains of interpreting and equip trainee interpreters and students of interpreting with the skills needed in each area of the field. Concise, accessible and written by leading authorities, they include examples from existing interpreting practice, activities, further reading suggestions and a glossary of key terms.

Drawing on recent peer-reviewed research in interpreting studies and related disciplines, *Dialogue Interpreting* helps practising interpreters, students and instructors of interpreting to navigate their way through what is fast becoming the very expansive field of dialogue interpreting in more traditional domains, such as legal and medical, and in areas where new needs of language brokerage are only beginning to be identified, such as asylum, education, social care and faith.

Innovative in its approach, this guide places emphasis on collaborative dimensions in the wider institutional and organizational setting in each of the domains covered, and on understanding services in the context of local communities. The authors propose solutions to real-life problems based on knowledge of domain-specific practices and protocols, as well as inviting discussion on existing standards of practice for interpreters. Key features include:

- contextualized examples and case studies reinforced by voices from the field, such as the views of managers of language services and the publications of professional associations. These allow readers to evaluate appropriate responses in relation to their particular geonational contexts of practice and personal experience;
- activities to support the structured development of research skills, interpreter performance and team-work. These can be used either in-class or as self-guided or collaborative learning and are supplemented by materials on the Translation Studies Portal;
- a glossary of key terms and pointers to resources for further development.

Dialogue Interpreting is an essential guide for practising interpreters and for all students of interpreting within advanced undergraduate and postgraduate/graduate programmes in Translation and Interpreting Studies, Modern Languages, Applied Linguistics and Intercultural Communication.

Rebecca Tipton is a Lecturer in Interpreting and Translation Studies at the University of Manchester, UK. Her publications include an entry on trust in interpreting in the *Routledge Encyclopaedia of Interpreting Studies* (Routledge, 2015).

Olgierda Furmanek is an Associate Professor and a Founding Director of a graduate programme in Interpreting and Translation Studies at Wake Forest University, North Carolina, USA. Her publications include *Emotions and Language Choices in Multilingual Discourse* (2005).

Dialogue Interpreting

A guide to interpreting in public services and the community

Rebecca Tipton and Olgierda Furmanek

Routledge
Taylor & Francis Group

LONDON AND NEW YORK

First published 2016
by Routledge
2 Park Square, Milton Park, Abingdon, Oxon OX14 4RN

and by Routledge
711 Third Avenue, New York, NY 10017

Routledge is an imprint of the Taylor & Francis Group, an informa business

British Library Cataloguing-in-Publication Data
A catalogue record for this book is available from the British Library

Library of Congress Cataloging-in-Publication Data
A catalog record for this book has been requested

ISBN: 978-1-138-78460-4 (hbk)
ISBN: 978-1-138-78462-8 (pbk)
ISBN: 978-1-315-64457-8 (ebk)

Typeset in Minion
by Wearset Ltd, Boldon, Tyne and Wear

The basic point about emancipatory translation is that trainees are of course taught translation norms, but they themselves are responsible for deciding how they will react to these norms.

Andrew Chesterman

Contents

Illustrations

Figures

Tables

Acknowledgements

We offer sincere thanks to our colleagues and friends who have provided helpful comments and insights throughout the process, in particular:

- Sally Barbour, Candelas Gala and Luis Gonzalez of the Department of Romance Languages, Wake Forest University, USA; Fabrizio Gallai, Dipartimento di Lingue, Letterature e Culture Moderne, University of Bologna, Italy (Introduction and general aspects);
- Maeve Olohan, Centre for Translation and Intercultural Studies (CTIS), University of Manchester, UK; Danielle D'Hayer, PSIT Network Group, London Metropolitan University, UK (Chapter 1);
- Luis Pérez-González, CTIS University of Manchester, UK; Jérôme Devaux, School of Humanities, Languages and Social Sciences, University of Salford, UK; Chiu-Yi O'Hagan, Court Interpreter, UK (Chapter 2);
- Kirsten Coope, CTIS University of Manchester, UK; Svetlana Carsten, Project Task Leader for Online Resources in Conference Interpreter Training, Vilnius University, Lithuania (Chapter 3);
- Linda Batiz Dorton, Manager of Language Services, Baptist Medical Center, Winston-Salem, NC, USA; Mireya Vera, Director of Interpreter Services and Community Relations, Holy Cross Hospital, Chicago, IL, USA (Chapter 4);
- Fran Hernandez-Herbert, Supervisor, Exceptional Student Services, Colorado Department of Education, USA; Mireya Vera, Director of Interpreter Services and Community Relations, Holy Cross Hospital, Chicago, IL, USA; Ana Soler, Medical and Educational Interpreting Curriculum Developer, Language Services Administrator, Gwinnett County Public Schools, GA, USA; Astrid Dinneen, Ethnic Minority and Traveller Achievement Service, Hampshire County Council, UK (Chapter 5);
- Anna Strowe, CTIS University of Manchester, UK; Clarisa Carvalho, Freedom from Torture, London, UK (Chapter 6);
- Fr Sergiusz Bałdyga, OFM, PhD, Vice-General Secretary for Formation and Studies of the Franciscan Order, Rome, Italy; Jonathan Downie, Interpreter and PhD Candidate, Heriot-Watt University, UK (Chapter 7);

- Stephanie Pellet and Edyta Oczkowicz, professors at Wake Forest University and Salem College, NC, USA, respectively, for their invaluable comments on the content and structure of the activities.

We are also grateful to:

- Brian Harris for his encouragement to focus on the emerging areas of dialogue interpreting;
- Cecilia Wadensjö, Kelly Washbourne and Christian Degueldre for their thorough reviews of the manuscript;
- Louisa Semlyen and Laura Sandford at Routledge for commissioning and assisting with the project;
- Amanda Tingley, our Student Research Assistant, Carol Cramer, our Librarian Specialist and Cyndy Brown for her editorial assistance;
- Carlos A. Fasola for carefully reading the proofs;
- our students for feedback on activities; and
- our families for their unstinting support throughout.

Permissions

The authors and publishers would like to thank the following for permission to reprint material:

Elsevier for permission to reproduce material from Brisset, C., Leanza, Y. and Laforest, K. (2013) 'Working with Interpreters in Health Care: a systematic review and meta-ethnography of qualitative studies', *Patient Education and Counseling*, 91 (2): 131–40.

Fabrizio Gallai for permission to reproduce a text extract from Gallai, F. (2013) 'Discourse Markers in Interpreter-Mediated Police Interviews: an interdisciplinary approach', unpublished PhD thesis, University of Salford.

inTRAlinea for permission to use some extracts from Vargas-Urpi, M. and Arumí Ribas, M. (2014) 'Estrategias de interpretación en los servicios públicos en el ámbito educativo', *inTRAlinea*, 16. URL: www.intralinea. org/archive/article/2040.

John Wiley and Sons for permission to reproduce a text extract from Davidson, B. (2002) 'The Interpreter as Institutional Gatekeeper: the sociallinguistic role of interpreters in Spanish-English medical discourse', *Journal of Sociolinguistics*, 4 (3): 379–405.

María Isabel Abril Martí for permission to reproduce material (translated by Monica Weber) from 'La Interpretación en los Servicios Públicos: caracterización como género, contextualización modelos de formación. Hacia unas bases para el diseño curricular', unpublished PhD thesis, University of Granada.

McGraw Hill Education, Open University Press for permission to adapt an extract from Parris, M. (2012) *An Introduction to Social Work Practice: a practical handbook*, Maidenhead: McGraw Hill, Open University Press.

Metropolitan Police, London, UK for permission to reproduce the interpreter's introductory statement.

FITSPos International Journal and Uldis Ozolins for permission to reproduce a table from Ozolins, U. (2014) 'Descriptions of Interpreting and their Ethical Consequences', *FITISPos International Journal of Public Service Interpreting and Translation*, 1 (1). Reprinted with permission of the editor.

Dina Refki for permission to reproduce material from Refki, D., Avery, M.P. and Dalton, A. (2013) 'Core Competencies for Healthcare Interpreters', *The International Journal of Humanities and Social Science*, 3 (2): 72–83.

Right to Remain, UK for permission to reproduce material from their website.

The Sector Skills Council, UK for permission to reproduce the table on social worker roles and standards.

We are grateful to UTSePress for permission to reprint some of the material included in Ikuko Nakane, 'The Myth of an "Invisible Mediator": an Australian case study of English–Japanese police interpreting', *The Space Between: languages, translations and cultures*, Special Issue guest-edited by Vera Mackie, Ikuko Nakane and Emi Otsuji (2009), *PORTAL Journal of Multidisciplinary International Studies*, 6 (1), DOI: http://dx.doi.org/10.5130/portal.v6i1.825 [http://epress.lib.uts.edu.au/journals/index.php/portal/article/view/825].

Every effort has been made to contact copyright-holders. Please advise the publisher of any errors or omissions, and these will be corrected in subsequent editions.

Abbreviations

AIIC	Association internationale des interprètes de conférence
ASL	American Sign Language
BSL	British Sign Language
CLAS	Culturally and Linguistically Appropriate Services
CLD	Culturally and/or Linguistically Diverse
CoP	Community of Practice
CPD	Continuing Professional Development
EAL	English as an Additional Language
ELL	English Language Learner
IEP	Individual Education Program
ILO	Intended Learning Outcome
LEP	Limited English Proficiency
LFP	Limited French Proficiency
LLP	Limited Language Proficiency
LPS	Limited Proficiency Speaker
PDP	Professional Development Planning
PSIT	Public Service Interpreting and Translation
RCO	Refugee Community Organization
RSMI	Remote Simultaneous Medical Interpreting
SWOT	Strengths Weaknesses Opportunities Threats
VCI	Video-Conference Interpreting
VCMI	Video-Conference Medical Interpreting

Introduction

1 Scope and purpose of this guide

Until recently the idea of carving out a full-time career as a dialogue inter-preter and translator in community-based organizations and state-run statu-tory services would have appeared unrealistic in many countries. However, the demand for public service interpreting and translation (PSIT) across the globe has steadily risen in recent decades and continues to do so,[1] leading to employment opportunities at the front line of interpreting and in the related activities of service organization, education, policy making, research and technologies development. Individuals attracted to work in these fields are commonly united by a belief that access to human services for limited-proficiency speakers through appropriately managed, professional trans-lation and interpreting services, forms part of a socially enlightened and ethically responsible approach to the complexities of migration. This includes an appropriate response to and understanding of the needs of users of lin-guistic and cultural services, be it linguistic minority populations, institu-tions or organizations.

The introduction of legislation such as the European Directive 2010/64/ EU on the Right to Interpreting and Translation in Criminal Proceedings and the publication of the document *Integrating Immigrant Children into Schools in Europe* (Eurydice Network 2009) are indicative of shifts toward understanding PSIT in rights-based terms. Such shifts are helping to consoli-date the professional status of PSIT together with increased evidence-based policy making, especially in the healthcare sector where timely provision has been found to contribute to better patient outcomes and reduced readmis-sion rates (Lindholm *et al.* 2012).

Whether interpreters are employed on a full- or part-time basis, as free-lancers or staff, an ongoing commitment to education and professional development forms the basis of reliable and quality services. This guide has been designed to support advanced students of interpreting and early-career interpreters in independently structuring their professional growth in core, developmental and domain-specific competencies of spoken language inter-preting and career planning in relation to a wide range of settings. Although the focus is on spoken language interpreting, written translation is discussed in a limited way where appropriate. The guide is intended as an accompaniment to and not a replacement for interpreter education; knowledge of basic interpreting modes, skills and preparation techniques is assumed from the outset.

Drawing on peer-reviewed research in translation and interpreting studies and other disciplines, the guide illuminates connections between research and education in order to support a structured approach to reflection – on practice (following Schön 1983) and professional development. In particular, it recognizes that although university-level programmes are now available in many countries, interpreter education is delivered by a wide range of providers and practising interpreters, not all of whom have access to the breadth of empirical research that has been carried out to date.

The approach is descriptive and designed to help interpreters reflect on their own practice as related to each specific institutional and/or community setting. Readers should be aware that key concepts have been shaped by different theoretical traditions and that the presented findings come from a range of methodological approaches, which are beyond the scope of this guide to discuss. Where appropriate, readers should refer to the recommended reading provided at the end of each chapter for further insight. Discussions are also supported by voices from the field through sources such as the publications of professional associations and practitioners' blogs.

The guide is underpinned by the principles of:

- **Holism**
  The idea that professional development entails more than a focus on language and discrete interpreting skills, and needs to take account of the wider context of practice, expectations of interlocutors, professional ethics and institutional, domain-specific and lay language use.
- **Reflection**
  The idea that professional and personal development is best achieved through an approach to the evaluation of the personal and professional self in all its complexity in a structured manner and on a regular basis.
- **Active professional engagement and exchange**
  The idea that professional development combines dedicated independent learning and a commitment to engage with and learn from peer interpreters and other professionals in the workplace.

2 Dialogue interpreting: terminology and taxonomy

The terminology used to refer to interpreting that takes place in public services and in community-based organizations has been in constant flux, leading to a mishmash that appears to defy resolution. Some may view these terminological complexities and meanderings as redundant, others as enriching, still others as simply an inconsistency impossible to avoid in a rapidly growing and changing field. It is well known that terminology continuously evolves as it is tried and tested, and moves in and out of different contexts. Since scholarly interest in the field of non-conference, non-business and non-diplomatic interpreting first emerged in the 1980s the following terms have appeared in ways that sometimes overlap or contradict: ad hoc *interpreting, community interpreting, public service interpreting, dialogue interpreting, liaison interpreting, bilateral interpreting, triad interpreting, discourse interpreting, cultural interpreting, intercultural interpreting* and *intrasocietal interpreting*. It is important to note, however, that defining and naming concepts should not happen in isolation from particular contexts where practices described by those names are used or not used. For example, the terms *interlinguistic medical mediator* in Spain and *bilingual patient navigator* (e.g. Simon *et al.* 2015) in the United States may mean the same thing.

As services have developed, scholars have started to examine the nature of response to multilingual interpreting needs around the world, which has influenced the debate on terminology and taxonomy. Researchers such as Abril Martí (2006), Toledano Buendía (2010) and Ozolins (2010), for example, have started to situate linguistic and cultural liaisoning, its normative systems and terminological variations in specific national or regional contexts. Although studies have tended to focus on Western contexts, the rise of indigenous/native interpreting in Latin America (Mexico, Chile, Argentina) and Asia is broadening the debate further. For example, language brokering needs that were limited in the past to business and diplomacy in South Korea and Malaysia have begun to take on new dimensions in the second decade of this century as migration patterns changed (see Ra and Napier 2013).

With regard to specific developments in terminology, Mason asserts that the labels applied to interpreting activity refer 'to slightly differing aspects of the process and are preferred according to the professional orientation of those involved' (2000: 215). Echoing this assertion, a more recent work by Ozolins offers a thorough study of terminological issues from an ethical perspective, intending to 'reveal some altogether clear distinctions that can help our understanding of differentiating and common elements in interpreting' (2014: 23). As summarized in Table I.1 below, which covers different forms of interpreting, 'the ethical implications of different descriptions are categorized to show that **ethical responsibility** in interpreting situations rests not with the interpreters alone, but with other players, particularly institutional players, in contracting language services' (ibid., emphasis in original).

It is worth noting that in some English-speaking contexts professionalization has led to a preference for the term *public service interpreting and translation*. This preference is in part a response to the negative connotations sometimes associated with the term *community*, namely amateurism, difference and hierarchy, and the risk that the term reinforces the notion that minority-speaking groups are marginalized in relation to the receiving society (see Edwards *et al.* 2006). In other national contexts, historical,

Table I.1 Who defines what kind of interpreting

Defined by the profession or professional literature (self-ascription varies; the most common is interpreting)	Defined by institutions (interpreters in these categories usually use the institutionally defined description)	Defined by others (interpreters in these categories often do not use the categories as self-ascription)
Interpreting		
Conference interpreting		
Community interpreting		
Liaison interpreting		
Monologic/dialogic		
Business interpreting		
Public service interpreting		
Court interpreting		
Health interpreting		
	Social interpreting	
	Interprétariat	
	'Locally recruited'	
	'Civilian'	
	(Inter-)cultural mediation	
	Linguistic mediation	
		Ad hoc interpreting
		Unprofessional interpreting
		Volunteer interpreting
		Natural interpreting
		'Fixer'

Source: Ozolins (2014: 35).

sociopolitical or purely linguistic reasons have shaped the preferred nomenclature. Table I.2 presents a representative sample of terms used in various geonational contexts. However, it remains questionable whether frequency of use alone should determine the acceptance of a particular term.

Another significant point is that conceptualization should precede terminological choices. This is the approach proposed by Pöchhacker (2011) in his article 'NT and CI in ITS: taxonomies and tensions in interpreting studies', which was based on an early taxonomy by Harris (1982). According to Pöchhacker (2011: 218), Harris described this taxonomy as his 'little 1982 glossary' in which he lists 'some twenty terms designating various types of interpreters'. This short piece by Harris and his unpublished *Taxonomic Survey of Professional Interpreting* (1994) that constitutes the foundation of

Table I.2 Terms used in various geonational contexts

Africa	**RSA:** *liaison interpreting*
Asia	**China:** 社区口译 (community interpreting) **Japan:** *komyunitī tsūyaku* (community interpreting) **Malaysia:** *interpretasi komuniti/pendatang dan kumpulan lain* (community interpreting/for migrants and other groups) **South Korea:** *keomyuniti tong-yeog* (community interpreting)
Australia and Oceania	**Australia:** *community interpreting* or *liaison interpreting*
Europe	**Austria:** *Kommunaldolmetschen* (community interpreting) **France:** *interprétation en milieu social* (social setting interpreting) **Germany:** *Sprach- und Kulturmittlung* (language and cultural mediation) or *Sprach- und Integrationsmittlung* (language and integration mediation) **Ireland:** *dialogue interpreting* or *community interpreting* **Italy:** *mediazione interculturale/linguistica* (intercultural/linguistic mediation) *interpretazione di trattativa* (liaison interpreting) **Poland:** *tłumaczenie środowiskowe* (social setting interpreting) or *tłumaczenie ustne dla służb publicznych* (public service interpreting) **Portugal:** *interpretação comunitária* (community interpreting) **Slovakia:** *komunitný tlmočenie* (community interpreting) **Spain:** *interpretación en los servicios públicos* (public service interpreting) or *mediación intercultural* (intercultural mediation) **Sweden:** *kontakttolk* (contact interpreting) or *dialogtolk* (dialogue interpreting) **UK:** *public service interpreting*
North America	**Canada:** *community interpreting* or *cultural interpreting* **Mexico:** *interpretación comunitaria* (community interpreting) **USA:** *community interpreting*
South America	**Argentina:** *interpretación en los servicios públicos* (public service interpreting) **Brazil:** *interpretação comunitária* (community interpreting)

Pöchhacker's (2011) discussion can be considered as the very first termino-logical categorization of interpreting practices and practitioners in the field.

Pöchhacker's (2011) survey of the terminological landscape of interpret-ing studies, not only contributes to a better understanding of subtypes of interpreting (by medium, setting, mode, languages, discourse, participants and interpreter), but also crucially assists in mapping them out. His graph 'Dimensions of interpreting' (2011: 228) is of particular relevance for further charting the metaterminological issues in interpreting research. In fact, meta-terminology and field conceptualization are two of the most promising areas in interpreting studies in general, but particularly with regard to community interpreting where etymology, ethnographic studies, social psychology and geolexicography, supported by corpus linguistics, can shed light on such issues as dialogue interpreting conceptualization and naming, e.g. hypon-ymy, regional usage and sociocultural preferences.

As seen in the above table, as of 2015 *public service interpreting* and *com-munity interpreting* are the two most common names for dialogue interpret-ing across geonational contexts. Given the broad spectrum of intended readership and for reasons of clarity, the following nomenclature is used in this guide:

- *dialogue interpreting (interpreter), community interpreting (interpreter)* and *public service interpreting (interpreter)* are used interchangeably;
- *interlingual/intercultural mediation (mediator)* and *community/public service interpreting (interpreter)* are used interchangeably;
- *domain (subdomain)* refers to the type (subtype) of interpreting such as legal, healthcare, educational;
- *mode* of interpreting refers to the way it is delivered, e.g. consecutive, simultaneous, escort, bilateral, sight translation, whispered interpreting (*chuchotage*).

The term **dialogue interpreting** is the authors' preferred term and was chosen as the title of this guide with an intention to reintroduce and revive the term that was proposed by Wadensjö (1992). The recently observed resurgence (e.g. Baraldi and Gavioli 2012; Wadensjö 2004)[2] of the particular interper-sonal angle of interpreting reflected in the term *dialogue interpreting* indi-cates a certain emphasis on equal, balanced, respectful communication and has broad appeal since it does not imply a specific setting or service. *Dialogue interpreting* also places emphasis on the meaning of the word (*logos*) and on mutuality (*dia*), which refocuses the action on the person in the Buberian tradition of philosophy of dialogue and of personalism, and calls for an openness to the Other in order to understand oneself. Then, and only then, can true communication and building of unity or community in a broader sense occur (Buber 1948, 1966).[3] It appears that in the coming decades other needs and settings are likely to emerge in which interlingual and intercultural interaction would expand beyond initial migrant resettlement phases and include contexts of more educational, social, faith-related or entertainment-related communication. The term *dialogue interpreting* is also therefore proposed as a means to encompass emerging areas of focus.

Additionally, one of the authors of this guide for the last ten years has been surveying her students in graduate and undergraduate courses at Wake Forest University (North Carolina, USA) in regard to which term they would prefer to describe the profession they are about to enter. In that survey six synonymous terms are presented. The description, reasoning and history behind each term and the concept described by each term are provided prior to the vote. The survey is conducted during the third week of the course and then repeated at the end of that one semester interpreting course. *Dialogue interpreting* has consistently and significantly gained first place in the ranking, followed by *community interpreting* (probably due to the national context and the frequency of the term, but also possibly due to the idealistic view of the profession that the students hold when choosing this career).

Looking toward the future, two new concepts and terms are introduced in the guide (Chapters 5 and 7): **semi-professional interpreting** and **fusion interpreting**. The addition of these terms is not intended to add to the above-described multiplication and fragmentation but rather is an attempt to find broader terms that include and give voice to interpreters working in domains that have been recently gaining visibility in research and practice, particularly but not exclusively in educational, social care and faith-related events.

For reasons of space the domains of *business* and *tourism* do not feature in this guide, despite the fact that these activities are sometimes included under community interpreting and employ dialogue interpreting modes. Another area not included is *sports interpreting*, which covers interactions between fans, between team members within the teams or with the members of the opposite teams, and with the press and local authorities where a sports event is organized. *Military interpreting, interpreting in conflict zones or disaster situations* are also not featured domains. Finally, while we recognize that intercultural and interlingual brokerage occurs in various geonational contexts, including between minority indigenous populations and the majority within the same country, or in intranational or intraregional migration related to conflicts (i.e. military interpreting in the field), the focus of this guide is on interpreting in community and public settings in receiving countries, with exception of Chapter 7 where missionary interpreting is also discussed.

3 Competencies

In line with a commitment to holism, this guide is designed to support the development of interpreting competencies that are categorized as core, developmental and domain-specific. Available documentation on interpreting standards and related discussions suggests some agreement on core competencies, which are also recognized and promoted by International Standard

ISO 13611 Interpreting – Guidelines for Community Interpreting, 2014,[4] as linguistic, thematic/discipline-specific, interpersonal, intercultural, technological and business-related/strategic. We do not attempt to provide additional specifications or categorizations of those competencies that have been discussed and organized by, among others, Abril Martí (2006), Kermis (2008) and Refki *et al.* (2013) but rather encourage readers to adopt a holistic and reflective approach to this list.

3.1 Core competencies

Linguistic
- advanced grammatical, lexical and syntactic knowledge of working languages;
- knowledge of domain-specific language protocols;
- awareness of register variation;
- awareness of changes in language use in all working languages;
- flexibility in relation to idiom and domain-specific expression;
- strategies for handling culture-specific references.

Thematic
- knowledge of how to identify relevant topics for assignments;
- confidence in extracting terminology and phraseology from relevant documentation;
- knowledge of how to identify gaps in and research cultural knowledge in relation to a limited proficiency speaker's (LPS) country of origin;
- sound knowledge of consecutive, liaison, sight-translation, simultaneous and whispered interpreting modes;
- note-taking techniques and strategies.

Interpersonal
- awareness of sources of bias and limits of competence (self-knowledge);
- knowledge of trust-building strategies;
- knowledge of strategies available to the interpreter to coordinate interaction and message transfer (including turn taking and communication breakdown);
- internalisation and application of relevant professional values and ethical codes;
- self- and peer-evaluation techniques;
- attention to personal care/self-care (psychosocial support).

Intercultural
- awareness of different types of social disadvantage;
- knowledge of cultural changes in service user countries of origin;
- awareness of the nature of power asymmetries operating in relevant domains;

- awareness of the nature of the professional intercultures generated between interpreters and institutional service providers.

Technological
- record keeping;
- archiving;
- terminology management (e.g. glossary);
- use of social media.

Business-related
- customer management/customer relations;
- accounting/finance;
- time management;
- assignment management;
- professional development;
- quality monitoring;
- membership in professional associations.

3.2 Developmental competencies

- managing lifelong learning;
- working with others;
- promoting professional values;
- intellectual flexibility;
- performance development;
- decision making and accountability;
- responding to pressure and change.

In this guide we place emphasis on the need for a more complex and broader understanding of thematic competencies in specific settings. As a result, we propose that such competencies be considered as a separate subset of competencies, and not as a subcategory of core competencies. Throughout the guide they are referred to as *domain-specific (or setting-specific) competencies*. These domain-specific competencies are outlined in the introduction of each chapter and are understood to build on core and developmental competencies and respond to the specific characteristics of interpersonal communication in the domains and settings discussed.

4 Combining independent and collaborative approaches to professional development

Throughout the guide, professional development is viewed as more than an inward-looking and introspective process. It places emphasis on feeding out, learning from others and actions that help to shape the wider profession. As a result, practitioners are encouraged to explore available opportunities for engaging with peers and other professionals in relevant domains and settings and to promote the exchange of good practice both within and beyond national borders, and on- and offline.

To some extent the collaborative approach to professional development in the guide is informed by the work of Wenger (1998) on Communities of Practice and its application to interpreter education (e.g. D'Hayer 2012). For Wenger, a Community of Practice (CoP) is more than a simple network of connections between people; it brings together people with shared interests and helps to facilitate improvements in practice by regular interaction.[5] The strategic importance of this approach is echoed in the words of Corsellis, who observes that 'it is essential that [public service interpreters and translators] all share a common grasp of the structures and the underlying principles that should govern their learning and practice so that they can share in the professional development process' (2008: 82). In this regard, meaningful interaction with the wider communities of interpreting practice needs to be viewed as a conscious part of professional development.

5 Approach to role

The nature of the interpreter's role has long been debated, not least because the label given to mediators in bilingual and bicultural situations varies across and even within geographical contexts, generating uncertainty over remit and responsibility. This guide emphasizes the importance of understanding the wider interactional and institutional parameters in relation to interpreter-mediated events in their sociocultural and sociohistorical context and the parties to the interaction, thereby leaving scope to identify and explore shifts in the positioning of the interpreter as the interaction evolves. In short, '**role-space**' (following Llewelyn-Jones and Lee 2014) as opposed to 'role' is foregrounded as a concept that better captures the fluidity and dynamism of the (re-)positioning processes in intercultural and interlingual mediation (Baraldi 2012).

A multidimensional approach to role also permits social structures and power configurations, which often seem to operate at a level beyond the interpreter's control, to be addressed. As discussed throughout the guide, a commitment to holism involves attending to the interconnections between so-called micro and macro levels of interpreter mediation, that is, what happens at the face-to-face level as well as connections to the wider institutional and organizational setting. Furthermore, if career planning is to involve practitioners taking an increasingly active role in shaping the profession and its perception in wider society, then developmental activity would naturally need to take account of the interpreter's agency beyond the act of interpreter mediation itself.

6 Ethics

Concerns over role are intimately connected to issues of interpreter involvement and intervention, which by extension concern understandings of the interpreter's responsibility. Ethical practice is something all members of a profession strive to achieve consistently but the form that ethical practice takes and needs to take is often difficult to articulate. It is not uncommon for interpreters in state-run institutions and community-based organizations to consider the ethics of their practice almost exclusively in relation to a code of conduct or code of ethics. However, such codes can be all too readily turned to for 'off-the-peg' solutions to a broad range of issues that arise in practice, usually with unsatisfactory outcomes (see Tate and Turner 1997). This is indicative of what is sometimes termed a *deontological* approach to ethics, that is, an approach based on preordained rules in which neutrality typically dominates. Such an approach can be limiting and, as Baker and Maier assert, also risks blinding interpreters 'to the consequences of their actions' (2011: 3).

While recognizing the importance of such codes in the development of a profession, a complementary perspective is developed here to support professional development (following Dean and Pollard 2011). This approach is described as *teleological* and focuses on the outcomes of decisions in context. It is considered a flexible and constructive approach to ethical decision making and advanced understanding of the interpreter's accountability to others in the course of her/his professional life. Such an approach is reflected inter alia in Chesterman's (2001) notion of 'norm-based ethics', according to which ethical behaviour is judged against the expectations particular to a specific cultural location or setting.

The aim of this guide, then, is not to present a checklist approach to the rights and wrongs of interpreter actions; instead, emphasis is placed on exploring choices that arise in particular situations and the range of responses available in ways that foreground accountability and transparency. An **emancipatory translation** approach (following Chesterman 2005) therefore invites critical reflection on the norms that impact interpreter mediation and the interpreter's responses to them both during and beyond interaction.

7 Statement on materials and their representativeness

The guide is divided into thematic chapters that highlight features of domain-specific language practices, protocols and interpreter performance. Due to limitations of space, the choice of examples is necessarily limited and does not claim to be exhaustive or representative of all contexts or language combinations. Further, many examples reflect the respective countries of the authors, namely the United Kingdom and the United States. Contextualized examples are provided to allow readers an opportunity to evaluate approaches in relation to their local contexts of practice and recognize areas of overlap and difference. Throughout the guide, key terms (when used for the first time) and key concepts are highlighted in **bold**, and terms that may be used as an alternative or synonym are written in *italics*.

8 Activities

Each chapter contains activities that are guided by a series of broad intended learning outcomes, namely the ability to:

- effectively research, plan and evaluate new learning in the context of professional development;
- develop and improve interpreter mediation skills across a range of practice settings;
- better understand service users' and service providers' perspectives on interpreted events.

Chapter 1 lays the foundations for continuing professional development and supports the approach to activities in later chapters; activities in this chapter are labelled Professional Development Planning (PDP).

Chapters 2–7 focus on specific domains and are designed as stand-alone chapters that can be read in any order. Discussions on the legal interpreting domain are spread over two chapters; the first focuses on aspects of language services in criminal justice procedures and the second in the subdomain of asylum procedures. Activities are divided into three main categories and are followed by a descriptive subheading of the activity. They appear throughout the chapters to help assimilate the topic under discussion. Supplementary materials and activities can be found on the Routledge Translation Studies Portal.

The activities are indicated by symbols. The circle denotes continuity, completeness, fullness of knowledge and understanding that come with research and a well-rounded view of a subject; the square denotes evenness and balance, and the idea of preparedness and a solid orientation based on skills. Finally, the triangle denotes triadic interaction that is characteristic of dialogue interpreting as well as cooperation and interconnection.

● **RESEARCH**
- domain-specific knowledge enrichment
- problem-solving enhancement
- informed decision making

■ **PERFORMANCE SKILLS**
- linguistic analysis
- situational awareness
- interaction strategies

- memory and recording techniques
- self-/peer evaluation
- ethics and accountability
- personal care/self-care

▲ COLLABORATIVE DIMENSIONS

- expectation management
- team work
- interpersonal trust
- event coordination
- users' education
- organizational work

9 Chapter overview

Chapter 1: Foundations for Continuing Professional Development focuses on how to prepare for effective independent learning and development, from initial entry into the profession to longer-term career progression. Readers are guided on how to identify their preferred learning styles, motivations for professional development, how to match desired learning outcomes with competencies and activities, and set timeframes and evaluation points. The chapter emphasizes the importance of domain specificity in developmental activity and skills of critical evaluation through reflective approaches to learning. Activities focus on skills of self-auditing, the development of self-knowledge, and on structuring approaches to both individual and collective professional development planning.

Chapter 2: Legal Interpreting I: Criminal Procedures focuses on interpreter mediation in police and court settings, with specific reference to criminal matters. It explores approaches to police interviews in selected countries and selected examples of language strategies and influencing behaviours used by law enforcement officers. Readers are guided to reflect on the potential impact of interpreter mediation on police and court procedure in relation to prevailing domain-specific norms, supported by examples of authentic interpreted events. The use of new technologies in legal settings is also discussed. Activities focus on developing a structured approach to pre-assignment preparation and post-assignment reflection-on-practice, language enhancement and strategies for handling remote interpreting.

Chapter 3: Legal Interpreting II: Asylum Procedures explores asylum as a subdomain of legal interpreting and discusses aspects of interpreted asylum interviews with adults and unaccompanied minors. Readers are guided on how to manage expectations in these settings, supported by analysis of examples of interpreter performance from different countries. A case study provides insight into the potential limits of the interpreter's role in appeal hearings and attention is drawn to the importance of personal care in this subdomain through trauma-informed approaches to interpreting. Activities are designed to develop advanced procedural knowledge, note-taking strategies and resilience building.

Chapter 4: Healthcare Interpreting discusses the problems affecting the professionalization of healthcare interpreting and the domain-specific competencies that are central to professional development in this domain. The chapter explores the nature and structure of the medical interpreting event and analyses key factors that affect the interpreter's performance in healthcare, namely time, trust, control and power. The chapter suggests ways in which various stakeholders could be engaged in the development of language support services in the healthcare sector. Activities are designed to encourage strategies for handling role conflict and reflection on approaches to users' education.

Chapter 5: Educational Interpreting describes the complexities of education-related communication with refugee and immigrant families, and the range of bilingual support mechanisms available in primary and secondary education contexts. Attention is given to interpreted parent-teacher communication, special educational needs assessments and interpreter recruitment processes. Two case studies are discussed: one concerns an initiative for young interpreters and a second looks at best practices developed in one school system. Among other aims, activities are designed to develop knowledge of local policies and needs assessment procedures, and strategies for engaging in users' education with regard to recruitment and role.

Chapter 6: Social Care Interpreting focuses on interpreter mediation in social care-related work in the statutory, non-profit, voluntary and charities sectors. The chapter describes selected issues in cross-cultural needs assessment, child welfare protection processes and fostering and adoption, and their implications for interpreted events. A case study on interpreter mediation in a charity providing specialist support for victims of torture is presented. Activities are designed to develop knowledge of relevant legislative and regulatory frameworks governing care services, understanding complex interpersonal relations in cases of suspected child neglect and abuse, and strategy development for interviews where disclosure of emotions and facts are problematic.

Chapter 7: Faith-related Interpreting explores oral translation provided during religious liturgies, ceremonies and prayer meetings, interpreting for preachers and religious and lay missionaries, and interpreting during pilgrimages and other faith-related gatherings such as congresses, synods and religious orders' chapters. Drawing on the history of interpreting in religious contexts, the chapter presents key concepts in faith-related interpreting, its subtypes, and examines the level of preparedness needed to work as an interpreter in this often overlooked setting. Volunteer work is discussed in contrast with service and ministry. A case study on Pope Francis's homily interpreted in consecutive mode illustrates some of the discourse and domain-level issues specific to religious settings.

Notes

1 The Bureau of Labor Statistics in the USA predicts for example a 46 per cent growth in the employment of translators and interpreters between 2012 and 2022 due to the increasing number of non-English speakers: www.bls.gov/ooh/media-and-communication/interpreters-and-translators.htm (accessed 16 July 2015).
2 Wadensjö proposes to capture the complex character of interpreter-mediated interaction as 'monologising practice in a dialogically organized world' (2004: 105).
3 See also Lévinas, E. (1981) *Otherwise Than Being: or, beyond essence*, Hingham, MA: Martinus Nijhoff Publishers; Scheler, M. (1973) *Selected Philosophical Essays*, Evanston, IL: Northwestern University Press; Wojtyła, K. (1993) *Person and Community: selected essays*, New York: Peter Lang.
4 International Standard ISO 13611, Interpreting – Guidelines for Community Interpreting: www.iso.org/iso/catalogue_detail.htm?csnumber=54082 (accessed 20 April 2015).
5 For more insight into Communities of Practice: http://wenger-trayner.com (accessed 14 March 2015).

References

Abril Martí, M. (2006) 'La Interpretación en los Servicios Públicos: caracterización como género, contextualización y modelos de formación. Hacia unas bases para el diseño curricular', PhD thesis, Granada: University of Granada.

Baker, M. and Maier, C. (eds) (2011) 'Ethics in Interpreter and Translator Training: critical perspectives', *Interpreter and Translator Trainer*, Special Issue: Ethics in the Curriculum, 5 (1): 1–14.

Baraldi, C. (2012) 'Interpreting as Dialogic Mediation: the relevance of expansions', in C. Baraldi and L. Gavioli (eds) *Coordinating Participation in Dialogue Interpreting*, Amsterdam/Philadelphia: John Benjamins Publishing.

Baraldi, C. and Gavioli, L. (eds) (2012) *Coordinating Participation in Dialogue Interpreting*, Amsterdam/Philadelphia: John Benjamins Publishing.

Buber, M. (1948) *Between Man and Man*, trans. R.G. Smith, New York: Macmillan Company.

Buber, M. (1966) *The Way of Response*, New York: Schoken Books.

Chesterman, A. (2001) 'Proposal for a Hieronymic Oath', *The Translator*, Special Issue: The Return to Ethics, 7 (2): 139–54.

Chesterman, A. (2005) 'Causality in translator training', in M. Tennent (ed.) *Training for the New Millennium: pedagogies for translation and interpreting*, Amsterdam/Philadelphia: John Benjamins Publishing.

Corsellis, A. (2008) *Public Service Interpreting: the first steps*, London: Palgrave Macmillan.

Dean, R.K. and Pollard, R.Q. Jr. (2011) 'Context-based Ethical Reasoning in Interpreting: a demand control schema perspective', *Interpreter and Translator Trainer*, Special Issue: Ethics in the Curriculum, 5 (1): 155–82.

D'Hayer, D. (2012) 'Public Service Interpreting and Translation: moving towards a (virtual) community of practice', *Meta: Translators' Journal*, 57 (1): 235–47.

Edwards, R., Alexander, C. and Temple, B. (2006) 'Interpreting Trust: abstract and personal trust for people who need interpreters to access services', *Sociological Research Online*, 11 (1). Online. Available at: www.socresonline.org.uk/11/1/edwards.html#alexander2004 (accessed 29 June 2011).

Eurydice Network (2009) *Integrating Immigrant Children into Schools in Europe: measures to foster communication with immigrant families and heritage language teaching for immigrant children*. Online. Available at: http://eacea.ec.europa.eu/education/eurydice/documents/thematic_reports/101EN.pdf (accessed 21 April 2015).

Harris, B. (1982) 'There is More to Interpreting than Conference Interpreters', *InformATIO*, 11 (3): 4–5.

Kermis, M. (2008) 'Translators and Interpreters: comparing competences', MA dissertation, Utrecht University.

Lindholm, M., Hargreaves, J.L., Ferguson, W.J. and Reed, G. (2012) 'Professional Language Interpretation and Inpatient Length of Stay and Readmission Rates', *Journal of General Internal Medicine*, 27 (10): 1294–9.

Llewelyn-Jones, P. and Lee, R.G. (2014) *Redefining the Role of the Community Interpreter: the concept of role-space*, Carlton-le-Moorland: SLI Press.

Mason, I. (2000) 'Models and Methods in Dialogue Interpreting Research', in M. Olohan (ed.) *Intercultural Faultlines: research models in translation studies*, Manchester: St Jerome.

Ozolins, U. (2010) 'Factors that Determine the Provision of Public Service Interpreting: comparative perspectives on government motivation and language service implementation', *Journal of Specialised Translation*, Issue 14.

Ozolins, U. (2014) 'Descriptions of Interpreting and their Ethical Consequences', *FITISPos International Journal of Public Service Interpreting and Translation*, 1 (1). Online. Available at: www3.uah.es/fitispos_ij/OJS/ojs-2.4.5/index.php/fitispos/article/view/9 (accessed 12 April 2015).

Pöchhacker, F. (2011) 'NT and CI in IS: taxonomies and tensions in interpreting studies', in M.J.B. Mayor and M.A.J. Ivars (eds) *Interpreting Naturally: a tribute to Brian Harris*, Bern: Peter Lang.

Ra, S. and Napier. J. (2013) 'Community Interpreting: Asian language interpreters' perspectives', *The International Journal of Translation and Interpreting Research*, 5 (2): 45–61.

Refki, D., Avery, M.P. and Dalton, A. (2013) 'Core Competencies for Healthcare Interpreters', *International Journal of Humanities and Social Science*, 3 (2): 72–83.

Schön, D.A. (1983) *The Reflective Practitioner: how professionals think in action*, New York: Basic Books.

Simon, M.A., Tom, L.S., Nonzee, N.J., Murphy, K.R., Endress, R., Dong, X. and Feinglass, J. (2015) 'Evaluating a Bilingual Patient Navigation Program for Uninsured Women with Abnormal Screening Tests for Breast and Cervical Cancer: implication for future navigator research', *American Journal of Public Health*, 105 (5): e87–e94.

Tate, G. and Turner, G.H. (1997) 'The Code and the Culture: sign language interpreting – in search of the new breed's ethics', *Deaf Worlds*, Special Issue on Interpreting, 13 (3): 27–34.

Toledando Buendía, C. (2010) 'Community Interpreting: breaking with the "norm" through normalisation', *Journal of Specialised Translation*, Issue 14.

Wadensjö, C. (1992) *Interpreting as Interaction: on dialogue interpreting in immigration hearings and medical encounters*, Linköping Studies in Arts and Science 83, Linköping: Department of Communication Studies.

Wadensjö, C. (2004) 'Dialogue Interpreting: a monologising practice in a dialogically organised world', *Target: International Journal of Translation Studies*, 16 (1): 105–24.

Wenger, E. (1998) *Communities of Practice: learning, meaning and identity*, Cambridge: Cambridge University Press.

1 Foundations for continuing professional development

1 Introduction

This chapter explores the nature and scope of professional development for dialogue interpreters, taking account of transition points in an interpreter's career trajectory from formal classroom learning to professional practice, and the relationship between informal or *lifelong* learning and **continuing professional development** (CPD). It places emphasis on **reflective practice** and **collaboration** as mechanisms to support structured professional development.

For early career interpreters the excitement of moving from the classroom into professional practice can sometimes be tempered by experiences that have not been encountered during initial interpreter education and for which there appear to be no readily available solutions. It is at that point when interpreters begin to confront the messy realities of human service industries that their professional identities really begin to take shape.

Idealized approaches to interpreter education, where everyone patiently waits his/her turn to speak and all parties implicitly understand the interpreter's position are routinely challenged by service providers who thrust the interpreter into the spotlight in unanticipated ways, often due to a lack of knowledge about professional interpreting and frameworks for judging standards. Regardless of the reason, interpreters can be left feeling unsure about their role, particularly if the impartiality of service delivery that seemed so clear-cut in the classroom appears all but impossible to achieve in professional practice. How to build resilience, assertiveness and understanding of others' perceptions and expectations are therefore key developmental issues in an interpreter's career.[1] Even experienced interpreters find it difficult to handle different attitudes to their occupation and problem solve on the job since the highly autonomous nature of dialogue interpreting can generate uncertainties with regard to decision making and professional accountability; it is not uncommon for experienced professional interpreters to regularly question the legitimacy of their actions and approach.

Professional development involves more than maintaining and updating competencies developed in initial interpreter education; it concerns deepening understandings of the many facets of human-to-human communication in complex social, institutional and organizational systems. At all levels of experience, practitioners confront questions of what constitutes 'professional knowledge' and how its acquisition and use relate to the different types of activity they perform. In this regard Eraut provides a helpful distinction between knowledge types:

> Although many areas of professional knowledge are dependent on some understanding of relevant public codified knowledge found in books and journals, professional knowledge is constructed through experience and its nature depends on the cumulative acquisition, selection and interpretation of that experience.
>
> (1994: 20)

It is the vitality of interpreting and its lack of a codified knowledge base that make the role of experience central to effective professional development. How such experience is articulated, appraised and built on forms the focus of this chapter. The sections that follow provide guidance on developing a structured and critical approach to professional development in which the importance of core, developmental and domain-specific competencies development is highlighted.

2 Professional development and lifelong learning

Professional development and lifelong learning are terms familiar to the modern workplace and are sometimes considered in relation to formal and informal learning respectively. Two types of professional development are identified, each of which can be broken down further into discrete phases in the interpreter's career trajectory.

- **Initial professional development**
  Initial professional development usually takes place in contexts of formal or institutional learning, both online and face-to-face, and leads to certification and accreditation through examination. At this stage, the focus is placed on acquiring interpreting skills, developing advanced language competence and contextual understanding, and on understanding how these translate from the classroom to the different settings of professional practice.
- **Continuing professional development**
  Continuing professional development (CPD) is understood in general terms as a commitment to maintain and develop core, developmental and domain-specific competencies and keep abreast of changes to the profession on an informal or formal basis throughout an individual's career.

Megginson and Whitaker describe CPD as 'a process by which individuals take control of their own learning and development by engaging in an ongoing process of reflection and action' (2007: 3). It can involve participation in formal learning opportunities to maintain and acquire new skills but informal learning through experience also plays an important supplementary role.

2.1 The role of professional bodies

Professional development is primarily an individual endeavour owing to the freelance nature of most dialogue interpreting provision. In this respect, professional bodies and interpreter associations provide important sources of support and, in fact, membership is often conditional on the completion and submission of an annual record of activity (typically 30–40 hours). A cursory examination of some of the world's leading professional bodies reveals considerable overlap in the nature and range of activities recommended:

- reading specialist publications;
- attending workshops and conferences;
- completing online tutorials;
- writing blogs and creating vlogs;
- giving presentations;
- participating in committees;
- coaching and mentoring.

However, the ability to ensure that activities are relevant, meaningful and contribute to medium- and long-term goals is often taken for granted. Without appropriate planning and personalization interpreters can feel that they are undertaking activities for the sake of the activity alone or simply to retain accreditation.

Professional development planning: Activity 1

A   Review the list of core competencies in the introduction to this guide and identify the activities recommended by professional bodies above that can help to support their development.

B   Identify the range of CPD opportunities currently available in your local area and the range of competencies they can help develop.

C   Reflect on other types of development activity (on- and offline, individual and collaborative) that can supplement the activities recommended by professional bodies.

3 Entering the profession and moving forward

3.1 Certification and standards

Initial entry to the interpreting profession typically depends on meeting a minimum set of performance standards determined by the relevant certifying and accrediting authorities,[2] although, as has been well documented, the lack of uniformity in this regard is a source of constant tension in public service and community interpreting. Hvlac observes that certification may be 'specified according to general or specialised ability, or mode and context of interlingual transfer (e.g. "healthcare interpreter certification", "telephone interpreter certification")' (2013: 32). This raises questions regarding levels of overall preparedness for the range of domains and settings that interpreters encounter, and underscores the importance of structured professional development. Hvlac also makes a distinction between standards understood in the narrow sense of 'demonstrated performance' and standards as 'organisational and policy features' that operate at the national and supranational level (ibid.: 34). The latter are described as 'the procedures that practitioners and agencies must uphold to present themselves to the market as a quality-assured product' (ibid.).

The professionalization of community interpreting has been doubtless strengthened by the development of national occupational standards. Efforts to create supranational standards have tended to focus on written translation rather than interpreting, although the situation is evolving (e.g. the recent International Standard ISO 13611 Interpreting – Guidelines for Community Interpreting). However, there is some uncertainty regarding the extent to which occupational standards serve to guide professional development, which helps to explain why competency-based approaches to interpreter education are becoming increasingly prominent.

3.2 Competency-based approaches to interpreter education and development

The list of competencies in the introduction to this guide reflects a wider trend in **competency-based learning** in translator and interpreter education, which is advocated, for example, by the European Masters in Translation (EMT) network under the auspices of the European Commission in relation to written translation. In general terms, the approach provides a coherent framework for education providers, students and practitioners to deal with the many facets of the occupation, from actual service delivery to effective preparation and business management.

However, competency-based approaches are not without their critics and some scholars claim that they do not train students to deal effectively with uncertainty and complexity (e.g. Kelly and Horder 2001). There is a risk that without appropriate support, interpreter practitioners may approach competency development in limited terms and, in particular, underestimate the potential of collaboration with peers and other human service professionals to support development at a more holistic level.

3.3 Complexity of competency development

Continuing professional development involves identifying areas for improvement and learning in relation to core, developmental and domain-specific competencies; the latter is typically much more challenging since initial interpreter education tends to focus only on such knowledge, skills and attitudes as the basics of pre-assignment preparation, terminological research, sight translation and whispered interpreting, interaction management, note taking and general ethical issues. Issues such as register variation in the courtroom, influencing behaviours of police officers in interviews with suspects, and the role of code-switching in child abuse interviews are examples of domain specificity that interpreters are often left to address on their own with varying levels of success. The following sections provide guidance on how to get started in the process.

4 Professional development planning: getting started

4.1 Skills audit and profiling

Professional development planning can usefully begin by taking stock of current skills and activity levels. Instead of simply reviewing a CV, creating a profile such as the one below (Figure 1.1) can provide a simple snapshot of current professional status and services offered.

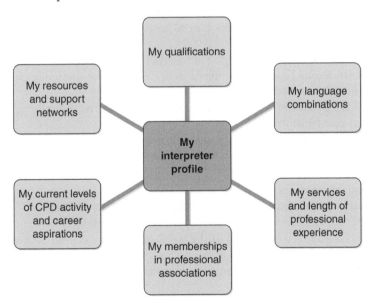

Figure 1.1 Sample profile.

4.2 Profile evaluation: SWOT analysis

Once created, the profile can be evaluated by using a basic SWOT analysis (strengths, weaknesses, opportunities and threats). This framework allows a distinction to be made between internal and external, and positive and negative factors that influence business activity. For example, opportunities and threats are more likely to be related to external factors like market conditions, and strengths and weaknesses are more likely related to internal factors like self-motivation. It can help to visualize these elements in a tabular format:

Strengths	Weaknesses
Opportunities	Threats

The questions below provide a series of prompts to support the analysis. What might have been a strength in the past may be a weakness in current market conditions, and so it is important to view professional identity as continually evolving. Similarly, what may be considered an asset in one domain can actually be a limitation in another.

A Early career interpreters

- Do my current qualifications allow me to access relevant interpreting opportunities in my local market?
- Are the services I offer in demand locally?
- Am I making the most of my membership of professional bodies?
- Do I have access to the resources I need to prepare appropriately for assignments?
- Is my current workflow providing a sufficient income?
- Are there situations I have encountered in my work where there is a gap in my knowledge and education?
- Is the reality of working as an interpreter meeting my expectations?
- Who is my competition?
- Am I working in contexts for which my interpreter education was not specifically designed?

B Experienced interpreters

- Are the services I am qualified to offer still relevant for the market?
- What CPD activities have been most helpful to my current work?
- In what ways have I contributed to the work of the professional bodies and associations I am a member of?
- What activities do I undertake to maintain and improve my language competence?
- Are my professional identity and my client base clear to me?
- Who is my competition?

- Am I up to date with new technologies and their role in my services?
- Is my current profile market-resilient or market-vulnerable?
- Am I taking assignments in areas that I feel less competent in while having access to or exploring enough the domains that could be my strengths?
- Have I been forced to work in certain interpreting contexts but in reality I have always wanted to work in a different setting (for various reasons)?
- Do I still enjoy what I do?

4.3 Self-knowledge: cultural bias and prejudice

Individuals who are attracted to working in multicultural and multilingual environments are likely to consider themselves as particularly open to others and Otherness in ways not necessarily reflected in the general population. However, this does not mean that interpreters are completely free of bias in their dealings with others; all humans harbour and exhibit bias in social life. Professional development planning benefits from reflection on aspects of the self that are seldom brought to the surface but that underlie an individual's attitudes, actions and reactions in the workplace.

As an extension to the SWOT analysis recommended above, reflection on the sources and types of bias that exist within us and that are encountered through social interactions is a useful foundation for professional development planning. It helps to understand emotional responses to everyday social life and the ways these impact the professional self; it also helps to make sense of the responses of others to the difficulties posed by intercultural communication in societies more generally. Finally, it can help develop the mental robustness and resilience needed for interpreting settings where the stakes for service users are often very high and emotions can run deep.

At the level of face-to-face interaction, negative attitudes toward limited language proficient (LLP) service users can be manifested by service providers (and vice versa) through behaviours such as poor eye contact, aloofness, impatience, a failure to explain procedures that are particular to that country, and even openly racist comments. Prior experiences with interpreters, both positive and negative, also have a bearing on approaches to interpreter mediation by both service providers and limited proficiency speaking service users. As a result, expectation management is particularly challenging and needs to be viewed as taking many forms (see the dedicated sections on users' expectations in Chapters 2–7).

Bennett's (1986) Developmental Model of Intercultural Sensitivity is a useful point of reference for evaluating the way in which people respond to cultural difference. The model sets out six stages of increasing sensitivity to difference: denial, defence, minimization, acceptance, adaptation and integration. The first three stages are described as *ethnocentric* since in these stages the individual tends to consider his/her culture as superior and/or view other cultures in terms of his/her own. The final three stages are described as *ethnorelative*, which means that an individual becomes increasingly able to view and contrast his/her own culture in relation to other cultures. When moving between stages, the following broad changes in sensitivity are considered to occur:

- from Denial to Defence: the person acquires an awareness of difference between cultures but tends to view the difference in a polarized way;
- from Defence to Minimization: difference becomes less polarized and a person arrives at intercultural sensitivity;
- from Minimization to Acceptance: a person comes to experience cultural difference in context;
- from Acceptance to Adaptation: a person begins to alter his/her behaviour and reorganize experience in ways that recognize another worldview;
- from Adaptation to Integration: a person makes an effort to become competent in new cultures.

(see Bennett 1993)

It is worth noting that the concept of **cultural humility** is also used to support approaches to difference in intercultural working and is promoted as a long-term commitment to others and the self through self-reflection and self-critique rather than as a discrete endpoint, which is a criticism of competency-based approaches mentioned earlier (Tervalon and Murray-García 1998).

Professional development planning: Activity 2

Read the following scenarios and, with a partner, reflect on the possible respective attitudes and responses of the institutional service provider and interpreter by imagining each individual at the Acceptance to Adaptation stage in Bennett's Model above.

A   Interpreter mediation is required for a meeting between a former asylum seeker and a housing officer during a tour of a house that has become available for rent; during the conversation the would-be tenant complains bitterly that it needs some paint and cleaning, and feels a bit small.

B   Interpreter mediation is required at a community centre for a group of refugees during a talk by a health visitor who mentions that the medical centre in the local area sees relatively few members of that particular community; one of the service users says that the community has little faith in the quality of services provided and often prefers to travel to another country to have treatment.

C   Interpreter mediation is required for a young patient in her twenties who is married and has three children. Due to her beliefs, the patient reacts negatively and strongly to the doctor's advice to take birth control measures. The doctor makes a derogatory comment in front of her about the approach of this particular immigrant group to having large families and at a young age, and tells the interpreter not to translate that side comment.

For further reflection: a common form of bias reported about the type of situations described above concerns the feeling that people in such precarious and vulnerable positions should be grateful for the assistance that is being offered and therefore simply accept it. What do you think about such a stance? What counterviews exist?

As mentioned earlier, bias and prejudice exist in all humans; recognizing that it exists and the forms it can take, regardless of how open to Otherness individuals believe they are, is an important part of developing self-awareness and managing interaction in the workplace (see Furmanek 2004). Reflection may not eliminate bias, but it can help reveal knowledge gaps about the groups and communities with whom interpreters interact. Furthermore, it can prompt research into aspects such as the power structures and institutional barriers that affect the ways in which socially disadvantaged groups are treated as well as their ability to access and benefit from certain types of knowledge and support (Advocates for Youth website).

Professional development planning: Activity 3

Personal bias manifests in assumptions made about interlocutors during assignments. Consider the assumptions that could be made by the interlocutors (about themselves and each other) in the following scenarios and the patterns of behaviour that may be manifested in the interpreted event as a result of these assumptions.

A   A mental health interview takes place involving a newly qualified, young and clearly nervous mental health practitioner who has never worked with an interpreter before.
B   In the waiting room of a law centre a service user strikes up conversation with the interpreter and starts asking very personal questions about religious beliefs and family circumstances.
C   A male doctor with poor command of the language of the receiving country and poor interpersonal skills has an interpreter-mediated consultation with a female patient who presents with mental health problems.

5 Professional development planning: empowerment through horizontal learning

Prior experience in institutional contexts of learning doubtless leads individuals to question what, why and how they have learned. The answers will vary depending on the intrinsic level of interest in a subject, motivation to learn, and extrinsic factors such as a requirement to complete a programme to retain accreditation, the manner in which information is presented, and the ways in which new knowledge is internalized and later employed.

Institutional learning is often described as **vertical learning** since it often promotes a 'top down' approach, according to which knowledge is passed from teacher to student. By contrast, **horizontal learning** describes a process through which the learner identifies and engages in opportunities to construct a body of knowledge appropriate for his/her goals and needs in ways that support his/her capacity to work in different contexts (Tynjälä 2008: 144). Under this approach learning is characterized as personalized, open ended and interactive; however, in practice, professional development is likely to include elements of vertical learning as described above. Building a personalized programme of development can be very empowering, but the lack of guidance currently available to interpreters makes the process particularly challenging. In the next section we explore insights from formal educational practice and their application to independent learning and professional development.

5.1 Identifying learning preferences, styles and motivation

Reflection on prior learning is a useful first stage in understanding how individuals learn most effectively and in ways they most enjoy. It entails thinking about the preferred means of acquiring knowledge, developing skills and problem solving. Awareness of different **learning styles** can also help uncover **learning preferences**, of which the most common are visual, auditory and kinaesthetic. Pritchard (2008) also draws attention to the impact of an individual's personality on his/her learning preference and the ability for preference to change over time.

Professional development planning: Activity 4

Identify your preferred learning style(s), drawing on available guidance online. Resources such as the VARK Guide to Learning Styles (http://vark-learn.com/home/) can help to support awareness and understanding of personal learning preferences. VARK stands for Visual, Auditory, Read/Write and Kinaesthetic and relates to a model developed by New Zealand scholar Neil Fleming.

Once one's learning styles and preferences have been identified, the choice of professional development activities is likely to be shaped by an individual's motivation for learning and, to a certain extent, by resources and opportunities available in her/his geonational context, even though many materials can be found online. Motivation is affected by intrinsic and extrinsic factors as the following activity demonstrates.

Professional development planning: Activity 5

Based on the SWOT analysis of your profile, list your current developmental needs and aspirations. Using the list of prompts below, consider the motivations that lie behind the type of activities you intend to prioritize in the short-medium term (e.g. the next three to six months) and longer-term (e.g. the next five years).

Rewards: is your motivation based on financial or personal reward, or perhaps both?

Opportunities: what activities are available to you on-/offline, and at the local, national, and international levels?

Resources: do you have access to relevant resources for your needs?

Networks: do you have access to reliable networks for learning (on-/offline)?

Age and seniority: how does your age and level of seniority in the profession affect your motivation for CPD?

Time: do you view CPD as an add-on to your activity or an integral part?

Previous occupational experience: have you seen a positive correlation between development activities and performance in the workplace?

Previous educational experience: what has your experience been of professional development activities (self-directed/institutional)? Have they been worth the time, effort and money?

Risk: to what extent do you view CPD as 'transformational'? Do you prioritize activities that help maintain current skill levels as opposed to breaking new ground?

Environment: where do you usually undertake development activity?

5.2 Aligning development needs, outcomes and activities

Aligned approaches to learning emphasize the connection between development needs and the intended learning outcomes (ILOs),[3] by ensuring that there is a good fit between aims and the type(s) of activity undertaken. Such approaches also include scope for evaluating the impact of activities. In order to understand the extent to which an individual's current approach to CPD is aligned, a good starting point is to evaluate a record of activities in relation to the connections between the purpose of CPD and the outcomes they are intended to achieve.

Professional development planning: Activity 6

Read the two sample extracts below on CPD activities for the period January to June, compare them and consider the extent to which they resemble your current approach to professional development.

Example 1

March: Read an article on perceptions of interpreters in the court system.
March–April: Familiarized myself with vocabulary on insurance fraud.
May: Attended a conference on marketing for interpreters and networked.

Example 2

February–March: Completed online training course on developing my brand (eight hours) and revised my social media presence.
January–April: Developed a toolkit for new interpreters working in my local hospital by working with the local agency that books interpreters.
March: Practised a new approach to note taking with a colleague to enhance telephone interpreting performance (evaluated effectiveness through peer observation).
May: Started to research maternal health issues in the local ethnic community and compile a list of articles/books on the topic (to support a webinar presentation later in the year).

Both lists provide examples of relevant CPD activities, but there are clear differences. In Example 1, the approach to professional development seems fairly passive and the outcomes of the efforts are unclear; for example, the second activity (on insurance fraud) is expressed in very imprecise terms – what does it mean to be 'familiar' with something? Can the person recall the new terminology and use it in context? Is there any intention to develop this activity further or review progress?

The second list suggests that the activities have been planned with a clear timetable in mind and clear end purpose. The activities show engagement with both independent and collaborative activities, and a commitment to contributing to the wider profession. Although most of these activities are more likely to be associated with an interpreter with several years of experience, they provide examples of an aligned approach to development. In sum, the end purpose of the activity is considered the main priority in planning; from that point, the learner can work backward to decide what activities will help him/her achieve the outcome and the manner of their execution, e.g. whether individual or collaborative. Both approaches can be further improved by considering the domain-specific competencies that need to be prioritized.

6 Reflective practice and performance dimensions

Reflective practice is increasingly used by human service professionals whose work involves complex service cultures and service users who bring a range of expectations, emotions and attitudes to interaction. The often unpredictable and highly context dependent nature of decision making requires flexible and critical thinking skills, and reflective practice is promoted as a practical means of structuring such skills development and dealing with change in the workplace (see Schön 1983). However, as Moon observes 'There is no one behaviour or one consistent set of behaviours that is reflective practice' (1999: 65) and, while it may not necessarily lead to the resolution of a particular problem or a change in behaviour, reflective practice can help to understand it (ibid.: 64).

In continuing professional development, reflective practice can be a useful way of evaluating experiences in the workplace as it encourages their externalization and verbalization. These processes can usefully be structured with reference to the five intertwined dimensions of interpreter performance described below:

1   **Involvement** in terms of the level and nature of interpersonal intervention and latitude for action, such as explaining cultural differences, negotiation of meaning (e.g. asking for re-phrasing), topic determination, sharing sources of communication breakdown.
2   **Visibility** in terms of both physical visibility, i.e. positioning (bodily/via screen image) in relation to the interlocutors, gaze behaviour and articulation of presence, i.e. making introductions, briefing, informing the users of how they should act (e.g. speaking directly to the other party, avoiding regional expressions), using self-distancing strategies.
3   **Transparency** in terms of decision making about what is being interpreted and what is not (e.g. purposeful omissions, summarizing, modifying register).
4   **Coordination** in terms of coordinating the interaction (e.g. requests to stop talking, monitoring turn taking, clarification, time management).
5   **Co-construction** of the event in terms of interpreter's interest in and commitment to the expected/intended outcome of the event, e.g. the mission to accomplish social integration and/or to resolve conflict, and her/his ability to achieve it in relation to the setting specific protocol and/or institutional environment.

The term **neutrality** does not appear in the list since it underlies all of the dimensions above. It is understood as something that interpreters need to enact and not simply embody; in other words it is a commitment to fair communicative exchange that evolves during interpreted events on the basis of carefully judged involvement and withdrawal, and the need for transparency in relation to some aspects of interpreter decision making.

A second underlying term is **co-power** that concerns the multi-dimensional impact that the interpreter has on the results of the interpreted event and is indicative of certain situations in which interpreters may, legitimately or not, have a level of power to influence outcomes. This occurs particularly in domains where there is a **shared responsibility** between interpreters and service providers to achieve specific goals (e.g. in cases of child protection discussed in Chapter 6, or preaching explored in Chapter 7) but can also be observed when an interpreter aligns with the primary service provider or service user. This is an important aspect of self-reflection and will be addressed in Chapters 2–7.

The use of journals or logs to maintain a regular written record of reflection is commonly recommended. These may take the form of 'free writing' that encapsulate the facts of a situation as well as the emotional and intuitive responses experienced at the time. A regularly kept diary provides a starting point to connect those real-life experiences with scholarly developments and findings that could help solve issues that seem difficult or particularly complex. Given the emotional rigours of much interpreting work, keeping a log of feelings and responses can help to develop mental robustness and promote regular attention to personal care. Other approaches to reflection concern a set of cue questions and can help evaluate isolated critical incidents. Finally, reflection does not need to take the form of a written record; the oral exchange of experiences with peers, either immediately after the interpreted event at the work place or retrospectively, also benefits from the approach suggested above.

Professional development planning: Activity 7

Drawing on your recent experiences, use the following guidelines to develop an approach to reflection that suits your educational or professional context of practice. Note that these are presented as examples/options only and not as pre-determined stages.

A Preliminary work
Identify:

1   The focus of reflection

- a range of issues over a particular time span (e.g. workflow, quality, and extent of pre-assignment preparation);
- a 'critical incident' (i.e. a particular aspect of an assignment that challenged you);
- a feature of your interpreting practice (e.g. handling of register variation).

2   The timing of reflection

- weekly
- at industry conferences
- on CPD courses.

3   The nature of reflection

- performance-related dimensions (e.g. involvement, visibility, transparency);
- strategies employed to overcome particular challenges during an assignment;

- mood, emotion and quality of interpersonal relations;
- ethical and moral questions arising from an assignment;
- outcome of interaction and extent to which interpreter mediation facilitated the conversation.

4   The mechanism of reflection

- discussions with a friend or peer;
- written journal or blog.

5   Future actions and development

- categorise problem areas and plan alternative approaches;
- revisit earlier reflections and actions.

B Prompts for reflection on practice

- How effective was my pre-assignment planning in meeting the range of challenges in the assignment (e.g. linguistic, cultural, interpersonal)?
- How did the service provider and service user respond to my presence? Did I make my role clear? Was my role challenged in any way and, if so, how did I respond?
- How did I feel during the assignment – tired, awkward, valued?
- What could I do differently if I were to work with this service user/in this type of setting again in the future?
- Did I feel a certain level of accomplishment in advancing a better understanding of interpreting services that will positively affect how the users approach an interpreted encounter/interpreters' work (my own work included) in the future?

7 Collaborative approaches to continuing professional development

Interpreters may feel reluctant to collaborate in professional development activities due to the competitive nature of the work and because they may not see a return on their personal investment, at least in the short term. Nevertheless, the isolation entailed by freelance working suggests that considerable advantages can be gained from collaborative approaches in both personal and professional development terms. The following categories are a point of departure for understanding the nature of collaboration in different types of CPD activity:

- **Collaboration-as-observation**: watching a webinar or a conference, accessing archived CPD material, reading blogs, vlogs, etc. In this type of activity collaboration is typically limited to administrative matters but can include feedback on the events observed.
- **Collaboration-as-engaged participation**: exchanges with others in the form of peer-to-peer discussion, comments and/or questions in on- and

offline CPD activities. It also extends to collaboration with other professionals to enhance understanding of interpreter mediation. Knowledge is created dynamically but the participant can control the amount s/he shares.

- **Collaboration-as-content creation**: sharing specialist knowledge with others either commercially or freely. The activity may be uni-directional (e.g. knowledge is transmitted via webinar) or dynamic (e.g. knowledge is transmitted and transformed through a workshop or discussion with others).
- **Collaboration-as-organization**: CPD activity that is instigated but not necessarily delivered by an interpreting practitioner. It could be a one-off event or series of events designed to bridge a knowledge deficit in the wider profession or address a domain-specific competency of concern for that individual. It may also involve creating a network.

These categories, which can be extended and/or adapted by individuals, can also be mapped onto an individual's learning preferences and styles, and used to identify appropriate support mechanisms for core, developmental and domain-specific competency development. The categories also allow individuals to judge their desired level of collaboration and participation in relation to the time they have available and support a holistic approach to development.

7.1 Communities of Practice

The concept of a Community of Practice (CoP) presented in the introduction to this guide serves as both a type of mental or virtual framework (e.g. a way for practitioners to conceptualize their belonging to a profession) and a practical mechanism for development. As such it has the potential to cut across all of the categories of collaboration mentioned above. A Community of Practice that is conceived as a loose and flexible network can help individuals to understand that competition between participants not only exists but is healthy, and that trusting in the relationships in the community over time can help to support meaningful development for the individual on both a personal and professional level.

Individuals may be motivated to join a particular community out of a sense of belonging and desire to consolidate professional identity rather than for reasons of specific competency development but these motivations are not mutually exclusive. It can be helpful, then, to think of Communities of Practice in the plural rather than in the singular and anticipate that over the course of an individual's career, s/he may be involved in several communities concurrently or consecutively. Communities may be public or private (e.g. think of a members-only discussion list in a professional association or group, e.g. LinkedIn), emergent or stable.

Professional development planning: Activity 8

A   Outline the benefits and drawbacks of collaborative approaches to CPD.
B   Consider the advice you might give to an early career interpreter on how to identify opportunities and incorporate collaborative approaches into their CPD activity.
C   Reflect on the Community/ies of Practice to which you currently belong and consider ways you can provide additional support and derive further benefit as a result of your involvement.

8 Conclusion

Professional development planning presented in this chapter addresses the lack of guidance available to interpreters for engaging with continuing professional development in a sustained and meaningful way. It promotes an aligned approach to development planning through which interpreters are encouraged to reflect on priorities for professional growth, the nature of support provided by professional bodies and opportunities available for participating in targeted activities that take account of prior learning experiences, learning styles and preferences, and motivations. Reflective practices can be particularly useful if structured with reference to the dimensions of interpreter performance: involvement, visibility, transparency, coordination and co-construction.

For both early career and more experienced interpreters, reflective and collaborative approaches to professional development are suggested as a means to connect professional experience to the wider context of knowledge creation and collaborative working environments. They also help to foreground issues of sensitivity to cultural difference, personal care and the enhancement of moral and professional accountability.

Notes

1   Professional associations such as the American Translators Association and the Institute for Translation and Interpreting in the UK offer mentoring schemes for new interpreters.
2   Hvlac observes that although there is little difference between 'certify' and 'accredit', there are differences in usage at the national level and it is not uncommon for certification to be subordinate to accreditation processes (2013: 35).
3   Intended Learning Outcomes have emerged through approaches to curriculum design in Higher Education founded on models of constructive alignment (e.g. Biggs 1996) in which coherence between all elements in a programme of learning is promoted.

References

Advocates for Youth, *Tips and Strategies for Taking Steps to Cultural Fairness*. Online. Available at: www.advocatesforyouth.org/publications/publications-a-z/480-tips-and-strategies-for-taking-steps-to-cultural-fairness (accessed 29 March 2015).

Bennett, M.J. (1986) 'A Developmental Approach to Training Intercultural Sensitivity', *International Journal of Intercultural Relations*, Special Issue on Intercultural Training, 10 (2): 179–86.

Bennett, M.J. (1993) 'Towards a Developmental Model of Intercultural Sensitivity', in R. Michael Paige (ed.) *Education for the Intercultural Experience*, Yarmouth, ME: Intercultural Press.

Biggs, J. (1996) 'Enhancing teaching through constructive alignment', *Higher Education*, 32 (3): 347–64.

Eraut, M. (1994) *Developing Professional Knowledge and Competence*, London: Routledge Falmer.

Furmanek, O. (2004) *Transparency or Intervention: the role of the interpreter based on the philosophy of dialogue*, 2nd American Translation and Interpreting Studies Association Conference, Amherst, MA.

Hvlac, J. (2013) 'A Cross-National Overview of Translator and Interpreter Certification Procedures', *Translation and Interpreting, The International Journal for Translation & Interpreting Research*, 5 (1): 32–65.

Kelly, J. and Horder, W. (2001) 'The How and the Why: competences and holistic practice', *Social Work Education*, 20 (6): 689–99.

Megginson, D. and Whitaker, V. (2007) *Continuing Professional Development*, 2nd edn, London: The Chartered Institute of Personnel and Development.

Moon, J.A. (1999) *Reflection in Learning and Professional Development: theory and practice*, London: Kogan Page.

Pritchard, A. (2008) *Ways of Learning: learning theories and learning styles in the classroom*, Abingdon and New York: Routledge.

Schön, D.A. (1983) *The Reflective Practitioner: how professionals think in action*, New York: Basic Books.

Tervalon, M. and Murray-García, J. (1998) 'Cultural Humility versus Cultural Competence: a critical distinction in defining physician training outcomes in multicultural education', *Journal of Healthcare for the Poor and Underserved*, 9 (2): 117–25.

Tynjälä, P. (2008) 'Perspectives into Learning at the Workplace', *Educational Research Review*, 3 (2): 130–54.

Recommended reading

Furmanek, O. (2012) 'Professionalization of Interpreters', *The Encyclopedia of Applied Linguistics*, Oxford: Blackwell Publishing Ltd.

Lyons, N. (ed.) (2010) *Handbook of Reflection and Reflective Inquiry: mapping a way of knowing for professional reflective inquiry*, London: Springer.

2 Legal interpreting I
Criminal procedures

People have vomited on my suit. I have stepped into puddles of urine on a cell floor. Nobody warned me that I would have to deal with such situations. I had to learn how to cope with them.

(Magdalena Katarzyna Głowacka, legal interpreter, UK)

1 Introduction

Interpreting in the legal domain has received increasing attention from both scholarly and professional constituencies in recent years, and collaboration between legal services providers and university research teams have significantly shaped debate and policy in relation to limited proficiency speakers' access to justice.[1] The wide range of interpreted events encompassed under the heading of legal interpreting has led to further divisions in the form of subdomains such as employment tribunals and asylum procedure, the latter of which forms the focus of Chapter 3. Despite some overlaps between domains and subdomains there is sufficient domain-specificity in matters of criminal justice to merit a dedicated chapter to interpreted events in police and court settings which are the focus here, primarily in relation to English-speaking contexts.

The right to interpreting and translation in criminal proceedings is currently not guaranteed for all. Despite provision in international instruments such as the International Covenant on Civil and Political Rights (1966) and the European Convention on Human Rights and Fundamental Freedoms (1950, Article 6), relatively few countries have formalized these rights at the national level (Gamal 2009: 64). Even in countries where rights have been formalized, they might not be 'backed up by practical mechanisms' (Mikkelson 2000: 11) or automatically extended to other areas of the legal system such as correctional facilities and rehabilitation programmes.

The implementation of EU Directive 2010/64/EU on the right to interpreting and translating in criminal proceedings, for example, faces considerable obstacles in terms of its implementation across all Member States because of differences in the availability of interpreter education and accreditation schemes. Furthermore, policy changes at the national level are making it possible for un- or under-qualified interpreters to work in court, even in countries where advanced level education and accreditation schemes are available.[2]

Given the pivotal role of language in law enforcement and protection, inconsistencies at the level of the regulation and organization of interpreting provision are a source of concern to many interpreters and legal practitioners, and to some extent explain the recent emergence of lobby groups in calls for more coherent approaches to regulation and standards in the profession, especially in the European context.[3] Such inconsistencies underscore the fact that issues of quality assurance and regulation have yet to be comprehensively addressed across the domain.

In seeking to support the development of domain-specific competencies in police and court settings this chapter places particular emphasis on activities that develop awareness of police interviewing models, language strategies and power relations. In relation to court interpreting, readers are given guidance on how to review their current level of preparedness for handling the very wide range of language strategies used by courtroom agents (with reference to adversarial systems) and increasing use of technologies (see Section 7). As Mikkelson (2000: 22) observes '[t]he role played by the interpreter in the different phases of litigation is a function of the legal system prevailing in the country in question' and, while it is beyond the scope of this guide to provide a comparison of legal systems, the activities across the chapter invite readers to consider the implications of their local contexts in professional development planning.

2 Legal interpreting: settings and modes

Interpreter mediation in the legal domain first came to prominence through the trials in Nuremberg and Tokyo following the Second World War (Baigorri-Jalón 2014; Gamal 2009), which served as a launch-pad to careers in conference interpreting in international organizations for some of the interpreters involved. In fact court interpreting remains a conference-interpreter-led activity in large international institutions such as the European Court of Human Rights and the International Court of Justice in The Hague. Special arrangements were put in place for simultaneous interpreting at the International Criminal Tribunals for the Former Yugoslavia (ICTY) and Rwanda (ICTR); the latter, held in Arusha, Tanzania, involved teams of externally accredited and locally recruited conference interpreters.[4] These settings are known for the high levels of emotional stress experienced by interpreters.

The association of simultaneous interpreting with court interpreting at the international level to some extent explains why a distinction is often made between court and other forms of legal interpreting in which dialogue interpreting is prominent. Simultaneous whispered interpreting (*chuchotage*) is often used in courtrooms to permit a limited proficiency speaking defendant or witness to follow proceedings, but the short consecutive mode tends to be favoured when that person takes to the stand, as courtrooms within particular national contexts are seldom set up with simultaneous equipment. Exceptions, have been made, for example, in the trials relating to the Madrid bombings in 2004 when simultaneous interpreting was provided for the first time, albeit through loudspeakers in the courtroom (Martin and Ortega Herráez 2013).

Beyond the court setting, interpreters are employed in a wide range of legal and quasi-legal events involving both adults and juveniles in police interviews, lawyer-client meetings (criminal and civil procedure), tribunals (employment, family, asylum/immigration), parole hearings, rehabilitation and probation programmes, victim support programmes (e.g. domestic violence) and mental health-related assessments, in all of which dialogue interpreting is the principal mode, supported with sight translation where appropriate. Interpreters may be appointed by the state (either directly or through a contract-holder) or through private agencies and companies.

3 Police interpreting: scope and nature

Interpreting in police settings involves working with detained persons, victims and witnesses in interviews and during the taking of invasive and non-invasive samples such as fingerprints, DNA, etc. Interpreters in this domain may find that not all work involves their presence at a police station; raids on homes and businesses, road traffic accidents, surveillance operations and interviews with victims and witnesses occur in a range of locations and, at times, interpreters may be exposed to levels of danger that lead to the preference of telephone over face-to-face interpreting.

Practice varies with regard to the involvement of interpreters in different stages of criminal procedure, beyond considerations of which agent (state or private) is responsible for appointing their services. In some countries interpreters who are involved in early stages of a criminal investigation with the police cannot be involved in later stages in court, for example, in order to ensure a **fair trial**. This is the practice for example in England and Wales, and Belgium, but it is not the case everywhere, e.g. Czech Republic, France and Germany (Directorate General Justice 2012). Exceptions may be made in cases of languages of limited diffusion for which there may be a limited number of interpreters available.

 RESEARCH

Activity 1: Interpreting and local norms

Consider the different norms that govern an interpreter's involvement at different stages of criminal procedure in your country (be aware that norms may differ within a single geonational context).

A   What impact might an interpreter have on a trial process if s/he has worked in the earlier phases of a criminal investigation?

B   Find out the approach to the norms that govern the employment of interpreters at different stages of criminal procedure in your country of practice by contacting the interpreting service coordinator at your local court, or a relevant professional association. Examples include: Association of Police and Court Interpreters (APCI) in the UK and the National Association of Judiciary Interpreters and Translators (NAJIT) in the US.

The epigraph at the start of this chapter draws attention to some of the less salubrious aspects of interpreting in police settings, which are also known for antisocial working hours and potentially long, intensive interviews with detained persons, witnesses and victims. The unpredictable and varied nature of police-related work is an aspect that many interpreters find attractive. However, such unpredictability raises issues for workflow management, working conditions and pay, especially if a particular language community is very small and dispersed geographically; not all recruiting agents will cover travel time and travel expenses, for example.

There are few dedicated education programmes and certification schemes for police interpreting. Some believe this is due to the setting being overshadowed by court interpreting in both research and development terms, and yet, as Gamal (2014a: 73) observes, 'the majority of legal interpreting is done for the police and not inside the court'. The need for research and training (especially for police officers) in these settings is highlighted by Gamal (2014b) who observes that the police might only realise they need an interpreter for a particular operation once it has begun, which often means that they use the first person who is identified as available by the interpreting service provider. Even if a qualified interpreter is made available, the level of experience and knowledge of interpreting in police settings may be limited, which can have unintended consequences for the police investigation. Gamal even suggests that a centralized register for interpreters may not be the best way to address needs in this subtype of interpreting, thereby drawing attention to the need for domain-specific education and professional development.

Within a single case, an interpreter may be involved in a range of activities including the translation of documents (e.g. letters rogatory) and monitoring of live criminal operations through wiretapping. The fast-paced nature of developments on a case therefore means that flexibility in both translation and interpreting skills is often desirable. However, interpreters should not be expected to complete complex translation work when on a call-out for an interpreting assignment. In some cases (e.g. the Metropolitan Police in the United Kingdom), the protocols for working with interpreters and translators are set out in police operational plans; where such plans do not exist, interpreters will need to be clear about their ability and preparedness to take on certain types of activity (e.g. appropriate levels of remuneration need to be considered).

Interpreters based in more rural locations may find that the nature of criminal activity is less variable, although no less complex, and in small communities it is not uncommon for interpreters to regularly interpret for the same individuals and families. This does not mean that their ability to act impartially is necessarily compromised; however, it does mean special attention is needed in relation to personal relationships outside of the legal setting and within the local community to maintain discretion and for reasons of self-protection.[5]

4 Interpreter-mediated police interviews

The limited attention in initial interpreter education and research to the specific characteristics of police interpreting to date makes it difficult for interpreter practitioners to know how to best plan the development of domain- and setting-specific competencies. To support this process, the sections that follow provide an insight into some of the setting-specific issues that confront interpreters, which include problems of communicating rights to limited proficiency speakers and aspects of police interview strategies. Readers are also guided to reflect on the performance dimensions outlined in Section 6 of Chapter 1 through examples taken from authentic interpreted events and consider the implications of the findings in relation to interpreter decision making and accountability in police settings.

4.1 Communicating the rights of the detained person

In many English-speaking Western countries detained persons are made aware of their legal rights through the communication of set texts, typically known as a 'caution' or 'warning'. Failure to communicate these rights appropriately can result in charges being dropped and/or evidence being considered inadmissible by the courts at a later stage, as documented by Berk-Seligson (1990/2002) in relation to the case of *People* v. *Diaz* (1983). However, these texts pose a number of challenges in both mono- and bilingual police procedures, not least in terms of comprehensibility and delivery (by both police officers and interpreters), which are discussed below.

A police caution is designed to protect suspects from making an 'inculpatory statement or confession that could be used against them in a criminal trial' (Davis *et al.* 2011: 88). However, concerns have emerged about the ability of all detained persons to sufficiently understand both the basic propositional content of texts and their legal implications to a sufficient extent to make informed decisions, such as whether or not to waive a right to silence. In some countries such as the United States, the wording of the text can take multiple forms as highlighted in a study by Rogers *et al.* (2007) that analyses 560 versions of the Miranda Warnings used in federal and state jurisdictions in the United States for comprehensibility among the general population. One of the versions formed the object of analysis by Ainsworth (2010: 115):

'You have the right to consult with, and have present, prior to and during interrogation, an attorney either retained or appointed.'

Ainsworth (2010) draws attention to features of this text that are problematic for hearers to process and comprehend. These include the use of conjoined verbs ('consult with'/'have present'), which means that the hearer must process each right separately, the fact that both verbs are not presented with a direct object immediately afterwards as is commonly the case in English and, finally, the word 'attorney' is followed by two adjectives, which are also not in their usual position, i.e. before the modified noun.

▪ PERFORMANCE SKILLS

Activity 2: Language analysis

Read the text of the police caution used in England and Wales prior to questioning a suspect about an alleged offence (under the Police and Criminal Evidence Act 1984, Code C, para. 10):

> 'You do not have to say anything. But it may harm your defence if you do not mention, when questioned, something which you later rely on in court. Anything you do say may be given in evidence.'

A   Compare this text with the text of the Miranda Warning discussed by Ainsworth above and identify similarities and differences in content and tone.
B   Identify the possible linguistic challenges (e.g. grammar, vocabulary, register) in the caution for both native speakers and limited proficiency speakers.

In addition to the complex use of language, these types of text present communicative challenges because they are primarily considered as oral texts (Eastwood and Snook 2012), which can lead them to be treated as a form of ritual (Nakane 2007). As a result, the way in which officers deliver the text in interpreted events varies: some officers deliver it in full in one go (i.e. it is effectively recited), whereas others deliver a small section before pausing for interpretation. Both approaches can pose difficulties for the interpreter.

▪ PERFORMANCE SKILLS

Activity 3: Memory-based vs sight translation

A   Ask a partner to read out the police caution used in England and Wales (see text in Activity 2) for you to interpret:

   •   the first time the caution should be read out in one go followed by the interpretation from memory;

- the second time, the caution should be read out in shorter chunks for interpretation after each chunk (it is up to the reader to decide when to pause for the interpretation).

B   Perform a sight translation of the caution to your partner.

C   Consider the impact of the three approaches on:

- your short-term memory;
- clarity and accuracy of output;
- experience for the interlocutor (listenability, comprehensibility).

Nakane's (2007) study on six interpreted police interviews in Australia highlights difficulties some police officers experience in paraphrasing the caution without using legal and technical terms. In some countries officers are encouraged to explain the meaning in their own words if they have any doubts about the ability of individuals to comprehend, but in doing so must draw on available guidance, as is the case in England and Wales. Attempts to simplify such texts, as Rock (2007) observes, can obscure the intended meaning, which strongly suggests that the decisions taken by interpreters when navigating the complexities of these texts need to be negotiated with the law enforcement officer and made transparent to all parties present.

The importance of negotiation and transparency in interpreting is also highlighted by Nakane (2007), who contrasts the phrase 'you do not have to say anything' with a simplified version 'you do not have to answer any of the questions'. She concludes that the second phrase restricts the limited proficiency speaker's understanding of the types of silence in the interview process. This example highlights the level of caution needed in relation to interpreting strategy. For instance, it is not uncommon for interpreters to silently perform an 'intralingual' translation (i.e. reformulation in the same language) before verbalizing the interpreted output, as this is believed to lead to more idiomatic expression in the target language.[6] However, the example shows that such reformulations can have consequences for a limited proficiency speaker's understanding and subsequent decision making. It may appear that the phrase 'you do not have to say anything' is synonymous with 'you have the right to remain silent', but in the cultural and legal context in which the phrase is spoken, such an assumption may distort the intended meaning and have consequences for legal procedure.

4.2 Limited proficiency speaker expectations and interpreter positioning

In police interviews, as in other institutional contexts, limited proficiency speakers exhibit a range of responses to the presence of an interpreter, and their perceptions about the interpreter's role boundaries shape the manner in which they approach interaction and disclose information, among other factors (see Section 4.4). Expectations can be managed to a degree if a statement is given about the nature of the interpreter's involvement prior to the interview commencing. The following is an example of an introductory statement delivered (in this case) by the interviewing officer:

> (Interpreter's name) is an interpreter. He/she is not a police officer. The interpreter is independent. He/she is a professionally qualified interpreter. Interpreters have strict rules about how they work. The interpreter will interpret everything we say. He/she will not add, leave-out or change the meaning of our words. The interpreter will not help you. The interpreter will not give his/her ideas. You must not talk privately to the interpreter. I will decide what the interpreter does.
>
> If we know the interpreter has broken any of these rules, we will take action to make sure it does not happen again.
>
> (Metropolitan Police 2007: 19–20)

 COLLABORATIVE DIMENSIONS

Activity 4: Negotiating introductions

Interpret the introductory statement to a partner who understands your working languages and together reflect on your approach.

A   Do you think it is important to retain the third person? Why/why not?
B   Do you think that the interpreter should be permitted to make a statement independently? If so, what impact do you think this might have on the limited proficiency speaker, if any?
C   Research the interpreter statements used in your local context of practice. With a partner discuss ways in which the text(s) could be amended and justify your reasons.

This type of statement helps to establish the preferred mode of interpreting and set clear parameters for communication; it also acts as a warning to interviewees not to disclose information that they prefer to remain confidential and protects interpreters from giving out any personal details that might compromise their safety (Directorate General Justice 2012: 19). Interpreters need to feel confident in the level of personal protection they are afforded in police settings and may therefore need to take action to ensure parameters are both set and respected from the outset, especially if no formal introductory procedure is used.

4.3 Police interviews: principles and models

Police interview processes have come under increasing scrutiny in relation to their potential for eliciting false confessions, primarily due to the particular vulnerabilities of certain individuals and the use of so-called accusatorial (interrogation-based) methods in some contexts (Meissner *et al.* 2010). In England and Wales, for example, the Police and Criminal Evidence Act of 1984 led to changes in police interview techniques and effectively ended the interrogation approach. The rights of suspects were strengthened through the right to have a legal advisor present in the room, and all interviews were henceforth recorded. However, interviews are not recorded in all countries and, consequently, interpreters cannot necessarily be called as a witness about their own interpreting if a case goes to court.

The aim of police interviews is to retrieve sufficient information for decisions to be taken on subsequent actions (such as to charge, detain or grant bail), prevent false confessions and miscarriages of justice. Several interview models have been developed to facilitate the process, among which the Reid and PEACE interview models are prominent examples in North America, and the United Kingdom and New Zealand (among others) respectively. The PEACE model involves the following stages:

- Planning and preparation
- Engagement and explanation
- Account
- Closure
- Evaluation.

Interpreters are not commonly involved in preliminary interview planning processes; however, the situation is evolving. The New Zealand Investigative Interviewing Suspect Guide, for example, places emphasis on pre-interview planning in conjunction with interpreters and is supported by the idea that 'quality interpreting means quality information' (2012: 33).

The PEACE model is underpinned by a 'cognitive interviewing' approach (also found in aspects of the Reid interview technique) which has increasingly superseded approaches based on a pre-set list of questions. Fisher and Geiselman (2010) describe how pre-set questions can be counterproductive since officers need to frequently interrupt interviewees to ensure they keep to the question asked. This has been shown to hamper memory retrieval and lead to interviewees feeling that the quality of their answers is not good enough. Cognitive approaches, by contrast, foreground the interviewee's emotional state at the time an event took place, which means that the sequence of questions is adapted to the interviewee and not the other way round. Fisher and Geiselman provide the following example: 'if the interviewer needs to learn about the rapist's knife but the victim is currently thinking about the rapist's odor, then the interviewer should defer asking about the knife until the victim is thinking about the knife' (2010: 323).

In practice, the implementation of the PEACE model varies due to issues such as time constraints and its use in *volume crimes* (theft, robbery and assault), which are often handled by less experienced officers who have been found to omit some stages of the process (Dando *et al.* 2008). The next section examines aspects of police interview processes and their implications for interpreted events in more detail.

● RESEARCH

Activity 5: Approaches to police interviews

A   What impact, if any, do you think the two approaches to interviewing (interrogative based on a pre-set list of questions or cognitive) could have on interpreted interviews? For example, consider issues of turn taking and how you might handle lengthy answers in the cognitive approach.

B   Would you adopt different preparation strategies for each and, if so, what might they involve?

C   Research the approach to police interviews in your local context of practice.

D   If you find it difficult to research interview techniques, consider inviting a law enforcement officer to talk to your class or a local meeting of your professional association; or arrange a dedicated CPD event in your region.

4.4 Police interviews: language strategies and influencing behaviours

In this section the discussion moves away from general approaches to interviews to focus on aspects of language use at the micro level and strategies that may be employed to influence different phases of the interview process. It is important to understand that influencing behaviours vary and can be construed both negatively (e.g. in terms of coercion) and in more general terms as moving an interview on to a different phase.

In some countries police interviews count as evidence in themselves and the words spoken are said to have a 'dual context' and perform a correlating 'dual function' (Haworth 2010: 169). 'Dual context' refers to the idea that interviews are 'produced' in the police interview room and the courtroom; 'dual function' means they can be both investigative and evidential, that is, they can be used for fact finding and as evidence in court proceedings.

The dual function of interviews highlights the importance of **audience design** and the problem of managing interaction for future multiple audiences (Haworth 2013). In practice, this means that officers may (re-)frame questions and information in ways that a court will recognize as evidence; the term 'dual function' also draws attention to the range of linguistic resources and strategies which interviewing officers use and the type of influencing behaviours they may adopt in the interview.

Haworth (2013: 56) shows how information can be added in interviews to specify the temporal location of an event through the example of an officer making reference to 'this morning' in a question before swiftly adding

'Saturday the 6th of January' for the benefit of future listeners. Gibbons (2003: 85), by contrast, shows how an officer's choice of language in recording a suspect's statement of events might be re-worded for reasons of clarity of evidence:

SUSPECT: I was walking down the road.
OFFICER: I was proceeding down the highway in a south-easterly direction.

Although this approach may seem a little exaggerated to the lay person, it helps to emphasize the constraints faced by future listeners who do not have access to the full interview setting. It is also noteworthy because it is indicative of what Johnson (2006: 666) describes as a clash between so-called legislative and conversational discourses that often occurs in police interviews. In this regard, 'legislative' refers to the type of police speak used by officers in the workplace. Officers are known for moving between the two during an interview, sometimes without even realizing it, which poses a number of challenges for interpreters.

 PERFORMANCE SKILLS

Activity 6: Handling register variation

Read the following extract from a monolingual police interview. The officer is taking notes while the witness is speaking and immediately seeks to clarify the information given.

WITNESS: We were driving along in our car in the fast lane pretty quickly; the car in front braked suddenly and we ran into the car in front.
OFFICER: The vehicle was proceeding at speed along the offside lane and had a secondary collision with another other vehicle, is that right?

Imagine interpreting the officer's utterance in the context of this interview for the limited proficiency speaking witness and, recognizing that the officer is repeating the same information in police speak (or 'legislative discourse'), would you:

• reproduce the officer's language and register? Why?
• reproduce the detained person's version in the belief it is likely to be more easily understood? Why?

Interviewing officers also draw on other linguistic strategies to construct evidential discourse. The following example from Holt and Johnson (2010: 27) shows how the word 'so' can be used in an English language interview for this purpose. In this case, Holt and Johnson explain that the word indicates the interviewee's responsibility to agree or disagree. It also serves as an example of influencing behaviour that an interviewing officer may employ at different stages of the interview to move it on to a different (in this case the closing) phase:

INTERVIEWER: And how many drinks did you have in the Indian restaurant?
INTERVIEWEE: One.
INTERVIEWER: So are you saying that all evening you had four pints?
INTERVIEWEE: Mm.

The nature of influencing behaviours, especially in interrogation-focused police interviews has come under increased scrutiny in recent years in both standard (monolingual) and cross-cultural (bilingual) interviews in order to investigate and challenge problems of coercion and understand linguistic and cultural issues affecting interaction with interviewees. This type of research can help interpreters to understand interview policy and procedure developed at the institutional level and how it is applied in interviews by officers. As a result, interpreters can develop a more holistic understanding of their position in the interaction and manage expectations of the institutional interlocutor's approach.

Influencing behaviour in police interviews has been investigated in several studies, e.g. Beaune *et al.* (2010) and Beaune *et al.* (2011) to evaluate the extent to which interviewing strategies impact on the nature and range of responses elicited in cross-cultural interviews with individuals from different cultures. The 2010 study was framed in terms of perceived cultural differences between the Netherlands, a *low-context culture* (one that values deductive thinking, explicit communication strategies that are highly individualized), and Morocco, as an example of a *high-context culture* (where indirect communication and group identity are more prominent socially).

One of the interviewing strategies evaluated in the study concerns the so-called 'reasoned and rational argumentation' strategy, which is reflected in questions of the kind: 'you said you haven't been in the bookstore, so how do you explain that we have a witness that saw you there?' (Beaune *et al.* 2010: 911). The researchers found that this strategy tended not to elicit responses from the Moroccan interviewees in ways that occur typically among the indigenous population in the Netherlands. Instead, interviewees seemed to respond more favourably (i.e. they tended to provide more detailed information) to approaches based on a strategy known as 'being kind', i.e. active listening.

Having insight into interview strategies employed in the interpreter's local context of practice can help understand why interviewees may respond to some interview questions better than others and suggests that interpreters need to explore research findings from other disciplines to support their development. The natural tendency for interpreters to assume that communication problems or a lack of response are solely due to them (e.g. as a result of a poorly formulated question or utterance) can be put into perspective through such knowledge.

A more specific example of this concerns the way in which an interpreter may construe the impact of her/his actions in cases where interviewees tend to agree with officers' questions in ways that appear to constitute agreement or even a confession (known as *acquiescence*). Simply agreeing to all questions might suggest to the interpreter that the interpretations have not been fully understood and that the interpreter needs to alter her/his approach. However, having insight into the wider (cultural) reasons acquiescence may be exhibited by an interviewee can help the interpreter to put the interviewee's responses into perspective. For example, research shows that high levels of acquiescence can be due to cultural differences in approaches to interpersonal communication that have their roots in specific cultures and social groups, e.g. those for whom the 'desire for surface harmony and the avoidance of interpersonal conflict' is very strong (Berk-Seligson 2009: 103).[7] Awareness of the impact of interview strategies and points of cultural tension between different social groups in interpersonal communication can therefore support the interpreter's decision making by helping prevent unnecessary attempts to clarify and/or reframe propositional content.

 PERFORMANCE SKILLS

Activity 7: Interviewing techniques in practice

A Interviewing a suspect
Scenario: A young male limited proficiency speaker has been arrested on suspicion of aggravated burglary and is interviewed by a police officer.

a   Role play the scenario using the approach of a pre-set list of questions based on your knowledge of the law in relation to this crime in your local context of practice.
b   Using the guidelines for the different stages of and approaches to a PEACE interview (see Appendix 1), role play the scenario again and reflect on the issues affecting interpreter mediation in both.

B Interviewing a victim and taking a statement
Scenario: A police officer interviews a 20-year-old female following the theft of her handbag in a restaurant during which she was also punched in the face. Using the guidelines to PEACE interviews, role play the discussion and statement-taking process.

For further guidance on interpreting in police interviews please see the materials on the Routledge Translation Studies Portal.

4.5 Interpreter performance

This section explores examples of authentic interpreted police interviews from the perspective of the performance dimensions discussed in Chapter 1

(Section 6). The aim is to highlight the complexity of interpreter decision making *in situ* and support approaches to pre-interview planning meetings with police officers. The extracts are also designed to stimulate reflection on interpreter accountability and decision making in relation to interpreter codes of conduct and on the importance of knowledge about some of the more intricate aspects of police procedure.

The first performance (or in this case, set of performances) concerns Krouglov's (1999) analysis of interpreted police interviews with four Russian-speaking sailors about a murder that had taken place in the port of an unspecified English-speaking country. Three of the sailors were interviewed in parallel using three different interpreters, followed by a fourth interview slightly later on with a fourth sailor and one of the interpreters used in the other interviews.

The findings, among other things, highlight the importance of socio-cultural and situational knowledge in the interpreting process, as exemplified by the problematic Russian phrase '*Ya tebya uroyu*'. In the three interviews with witnesses held in parallel, the phrase was interpreted as: 'I'll kill you', 'I'll get you' and 'I will stitch you up'. The phrase was particularly problematic for the interpreters due to differences in the length of time the witnesses had spent working as sailors and because it is a phrase associated with sailors' jargon. Krouglov (1999: 288–9), for example, shows how the use of the phrase suggests conflicting positions on the part of the interviewees, which makes it particularly difficult to interpret. He explains that if the phrase is used in a way that corresponds with commonly used sailors' jargon it can be considered more of a throwaway comment that constitutes no threat to the interviewee's face (see Section 6.3 for a discussion of face). By contrast, one of the interviewees exhibited a higher level of education but limited experience as a sailor compared to the others interviewed. As such, the use of the phrase in this particular interview could be construed as more aggressive and face-threatening due to the limited exposure to sailors' jargon.

The analysis leads Krouglov to make a series of recommendations for interpreters, namely that during interaction an interpreter's output should take account of: (1) the relative social status of the interlocutors; (2) the tenor of the discourse, that is, the nature of participant relations; and (3) cultural factors such as cultural inheritance and life experience. Krouglov also recommends that the interpreter explain linguistic issues as they arise to interviewing officers, thereby emphasizing the importance of transparency in the interpreter's performance. In the fast-moving context of the police interview, especially in cases where a witness might say something that changes her/his status into a suspect, the interpreter's intervention and contribution in the ways suggested above are considered warranted.

In this particular study, a briefing with officers prior to the fourth witness being interviewed helped to shape the interviewing officer's approach, especially with regard to the critical phrase *Ya tebya uroyu*, which had been interpreted differently in each of the three previous interviews. Krouglov adds that the example in question was played in court, which means that scope is available for an expert witness linguist to provide further analysis and interpretation on the language in the interview later in the legal process. Not all of the interpreters involved in this case were necessarily aware that this phrase had particular connotations when used among sailors, which highlights their limited scope for reflection on aspects of tenor or participant relations *in situ*.

A second example of an interpreted police interview concerns issues of involvement and transparency relating to the problem of 'repair', and draws on Nakane's (2009) study involving Japanese speakers in Australia. The example highlights tensions that can emerge when interpreter performance and decision making are almost exclusively evaluated in deontological terms, that is, in relation to a code of conduct.

The first extract from the study highlights the extent to which interpreters think that responses such as 'what's that?' or 'what do you mean?' to their interpretations are being directed at them as though they had created the problem, leading to the need for correction or 'repair'. The issue is also common to monolingual interactions as Nakane shows by drawing on Heydon (2005). In monolingual sequences, repair commonly takes the form of a four-part sequence exemplified as follows:

POLICE OFFICER: (Question 1, trouble source) Did you get into the car with the girl?
SUSPECT: (Question 2, next turn repair initiator) Did you say 'the car'?
POLICE OFFICER: (Answer 2, question 1 repair) Yes.
SUSPECT: (Answer 1) No I didn't get into the car.

In interpreted events, by contrast, the four-part sequence becomes an eight-part sequence, as in Nakane's (2009: 5) example:

Extract 1
POLICE OFFICER: What did you do with this, (0.2) form? (0.6) when you filled it out. (1.4)
INTERPRETER: *Kono shoshiki o kinyuu shita toki ni,* (1.0) *kono shoshiki ni tsuite nani o shimashita ka? = Kono shoshiki o dō shimashita ka?*
(translation): 'When you filled out this form, what did you about this form? (*sic*) What did you do with this form?'
INTERVIEWEE: *Ah? Mō ikkai, mō ikkai.*
(translation): 'Ah? Again, again.'
INTERPRETER (TO THE POLICE OFFICER): Could you repeat the question again?
POLICE OFFICER: After you filled this form out, did you give it to anyone?
INTERPRETER: *Kono shoshiki o kinyuu shita ato ni, dareka ni watashimashita ka.*
(translation): 'After you filled this form out, did you give it to anyone?'
INTERVIEWEE: *Watasanai.*
(translation): 'I didn't give it [to anyone].'
INTERPRETER: No, I didn't.

In this sequence, Nakane describes the interpreter as playing the role of an *animator*, that is, a person who speaks entirely on behalf of the primary interlocutors in an approach that is designed to preserve and emphasize impartiality. The ability of the interpreter to consistently maintain this approach throughout the interview is examined through the analysis of later sequences of talk. In the extract below (Nakane 2009: 7), information in bold typeface denotes information not available to the police officer.

Extract 2
POLICE OFFICER: How long have you been a jeweller?
INTERPRETER: *A, donokurai hōsekishou o itonanderasshaimasu ka?*
(translation): 'Uh, how long have you been a jeweller?'
INTERVIEWEE: *Ie anō hōseki wasukoshi nandesu kedo.*
(translation): 'No um actually [I deal with] jewellery a little.'
INTERPRETER: *Hai.*
(translation): Yes.
INTERVIEWEE: *ato tokei da toka=*
(translation): 'And [I deal with] watches or'
INTERPRETER: =Ano kikan wa dorekurai desu ka?
(translation): 'Um how long was the duration?'
INTERVIEWEE: *Ētto juunen kurai.*
(translation): 'Uhm about ten years.'
INTERPRETER: 'Uh I have been a jeweller for the last ten years.'

The salient aspects of this extract concern the nature of the repair which takes the form of an 'off-the-record repair' (i.e. it is not available to the police officer), the attempt by the interpreter to provide the police officer with an answer that is deemed acceptable (i.e. that answers the officer's original question) and the extent to which the interpreter complies with the (Australian) National Accreditation Authority for Translators and Interpreters Ltd (NAATI) code of conduct. In this example the interpreter's actions are deemed to violate the principle of accuracy in the code because the interpreter omitted to mention the reference to the watches in the interpretation, and the principle of impartiality due to the level of filtering in the interpretation.

The third example of an interpreter's performance in a police interview is taken from Gallai (2013: 195) and concerns the use of discourse markers (words like 'so' and 'well') and discourse operators ('right' and 'okay') in interpreted police events. Research in court interpreting (e.g. Hale 1999), has found that interpreters regularly omit these words, which Gallai's findings – based on a relevance-theoretic study on interpreted police interviews – appear to corroborate. The impact of omissions on the police interview are examined in the following discussion of an extract concerning an interview with a vulnerable child, Manuel, the alleged victim of a robbery in a park, which lasted about 25 minutes.

The interview is defined as a *vulnerable witness interview*[8] and is held with only Manuel, the interpreter and the police officer present in the room. The extract is taken from the rapport-building phase early in the interview, which is designed among other things to explore the child's understanding of truth and lies and to estimate the child's level of knowledge and linguistic competence. The extract shows the interpreter taking the role of principal interlocutor and becoming a **co-participant** or even co-investigator (displaying co-power), omitting discourse markers and implementing strategies that go beyond what Gallai considers to be an ethically acceptable level. Translations are provided in italics.

35	P	Okay (.) er:: (..) I'll just (.) ne:ed to make sure we get everybody introduced **so** Mariza can you just say what your name is and what your role is...
36	I	°Er°
37	P	Today please
38	I	My name is Mariza (.) João and I'm the interpreter
39	P	Okay thank you (..) er:: and er can you just give me your name and date of birth please?
40	I	Podes dizer o teu nome e a tua data de nascimento [por favor?] *Can you give your name and your date of birth [please?]*
41	M	[em português] ou em inglês? *[in Portuguese] or in English?*
42	I	O que é com- como tu quiser! (.) he:'s asking should I answer in Portuguese or in English? *Whatever yo- as you wish!* and I said whichever one you want
43	M	I can say in (..) in English
44	I	Just say it in Portuguese fala em português ((chuckles)) *speak Portuguese*

Of note in this extract is the interpreter's decision to disregard the officer's opening line and the discourse marker 'so', which means she switches from being an *animator* (i.e. speaking on behalf of another person) to principal interlocutor who provides a direct response. The interpreter is also seen to omit *'okay'* in 39. As Gallai explains, 'okay' and 'right' are the most commonly used discourse operators in interviews and are similar to non-linguistic expressions like *mh mh* and *uhm*. They serve as a means to verbalize the listener's attention (also known as *discourse particles*) and as an unwarranted means of managing the turn-taking system, due to poor memory retention.

Gallai describes how the word *'okay'* used by the officer in 35 and 39 can be analysed in procedural and not in translational terms as an expression which leads the hearer to an interpretation. In this case, the use of 'okay' indicates that Manuel has identified (what he takes to be) the intended contextual effects or that he believes that all participants have understood each other in that they have recovered the intended effects of the utterances made so far. However, it is important to note that the speaker may be wrong to assume the interview is going okay. Gallai concludes that the omission by the interpreter has a major effect on the officer's investigative techniques, particularly, rapport building.

Lastly, the extract contains instances (42 and 44) where the interpreter stops interpreting and starts talking as a third party, which further disrupts the rapport between the interviewer and child. This is highlighted through Manuel's request for clarification as to which language he must adopt (41) which is confronted by the interpreter's rather abrupt response 'As you wish!' (42). When the child tentatively tries to speak English, the interpreter again intervenes, this time suggesting to '[just] say it in Portuguese' with a chuckle. Although Manuel's statement in (43) was ignored and found amusing by the interpreter, Gallai observes that it constituted an important piece of information. If the interpreter had not interrupted the child, a longer narrative regarding the child's level of knowledge and linguistic competence may have been elicited. Instead, the police officer is left to accept the interpreter's decision in (44).

The examples of interpreter performance in this section draw attention to the complexities of interpreter decision making in police interviews. The recommendations made by Krouglov in relation to interpreter involvement based on the socio-cultural characteristics of the interview in question suggest a framework within which interpreters can work that will allow decisions to be transparent and for the interpreter to hold her/himself accountable. However, the practicalities of developing the desired levels of awareness prior to the interview as recommended by Kruglov raise further developmental issues for both the law enforcement and interpreting professions to address. The approach adopted in New Zealand mentioned earlier is perhaps something for other police systems to consider as good practice.

The examples also suggest that in order for the interpreter to have better control of her/his accountability and decision making, knowledge of police procedure at a fairly fine-grain level is needed to ensure institutional procedures unfold with minimal compromise. The seemingly inconsequential exchange between the interpreter and the child described above is indicative of the need for such awareness.

5 Court interpreting: scope and nature

5.1 Court hearings

The scope and nature of interpreting in court settings are shaped by the overarching principles governing the system in question, e.g. whether accusatorial (in common law countries), inquisitorial (in civil law countries) or other, and the extent to which more than one legal tradition may operate

(Mikkelson 2000). Eades (2010) demonstrates how the scope and nature of court interpreting can be investigated by outlining the range of events that take place within the criminal courtroom, among which the trial is considered the most significant, especially in adversarial systems. Furthermore, she observes that 'Despite having different legal purposes, these events are mostly consistent in their ways of speaking, including the use of routinised formalities' (2010: 34). However, the sense of routine can sometimes lead interpreters to underestimate the complexities of courtroom language use and asymmetries of power relations in their professional development, especially in countries where the adversarial system is used. In fact, the 'asymmetrical distribution of interactional power in these settings is one of the core issues in the study of dialogue interpreting' (Pérez-González 2006: 393), and possibly one of the most neglected in initial interpreter education.

De Jongh (2012: 42) also provides a useful overview of the scope and nature of court interpreting in criminal proceedings by setting out pre-trial proceedings in Criminal Actions in the United States: arrest, citation, complaint, information or indictment; initial appearance; bail or detention hearing; discovery and motions, plea negotiations, change of plea hearing or trial. Although terminology and procedure differ according to judicial system (e.g. not all systems allow plea negotiations),[9] a key point is that the length of hearings in pre-trial phases can vary significantly, with some lasting no more than ten minutes. However, as de Jongh observes, some hearings regarding decisions about bail and detention can be lengthy, especially in cases involving more than one defendant (ibid.: 58–9). Since many cases are resolved before going to trial, these shorter hearings often constitute a high proportion of the court interpreter's workload, but they raise important issues for interpreters in terms of payment structures.

5.2 Developing setting-specific competencies

At the national level, the range of certification schemes, education programmes and resources for court interpreters currently appears to far outstrip those available in relation to police settings. However, practitioners in some countries (e.g. Beresford 2011 in relation to the UK) have expressed concerns about the extent to which initial interpreter education provides sufficient depth of core, developmental and domain-specific competency development (see Introduction, Section 3) and the extent to which it sets the foundations for effective continuing professional development. These concerns are supported by evidence from research (e.g. Hale 1997, 2007, 2010, 2014) which finds in particular a lack of awareness among interpreters of the strategic use of language in the courtroom and of the impact of modifications to questions, unwarranted interruptions and the omission of important information, even among trained interpreters.

Hale's research highlights two areas of language use in cross-cultural court interpreting that appear particularly challenging for interpreters. The first concerns possible misunderstandings in relation to the ways in which 'different languages express pragmatic intention' (an example of which is the use of the imperative form in making a polite request in English as in 'give me your name' vs 'can you tell me your name please?'); the second concerns possible misunderstandings caused by 'different types of behaviour considered appropriate in certain settings by different languages and cultures' (Hale 2014: 323–4).

The reasons for the lack of linguistic awareness are many and complex but in some countries the models used to deliver initial interpreter education (especially where interpreter education is delivered outside of the university system) may partly explain the situation. This particularly concerns programmes where teaching is almost exclusively carried out through the medium of the receiving country language and language-specific input is minimal. In such cases interpreters are effectively left to develop domain-specific language competency skills on their own. The variability in literacy and prior educational experience among some trainee interpreters can also mean that peer feedback on matters of language use may not serve to support development appropriately. The time dedicated to developing self-knowledge in initial interpreter education and its importance for self-reflexive practice (i.e. the ability to incorporate cultural awareness and humility into practice) appears, anecdotally at least, very limited.

Although it is beyond the scope of this guide to address such issues in depth, the sections that follow are designed to assist structured reflection on current core and developmental competencies and planning for setting-specific professional development.

6 Interpreting in court: key issues

6.1 Preparing for court: learning to think forensically

As mentioned above, some interpreters have expressed concerns about opportunities for setting-specific competencies development in the legal domain, which is why the concept of thinking forensically is promoted to support independent approaches to continuing professional development (see Introduction, Section 3). The concept is used in general terms here to denote an approach to practice that is underpinned by a scientific eye for detail and systematic thinking. For example, understanding the street talk of a criminal gang in relation to the procurement of weapons and the technical descriptions of ballistics by an expert witness in a courtroom demand a level of knowledge and linguistic flexibility that go far beyond a basic glossary of key words that might be recommended in initial interpreter education.

Knowing where to begin to develop linguistic knowledge is not always self-evident but the availability of online resources means that the situation is evolving rapidly. Part of professional development in relation to core competency development therefore concerns advanced information mining skills and the ability to organize sources in ways that support specific activities. Miguélez (2001: 4), for instance, draws on publicly available information (in the form of authentic transcribed courtroom testimony) through which passives, multiple negatives, misplaced or intrusive phrases and unusual prepositional phrases and clauses are highlighted as characteristic of English legal language. This sort of close linguistic analysis is a good example of the systematic approach and eye for detail mentioned above.

Deepening awareness of language in use in legal settings in general terms can be complemented by reflection on specific features of language that can be impacted by fragmented delivery in interpreted events. Hale (2010: 447), for example, explores this by focusing on the way which Spanish and English speakers express the manner of motion, drawing on a study by Filipovic (2007) on witness testimony.

WITNESS: pero ... salió por la seven.
literal translation: *But ... (he/she/you formal) exited via the seven.*
INTERPRETER: The suspect ran up 7th street.

In this example Hale observes that in certain English-speaking jurisdictions, questioning practices place emphasis on the manner in which an action takes place, which contrasts with the Spanish language where such detail tends to be absent. Hale claims that in situations like this the fragmentation of delivery often leads interpreters to feel the need to add descriptions of manner, as in the example above where the verb *salió* (went out) is interpreted as 'ran up'.

From this short extract, Hale concludes that the interpreter's output is a reflection of her/his own perception of the event, which, crucially, may differ from the actual reality being described by the witness. She also highlights that although the interpreter's actions show an attempt to render the information idiomatically and in a way that reflects language as it is actually used, the content is affected. In other words, we do not know whether the person did actually run at this point in the interaction. For interpreters working between Spanish and English, then, descriptions of manner would be an appropriate sub-topic for reflection (see also Section 6.5 on ambiguity).

Insight into these features of language and/or domain-specific language analysis is not readily available through textbooks on language and the law, which underscores the importance of observing court hearings, where permitted, and scrutinizing publicly available documentation and other materials (e.g. videos of authentic courtroom interaction available online).

● **RESEARCH**

Activity 8: Legal language in use

Reflect on recent interpreting assignments in court, or, if you have never inter-preted in such settings, search online for video materials of authentic/mock interactions in legal settings in your working languages.

A   Note down concepts that are/were crucial to the case in question (e.g. consent, liability, intent …) and key phrases/features of language.
B   Consider the extent to which a particular concept/feature of language has an identifiable equivalent in the other language and culture, and the extent to which a verbatim translation might be needed in place of a more idiomatic rendering in order to convey a cultural particularity. Note that you may need to conduct research on practice in more than one country where your working languages are spoken.
C   Develop your understanding further by searching for examples of judgments and rulings in cases involving the concepts you have high-lighted to understand how the concepts have been used in context and what was at issue in the case. Examples of useful online resources (cover-ing a wide range of legal cases and not just criminal cases) from English-speaking contexts include:

> The Supreme Court, UK: www.supremecourt.uk/decided-cases/index.html
> The Oyez Project at the Chicago-Kent College of Law, USA: www.oyez.org/cases/

6.2 Environment, status and expectations

The physical environment of the courtroom impacts on interpreting in ways that are often beyond the interpreter's control. Regardless of the courtroom layout, the interpreter is a highly visible agent as a result of swearing in, jury selection and clarification processes (Berk-Seligson 1990/2002: 56); further-more, the triadic configuration common to so many encounters in com-munity and public service interpreting is typically broadened to include multiple interlocutors with very different needs and motivations for being present.

When not giving evidence, defendants may be seated in an open dock accompanied by an interpreter and security personnel. In some courtrooms the dock is made of glass with openings in the side through which the inter-preter must communicate, or a metal cage. The layout of the courtroom, then, can therefore pose a range of physical challenges for the interpreter, not least the ability to hear everything clearly. For instance, interpreters can find them-selves sat behind legal personnel who are facing away from the interpreter and toward the judge, which, in addition to poor acoustics, can generate considerable strain when providing whispered interpreting (*chuchotage*).

Some jurisdictions, however, operate a policy of strict separation between interpreters and defendants in the courtroom, e.g. in Austria (Morris 1999). This creates additional constraints in that interpreting is limited to occasions where the defendant is directly addressed. In other words, it prevents simultaneous interpreting of other court interactions and limits the defendant's opportunity to alert her/his counsel to any problems in relation to interpreter mediation. Portable interpreting equipment (e.g. bidule interpreting) may be available to interpreters and some jurisdictions permit interpreters to use their own equipment (Morris ibid.). This can be useful in cases where an interpreter is required to interpret aspects of court business simultaneously for more than one defendant. In Section 7.2.2 recent innovations in technologies are discussed that are leading to more use of simultaneous interpreting in the courtroom.

The status of the interpreter can also vary between jurisdictions, with some considering interpreters as 'officers of the court', which has a number of implications for court procedure. First and foremost this status serves as a reminder to those present that the interpreter is in court to interpret for all parties needing interpretation and is not on either the defendant's or prosecution's side. Rosado (2015), for example, explains how 'officer' status can impact on the administration of the interpreter's oath in some courts in the USA to the extent that some interpreters are required to take the oath every day, or once for an entire case, and in other cases (for both staff and contract interpreters) it is just administered once and kept on file. Rosado considers such practices demeaning to the professionalism of interpreters and he reports on comments made by Judge Ruben Castillo (co-chair of the American Bar Association Section of Litigation's Trial Practice Committee), which suggest that interpreters take their job more seriously when the oath has been administered for each case. However, it is worth noting that the practice of swearing an oath only once has been common practice in other countries such as Germany for many years, and so cross-national comparisons in this regard would be a useful subject for further research.

Similar to police contexts, court-appointed interpreters are often not permitted access to prehearing preparations, chiefly out of concern for impartiality. While this might be of less importance in relation to very short hearings (e.g. plea and directions, committal of a case to a higher court, and sentencing), for which a simple charge sheet can supply sufficient information, in longer proceedings such as trials, the lack of prior awareness of the topic, terminology and chronology of a case is considered a potentially serious impediment to performance. This is because it risks generating more need for questions and clarifications on the part of the interpreter in ways that might unnecessarily interrupt court proceedings (Gamal 2009: 65).

In a report on a national survey of interpreter policies, practices and protocols in the Australian court system, Hale (2011: xiii) finds that

> [a]djournments are more likely to occur when interpreters are not pro-
> vided with materials; [judicial officers or JOs and tribunal members]
> who accept interpreters regardless of their qualifications are less likely to
> provide them with preparation materials and JOs who explain the inter-
> preter's role are more likely to provide background materials.

An example of good practice in this regard is taken from the Judicial Council of Georgia's guidelines on working with interpreters in courts: 'when pos-sible allow the interpreter to review case file information in advance'.[10]

Limited access to information about a case reflects the well-documented legal professionals' desire for access to 'unprocessed' materials (Morris 1999). This desire is reflected in surveys conducted among court personnel (e.g. Hale 2004; Lee 2009) that show some legal professionals view accuracy as being achieved through literal (or verbatim) approaches to interpreting at the word level. This has become normalized in some jurisdictions where court inter-preters are guided to perform literal interpretations, an example of which will be explored later (see Section 6.3). In addition, Lee's (2009) survey reveals expectations that interpreters will place more emphasis on reproducing coun-sel's speech style than on a witness's style in the Australian adversarial system, suggesting a strong concern by legal professionals for interpreter mediation not to disrupt established power relations in the courtroom.

However, as in other domains discussed in this guide, research shows that interpreting practice regularly deviates from established guidelines or norms, whether explicitly or implicitly, largely as a result of the interpreter's own understanding of their role and how it should be executed (Paulsen Chris-tensen 2008; Shlesinger 1999). Although some interpreters' actions may be construed as a form of deviation in a negative sense, they need to be evalu-ated taking into account several factors: first, that most work alone in such settings; second that the level and nature of the education received by inter-preters whose work has been the object of research is often unknown or not reported in any depth; and third, interpreters' responses can be affected by unexpected deviations from court norms by legal personnel (e.g. judges who switch between reported and direct speech).

 RESEARCH

Activity 9: The interpreter's oath/affirmation

Compare the following examples of court interpreter oaths:

1   England and Wales

> 'I swear by Almighty God (or I do solemnly declare) that I will well and
> faithfully interpret and make true explanation of all such matters and
> things as shall be required of me according to the best of my skill and
> understanding.'

2   Tennessee Supreme Court

> 'Do you solemnly swear or affirm that you will interpret accurately, completely and impartially, using your best skill and judgment in accordance with the standards prescribed by law and the Rules of Ethics for Spoken Foreign Language Interpreters in Tennessee Courts; that you will follow all official guidelines established by this court for legal interpreting or translating, and discharge all of the solemn duties and obligations of legal interpretation and translation?'

3   Canada

> 'Do you solemnly swear/affirm to translate accurately from English/ French to XXX (the language of the person concerned) and from XXX to English/French every thing that is said during the hearing and every document that is presented in evidence?'

A   In the first oath (England and Wales), how do you think interpreters and other courtroom participants are to understand the words 'and make true explanation'? To what extent might an interpreter construe these words as being at odds with codes of ethics that specify no additions should be made to utterances?
B   Do you think the oath should make it explicit whether the interpreter is an 'officer of the court'? Why/Why not?
C   To encourage international comparisons and dialogue, set up an online forum and discuss the approaches to the interpreter's oath in courts in your local context of practice in terms of the content of the text and the way it is administered.

6.3 Face

A recurring theme in intercultural communication in the courtroom concerns the visibility of the interpreter (in terms of her/his physical presence) and tensions inherent in representing another's voice in open court. The concept of **face** in court interpreting in criminal cases has received considerable scholarly attention, not least because of its importance to defendants' and witnesses' ability to give a credible account of themselves to the judge and courtroom (e.g. a jury), but also because of the interpreter's need to maintain others' confidence in them as translators and interpreters (Jacobsen 2008: 129).

In general terms, face is understood as the ways in which (linguistic) politeness impacts on interpersonal communication, that is, on how meanings are exchanged and negotiated (Mason and Stewart 2001), and on the extent to which individuals signal their identification with another person. Early research on court interpreting (e.g. Berk-Seligson 1990/2002) revealed a tendency for interpreters to elevate the register of witness testimony using a uniformly hyperformal style, motivated by a desire to be seen in a favourable light and a competent interpreter by the courtroom.

There are various ways in which a defendant's and a witness's face may be threatened in the adversarial courtroom; these include requests for information that the witness or defendant is unwilling or unable to give, questions designed to challenge a person's positive self-image as someone who is cooperative and trustworthy, and questions that suggest the inability to provide information is an attempt to mislead the court (Jacobsen 2008: 133).

A study that analysed interpreter mediation for a witness (Rosa López) in the trial of OJ Simpson by Mason and Stewart (2001: 56–7), for example, shows how an established norm of the federal court – according to which interpreters are to provide a literal interpretation – can impact on face and the way in which a witness is represented. Under cross-examination during the testimony in question, the witness is challenged about a claim that she had reserved a flight back to El Salvador. When pressed by the attorney to explain why she had just told the court she had made a reservation, the response is:

> 'No pero voy a hacerlo no mas salir de aqui (xxx) tiempo para salir (waves arm). No voy a hablar a las diez/a la una de la mañana…'. This was interpreted as 'No but I am going to do it as soon as I leave here (xxx) time to leave. *I am not going to* speak at ten/at one in the morning…'
>
> (2001: 61, emphasis in the original)

The part of the sentence highlighted in italics is crucial to the issue of face in this extract. Mason and Stewart assert that the interpreter's literal approach required by the court reduces the face-threatening force of the witness's response in two ways: first, it presents the witness as being unable – and not unwilling – to phone the agency at 1am and, crucially, it obscures the fact that the nature of the response was designed to reject the attorney's line of questioning. In short, as Mason and Stewart (2001) observe, by following the court's requirements for literal interpretation, the attempted face-saving response of the witness, which idiomatically might be translated as 'I'm hardly going to phone at one in the morning', and implicated admission of guilt are lost.

6.4 Question styles in the adversarial courtroom

Pöchhacker and Shlesinger (2008) stress that the manner in which questions are posed in the courtroom is as important for procedure as the content of the questions themselves. However, they present a number of challenges for interpreters, particularly in the adversarial courtroom. Pérez-González (2006: 395), for example, observes that certain codes of ethics encourage interpreters to refrain from 'explicating or clarifying those elements which are deliberately or inadvertently left ambiguous, implicit or unclear in the counsel's original formulation'. In fact, attempts to clarify lawyers' questions in court are often viewed as disruptive to established power relations (Berk-Seligson 1990/2002: 78).

In adversarial systems questions are posed during examination-in-chief and cross-examination; the different purpose of each entails a different approach to question forming and tone. Under the former, as Hale (2004: 33) observes, witnesses are typically questioned in a non-confrontational manner and in a way that invites open narrative and detail, whereas under the latter, the purpose is to challenge and potentially discredit evidence. The tone is more aggressive and individuals are given a much narrower range of response options. The typical sequences for each according to Hale (ibid.) are:

EXAMINATION-IN-CHIEF:
1   Elicitation of personal details.
2   Framing the evidence (setting the scene) – usually achieved through short, closed questions that elicit a yes/no response.
3   Elicitation of the witness's version of events – usually open-ended questions.

CROSS-EXAMINATION:
1   Re-establishment of undisputed information – usually through short, leading questions to elicit yes/no answers.
2   Clarification of disputed facts.
3   Presentation of disputed facts and open confrontation – usually taking the pattern of short yes/no questions, followed by declarative question types with tags.

The question and answer format is central to the power dynamics in the adversarial courtroom, with laypersons being excluded from posing questions (Hale 2001). Commonly used question types in the English adversarial courtroom include closed questions (e.g. yes/no questions) and open or information-seeking questions. According to Hale (ibid.: 27), within the first category, two subcategories exist, namely 'tag questions' (typically comprising a statement with a tag question at the end, as in 'you left the restaurant at 8.30, did you?') and 'declarative questions', formulated by making a statement with a rising intonation at the end.

Question forming can pose problems at the level of equivalence (grammatical, pragmatic, among others) as Hale's research shows. Close scrutiny of court interaction (whether live court hearings where permitted or using online materials) can help interpreters to anticipate issues in their working languages and is part of the forensic thinking approach to professional development.

6.5 Ambiguity

Coping with ambiguity is difficult in cases involving spoken evidence as Shuy (2012) observes. As discussed above, the fragmentation of spoken language delivery often observed in interpreter mediation can generate uncertainty and ambiguity about context and meaning (see Section 6.1). Although ambiguity can also be a strategy on the part of the witness and counsel in examination processes, interpreters need to be alert to instances where such strategies are being employed and those where they occur unintentionally, and thus where warranted intervention to clarify might arise.

Ambiguity typically arises as a result of different interpretations of events described by individuals. Shuy provides the example of the phrase 'we'd been carrying on and carrying on' spoken by a female complainant in a sexual misconduct case, which was interpreted by the accused as a reference to 'the playful but improper touching and flirting that he willingly admitted' (2012: 220). However, the female in question had made an accusation of indecent exposure and assault and battery, which contrasted starkly with the male's own interpretation of events. As Shuy observes, 'when [the male] said "it will never happen again", the unspecified meaning of "it" in this sentence had very different meanings to the police' (ibid.).

In sexual misconduct cases, the use of vague terms to avoid explicit language and descriptions is commonplace. Shuy discusses a case where the phrase 'it was a mistake' led to an individual being indicted for molesting a child because of ambiguity as to whether (in this case) 'it' referred to the child's dreams or real events. Similarly, the individual's use of 'I'm sorry for that' meant that there was ambiguity around what the person was sorry for.

There are no specific guidelines for interpreters on how to deal with ambiguity but it can be helpful to consider strategies in relation to the performance dimensions mentioned in Chapter 1. Consultation with other professional participants in the event leading to transparency of decision making is recommended in cases where doubts about speaker intention arise.

6.6 Interpreting expert witness testimony

Finally, this section explores expert witness testimony as a feature of courtroom interpreting. Although such testimony follows the same question and answer format as in other courtroom events, it poses particular challenges for interpreters in terms of performance and preparation, especially in relation to the simultaneous interpreting mode.

An expert witness is a person who possesses knowledge or experience of a particular field (beyond that expected of a lay person) and who makes that knowledge and experience available to a courtroom. Expert testimony can cover a very broad range of subject areas from anaesthesiology, serology and blood typing to geology, minerology, crime scene management and family therapy, and is used in both civil and criminal cases. The purpose of an expert witness is to help a court 'understand the issues of a case and reach a sound and just decision'.[11] This means that the expert's duty is first and foremost to the court and might mean that the testimony runs counter to the client's case. As witnesses might be on the stand for long hours, it is a particular test of stamina for interpreters, especially since it is one of the most dense types of speech or 'text' that interpreters can encounter in court (Palma 1995).

A study on expert witness testimony by Miguélez (2001) in the United States of America analysed approximately 75,000 words of publicly available transcripts, which revealed a surprisingly low amount of technical jargon used by expert witnesses. The study also draws attention to the fact that specialized speech of the kind expert witnesses deliver is likely to contain just as many inconsistencies of the type observed in other spontaneous speech. However, the analysis reveals the need for interpreters to be aware of common terms taking on unfamiliar meanings in a specialized context. Examples from Miguélez's study include: 'what is the proximation?' (i.e. distance) and 'we were able to lift latent prints from several surfaces' (i.e. get a copy of fingerprints) (2001: 8).

 PERFORMANCE SKILLS

Activity 10: Preparing to interpret expert witness testimony: *chuchotage* and peer evaluation

A   Gather examples of expert witness testimony in your working languages. Although it is possible to access transcripts of expert witness speech from courts, there is usually a fee involved. Sample written texts of cross-examination of expert witnesses are available (in English) for example at:

> http://defensewiki.ibj.org/index.php/Sample_Cross-Examination_
> Transcripts#Cross-Examination_of_Pathologist

Video material is also available online through a range of non-subscription channels, for example on YouTube. Type 'expert witness testimony in court' into the search facility and a range of materials will be listed that will serve as a guide to cross-examination techniques and language styles. Short excerpts can be transcribed (and translated) to create exercises in your working languages.

B   Select excerpts from the materials collected to use in small group work. Ideally working in groups of three, take turns at the same material with one person reading while another simultaneously interprets for the third person. It is suggested that the group use short and relatively straightforward excerpts (at least initially) and stop frequently to peer evaluate the interpreter's performance, before moving on to more complex materials.

Note: This activity is not recommended for interpreters who have not been trained in simultaneous interpreting techniques.

For further guidance on developing confidence in whispered simultaneous interpreting, please see the materials on the Routledge Translation Studies Portal.

7 Technology and interpreter mediation in legal settings

Modern policing is increasingly using new technologies, from roadside mobile devices that check driver credentials and insurance, to camera technology fitted to officers, and tablet devices to facilitate administrative duties out on the road; it is also increasingly a feature of interpreter mediation in police settings. The discussion in this section focuses on issues of first and third person interpreting and the difficulty of coordinating turns at talk and handling non-verbal communication, aspects that fall under the performance dimension of coordination of the interpreted event.

Remote interpreting through telephone or videoconferencing is used in particular when face-to-face arrangements cannot be provided in a timely manner, e.g. drink/drug-driving procedures in the street and in situations deemed too dangerous for face-to-face interpreting. However, it is advised against in some situations such as in the initial in-depth interviewing of suspects, and in cases involving minors and vulnerable adults.

7.1 Remote interpreting: telephone interpreting in police settings

Telephone interpreting is a well-established method of remote interpreting service delivery in public, community and business settings; however, issues of sound quality, poor regulation of turn taking, relinquishing the phone to another user before the interpreter has finished speaking are commonly reported, meaning that it is often viewed less favourably than face-to-face interpreting. Several configurations of participation are possible (Ozolins 2011): three-way conversations where everyone is on a separate phone or a configuration involving primary participants (e.g. service provider and limited proficiency speaker) are in the same room and use a speaker phone or pass a phone between them.

This form of interpreting entails a greater reliance on auditory clues for receiving and transmitting information such as tone of voice, volume and pronunciation (Kelly 2008), and can place the interpreter under added pressure, especially if the encounter is lengthy. Additionally, the clarity of speech of limited proficiency speakers – be they witnesses, victims or suspects – can be affected by a range of emotions such as fear and anger in the aftermath of an incident.

The use of first person in telephone interpreting is something that interpreters may find interferes with the need for interpreter-initiated communications at the periphery of interaction in this mode of delivery. Research (e.g. Lee 2007) has found that interpreters often privilege the third person, chiefly as a response to the lack of eye contact between interlocutors and the need to (re-)establish turn taking and the narrative thread of the conversation when the floor is handed to a different interlocutor. Furthermore, in dealing with the emotional states of individuals, the interpreter may find it helpful to act assertively to guide communication in ways that are also more likely to lead to the use of the third over the first person, as in 'I know this is difficult for you, but I need to ask you to try and speak more slowly so that I can communicate all of the details to the officer accurately'. The use of the third person may also arise as a result of comments on technical issues, such as problems with the line quality (see Kelly 2007, 2008).

By contrast, issues of non-verbal communication in telephone interpreting are highlighted among others in a study by Wadensjö (1999) of an interpreted police interview in Russian and Swedish with a victim of domestic assault in which the victim reported a preference for the interpreter to be present in the room after having an opportunity to experience both remote and face-to-face interpreting. The study shows the officer in question's awareness of the disadvantage of the interpreter not being in the same location as the victim and helped to communicate aspects of non-verbal communication where necessary (e.g. when the victim was demonstrating how a knife had been used). The officer also indicated how the interpreter should 'interpret' longer stretches of silence, as in:

POLICE OFFICER: Nu skriver jag så det blir tyst ett tag.
(translation): Now I write a little so it'll be silent for some time.

The study also highlights the importance of conversational rhythm and synchronicity (i.e. how participants coordinate their contributions) in situations where a (victim's) story is being told and the impact of telephone interpreting on the process. In particular, the study shows how the victim provided more details in the face-to-face interview where the other participants were more readily able to give 'feedback' through signs of agreement or indications of understanding (e.g. 'mm, do go on'), and synchronize their turns at talk by reading the non-verbal gestures of the others present. This type of research can help interpreters manage telephone-mediated interpreting events by providing cues to the sort of information that the interpreter will find valuable in managing their part in the process and that they can draw on to negotiate interview parameters prior to it commencing as part of a shared responsibility to the limited proficiency speaker.

7.2 Remote interpreting: videoconferencing

7.2.1 Police settings

Video-conference interpreting (VCI) is a fairly recent development in police settings. For example, a project was introduced by the Metropolitan Police in London, UK (2011) involving eight video interpreting centres or 'hubs', used in cases ranging from theft to drug offences and domestic assault. Early evaluations of the project reveal significant savings on interpreter travel time; however, the impact on delivery and fairness of justice is still under investigation, e.g. through the AVIDICUS project.[12] As Braun and Taylor, assert 'Procedural fairness is closely linked to the quality of communication, and in national and transnational cases involving more than one language the quality of the interpretation is a crucial element' (2011: 85). However, as this section shows, there are distinctions to be made between an individual's perception of technology on interpreter mediation and its actual impact.

A study on the use of VCI technologies in police interviews by Rombouts (2011: 141) reports on difficulties encountered by interviewers as a result of the distance from the other interlocutors, namely, the ability to express empathy, adjust communication channels, convey messages to and interpret messages communicated by the interviewee, some of which were also present in Wadensjö's (1999) study discussed above. The primary interlocutors in the interview also found that having the interpreter present in the same room made a difference to the communication in that it appeared more direct and familiar.

In order to move beyond perceptions of the impact of interpreter presence/absence discussed in Rombouts' (2011) study, Braun and Taylor (2011) investigated the impact of remote interpreting on police interviews by comparing face-to-face and remote delivery. The authors conducted a quantitative analysis of 16 interviews based on language-based and non-verbal categories. The language-based category included elements such as omissions, additions, inaccuracies, lexical and terminological problems; the non-verbal category involved issues such as problems with gaze and individuals being out of shot.

As anticipated by the researchers, the number of problems identified in relation to both categories was higher in the remotely interpreted interviews, albeit to varying degrees. It appeared that in terms of inaccuracies observed, there was very little difference between the two modes. However, on closer inspection, when the inaccuracies were broken down into further categories (e.g. distortions, minor distortions, minor other inaccuracies, inaccurate names and numbers), greater differences emerged, the most salient of which were 'distortions' (the most problematic category), which occurred twice as frequently in the remote mode. Examples include:

1   **Mishearing:**
    DETAINED PERSON: Elle m'accusait devant tout le monde.
    (translation): She was accusing me in front of everybody.
    INTERPRETER: And she was abusing me in front of everybody.
2   **Summary rendition:**
    POLICE OFFICER: Then I said, 'The people at the cab office said you
        did [hit Ms Jones].'

INTERPRETER: Ensuite-, ensuite, euh, j'ai dit, euh, ce que les employés ont dit.

(translation): Then, then, uh, I said, uh, what the employees at the taxi stand said.

(Braun and Taylor 2011: 93)

7.2.2 Court settings

The use of VCI in court settings is becoming a feature of the court interpreting landscape around the world. It has been used, for example, in Singapore for many years (Ozolins 1998) and sporadically elsewhere (see Section 2), but is only more recently beginning to be implemented in other jurisdictions.

For example, VCI technology was piloted in some courts in England and Wales in 1998–2000 before being rolled out more widely. It involves several configurations with the interpreter either in the prison building with the limited proficiency speaker or in the courtroom. The system has received considerable criticism, not least due to issues of reliability with the equipment. One court interpreter in the UK reported an instance where the screen had frozen, leading the court to believe the limited proficiency speaker had fallen asleep (Devaux forthcoming).

In the United States, the Ninth Judicial Circuit of Florida has responded to a significant rise in demand for court interpreting through the development of remote interpreting using videoconferencing technology, as its eight staff interpreters who were covering 67 court rooms spread across 2,229 square miles could not meet the demand. As an indication of the scale of demand, in 2009/10 the Circuit provided interpreting (Spanish/English) for more than 25,000 court hearings (Ninth Judicial Circuit of Florida website).

The interpreter works at a separate location to the court and, using a Web-based system, speaks to the courtroom via loudspeakers and to the limited proficiency speaker through a headset (the interpreter needs to manipulate the microphone when switching between audiences to ensure the responses from the limited proficiency speaker can be heard in the open courtroom). Facilities also exist to permit counsel to communicate with their clients through the interpreter without the rest of the court hearing the conversation.

According to the Judicial Circuit's website, the system is used in relation to a limited number of hearings, including: initial appearances, arraignments, traffic and misdemeanour cases, and felony pre-trial hearings. The benefits for the court include increased operational effectiveness and no undue delays due to having to wait for an interpreter. Significant cost reductions have been achieved as a result of paying-per-minute instead of a minimum two-hour callout, and there are plans for the system to become state-wide, thereby permitting increased pooling of interpreters and increased efficiency savings.

RESEARCH

Activity 11: Impact of technologies

A   With a partner discuss some of the implications of a Web-based interpreting system like the one in the Ninth Judicial Circuit of Florida for: a) interpreters (education and practice) and b) limited proficiency speakers (nature of their participation).

B   Why do you think the system in Florida is limited to certain types of hearing? Could it be extended to other hearings?

C   Do you think remotely delivered services impact on the notion of the interpreter being an 'officer of the court' as described earlier in relation to certain jurisdictions?

D   Discuss the pros and cons of different payment models for interpreters in such systems (e.g. a pay-per-minute model vs a minimum hourly rate).

7.3 Adapting skills to meet service users' needs

Despite preferences for face-to-face interpreting in many legal settings, remote interpreting is swiftly becoming a feature of the interpreting market in both public service and conference-based settings, which has implications for managing the different performance dimensions highlighted in Chapter 1 and professional development planning (see also Chapter 4, Section 2).

The idea of the interpreter as a coordinator of others' talk and not simply a conduit of others' talk has become a well-acknowledged description of what interpreters actually do (introduced by Wadensjö 1998). However, remote interpreting requires interpreters to cast fresh light on how they view their coordinating role and acknowledge the need to be involved more explicitly during remotely interpreted events as necessary. This may entail giving assurances to all parties that interpersonal communication channels are indeed open (rather than expecting everyone to assume they are) and ensuring that emotions such as empathy (e.g. through discourse particles) are expressed to enable all parties to feel they are fully participating in the interaction.

Preparation for this type of work is best achieved experientially, that is, learning by doing. Training is often provided by the larger telephone interpreting providers, but an interpreter may not be aware of all of the possible pitfalls such as the extent to which the quality of their own hearing might impact on their ability to interpret. Some of the examples given above of inaccuracies in interpreting could be due to technical issues, but they could also be physiological (e.g. fatigue, hearing impairment and stress levels).

■ PERFORMANCE SKILLS

Activity 12: Remote interpreting in police settings

A For each of the scenarios described below make a list of potential challenges for the remote interpreter and reflect on the range of strategies available to mitigate their impact on communication:

1 A driver of a large pick-up truck has collided with a car on a motorway pushing the car into its path. The police arrive at the scene and the drivers of both vehicles are able to move their respective vehicles to the hard shoulder. The driver of the pick-up does not speak the language of the country in which s/he is working.

The law enforcement officer communicates with the driver through an interpreter using a mobile phone. The interpreter suspects that the driver is under the influence of alcohol from the way s/he speaks.

2 A raid on an apartment block finds two women apparently being used as domestic slaves. A neighbour called the police and alerts them to the situation and the lack of language proficiency.

As there are no local interpreters who speak the language of the women, you are contacted to do a telephone-interpreting encounter. The police officer uses a mobile phone with the speaker-phone facility switched on. The women are emaciated, covered in bruises and are in a highly agitated state.

3 An interpreter is called to establish a video link with a police station where a suspect is to be interviewed by a police officer about bags of what look like stolen laptop computers found in the boot of a car, the driver of which was stopped after it had been reported stolen.

B Working in a group of three, improvise a conversation based on each scenario using mobile phone technologies or video-based internet technologies to simulate practice. Review each interpreter's performance in relation to some of the issues listed in this section and discuss the range of strategies used to address them.

8 Conclusion

Interpreting in police and court settings typically falls under the less involved end of the spectrum compared to other domains due to the strict procedural constraints that underpin interaction. However, this chapter provided evidence to suggest that approaching interpreter mediation from a perspective of **shared responsibility** is gaining ground in relation to pre-event preparation (in both police and court settings), premised on the idea that quality information for the institutional interlocutors is more likely to lead to quality interpreting. We extended such thinking to professional development planning in the belief that quality information on technical aspects of police interviews can usefully support the process. Similarly, local approaches to cultural difference in question forming can usefully support improvements across performance dimensions.

Understandings of **involvement** and **visibility** were also shown to be evolving in these settings due to an increased use of remote interpreting with implications for the level of the interpreter's **co-power**. We suggested that shared responsibility can increasingly be viewed as a feature of the interpreted event, i.e. during interaction and not just prior to it (pre-event) in remote modes, but the limited amount of research in this area means that the frameworks for developing relevant competencies require attention.

In terms of developing a subset of domain-specific competencies in face-to-face interaction, evidence of limited attention to core linguistic competencies in some initial interpreter education and its consequences in the police interview room and courtroom supports the promotion of a more systematic or **forensic** approach to thematic and linguistic knowledge enhancement. Progress in these areas rests on structured independent learning, but both intra- and interprofessional collaboration were highlighted as an important adjunct.

Notes

1 See for example the AVIDICUS project: www.videoconference-interpreting.net, Building Mutual Trust project www.building-mutual-trust.eu and SOS-VICS on domestic violence, University of Vigo, Spain http://cuautla.uvigo.es/sos-vics/ (accessed 25 May 2015).

2 For a discussion of some of these issues in the UK for example, consult the House of Commons Justice Committee report *Interpreting and Translation Services and the Applied Language Solutions Contract*, Sixth Report of Session 2012–13. Online. Available at: www.publications.parliament.uk/pa/cm201213/cmselect/cmjust/645/645.pdf (accessed 10 May 2015).

3 Examples of such groups include the Professional Interpreters' Association (PIA), Interpreters for Justice in the UK, and Fair Trials International and Rights International Spain.

4 For more information on interpreting at ICTY see Elias-Bursać (2015) and on interpreting at the ICTR, visit www.tribunalvoices.org (accessed 14 April 2015).

5 See 'The Rural Interpreter' (2012), NAJIT website: http://najit.org/blog/?tag=rural (accessed 2 April 2015).

6 This is similar to processes of 'deverbalization' described in the conference interpreting literature where interpreters are said to mentally strip away the form of the words to access meaning or 'sense' (see Seleskovitch and Lederer 1984).

7 Berk-Seligson (2009) discusses the case of Spanish-speaking Miguel Peralta, a 20-year-old US Latino male, who was convicted for the murder of an elderly lady, Louise Patterson, in the United States of America. The level of acquiescence revealed in the interview is shown to a type of response that is considered to have its roots in particular cultural contexts and social groups for whom the 'desire for surface harmony and the avoidance of interpersonal conflict' is very strong (Berk-Seligson 2009: 103).

8 As defined by section 16 of the Youth Justice and Criminal Evidence Act 1999 (as amended by the Coroners and Justice Act 2009), children are defined as vulnerable 'by reason of their age' (section 16(1)).

9 Key to terminology: a citation is a charge usually relating to a petty misdemeanour, a complaint usually comes from an individual asking the prosecutor to initiate charges, an information concerns a charge brought by a prosecuting attorney and an indictment are charges brought through a grand jury (de Jongh 2012: 42). Discovery concerns the exchange of information about witnesses and evidence that will be presented at trial (ibid.: 39) and motions concern requests by parties for a judge to make a ruling on a legal matter of dispute (ibid.: 60).

10 See http://w2.georgiacourts.gov/coi/files/Brochure%20Working%20with%20 Interpreters%20PDF.pdf (accessed 1 April 2015).

11 See www.ukregisterofexpertwitnesses.co.uk/AboutExpertWitnesses.cfm (accessed 2 January 2015).

12 Consult the project website for information on the project aims and findings: www.videoconference-interpreting.net (accessed 14 April 2015).

References

Ainsworth, J. (2010) 'Curtailing Coercion in Police Interrogations – the failed promise of *Miranda* v. *Arizona*', in M. Coulthard and A. Johnson (eds) *The Routledge Handbook of Forensic Linguistics*, Abingdon and New York: Routledge.

Baigorri-Jalón, J. (2014) *From Paris to Nuremberg: the birth of conference interpreting*, Trans. H. Mikkleson and B. Slaughter Olsen, Amsterdam/Philadelphia: John Benjamins Publishing.

Beaune, K., Giebels, E. and Taylor, P.J. (2010) 'Patterns of Interaction in Police Interviews: the role of cultural dependency', *Criminal Justice and Behavior*, 37 (8): 904–25.

Beaune, K., Giebels, E., Adair, W.L., Fennis, B.M. and Van der Zee, K. (2011) 'Strategic Sequences in Police Interviews and the Importance of Order and Cultural Fit', *Criminal Justice and Behavior*, 38 (9): 934–54.

Beresford, K. (2011) 'Slash and Burn', *ITI Bulletin*, September–October: 13.

Berk-Seligson, S. (1990/2002) *The Bilingual Courtroom: court interpreters in the judicial process*, Chicago and London: University of Chicago Press.

Berk-Seligson, S. (2009) *Coerced Confessions: the discourse of bilingual police interrogations*, Berlin and New York: Mouton de Gruyter.

Braun, S. and Taylor, J.L. (2011) 'AVIDICUS Comparative Studies – part I: traditional interpreting and remote interpreting in police interviews', in S. Braun and J.L. Taylor (eds) *Videoconference and Remote Interpreting in Criminal Proceedings*, Guildford: University of Surrey.

Dando, C., Wilcock, R. and Milne, R. (2008) 'The Cognitive Interview: inexperienced police officers' perceptions of their witness/victim interviewing practices', *Legal and Criminal Psychology*, 13 (1): 59–70.

Davis, K., Fitzsimmons, C.L and Moore, T.E. (2011) 'Improving the Comprehensibility of a Canadian Police Caution on the Right to Silence', *Journal of Police and Criminal Psychology*, 26 (2): 87–99.

De Jongh, E.M. (2012) *From the Classroom to the Courtroom: a guide to interpreting in the U.S. justice system*, American Translators Association Scholarly Monograph Series XVII, Amsterdam and Philadelphia: John Benjamins Publishing Company.

Devaux, J. (forthcoming) 'Interpreting for Better or for Worse: ethics and the use of videoconference interpreting in court settings', in C. Valero Garcés and R. Tipton (eds) *Translating Conflict: ethics and ideology in public service interpreting and translation*, Clevedon: Multilingual Matters.

Directorate General Justice (2012) *Improving Police and Legal Interpreting (ImPLI)*, Final Report (2011–12). Online. Available at: http://impli.sitlec.unibo.it/pdf/ImPLI2012Final_Report.pdf (accessed 10 May 2015).

Eades, D. (2010) *Sociolinguistics and the Legal Process*, Bristol, Tonawanda, Ontario: Multilingual Matters.

Eastwood, J. and Snook, B. (2012) 'The Effect of Listenability Factors on the Comprehension of Police Cautions', *Law and Human Behavior*, 36 (3): 177–83.

Elias-Bursać, E. (2015) *Translating Evidence and Interpreting Testimony at a War Crimes Tribunal: working in a tug-of-war*, Basingstoke and New York: Palgrave Macmillan.

Filipovic, L. (2007) 'Language as a Witness: insights from cognitive linguistics', *International Journal of Speech, Language and the Law*, 14 (2): 245–62.

Fisher, R.P. and Geiselman, R.E. (2010) 'The Cognitive Interview Method of Conducting Police Interviews: eliciting extensive information and promoting therapeutic Jurisprudence', *International Journal of Law and Psychiatry*, 33 (5): 321–8.

Gallai, F. (2013) 'Discourse Markers in Interpreter-Mediated Police Interviews: an interdisciplinary approach', PhD thesis, University of Salford, UK.

Gamal, M.Y. (2009) 'Court Interpreting', in M. Baker and G. Saldanha (eds) *Routledge Encyclopedia of Translation Studies*, 2nd edn, Abingdon and New York: Routledge.

Gamal, M.Y. (2014a) 'The World of Police Interpreting', in A. Arnall and A. Gentile (eds) *AUSIT 2012: Proceedings of 'JubilaTIon 25'*, Biennial Conference of the Australian Institute of Interpreters and Translators, Newcastle: Cambridge Scholars.

Gamal, M.Y. (2014b) 'Police Interpreting: a view from the Australian context', *International Journal of Society, Culture and Language*, Special Issue on Translation, Society & Culture, 2 (2): 77–88. Online. Available at: http://ijscl.net/article_7724_848.html (accessed 4 May 2015).

Gibbons, J. (2003) *Forensic Linguistics: an introduction to language in the justice system*, Oxford: Blackwell.

Głowacka, M. (2012) 'Violent Clients, Traumatised Victims, Late Payment – the life of a court interpreter', *Guardian*, 15 March 2012. Online. Available at: www.theguardian.com/law/2012/mar/15/court-interpreters-protest-over-contract (accessed 20 May 2015).

Hale, S.B. (1997) 'Interpreting Politeness in Court: a study of Spanish–English interpreted proceedings', in S. Campbell and S. Hale (eds) *Proceedings of the 2nd Annual Macarthur Interpreting and Translation Conference 'Research Training and Practice'*, Milperra: UWS Macarthur/LARC.

Hale, S.B. (1999) 'The interpreter's treatment of discourse markers in courtroom questions', *Forensic Linguistics: The International Journal of Speech, Language and the Law*, Special Issue on Legal Interpreting, 6 (1): 57–82.

Hale, S.B. (2001) 'How are Courtroom Questions Interpreted? an analysis of Spanish interpreters' practices', in I. Mason (ed.) *Triadic Exchanges: studies in dialogue interpreting*, Manchester: St Jerome.

Hale, S.B. (2004) *The Discourse of Court Interpreting: discourse practices of the law, the witness, and the interpreter*, Amsterdam and Philadelphia: John Benjamins.

Hale, S.B. (2007) *Community Interpreting*, Hampshire: Palgrave Macmillan.

Hale, S.B. (2010) 'The Need to Raise the Bar: court interpreters as specialized experts', in M. Coulthard and A. Johnson (eds) *Handbook of Forensic Linguistics*, London and New York: Routledge.

Hale, S.B. (2011) *Interpreter Policies, Practices and Protocols in Australian Courts and Tribunals: a national survey*, Melbourne: Australasian Institute of Judicial Administration Incorporated.

Hale, S.B. (2014) 'Interpreting Culture: dealing with cross-cultural issues in court interpreting', *Perspectives: Studies in Translatology*, 22 (3): 321–31.

Haworth, K.J. (2010) 'Police Interviews in the Judicial Process: police interviews as evidence', in M. Coulthard and A. Johnson (eds) *Handbook of Forensic Linguistics*, London and New York: Routledge.

Haworth, K.J. (2013) 'Audience Design in the Police Interview: the interactional and judicial consequences of audience orientation', *Language in Society*, 42 (1): 45–69.

Heydon, G. (2005) *The Language of Police Interviewing: a critical analysis*, Basingstoke: Palgrave.

Holt, E. and Johnson, A. (2010) 'Legal Talk. The sociopragmatics of legal talk: police interviews and trial discourse', in M. Coulthard and A. Johnson (eds) *The Routledge Handbook of Forensic Linguistics*, London: Routledge.

Jacobsen, B. (2008) 'Interactional Pragmatics and Court Interpreting: an analysis of face', *Interpreting*, 10 (1): 128–58.

Johnson, A. (2006) 'Police Questioning', in K. Brown (ed.) *The Encyclopedia of Language and Linguistics*, vol. 9, Oxford: Elsevier.

Judicial Council of California (2013) Professional Ethics and Standards for California Court Interpreters, 5th edn. Online. Available at: www.courts.ca.gov/documents/CIP-Ethics-Manual.pdf (accessed 19 May 2015).

Kelly, N. (2007) *Telephone Interpreting: a comprehensive guide to the profession*, Victoria, CA: Trafford Publishing.

Kelly, N. (2008) *A Medical Interpreter's Guide to Telephone Interpreting*. International Medical Interpreters Association. Online. Available at: www.imiaweb.org/uploads/pages/380.pdf (accessed 20 May 2015).

Krouglov, A. (1999) 'Police Interpreting: politeness and sociocultural context', *The Translator*, Special Issue on Dialogue Interpreting, 5 (2): 285–302.

Lee, J. (2007) 'Telephone Interpreting – seen from the interpreters' perspective', *Interpreting*, 9 (2): 231–52.

Lee, J. (2009) 'Conflicting Views on Court Interpreting Examined through Surveys of Legal Professionals and Court Interpreters', *Interpreting*, 11 (1): 35–56.

Martin, A. and Ortega Herráez, J.M. (2013) 'From Invisible Machines to Visible Experts: views on interpreter role and performance during the Madrid train bomb trial', in C. Schäffner, K. Kredens and Y. Fowler (eds) *Interpreting in a Changing Landscape: selected papers from Critical Link 6*, Amsterdam/Philadelphia: John Benjamins.

Mason, I. and Stewart, M. (2001) 'Interactional Pragmatics, Face and the Dialogue Interpreter', in I. Mason (ed.) *Triadic Exchanges: Studies in Dialogue Interpreting*, Manchester: St Jerome.

Meissner, C.A., Redlich, A.D., Bhatt, S. and Brandon, S. (2010) *Interview and Interrogation Methods and Their Effects on True and False Confessions*, Oslo: The Campbell Collaboration. DOI: 10.4073/csr.2012.13.

Metropolitan Police (2007) *Working with Interpreters and Translators: standard operating procedures*. Online. Available at: www.met.police.uk/foi/pdfs/policies/interpreters_and_translators_sop.pdf (accessed 24 February 2015).

Miguélez, C. (2001) 'Interpreting Expert Witness Testimony', in I. Mason (ed.) *Triadic Exchanges: Studies in Dialogue Interpreting*, Manchester: St Jerome.

Mikkelson, H. (2000) *Introduction to Court Interpreting*, Manchester: St Jerome.

Morris, R. (1999) 'The Gum Syndrome: predicaments in court interpreting', *International Journal of Speech, Language and the Law: Forensic Linguistics*, Special Issue on Legal Interpreting, 6 (1): 6–29.

Nakane, I. (2007) 'Problems in Communicating the Suspect's Rights in Police Interviews', *Applied Linguistics*, 28 (1): 87–112.

Nakane, I. (2009) 'The Myth of an "Invisible Mediator": an Australian case study of English-Japanese police interpreting', *PORTAL: Journal of Multidisciplinary International Studies*, 6 (1). Online. Available at: http://dx.doi.org/10.5130/portal.v6i1.825 (accessed 20 May 2015).

New Zealand Investigative Interviewing Police Unit (2012) *New Zealand Investigative Interviewing Suspect Guide*. Online. Available at: https://fyi.org.nz/request/244/response/2484/attach/5/Investigative%20interviewing%20suspect%20guide.pdf (accessed 17 April 2015).

Ozolins, U. (1998) *Interpreting and Translating in Australia: current issues and international comparisons*, Victoria: The National Languages and Literacy Institute of Australia.

Ozolins, U. (2011) 'Telephone Interpreting: understanding practice and identifying research needs', *The International Journal for Translation and Interpreting Research*, 3 (1): 33–47.

Palma, J. (1995) 'Textual Density and the Judiciary Interpreter's Performance', in M. Morris (ed.) *Translation and the Law*, American Translators Association Scholarly Monograph Series Volume VIII, Amsterdam and Philadelphia: John Benjamins.

Paulsen Christensen, T. (2008) 'Judges' Deviation from Norm-based Direct Speech in Court', *Interpreting*, 10 (1): 99–127.

Pérez-González, L. (2006) 'Interpreting Strategic Recontextualisation Cues in the Courtroom: corpus-based insights into the pragmatic force of non-restrictive relative clauses', *Journal of Pragmatics*, Special Issue on Translation and Context, 38 (3): 390–417.

Pöchhacker, F. and Shlesinger, M. (eds) (2008) 'Doing Justice to Court Interpreting', Special Issue of *Interpreting*, 10 (1): 1–7.

Rock, F. (2007) *Communicating Rights: the language of arrest and detention*, Basingstoke, London: Palgrave Macmillan.

Rogers, R., Harrison, K., Shuman, D., Sewell, K. and Hazlewood, L. (2007) 'An Analysis of Miranda Warnings and Waivers: comprehension and coverage', *Law and Human Behavior*, 31 (2): 177–92.

Rombouts, D. (2011) 'The Police Interview using Videoconferencing with a Legal Interpreter: a critical view from the perspective of interview techniques', in S. Braun and J.L. Taylor (eds) *Videoconference and Remote Interpreting in Criminal Proceedings*, Guildford: University of Surrey.

Rosado, T. (2015) 'Is this Practice Demeaning to Court Interpreters?', Blog entry, 26 February 2015. Online. Available at: https://rpstranslations.wordpress.com/2015/02/ (accessed 20 July 2015).

Seleskovitch, D. and Lederer, M. (1984) *Interpréter pour Traduire*, Paris: Didier Érudition.

Shlesinger, M. (1999) 'Norms, Strategies and Constraints: how do we tell them apart?' in A.A. Lugris and A.F. Ocampo (eds) *Anovar/Anosar: Estudios de Traducción e Interpretación*, Vigo: Universidade de Vigo.

Shuy, R.W. (2012) *The Language of Sexual Misconduct Cases*, Oxford: Oxford University Press.

Wadensjö, C. (1998) *Interpreting as Interaction*, London: Longman.

Wadensjö, C. (1999) 'Telephone Interpreting and the Synchronization of Talk in Social Interaction', *The Translator*, 5 (2): 247–64.

Recommended reading

De Jongh, E.M. (2012) *From the Classroom to the Courtroom: a guide to interpreting in the U.S. justice system*, American Translators Association Scholarly Monograph Series XVII, Amsterdam and Philadelphia: John Benjamins Publishing Company.

Eades, D. (2010) *Sociolinguistics and the Legal Process*, Bristol, Tonawanda, Ontario: Multilingual Matters.

Elias-Bursać, E. (2015) *Translating Evidence and Interpreting Testimony at a War Crimes Tribunal: working in a tug-of-war*, Basingstoke and New York: Palgrave Macmillan.

Mulayim, S., Lai, M. and Norma, C. (2014) *Police Investigative Interviews and Interpreting: context, challenges, and strategies*, Boca Raton, London, New York: CRC Press.

Nakane, I. (2014) *Interpreter-mediated Police Interviews: a discourse-pragmatic approach*, Basingstoke and New York: Palgrave Macmillan.

Rosado, T. (2012) *The New Professional Court Interpreter: a practical manual*, Create Space, Independent Publishing Platform.

Tiersma, P.M. and Solan, L.M. (2012) *The Oxford Handbook of Language and Law*, Oxford: Oxford University Press.

3 Legal interpreting II

Asylum procedures

Every 4 seconds someone is forced to flee.

(UNHCR 2014)

1 Introduction

This chapter explores interpreted events concerning claims for asylum that are often described as belonging to a 'grey zone' (following Bancroft *et al.* 2013) in the legal interpreting domain and for which a lack of specialized interpreter education has been identified. Although some interpreted events in asylum procedures take place in courtrooms, the chapter focuses on the initial phases of a claim, which are the most bureaucratically complex and linguistically important, and which can take place in a range of settings. The chapter is limited to asylum procedures in receiving countries but recognizes the work of humanitarian field interpreters working in areas of violent conflict, whose work may impact on asylum seeking processes (see Moser-Mercer *et al.* 2014).

Drawing on empirical research and studies by national and international organizations, the chapter illuminates aspects of interpersonal relations and language practices in asylum procedures around the world and their implications for interpreting practice and process. The aim is to help interpreters manage expectations about the interlocutors with whom they work, understand their position and positioning (by themselves and by others) and reflect on selected competencies in these settings. The chapter examines aspects of the account-giving process and issues affecting interpreter performance with regard to, among other things, note taking, management of turn length, and narrative sequencing. Attention is given to the emotional pressures faced by applicants as a result of (re-)telling stories of escape, torture and persecution, and the impact this can have on crucial interview stages.

The chapter includes a case study on the role of the interpreter in an Asylum and Immigration Tribunal appeal hearing in the United Kingdom, and the legal determination made with regard to the limits of the interpreter's involvement in the case. It also discusses the specific sensitivities in asylum encounters involving children and draws on established interview protocols developed by leading international and national bodies in exploring good practices for interpreters.

Finally, since interpreters and interviewing officers also risk stress and burnout in this subdomain, the chapter explores aspects of personal care and resilience building. In so doing, it draws on the latest developments in trauma-informed approaches to interpreting.

2 Interpreting in asylum procedures: settings and modes

This subdomain of legal interpreting involves interpreted events with different categories of migrants, from those who have left voluntarily to those forced to flee conflict situations or forces of nature that have made life unsustainable in their country of origin. Interpreters are employed in a wide range of institutional events, from initial asylum claims at ports of entry to appeal hearings, interviews for visa and residency applications, and meetings at reporting and detention centres involving individuals, families and unaccompanied children. The majority of interpreted events in these settings are conducted face-to-face in the bilateral mode and may involve some sight translation and telephone interpreting; this chapter focuses on face-to-face interpreting.

Due to the highly unpredictable nature of migrant flows, it is not uncommon for shortages of interpreters with particular language combinations to arise, leading authorities to go with whomever is available (Valero Garcés 2010). Individuals who are called on to interpret in such circumstances can soon find themselves in demand elsewhere and in some cases may never receive formal interpreter education, which explains to some extent why professionals and non-professionals continue to work side by side in this and other domains.

National politics of immigration and migration that are characterized by increasingly restrictive policies in many countries are likely to impact initial determinations of status more significantly than interpreter mediation; however, the importance of interpreter mediation cannot be underestimated, as Barsky claims: 'To state that minor errors made by the interpreter could be fatal is no overstatement' (1994: 41). In addition, an individual's journey through the asylum procedure can involve many interpreters from different backgrounds and with different levels of education; mistakes made early in the process can and often do remain unresolved as the examples discussed later show, thereby impacting determination and appeal processes.

In general terms, asylum procedure can be described as highly constrained, to the extent that some institutional settings strictly govern what is 'sayable'. Barsky reminds us of this in his work on Convention refugee hearings in Canada, where individuals are 'called upon to say certain things and not others' (1994: 101). The fact that initial interviews are not routinely video or audio recorded, leading to reliance on written accounts, is another example of the type of constraints imposed on the voice of the applicant, as Maryns (2006) observes. The constraints of the institutional setting are often compounded by the lack of supporting documentation in the possession of individuals on arrival, leading to a situation in which 'far-reaching legal decisions often have to be made on very limited grounds' (Maryns 2006: 1).

3 Interpreting in asylum procedures: scope and nature

The Asylum Trends 2014 report published by The Office of the United Nations High Commissioner for Refugees (UNHCR) draws attention to the recent sharp increase in asylum applications in the industrialized world, with estimates of around 866,000 applications in 2013–14 alone. The top five receiving countries are Germany, the United States, Turkey, Sweden and Italy; together these countries 'accounted for six out of ten new asylum claims submitted in the 44 industrialized countries' (UNHCR 2014: 3). These figures attest to the continuing levels of instability and conflict in the world, and highlight the high level of ongoing need for qualified interpreters in asylum procedures, among other reception and resettlement services. The following sections examine aspects of the international and national contexts of asylum as a background for exploring interpreter mediation in this subdomain.

3.1 Asylum and international protection

Although it is beyond the scope of this guide to provide an introduction to international law relating to asylum, The Office of the United Nations High Commissioner for Refugees (UNHCR), or UN Refugee Agency as it is commonly known, merits particular attention for its role in shaping approaches to refugee protection at the international level. Two key instruments underpin its work:

1   1951 United Nations Convention relating to the Status of Refugees and Exiles.
2   1967 Protocol to the Convention.

The 1951 Convention, which entered into force in 1954, is grounded in Article 14 of the Universal Declaration of Human Rights (1948). It recognizes the right of persons to seek asylum from persecution in other countries. The Convention was initially designed to protect people fleeing events prior to 1 January 1951 and only applied within Europe; these restrictions were revised in the 1967 Protocol, thereby broadening its coverage. Article 1A(2) of the 1951 Convention (as completed by the 1967 Protocol) defines a refugee as any person who owing to a well-founded fear of persecution for reasons of race, religion, nationality, membership of a particular social group or political opinion, is outside the country of his nationality and is unable, or owing to such fear, is unwilling to avail himself of the protection of that country; or who, having a nationality and being outside the country of his former habitual residence, is unable, or owing to such fear, is unwilling to return to it.

However, neither the 1951 Convention nor the 1967 Protocol make specific reference to asylum or the procedures governing how individuals obtain refugee status. As Lambert observes, 'Contracting Parties are, therefore, free to interpret the terms of the Convention/Protocol and to set up their own national procedures, subject to various instruments' (1995: 4). Furthermore, neither the Convention nor the Protocol provide a definition of persecution, in part due to the political context in which the Convention emerged (e.g. after the Second World War and during the cold war) when agents of persecution were understood to be the state (McFadyen 2012: 13). This means that persecution has been subject to very different interpretations (see UNHCR 2001), and can concern non-state actors such as rebels and militia (McFadyen 2012: 15).

The Convention is underpinned by the three key principles of non-discrimination, non-penalization and non-refoulement, and sets out the basic minimum standards for the treatment of refugees by states (UNHCR 2010a).

The principle of non-discrimination concerns discrimination on the grounds of race, religion or country of origin (as set out in the Convention) and international human rights law that includes discrimination on grounds of sex, age, disability, sexuality or other prohibited grounds of discrimination.

The principle of non-penalization means that individuals cannot be subject to prosecution (save for specific exceptions) for illegally entering or staying in a country. Penalties that are prohibited could include being charged with immigration or criminal offences relating to the seeking of asylum.

The principle of non-refoulement is deemed such a core principle that no exceptions or derogations may be made to it. According to this principle, no one can expel or return a refugee against her/his will to a territory where s/he fears threats to life or freedom (UNHCR 2010a: 3).

Since the Convention was first drafted, additional instruments have been developed that address specific situations for which the definition of a refugee under the terms of the Convention is considered insufficiently broad. For instance, states in Africa and Latin America have expanded the definition of a refugee through Article 1(2) of the 1969 Organization of African Union (OAU) Convention and Article 3 of the Cartagena Declaration respectively (see the Office of the High Commissioner for Human Rights, OHCHR, Factsheet 20, Human Rights and Refugees).[1]

RESEARCH

Activity 1: Refugees of the future and international protection

A   Research the changing dynamics of population displacement. Useful resources include:

United Nations: www.un.org
Forced Migration Online: www.forcedmigration.org
International Organization for Migration: www.iom.int
The Migration Observatory: www.migrationobservatory.ox.ac.uk

B   Discuss some of the pros and cons of extending the list of grounds for refugee status listed in the UN Convention to take account of anticipated changes in the triggers for population displacement.

It is also important to note that countries may need to invoke special procedures to offer temporary protection to assist individuals involved in mass displacements, an example of which is the 2001 EU Directive on Temporary Protection that was created following the conflicts in the former Yugoslavia in the 1990s. Governments can also grant other forms of humanitarian protection to individuals who are very vulnerable but do not meet the criteria for refugee status.

 PERFORMANCE SKILLS

Activity 2: Using case law to understand asylum seeker experiences and prepare for assignments

Read examples of asylum case law and identify key issues at stake for asylum applicants and the ways in which the information could serve as part of pre-assignment preparation (e.g. glossary creation, expectation management, etc.).

Recommended databases:
The European Database of Asylum Law (EDAL): www.asylumlawdatabase.eu
Centre for Gender and Refugee Studies (US case law): http://cgrs.uchastings.edu
RefWorld (maintained by UNHCR): www.refworld.org/docid/47dfc8e32.html
A thematic search is recommended using keywords. Examples include:
Family ostracism or victimization as a result of being trafficked;
Domestic violence and lack of state protection;
Membership of a social group.

3.2 Asylum procedure at the national level

Differences in asylum policy and procedure at the national level mean that the regulations governing legal representation, detention, right(s) of appeal, and the provision of professional interpreting and translation services, among others, will vary across geonational contexts. In the UK, for example, the United Kingdom Border Agency in the Home Office is responsible for interviewing and assessing asylum claims. Applicants first undergo a screening or *preliminary* interview, which is held at an Asylum Screening Unit, local immigration office, or port, and is conducted by an immigration officer. This interview establishes basic information such as information on health and a few details on the reasons for claiming asylum. Qualified interpreters are provided in these interviews.[2] The information from the screening interview is used to determine which category an individual's case falls into for subsequent handling. At the time of this writing, a case could be categorized under general casework, detained fast track (DFT), detained non-suspensive appeal (DNSA), children or Dublin/Third Country. A substantive or personal interview in which the details of the claim are set out in depth occurs at a later stage. The following descriptions of case categories are designed as a guide only and do not constitute a definitive legal definition.

Categorizing a case as *detained fast-track* means that the assessment of the claim takes place on a very short timescale, and an individual can be taken to a detention centre where an interview and initial decision usually occur within a few days.[3]

The *non-suspensive category* indicates that individuals have no right to appeal within the UK. The decision to categorize a case in this way is based on the fact that the authorities believe the asylum seeker is from one of a list of countries deemed safe by the government.

Cases categorized as *Dublin/Third Country* (if a person has travelled through a safe (or 'third') country on her/his way to the UK), are not normally heard in the UK. This person can be obliged to return to that country to have the asylum claim heard there.

 RESEARCH

Activity 3: Enhancing knowledge of policy and procedure

Awareness of asylum procedure is important for understanding the nature of events requiring interpreter mediation and where a particular event fits within the asylum seeker's administrative journey. How familiar are you with the structures (e.g. international and national policy and procedure) governing asylum applications and the terminology in the country where you practice?

Research the legislation and procedure in force in your country, bearing in mind that legislation changes frequently and procedures may be subject to change. Pay particular attention to the different stages of status determination, the timescales involved, the location of interviews, right(s) of appeal, access to social welfare and support, and provision of interpreting and translation services in the processes of reception, status determination, detention, resettlement and deportation. Useful sources include government information available on the Web, refugee and migrant advice groups (e.g. www. refugee-action.org.uk) and national and local media sources.

4 Asylum interviews: key concepts

The *personal interview* forms the basis on which an applicant's claim for asylum is usually determined. The oral accounts produced in these interviews, in which interpreting frequently plays a crucial role, are routinely written up into a report for scrutiny by the determining authorities. Policy varies with regard to the provision of interpreters for personal interviews. In some countries applicants are entitled to interpretation but may be responsible for finding an interpreter themselves (e.g. in the United States); in others, professional interpretation may be provided (e.g. in the Netherlands, Australia and the United Kingdom), although not necessarily from the start of the process.

4.1 Personal interviews and credibility

The success or failure of an asylum application typically rests on the **credibility** of the account provided in support of the claim of a well-founded fear of persecution for reasons of race, religion, nationality, membership in a particular social group, or political opinion. Assessments of credibility may involve evaluating accounts for what is termed their internal and external credibility. Internal credibility concerns the applicant's own evidence provided during the interview and consistency with claims made in the past (*internal coherence*), whereas external credibility is based on the level of correspondence between material facts claimed and generally known facts, and official information sources used in compiling country profiles (*Asylum Decision-Making Guidance*, UK Visas and Immigration 2012).

In addition to scrutinizing the internal coherence of accounts, the determining authorities pay particular attention to the level of detail and its specificity. However, as the following quotation suggests, the process of account making and account receiving is far from straightforward:

> The memory for these peripheral details can be poor or even absent....
> Failure to remember such details (e.g. description of uniforms, number
> of people present during torture, duration of an event) during the
> asylum interview, often leads to the asylum account being rejected on
> the basis that it is not credible.
>
> (Bloemen *et al.* 2006: 57)

The impact of a poor recollection of peripheral details is highlighted in the following extract from an asylum refusal letter sent to a claimant by the Home

Office in the United Kingdom. The extract highlights what was not considered a reasonable lapse in the individual's memory in the circumstances:

> You were asked what materials the carpets were made from. You stated they were made from a material called xxx in 3 different colours. You were then asked what plant or animal this material came from; you replied you did not know. It is not accepted that someone who claims to have been weaving carpets since the age of 10 would not know whether the materials used to weave the carpets were of plant or animal origin.
>
> (Right to Remain website)

As Kagan asserts,

> Assessing the believability of refugee testimony is not a simple matter of analysing answers given by a witness. In real life, credibility assessment involves many more factors, including not just the answers but also *the questions, the way the questions are asked,* and *the environment in which they are asked.*
>
> (2010: 1183, authors' emphasis)

To this must be added how questions (and their answers) are interpreted and the extent to which interpreter mediation impacts the process of account giving, elements not routinely considered by the determining authorities when scrutinizing accounts (see Tipton 2008a).

4.2 Shared responsibility

A UNHCR (2010b) research project on the application of key provisions of the Asylum Procedures Directive draws attention to interviewing competencies and observes inconsistencies in the recruitment and pre-interview preparation processes of interviewing officers in different Member States of the European Union. The project report highlights the often limited amount of time available for officers to prepare for interviews due to high caseloads and the pressures generated by the need to conduct a high volume of interviews each day. As a result, the extent to which officers are aware of specific cultural issues likely to arise in interviews and confidence in probing responses varies, and may explain why interpreters sometimes feel obligated to intervene in ways that appear to go beyond their anticipated remit (e.g. as specified by the employer; see UHNCR interpreter guidelines below).

It is not uncommon for national policy guidelines to place an emphasis on non-adversarial interviewing. Guidance for interviewing officers in the UK, for example, describes the process as a **shared responsibility**, although it also emphasizes that cooperation should not be confused with helping since officers are concerned first and foremost with the objective assessment of material facts:

Whilst a claimant must substantiate their claim, the interview is a cooperative process in which caseworkers should assist the claimant by:

- ascertaining the relevant aspects of the claim;
- encouraging disclosure of all relevant information;
- obtaining and assessing all the available information relevant to the claimant's case.

(*Asylum Policy Instruction: Asylum Interviews*, Home Office 2015: 12)

In practice, a non-adversarial approach may take different forms. Advice for interviewing officers in the United States (United States Citizenship and Immigration Services 2013b), for example, highlights good practice for interviewers as not arguing in opposition of the applicant's claim, taking sides or questioning applicants in a hostile manner. Some of these principles are reflected in UNHCR (2010b: 115) guidelines on appropriate communication in interpreted personal interviews, according to which the preference is for **gender sensitive** provision. The guidelines also recommend that the interpreter:

- posses competent interpreting skills, for instance, interprets accurately without addition or omission, uses the same grammatical person as the speaker, takes notes, etc.;
- be neutral in her/his interpretation;
- be impartial;
- not provide any kind of supplementary sociological, anthropological or historical information as a contribution to the case for which s/he is interpreting, and does not comment on the applicant's testimony; and
- not provide procedural or legal advice to the applicant.

Despite UNHCR's recommendation that the services of a competent interpreter be provided throughout the determination process, in practice it has found that, as with interviewing officers, recruitment, training and practice vary in quality and consistency according to the country. Its findings, which are based on observations of interpreted events in Member States of the European Union, highlight gaps between the guidelines above and actual practice, as the following examples show:

- The interpreter extensively modified the statements of the applicant by summarizing, paraphrasing or only interpreting the conclusions of the answers given by the applicant.
- The interpreter added her/his own comments or personal observations. For example, the interpreter added comments such as: 'Should I ask him whether he is all right in the head?' or 'This seems quite strange'.
- The interpreter did not adopt a position of neutrality but was instead hostile towards the applicant.

- The interpreter took over the role of the interviewer and asked the applicant questions.
- The interpreter took over the role of the interviewer and explained aspects of the procedure or answered questions posed by the applicant regarding the procedure without interpreting the questions for the interviewer to answer.
- The interpreter took over the role of the applicant and answered the interviewer's question, which was directed to the applicant.
- In several cases, without guidance from the interviewer, the interpreter advised applicants and instructed them as to how to complete the application form.
- The interviewer and the interpreter exchanged comments in an aside, or the interpreter and the applicant exchanged comments that were not interpreted for the interviewer.
- The interpreter undertook or was asked to undertake tasks beyond their duties, e.g. to call the applicant in, or bring tissues or water.

(Adapted from UNHCR 2010b: 122–3)

While it is clear that some of the actions reported above stem from the likelihood of poor, or even a lack of, interpreter education, it is important to note that the desirability for interpreter neutrality set out in UNHCR recommendations is contingent on all parties to the interview understanding what it entails and being able to monitor it on an ongoing basis. There is little evidence that this occurs in practice. Furthermore, the level of permissiveness shown by some interviewing officers in relation to interpreters transgressing institutional protocol on role boundaries and neutrality that are implied in some of the examples above may help explain some of the interpreters' actions; this theme is further explored later (see Section 5.3).

The very noisy and cramped working conditions in which some interviews were found to take place cannot be discounted as factors contributing to lapses in adherence to the guidelines, especially with regard to hostility of tone and role shifts evidenced by some of the interpreters observed. In fact, the impact of working conditions on interpreted events is something that merits further scholarly investigation. Additionally, discussions in online communities and other discussion forums with regard to working conditions may lead to positive changes for all parties to these events in the future, and ensure that the concept of shared responsibility in asylum procedure extends to the recruitment and education of interpreters.

▲ COLLABORATIVE DIMENSIONS

Activity 4: Interpersonal negotiation

Imagine interpreting in an interview between an asylum applicant and her/his legal representative. During the interview the legal representative turns to the interpreter and says: 'That is not good enough.'

A   With a partner, reflect on the possible reasons for the interviewer's response.
B   Consider to whom the comment is being addressed. If it is directed at the interpreter, is s/he meant to view it as a directive to the applicant to come up with something better, or simply consider it as a side comment that should not be interpreted directly to the interviewee?
C   How would you interpret the comment and manage the situation?

4.3   Applicants' expectations and power asymmetries

Trusting a third party to provide a sufficiently detailed personal account in support of an asylum application is just one of many hurdles facing applicants:

> The fact that they are seeking safety ... does not automatically mean that they should understand the asylum interview process or trust the interviewer whom they have never previously met. Many distrust government officials, having experienced persecution at the hands of officials in their country of origin.
>
> (Crawley 1999: 32)

Issues of trust, however, constitute one among many other forms of linguistic and social disadvantage faced by applicants in asylum procedures, which have been the subject of scholarly research. For example, research by Barsky (1994) on Convention refugee hearings in Canada, Pöllabauer (2004) on the Austrian asylum procedure, Maryns (2006) on the Belgian asylum procedure, and Inghilleri (2005) and Tipton (2008a) on asylum procedure in the United Kingdom, has highlighted elements that appear to arise regularly across geonational contexts. In many cases applicants:

- often do not know how to respond in interviews or what is expected of them;
- cannot correct misunderstandings as they occur in interpreter mediation (and often fear challenging an interpretation);
- lack familiarity with (Western) argumentation strategies;
- are often not made aware of the motives behind certain interview questions;

- are often unaware that the initial interview account is one of several versions that are 'recontextualized' by the institution in the different reporting phases, and subject to scrutiny by others not including the interviewing officer.

The findings show the level of difficulty that applicants experience in producing accounts that are considered institutionally acceptable, that is, accounts that contain a level of detail and cohesiveness that is likely to lead to the determining authorities finding the claim credible (see also Jacquemet 2005). The impact of institutional procedure on the determination of status is powerfully illustrated through, for example, the work of Maryns (2006) in relation to the Belgian asylum procedure. Maryns shows how oral accounts produced in asylum interviews are converted into written texts in ways that meet institutional requirements but that often marginalize the true voice of the applicant. The resulting written reports effectively draw a veil over the impact of interpreting on the storytelling process and identity construction of the applicant, and serve as an example of particular configurations of power that operate beyond the interpreter's control. For example, lack of proper coordination of the event by the interpreter such as poor management of turn taking (e.g. due to disruptions for clarification) can lead to important aspects of the story remaining unexplored and/or content may be filtered (through unconscious censorship on the part of the interpreter or simple omission).

Applicants' lack of awareness of institutional context and procedure can be further impacted as a result of the trauma of account giving. The United States Citizenship and Immigration Services (2013a: 20–1) draw attention to the range of behaviours that survivors of torture and trauma might manifest in personal interviews. For example, they suggest that survivors may, among other things, avoid discussing events; be more willing to discuss physical symptoms than psychological symptoms; or employ defensive techniques to avoid reliving events, such as denying they occurred or temporarily forgetting they occurred, minimizing them or blocking them out. They may also lose composure and laugh at inappropriate moments or cry.

In addition to highlighting the vulnerability of the asylum seeker, these observations evidence the considerable pressure on interviewers to navigate their way through these challenges and manage the production of a coherent account in ways that avoid directly shaping it. It is worth noting, however, that interpreters can also find it difficult to handle mediation due to both the trauma-affected behaviours listed above and the lack of in-country knowledge of the applicant about the asylum process, leading them in some cases to attempt to (over-)compensate through a range of personal interventions during interaction.

5 Interpreter mediation in asylum interviews

5.1 Social relations in cross-cultural asylum interviews

By developing an understanding of the nature and range of relations between participants in asylum procedures interpreters can be better prepared to manage expectations of an ethical, emotional, procedural and linguistic nature, and plan professional development activities accordingly. In this section, the range of participant relations (*tenor*) in interpreted asylum events is explored with particular emphasis on the 'intercultures' that are generated between the different pairings in the encounter:

1   asylum claimant–interpreter
2   interviewing officer[4]–interpreter
3   interviewing officer–asylum claimant (child/adult)

Although the pairings are not considered to carry any special privilege in interaction, they are noteworthy because of the differences in the level of social solidarity and distance they entail. At issue is the degree of overlap between the interpreter and the applicant/interviewer's linguistic and cultural background, the degree of the interpreter's exposure to the relevant national asylum procedure in terms of personal experience, and length of exposure to the procedure as a professional interpreter.

Social solidarity can be said to operate along a continuum from high to low and is not necessarily understood as synonymous with empathy, although empathy (and sympathy) may be a feature of the relation; nor is it necessarily indicative of the likelihood that the interpreter will operate as an advocate. Instead, it is understood in more general terms as a means of anticipating levels of shared understanding and contextualization problems in the interview process.

5.1.1 Asylum claimant–interpreter

Higher levels of solidarity are likely to occur when:

- interpreters are former asylum seekers and share the same linguistic and cultural background (e.g. from the same region, city, or clan);
- interpreters have prominent roles within a particular language community in the receiving country and assist claimants in finding legal representation, even serving as an interpreter for them.

Lower levels are likely to occur when:

- language is shared but not cultural background;
- language and culture are shared, but the interpreter may be unaware of how the situation has changed since s/he was last in the country;

- language and culture are shared, but the interpreter and claimant are from different (and even opposing) ethnic groups and/or social classes;
- language and culture are shared, but educational levels differ;
- there are problems of trust (claimant) and/or compassion fatigue (interpreters).

5.1.2 Interviewing officer–interpreter

Higher levels of solidarity are likely to occur when:

- both share the same cultural and linguistic background;
- the interviewing officer has undergone training on working with interpreters;
- both have prior experience of working with the other.

Lower levels are likely to occur when:

- there is asymmetric understanding of the communicative norms of the setting;
- interviewers have received little or no training on working with interpreters;
- interviewers and interpreters share a linguistic but not cultural background.

Note: even the nature of the shared linguistic background can vary if the interpreter speaks a non-standard variety of the interviewer's language.

5.1.3 Interviewing officer–asylum claimant

Higher levels of solidarity are likely to occur when:

- interviewing officers display a commitment to providing the fairest conditions in which a determination can be made;
- interviewing officers have some knowledge of the claimant's language.

Lower levels are likely to occur when:

- there is asymmetry in knowledge about institutional context and practices;
- there are asymmetries in knowledge about local political structures, kinship ties, time and social space;
- there are problems of interpersonal trust (both parties) and compassion fatigue (interviewing officers).

The above examples do not constitute an exhaustive list of characteristics, nor do they imply a particular outcome to encounters; nevertheless, they encompass commonly observed features and underscore the potential fragility of the 'macro interculture' formed between the three (or more) participants in the interpreted event. Such fragility is manifested, for instance, by interpreters who share both a cultural and linguistic background with applicants but who at times distance themselves from the claimant if s/he is perceived to come from a lower socioeconomic group. In these cases interpreters may filter claimant answers that seem particularly critical of the country of origin in order to present it in a more favourable light (United States Citizenship and Immigration Services 2013b: 16). To counter these and other potentially negative influences on procedure, some authorities screen interpreters (e.g. Belgium) and do not employ those found to have been politically active in their country of origin (assuming that the interpreter is not from the indigenous population of the receiving country).

 RESEARCH

Activity 5: Identifying factors that impact on levels of social solidarity and distance: gender-sensitive interviews

Read the following extract taken from *UNHCR Guidelines on International Protection No 1: gender-related persecution* (2002: 8), available at: www.unhcr.org/3d58ddef4.pdf.

> The image of a political refugee as someone who is fleeing persecution for his or her direct involvement in political activity does not always correspond to the reality of the experiences of women in some societies. Women are less likely than their male counterparts to engage in high profile political activity and are more often involved in 'low level' political activities that reflect dominant gender roles. For example, a woman may work in nursing sick rebel soldiers, in the recruitment of sympathisers, or in the preparation and dissemination of leaflets. Women are also frequently attributed with political opinions of their family or male relatives, and subjected to persecution because of the activities of their male relatives. While this may be analysed in the context of an imputed political opinion, it may also be analysed as being persecution for reasons of her membership of a particular social group, being her 'family'. These factors need to be taken into account in gender-related claims.

A   Identify two groups of asylum seekers in your country and compare the social roles of women in each with the role of women in your country.

B   Identify the ways in which gender-sensitive interpreting (e.g. matching the gender of interpreter and applicant) may support the asylum seeker in the interview process.

5.2 Home narratives

This section examines the asylum account giving process in order to explore how and why – in addition to the impact of trauma – coherence can be lacking or compromised, and the extent to which interpreting impacts on account giving and account receiving.

The work of Blommaert (2001) in relation to the Belgian asylum procedure investigates issues of **narrative inequality** in the account-giving process and highlights the problems of coherence and credibility that can arise in official personal interviews. His study concerns asylum seekers who were invited to recount their stories of escape as part of a fieldwork exercise and therefore do not directly reflect official interview procedure, although there are many common features. In this particular study the interviews did not involve interpreter mediation, but the findings help to understand the extent to which interpreting can impact the process.

The study shows how applicants often provide dispreferred responses to short and simple questions, that is, responses that do not appear to directly answer the question. Instead, responses are often provided that Blommaert describes as rich in contextual information, such as information about local politics and other details that go beyond the type and amount of information elicited by the interviewer. These stories or **home narratives** are 'triggered by an awareness that [the applicant's] story cannot be fully understood unless other people know some details about the society they come from' (2001: 428). They serve several important functions, including sense making, explanatory and argumentative functions, and are a means of combating the perceived ignorance of the interviewing officer about the situation in the applicant's country of origin.

The different functions of these narratives also affect the way they are constructed and reported by asylum applicants. Very often, as Blommaert observes, the sequencing of the narrative is confused; applicants mix information on the current situation in the country of origin, the receiving country, and information concerning events in the recent and distant past. Blommaert's analysis also highlights the importance of audience design in the telling process, as illustrated through the use of fillers such as 'You must know that…' or 'You see, in my country…', which are directed at the hearers or audience of the story and help applicants to personalize and localize the narrative at particular points in time and space. There is a risk, however, that such features are filtered out of the interpretation as a result of attempts to privilege the main message only, which means that the home narrative presents particular challenges for interpreters. Although exchanges in asylum interviews can often be short and easily retained in the memory, the use of notes is always recommended in professional practice because the length of turn is difficult to predict. The home narrative is a case in point.

■ **PERFORMANCE SKILLS**

Activity 6: Note taking and home narratives

Ask a partner to read the following extract as you take notes. The extract should be read as naturally as possible, but in full.

INTERVIEWER: Why did you escape?

ASYLUM APPLICANT: Well, you see, it is difficult for people to understand the politics of my country ... really difficult. We have only had multiparty democracy since 1991 when the president formed a coalition ... we were hopeful when the elections came in 2006 that it would be a new start but things are difficult ... there is no money and there is corruption – everyone does what they can ... my father died in the conflict in ninety-seven, no ninety-eight when he crossed the border and me and my brothers came to look for him and stayed in the north ... we joined the rebel forces and moved around but I couldn't carry on ... the MONUC* were there but they couldn't really do anything.... I wanted to be a businessman ... you know, like my brother who now owns a small restaurant in the business district ... he helped me to leave when he found out the authorities were looking for me.... I wanted change, you know, we all did ... it was me that organized the meeting in 2000 in my village to set up an opposition party ... the military found out about it and fired shots into the crowds to break them up and soon after they started looking for me so I had to leave.

A   Perform your interpretation from your notes to your partner and/or record yourself. It is recommended that you simply work in English initially – the exercise can be repeated later in your other language(s).

B   Evaluate your performance in terms of:

- completeness (factual accuracy and narrative accuracy);
- coherence (i.e. does the coherence/incoherence in your performance mirror the source?);
- language use (especially register).

C   Review your notes, paying particular attention to:

- the areas where changes occur in the narrative in relation to time-frames, agency and places, and how these are signalled in your notes;
- the perspective of the different agents and bodies mentioned. How easy/difficult was it to recreate the relations between these elements in a) the note-taking process and b) your performance? What impact does the speed of delivery have on your ability to note the relations?

* MONUC is the name of a UN peacekeeping mission.

- the relevance of key terms in the narrative such as 'brother', 'restaurant', 'opposition', 'meeting' – what are the connotations of such terms in your country and in the country of individuals you interpret for? Might any ambiguities arise in using these terms, and do alternatives need to be considered? For example, in some countries 'brother' may not indicate a filial relation, and 'restaurant' may denote a food-related outlet that is no more than a street stall (what impressions of personal wealth are created through this term?);
- the gaps in your performance. Can gaps in the performance be easily categorized (e.g. do you tend to omit verbs/indicate verb tenses/are points separated clearly)? What actions could you take to overcome these difficulties if you repeated the exercise?

For further guidance on developing communication strategies in asylum interviews please see the materials on the Routledge Translation Studies Portal.

5.3 Interpreter performance

This section draws on research that examines examples of interpreting and considers the possible motivations for and impact of interpreter decision making. For example, Pöllabauer's (2004) research highlights approaches adopted by interpreters based on the analysis of recordings of 20 authentic asylum hearings in the Federal Asylum Office in Graz, Austria. The study highlights the extent to which interpreters play a central role in 'this unequal and asymmetrical interactive situation' (2004: 148) and the extent to which officers' handling of interpreter mediation impacts procedure.

Pöllabauer's findings reveal that interpreters are 'granted a much wider scope of influence than is generally assumed' within the interaction, and that they often 'take the lead and elicit information they regard as necessary for the outcome of hearings or for establishing favourable communicative relations' (2004: 154). In this respect, the findings corroborate some of the practices observed by UNHCR mentioned earlier. However, the findings also show that interpreters can be strongly influenced by the officers' expectations, and that neither the interviewing officers nor the applicants seemed to regard the interpreter as a neutral mediator, thereby underscoring a view of neutrality as something that is enacted and responded to as opposed to simply being 'possessed' and taken for granted (see Tipton 2008b).

A key question concerns the motivations behind this approach and the tendency – at least in the case of this study – for interpreters to align themselves with the institution, that is, act in ways that promote the institutional perspective and priorities. Pöllabauer believes the motivation stems from the interpreters' 'extensive knowledge of the archetypal structures and make-up' of the hearings that led them to know what information is relevant to interviewing officers at the various stages of the procedure (2004: 154).

Motivation is also influenced by the permissiveness of interviewing officers, who are reported to routinely view interpreters as institutionally aligned and as persons who seek to promote approaches to interpreting that assist the institution in its task. To some extent this attitude is to be expected as the institution is the commissioner of the language service, but it is not a formal protocol and risks distorting the principle of the publicly neutral space that exists between applicants and interviewing officers.

In addition, the study identifies the following key points:

- interpreters' interruptions to seek clarification are not always successful, and the loss of conversational thread caused by the interruption can lead the applicant to repeat aspects of their story to the point that the account may seem very long-winded;
- the interpreters in the study very rarely took notes, which led to the loss of information in sections of the interview that concerned home narratives;
- lengthy answers were frequently reduced to gist statements by interpreters (possibly due to the lack of note taking);
- interpreters were seen to adopt face-saving strategies[5] when their competence appeared to be in question (e.g. by adopting a higher register when interpreting the applicant's utterances).

Pöllabauer asserts that her aim was not to evaluate the errors and mistakes in the interpretation process, but instead to look at the interaction more holistically to identify trends and gaps in practice. Her work shows that the interviews were impacted by both the interpreter's attempts to intervene in a professional manner (e.g. to seek clarification) that were not always handled well by the interviewer, and by the interpreter's approach to handling some of the exchanges (e.g. filtering), and response to perceived challenges to their own position in encounters (e.g. as a competent linguist). The study illustrates the dynamic nature of the performance dimensions discussed in Chapter 1 and the need for professional development to enhance self-knowledge and capacity for critical reflection on motivations for decisions *in situ*.

5.3.1 Communicative intent

Other research that evaluates interpreted asylum events show the ease with which participants can misread the communicative intent of the situation. Blommaert (2001) highlights this issue in relation to monolingual conversations that resonate with interpreted events. In the following extract (translated by Blommaert from Dutch), the interviewer is attempting to give the interviewee some instructions about the interview:

INTERVIEWER: I think it would be easiest if you start/with how you got here ehr
INTERVIEWEE: = by plane

INTERVIEWER: Yes/why wh=why you came here/her/and how you got here/
that you just/we won=we won't be asking many questions/it's what/that
you just/talk a bit

(Blommaert 2001: 422)

The interviewee's response ('by plane') shows a failure to understand the
nature of the interviewer's communicative intent because the first line is
interpreted as a question and not 'as part of a set of preliminary instructions'
(Blommaert 2001: 422). In this case, it is clear that the interviewee has pre-
empted matters and responded too soon. However, this can also arise in
interpreter mediation where a speaker's pause for interpretation is taken to
mean that the floor is being handed over to the next speaker, rather than as a
sign that the rest of the idea is still to be completed. The result is that a
response is offered in places where it is not solicited, leaving the interpreter
in a difficult position if s/he realizes that key aspects are not revisited and
probed by the interviewing officer in the process of rectifying the
breakdown.

A second example of the problem of communicative intent is taken from
Mason (2005). In this example, the issue of **footing** is highlighted. *Footing* is
a term coined by Goffman (1981) and concerns an individual's basic alignment with the event discussed (e.g. as a hearer or message giver), which
Goffman shows often shifts within an exchange. In interpreter mediation, it
is common for the interpreter to align with the original speaker's orientation
as the message is interpreted.

INTERVIEWING OFFICER (*addressing the interpreter in English*): Does he under-
stand why he is here?
INTERPRETER (*to the officer*): Yes, he does. (*To the immigrant in Polish*): You
understand why you're here, don't you?
IMMIGRANT (*in Polish*): Yes.
INTERPRETER (*in English*): Yes, he does.

(Mason 2005: 34)

As Mason observes, it is not unsurprising that the interpreter answers the
question directly even though the question is meant as a request for information from the immigrant, because 'questions invite answers' (ibid.: 35), and
the interpreter is responding spontaneously to that process.

▉ PERFORMANCE SKILLS

Activity 7: Evaluating the impact of interpreter involvement

A   Consider the impact of the interpreter's actions in the extract from Mason
(2005) above. The direct answer constitutes a clear shift in the interpreter's status as a participant in the event, from what might be termed a

secondary to a primary interlocutor. What are the consequences of this shift for the next part of the conversation in terms of the interpreter's involvement?

B   If, on the other hand, the interpreter had resisted this spontaneous response and changed the footing by formulating the question in the first person, as in 'Do you know why you are here?' what consequences might this have had on perceptions of the interpreter's level of involvement, e.g. approach to transparency of decision making and establishment of role boundaries, on the rest of the conversation?

5.3.2 Reformulation

With regard to other interpreting strategies in asylum settings, reformulation is commonly used as a mechanism to achieve idiomatic and clear output. However, the importance of detail and accuracy in such settings means that reformulation strategies need to be weighed carefully against the communicative purpose of the interviewer's questions. For example, Pöllabauer's study cited above shows that interpreters' strategies to explain or reformulate are not always successful, however well intentioned they may be.

EXAMPLE 1: REFORMULATION AT WORD LEVEL

INTERVIEWING OFFICER: What is her nationality?

INTERPRETER: Which nationality do you have? What is your nationality?

CLAIMANT: Nationality. I don't understand the question.

INTERPRETER: Your citizenship. You understand that?

CLAIMANT: No.

INTERPRETER: The/you but you are a citizen of Nigeria, aren't you?

CLAIMANT: Yes.

INTERPRETER: Okay. You don't understand the word citizenship or nationality?

CLAIMANT: I don't understand it because I have/I didn't travel before.

(Pöllabauer 2004: 172)

This example highlights the lower level of social solidarity between the two individuals as a result of sharing the same linguistic but not cultural background. In this case the interpreter's decision to add a question of her own led to a failed attempt at reformulation. Pöllabauer observes that in this exchange the final intervention by the applicant was not interpreted, meaning that the interviewing officer missed out on an important insight into the potential communicative difficulties that could impact later parts of the interview. The interpreter's intervention could therefore be construed chiefly as a face-saving exercise, as Pöllabauer claims (see Chapter 2, Section 6.3 for a discussion of face).

EXAMPLE 2: REFORMULATION OF QUESTION FORMS
Compare:

'Were you unaware of the lorry's destination?' with
'Did you know where the lorry was going?'

This example from Warren and York (2014: 16) concerns a young person who had crossed Europe hidden in a lorry and did not know at any point which country he was in. The interviewer asked: 'Were you unaware of the lorry's destination?' and the young person responded 'No' following the interpretation. Upon checking with the interpreter, it transpired that question had been reformulated as 'Did you know where the lorry was going?' to which the answer was indeed 'No'.

It is unclear why the interpreter reformulated the question in this way since this information is not available in the report cited, nor is the language of the interview known, which might have helped explain why the reformulation was handled as it was. It is possible that the interpreter's approach tried to take account of the age of the interviewee and the reformulation was deemed necessary to sound less bureaucratic and intimidating (as implied in the phrase 'were you unaware'). The example highlights the need for interpreters to keep others informed of linguistic decisions that might affect the core of the asylum claim, so that these could be (re-)negotiated as necessary with the interviewing officer.

EXAMPLE 3: CALQUES
Compare:

'I am an animator from Kinshasa' with
'I am an *animateur* from Kinshasa'.

In the first example, the word 'animator' appears as a lexical calque from the French and gives the impression that the applicant makes cartoons for a living since the interpreter provides no additional contextual information. The second example retains the source term and pronunciation, highlighting that it is particular to the applicant's cultural context: in this case, a person involved in organizing political rallies.

The first approach to the term had been used in the initial personal interview, which had been conducted prior to this interview that was part of the appeal preparation. The interpreter drew attention to the discrepancy and a note was made by the legal representative. This is an example of the sort of detail that might be viewed as a key discrepancy by the determining authorities since it is central to the claim, and emphasizes the warranted nature of the interpreter's intervention. The example also draws attention to the possibility of distortions due to the involvement of multiple interpreters in asylum procedure.

5.4 Case study from an asylum tribunal

In this section we return to the theme of the interpreter's understanding of her/his role boundaries in asylum-related encounters and related issues of co-power, and the impact of others' expectations of their performance on the interpreted event. As Hale observes, 'When interpreters are not clear about their own role, they are likely to be swayed by the pressures that confront them from the different spheres: the institutional, the professional and the interpersonal' (2005: 15). UNHCR's observations and Pöllabauer's (2004) study provide ample evidence of this.

In asylum settings interpreters are frequently faced with questions from interviewing officers about the identity of applicants. In the paragraphs that follow, the case of a court interpreter in the Asylum and Immigration Tribunal in England is presented in regard to a decision made about the use of interpreters in matters of language diagnosis.[6] The example highlights different responses by the interpreters to legal representatives' requests to comment on the country of origin, and the outcomes of the interpreters' decisions. The case concerns *Somalia* v. *Secretary of State for the Home Department*, [2008] UKAIT 00029, United Kingdom: Asylum and Immigration Tribunal/Immigration Appellate Authority, 9 April 2008, in which the court determined that

> it is no part of an interpreter's function to report on the language or dialect used. The expertise needed to identify a language or dialect is not typically the expertise of an interpreter. In any event, an interpreter should not be in the position of giving, or being asked to give, evidence on a contested issue.

Background

The case concerned a citizen of Somalia who, having been granted leave to remain in the United Kingdom as an unaccompanied minor, applied for variation of her leave on asylum grounds. The respondent (Secretary of State for the Home Department) refused her application. The appellant appealed (first appeal hearing), and in a determination sent out on 25 May 2007 an immigration judge dismissed her appeal. The appellant sought and obtained an order for reconsideration. The appellant's claim concerned her membership in a minority clan, and her belief that if she were able to establish that fact her appeal should succeed.

During the Substantive Appeal (first appeal hearing) the issue of language diagnosis was raised and the appellant's counsel requested the court interpreter to confirm or deny that the appellant was speaking the Reer Hamar dialect. The request was rejected by the court interpreter, who stated this was not part of his job, and when the appellant's counsel asked the judge to intervene and request the interpreter to confirm or deny the language, the judge also refused. The interpreter supplied by the appellant's solicitor was then asked to confirm or deny the language and the interpreter provided comment. However, the judge rejected the evidence provided by this interpreter since the interpreter's status as an independent witness was rejected and there was a lack of evidence to prove his status as an expert linguist. The appellant's counsel cited two cases in which a court interpreter was given permission to provide assistance on a matter of language diagnosis, which were taken into account in the determination. The determination included the following key points:

> An interpreter's function is to comprehend and communicate, not to assess or analyse. A person's skills in interpretation lie in his ability to understand what is being said to him in one language (or dialect) and communicate it accurately in another language (or dialect). It is simply wrong to say that the abilities of an interpreter necessarily import an ability to distinguish accurately between different dialects and to be able to attribute dialects to different sources...

> As an interpreter he may widen his vocabulary base and his understanding of different accents and dialects so that he can cope with whatever version of English is used by the person for whom he is interpreting, without needing or wanting or being required to consider or work out what the dialect is, but merely to do his own job of understanding and communicating. Of course an interpreter may know (or think he knows) something about the type of language or dialect the person for whom he is interpreting is using: but that is quite a different matter. It is not part of his function as interpreter...

> For these reasons we reject Mr. Schwenk's [the appellant's counsel] submissions that the interpreter ought to have been regarded as an expert, able to give evidence as an expert, and ought to have been required to give his view on the language or dialect being spoken by the appellant. We also reject his submission that what occurred at the hearing was unexpected or unfair. There was no proper reason to assume that the Court Interpreter would become an expert witness in the case.

> (United Kingdom: Asylum and Immigration Tribunal/Immigration
> Appellate Authority 2008)

 RESEARCH

Activity 8: Enhancing knowledge of norms in asylum tribunal hearings

A   What is the position in your country regarding the involvement of asylum and immigration court interpreters in matters of language diagnosis?

B   Can you find evidence of cases where language issues have been essential in the claim for asylum? What was the outcome?

C   How would you have responded to the request for clarification regarding dialects/languages if you were the court interpreter or the appellant's solicitor's interpreter in this case? Why?

6 Interpreting for unaccompanied minors in asylum settings

This section explores interpreter mediation involving unaccompanied minors and is set against the backdrop of Article 3(1) of the UN Convention of the Rights of the Children, which places emphasis on respect for the child's own opinion and states that: 'in all actions concerning children, whether undertaken by public or private welfare institutions, courts of law, administrative authorities or legislative bodies, the best interests of the child shall be a primary consideration'. Although not all countries have signed the Convention, it has helped to shape guidance on interviewing unaccompanied children in many areas of the world.

Working with children presents special sensitivities in any interpreted event, but interviews with unaccompanied minors in asylum settings are particularly challenging because a child's ability to participate is often affected by a range of complex and often intertwined issues. The United States Citizenship and Immigration Services (2009: 13–14) has listed issues as concerning chronological age; physical and emotional health; physical, psychological and emotional development; societal status and cultural background; cognitive processes and educational experience and language ability. Furthermore, it highlights chaotic social conditions, experience with different forms of violence, lack of protection and care by significant adults, nutritional deficits, and physical and mental disabilities as having the potential to impact child development.

Interviewing children therefore involves interviewers and interpreters developing awareness of discrepancies that can arise between the child's outer behaviour and the level of psychological development and emotions (Finnish Directorate of Immigration 2002). Zwiers and Morrisette (1999: 3) provide an indication of the form these discrepancies can take by highlighting that children have cognitive and linguistic abilities that differ from the professionals who may inadvertently talk either above or below a child's level; they further assert that children may have misconceptions about the role of the professional and may have some form of communication disorder.

The significant rise in the number of unaccompanied minors seeking asylum around the world in recent years, in particular at the US and Mexican border where numbers peaked at 10,622 in June 2014 (Rosenblum 2015: 1), brings into sharp relief the need for interpreter education suited to events involving children who present 'unique vulnerabilities and requirements' (Rosenblum ibid.). The sections that follow explore some of these vulnerabilities in more detail and provide insight into the communication protocols developed around the world to support child-focused interviewing.

6.1 Unwarranted interpreter intervention

Research by Keselman and associates has been instrumental in shedding light on interpreting in asylum interviews with unaccompanied minors, specifically in relation to the accuracy of question forming (2008) and a child's ability to participate in the interview process (2009, 2010).

Keselman *et al.* (2010), for example, report on a study involving recordings of 26 interpreted interviews with Russian-speaking unaccompanied children that took place in Sweden. The study investigates the ways in which interpreters may challenge children's ability to participate in asylum interviews by focusing on the nature and frequency of so-called **side sequences**. The term *side sequence* concerns monolingual conversations between participants that occur at the margins of the main interview. In such sequences the authors found the interpreters regularly 'assume the role of the main speaker or author' (Keselman *et al.* 2010: 101). Most side sequences analysed in the data concerned some form of repair, for example, the need to clarify a point of culture (e.g. kinship ties). However, the authors found examples of sequences that went beyond this basic type of repair and led to the child's voice being 'either excluded from interaction or guided' (ibid.: 89), constituting an example of the interview being conducted in ways that are not considered to be in the child's best interest.

One example concerns a monolingual conversation between a Swedish-speaking lawyer and caseworker that took place in front of a young male asylum applicant and an interpreter before the main meeting commenced. The conversation discussed the possibility of tracing the applicant's father through a voluntary organization. As the conversation developed, the young male asked the interpreter to interpret what was being said. The interpreter's response reveals an attempt to position herself as an expert about what the child needs to know:

INTERPRETER (*translation from Russian*): They discuss their own problems. That is not necessary for you to know. She says that they will contact, that the guardian will have an assignment to contact some organisation that deals with finding missing persons.

(Keselman *et al.* 2010: 91)

The extract strongly suggests that the interpreter's presence had particular consequences for the dynamics of interaction and interpersonal trust in this event. The authors highlight other examples of lengthy exchanges between the interpreter and the child in the same interpreted event that are neither challenged nor curtailed by the caseworker. This leads to the suggestion that the lack of intervention by the caseworkers may be 'due to a tacit understanding of asylum seeking children as less skilled and pragmatically disadvantaged interlocutors, whose accounts need to be reformulated and even corrected' (Keselman *et al.* 2010: 101).

Here again, the level of permissiveness on the part of the primary interviewing officer is viewed as potentially problematic and suggests that more training of officers on how to work with interpreters in such cases is needed. Of note, however, is that all examples from the study in relation to the exclusion or distortion of the child's voice concern the involvement of *unauthorized* or non-professional interpreters, leading the authors to recommend that only accredited interpreters be involved in such cases. However, even accredited interpreters who have not received specific training on working with children risk adopting similar approaches, believing it is a natural response to the vulnerability of the child's position in the encounter. This highlights the need for domain specificity in professional development terms.

6.2 Establishing interview parameters: building rapport and taking notes

The complex judgements interviewers need to make in relation to a child's cognitive capacity and potential levels of emotional detachment require careful management in interpreted events. This highlights the importance of interpersonal trust in the rapport building phases of the interview, which might take the form of questions about hobbies or an opening statement by the interviewer, depending on the child's age.

With regard to establishing other parameters in interpreted interviews with unaccompanied minors, note taking is salient. Note taking (by interviewers) is sometimes advised against because it may discourage the child from talking (for fear that they are disturbing the adult) and/or it may lead to suspicion regarding what the notes are for. In such cases, interviews are usually recorded and analysed at a later stage (Finnish Directorate of Immigration 2002: 5). Interpreters therefore need to be aware of the institutional norm in this regard and in cases where interviewing officers do not use notes, it is important that there is an opportunity for either the interpreter or interviewing officer to explain to the child why the interpreter needs to take notes and what they are used for. Please see the Routledge Translation Studies Portal for further guidance on introductory sequences in interviews involving children.

6.3 (Re-)formulation of interview questions

Although reformulation is an inherent feature of the interpreting process (see Section 5.3.2), particular attention is needed in child-focused interviews to avoid undermining the intended outcome of the question. The following are recommended as examples of good interview practice that also serve as helpful guidance for interpreters:[7] use short and clear questions (and avoid compound questions); ask a child to define a term/phrase to check his/her understanding of it; use simple words like 'hurt', 'do/say bad things' instead of 'persecution', and words like 'show' and 'tell me about' rather than complex words like 'depict', 'describe' or 'indicate'; avoid leading questions that create suggestibility: e.g. 'The soldier hit him, didn't he?'; use the active voice when asking a question (e.g. 'Did the man hit your brother?') and avoid the passive voice (e.g. 'Was your brother hit by the man?').

The extent to which interpreters are able to follow these guidelines will depend on the language combination in question. Interpreters should share any doubts with the interviewing officer so that culturally and linguistically appropriate solutions can be found and, ideally, interviews with minors should be preceded by a lengthy briefing so that expectations between interviewers and interpreters can be established and negotiated away from the interview itself.

6.4 Handling unresponsiveness and checking understanding

According to Zwiers and Morrisette, 'in some cultures, children quickly learn and begin to apply social display rules', leading them in some cases to mask 'inner thoughts and feelings because it is expected of them' (1999: 9). This draws attention to the problem of disclosure in child-focused interviews. Interviewing officers are usually advised to avoid forcing a child to talk; the same applies to the interpreter. Interpreters should not see it as a personal failure of their interpreting skills if a child is reluctant to open up or even rejects their presence in the interview room.

Furthermore, interviewing officers are often advised to tolerate periods of silence, even if they are fairly long; interpreters should do the same and avoid jumping in with the same question or a reformulation too quickly in the belief that the child has not understood. Asking the same question multiple times can give a child an impression that their first or previous answer was not good enough. Interpreters need to allow scope for interviewers to make it clear why a question might need repeating (e.g. to ensure the interviewee has understood things clearly). Interviewing officers employ a range of techniques to help communication and encourage children to open up. This means that in some cases interpreter mediation may not take the recognizable format of the *triadic exchange* common to other situations. Playing a game in the interview room with a child can be an important process of interpersonal trust building and should not be rejected by interpreters on the basis that it compromises interpreter neutrality or is beyond their role boundaries. It is merely a reflection of the more limited range of verbal and trust-building resources available to primary interviewers in such circumstances.

Finally, asking questions like 'Do you understand?' is not advisable in interviews with children because such questions are considered leading questions that children are likely to answer 'Yes' even if they have not understood. A commonly used strategy is to ask the child to repeat what the interviewer has said so that any issues can be clarified. Here again it is important for interpreters to not pre-empt this checking process by asking the question themselves, as they might do in events involving adults.

■ **PERFORMANCE SKILLS**

Activity 9: Interpreter intervention and self-awareness

It is a common principle of ethical codes that interpreters should not respond to requests for views or opinions on substantive matters in interview processes. However, in interviews with children it is helpful to consider the extent to which such a principle risks running counter to the principles of acting in the best interests of the child.

A   What actions do you think are open to the interpreter through the interpreting process to clearly signal to the interviewer that the child may be emotionally detached?

B   At what point in the process might you feel it appropriate to alert the interviewer to any issues (e.g. direct communication at the side of the interaction)?

7 Trauma-informed interpreting

The introduction to this chapter highlighted the potential for vicarious or secondary trauma and burnout on the part of individuals exposed to the traumatic experiences of others on a sustained basis. This is not to assume that unmanageable levels of stress and anxiety will affect all interpreters; in fact, many thrive on the positive feelings derived from playing a part in helping to relieve the distress of a fellow human being caught up in events beyond her/his control. Furthermore, it is well documented that people who are attracted to working in risky or challenging environments tend to have the ability to adapt in ways that keep them psychologically healthy (Vergara and Gardner 2011). However, despite the low likelihood that interpreters will develop post-traumatic stress disorders as a result of working in asylum settings, the cumulative effects of working with individuals who have been exposed to the horrors of war and suffering across a range of services mean that psychosocial health and well-being are a vital part of personal and professional development.

Across the globe, human service organizations are increasingly recognizing the vulnerability of individuals exposed to the trauma of others. In response, they have developed what is termed **trauma-informed** approaches to organizational life. In simple terms, this is a framework for care work that takes account of the impact of trauma by placing emphasis on the physical and psychological safety of both limited language proficient (LLP) service users and primary service providers.

7.1 Emotions and interpreter mediation

For many professional interpreters, concerns over impartiality and neutrality can lead to a denial of the self in ways that are not helpful to long-term career and personal development, as the following quotation illustrates:

> The first thing they tell us, when you actually become an interpreter, you've got to become very impartial, you've got to try, it's not like you don't try, you do, but there is a side of you that is much stronger than what you actually [are] as a professional acting and feeling for your client.
>
> (Interpreter working in asylum settings, Splevins *et al.* 2010: 1710)

Empathy is sometimes viewed as compromising neutrality and therefore as something to be avoided or kept secret; in practice, however, it can be a powerful element of trust building with others and sense making for the interpreter. Studies have shown that interpreters may initially identify with others' negative experiences and develop feelings of hopelessness and even anger, anxiety and sadness. However, in many cases such feelings were reported as short-lived and gave way to more positive feelings, including among interpreters who had experienced trauma similar to that of their clients (see Butler 2008; Miller *et al.* 2005). By contrast, Lor's (2012) study illustrates the potential for more serious and longer-term emotional effects of asylum-related work on interpreters, especially for those whose own experiences of trauma are reactivated through others' stories.

 COLLABORATIVE DIMENSIONS

Activity 10: Evaluating emotional stress and seeking support

Reflect on (an) encounter(s) that you have experienced and that triggered a particularly negative emotional response:

A   Identify the triggers and how the experience made you feel at the time and in the days/weeks afterward.
B   What coping strategies, if any, did you use to deal with the emotional response experienced?
C   How could peer interaction with fellow professional interpreters enhance the development of coping strategies, if at all?

7.2 Trauma-informed interpreting

In addition to managing emotions and empathy, trauma-informed approaches are designed to address issues such as secondary trauma, burnout and compassion fatigue. **Compassion fatigue** is often referred to as physical, emotional and spiritual depletion, or 'stress resulting from helping or wanting to help a traumatized or suffering person' (Figley 1995: 7), and is a feature of caregiving and crisis response services. Conrad and Kellar-Guenther (2006) make a distinction between burnout and compassion fatigue, highlighting that while both can lead to feelings of helplessness, anxiety and depression, they have different causes. **Burnout** usually results from extended periods of exposure to stress (of which compassion fatigue can be a contributing factor), and compassion fatigue can occur as a result of exposure to a single traumatic event.

Although the concepts of retraumatization and vicarious or secondary trauma are receiving increased attention in interpreting studies (e.g. Ndongo-Keller 2015), it remains a neglected aspect of interpreter education and professional development. In this regard, the pioneering work of the non-profit US organization The Voice of Love merits special mention for developing trauma-informed approaches to what it terms **extreme interpreting** events, that is, events that typically involve working with survivors of torture, war trauma and sexual violence.[8] Trauma-informed approaches also focus on practices that build resilience, help individuals make sense of their trauma history and current experiences, and plan ahead to achieve good psychosocial balance in occupational life.

 RESEARCH

Activity 11: Understanding the emotional stress experienced by new arrivals

Service users bring a range of emotions to interpreted asylum events as a result of past trauma and as a result of their experiences in the new social environment. Understanding the reasons for low mood or mood change can be helpful for interpreters in relation to expectation management in the interpreted event. For each of the following terms, research issues impacting newly arrived asylum seekers in your country, including but not limited to:

- destitution
- detention
- dispersal
- financial support
- employment (restrictions, opportunities)
- neighbourhood relations
- healthcare
- housing/temporary accommodation (e.g. regulations for housing female asylum seekers in the later stages of pregnancy)
- public attitudes to migrants.

7.3 Developing resilience

The interpreters interviewed in Splevins *et al.*'s (2010) study mentioned above commonly reported a motivation to develop strategies as a result of their experience of working with refugees, which typically combine externally sourced and personal coping techniques. To understand what these might entail and help structure reflection on interpreter well-being, this final section draws on studies and guidelines given to healthcare professionals who work in conflict zones. The discussions are meant as a basic guide only and are not a substitute for medical advice.

To a large extent, an individual's resilience depends on her/his adaptability. Some people are naturally quite resilient in that they tend to have a positive outlook on life and thrive on challenges; they may be more adaptable in difficult situations. The ability to adapt to different situations and deal with stress can be broken down into two main categories: (1) problem-focused coping strategies that focus on resolvable controllable sources of stress, and (2) threat-minimization strategies that are less adaptive since they tend to focus on avoiding, delaying or denying stressful demands (Folkman and Moskowitz 2000; Vergara and Gardner 2011). Palmer (2002: 172–3) outlines a number of responses that are typical of the two categories outlined above, according to which adaptive individuals are more likely to:

- sit and reflect on a situation constructively;
- express emotions with friends;
- get appropriately angry;
- talk to as many close friends as is reasonable;
- look for the good in the experience and what can be learned from it;
- seek help, both practical and supportive.

By contrast, individuals that tend to focus on threat-minimization strategies are likely to:

- keep themselves busy by throwing themselves into tasks;
- engage in activities that do not require a great deal of reflection, such as activities that are physically exerting;
- bottle things up and 'explode';
- be irritable/irascible;
- seek distractions by treating themselves.

Palmer makes a number of practical recommendations for developing resilience, such as making sure time is set aside for personal care, sufficient exercise is taken, and friendships and a balanced diet are maintained. Furthermore, he asserts that 'dealing with stress means accepting reality and acknowledging the source of the stress' and 'letting the past go', although these may be areas in which interpreters might need to seek external support.

For interpreters whose main or sole occupational focus is in the sub-domain of asylum, attention to personal care demands conscious effort. Free-lancers who work in different domains and perhaps combine interpreting with other activities can mitigate the accumulation of stress by creating a balanced portfolio of weekly activities to allow the mind to switch focus to less emotive topic areas and situations. Nevertheless, they may find that access to structures of support is more difficult than for interpreters based within an organization, and consequently relegate personal care to a lesser plane. This is where identifying the structures that help foster Communities of Practice (on- or offline) can create a safe environment for these aspects to become part of regular reflection on practice.

 PERFORMANCE SKILLS

Activity 12: Developing approaches to personal care

A   Reflect on your weekly schedule and the extent to which you make time for developing some of the strategies outlined above.

B   Reflect on your volume of exposure to traumatic stories and the triggers of work-related stress (Note: these may lie beyond the asylum setting).

C   Reflect on your personal level of resilience and the extent to which you are in a position to help others or know where to find appropriate support.

8 Conclusion

Variability in relation to interpreter education, recruitment and working conditions in asylum settings has significant impact on levels of **cultural humility** and **self-reflexivity** in this subdomain of legal interpreting. At the more serious end of the spectrum these shortcomings affect asylum procedures and life chances and in more general, but no less important, terms the dignity and well-being of applicants.

With regard to domain-specific competency development, we suggested that despite the often highly routinized nature of asylum procedures, account-giving processes often place particular burdens on the interpreter which they are sometimes ill-equipped to handle, in part due to over-confidence about short-term memory capacity and underestimation of the complexity of nar-rative construction. In addition, working with children presents special sens-itivities that call for reflection on the level of transferability of approaches between adult and child-focused interviews.

Since the interpreter's role boundaries are circumscribed and monitored to a greater extent in some interpreted asylum events than others, the concept of **social solidarity** in participant relations can benefit reflection on performance dimensions depending on the context. Greater awareness of the wider socio-political and sociocultural features that shape institutional interview practices invite a re-evaluation of issues of **neutrality** and **co-power** in some inter-preted events, particularly but not exclusively in relation to understandings of what constitutes **shared responsibility** in this subdomain.

The importance of personal care for interpreters, as demonstrated by the often extreme nature of interpreting activity in asylum procedures supports approaches to professional development based on reflective practice and tar-geted action to build **emotional resilience**.

Notes

1 Factsheet 20 available at: www.ohchr.org/Documents/Publications/FactSheet20en.pdf (accessed 29 March 2015).
2 See www.refugeecouncil.org.uk/assets/0002/0701/Applying_for_asylum_March_2012_English.pdf (accessed 29 March 2015).
3 Of note is that some individuals are excluded from the process, such as children (see www.gov.uk/government/uploads/system/uploads/attachment_data/file/257435/detained_fast_processes.pdf (accessed 14 July 2015)), and in June 2015 the DFT pro-cedure as it had been operating was held to be unlawful, see *Detention Action* v. *First-Tier Tribunal (Immigration and Asylum Chamber) & Ors*: www.bailii.org/ew/cases/EWHC/Admin/2015/1689.html (accessed 14 July 2015).
4 In some interviews other individuals may be present, such as a social worker.
5 The concept of face is discussed in Chapter 3 (Section 6.3). In this case, the interpreter perceives the applicant's actions to question her/his level of competency and the response reflects the desire to be seen as competent (i.e. in a more favourable light).
6 For information on language analysis in relation to questions of national origin, see Eades, D. (2010), 'Nationality Claims: language analysis in asylum claims', in M. Coulthard and A. Johnson (eds) *Handbook of Forensic Linguistics*, London and New York: Routledge.
7 Examples are taken from *Guidelines for Interviewing (Separated) Minors*, Direct-orate of Immigration, Finland, 2002 www.refworld.org/docid/430ae8d72.html; and United States Citizenship and Immigration Service, *Guidelines for Children's Asylum Claims*, 2009 www.uscis.gov/sites/default/files/USCIS/Humanitarian/Refugees%20%26%20Asylum/Asylum/AOBTC%20Lesson%20Plans/Guidelines-for-Childrens-Asylum-Claims-31aug10.pdf (accessed 25 May 2015).
8 The Voice of Love website: http://voice-of-love.org (accessed 26 April 2015).

References

Bancroft, M., Bendana, L., Bruggeman, J. and Feuerle, L. (2013) 'Interpreting in the Gray Zone: where community and legal interpreting intersect', *Translation and Interpreting*, 5 (1): 94–113.
Barsky, R. (1994) *Constructing a Productive Other: discourse theory and the conven-tion refugee hearing*, Amsterdam/Philadelphia: John Benjamins.
Bloemen, E., Vloeberghs, E. and Smits, C. (2006) *Psychological and Psychiatric Aspects of Recounting Traumatic Events by Asylum Seekers*. Online. Available at: www.evasp.eu/index.php?option=com_content&view=article&id=104%3Apsychol ogical-and-psychiatric-aspects-of-recounting-traumatic-events-by-asylum-seekers&Itemid=117&lang=en (accessed 12 April 2015).
Blommaert, J. (2001) 'Investigating Narrative Inequality: analyzing African asylum seekers' stories in Belgium', *Discourse & Society*, 12 (4): 413–49.

Butler, C. (2008) 'Speaking the Unspeakable: female interpreters' response to working with women who have been raped in war', *Clinical Psychology Forum*, 192: 22–6.

Conrad, D. and Kellar-Guenther, Y. (2006) 'Compassion Fatigue, Burnout, and Compassion Satisfaction among Colorado Child Protection Workers', *Child Abuse & Neglect*, 30 (10): 1071–80.

Crawley, H. (1999) *Breaking Down the Barriers: a report on the conduct of asylum interviews at ports*, Immigration Law Practitioners' Association, London: Russell Press.

Figley, C.R. (ed.) (1995) *Compassion Fatigue: coping with secondary traumatic stress disorder in those who treat the traumatized*, New York: Brunner/Mazel.

Finnish Directorate of Immigration (2002) *Guidelines for Interviewing (Separated) Minors*. Online. Available at: www.refworld.org/docid/430ae8d72.html (accessed 17 May 2015).

Folkman, S. and Moscowitz, J.T. (2000) 'Positive Affect and the Other Side of Coping', *American Psychologist*, 55 (6): 647–54.

Goffman, E. (1981) *Forms of Talk*, Philadelphia: University of Pennsylvania Press.

Hale, S. (2005) 'The Interpreter's Identity Crisis', in J. House, M. Rosario, M. Ruano and N. Baumgarten (eds) *Translation and the Construction of Identity*, IATIS Yearbook 2005, Seoul: International Association of Translation and Intercultural Studies.

Home Office (2015) *Asylum Policy Instruction: asylum interviews*. Online. Available at: www.gov.uk/government/uploads/system/uploads/attachment_data/file/410098/ Asylum_Interviews_AI.pdf (accessed 12 April 2015).

Inghilleri, M. (2005) 'Mediating Zones of Uncertainty: interpreter agency, the interpreting habitus and political asylum adjudication', *The Translator*, 11 (1): 69–85.

Jacquemet, M. (2005) 'The Registration Interview: restricting refugees' narrative performance', in M. Baynham and A. De Fina (eds) *Dislocations/Relocations: Narratives of Displacement*, Manchester: St Jerome.

Kagan, M. (2010) 'Refugee Credibility Assessment and the "Religious Imposter" Problem: a case study of Eritrean Pentecostal claims in Egypt', *Vanderbilt Journal of Transnational Law*, 43 (5): 1179–1233.

Keselman, O., Cederborg, A.-C., Lamb, M.E. and Dahlström, Ö. (2008) 'Mediated Communication with Minorities in Asylum Hearings', *Journal of Refugee Studies*, 21 (1): 103–16.

Keselman, O., Cederborg, A.-C., Lamb, M.E. and Dahlström, Ö. (2009) *Asylum-seeking Children: conditions of restricted participation. Communicative aspects of interpreter-mediated asylum hearings in Sweden*, Linköping University: Department of Behavioural Sciences and Learning.

Keselman, O., Cederborg, A-C. and Linell, P. (2010) ' "That's not Necessary for you to Know!": negotiation of participation status of unaccompanied children in interpreter-mediated asylum hearings', *Interpreting*, 12 (1): 83–104.

Lambert, H. (1995) *Seeking Asylum: comparative law and practice in selected European countries*, Dordrecht: Martinus Nijhoff.

Lor, M. (2012) 'Effects of Client Trauma on Interpreters: an exploratory study of vicarious trauma', *Masters of Social Work Clinical Research Papers*, Paper 53. Online. Available at: http://sophia.stkate.edu/msw_papers/53 (accessed 11 April 2015).

Maryns, K. (2006) *The Asylum Speaker: language in the Belgian asylum procedure*, Manchester: St Jerome.

Mason, I. (2005) 'Projected and Perceived Identities in Dialogue Interpreting', in J. House, M. Rosario, M. Ruano and N. Baumgarten (eds) *Translation and the Construction of Identity*, IATIS Yearbook 2005, Seoul: International Association of Translation and Intercultural Studies.

McFayden, G. (2012) 'The Contemporary Refugee: persecution, semantics and universality', *eSharp* Special Issue: The 1951 UN Refugee Convention – 60 Years On: 9–35. Online. Available at: www.gla.ac.uk/media/media_234569_en.pdf (accessed 29 March 2015).

Miller, K.E., Martell, Z.L., Pazdirek, L., Caruth, M. and López, D. (2005) 'The Role of Interpreters in Psychotherapy with Refugees: an exploratory study', *American Journal of Orthopsychiatry*, 75 (1): 27–39.

Moser-Mercer, B., Kherbiche, L. and Class, B. (2014) 'Interpreting Conflict: Training Challenges in Humanitarian Field Interpreting', *Journal of Human Rights Practice*, 6 (1): 140–58.

Ndongo-Keller, J. (2015) 'Vicarious Trauma and Stress Management', in H. Mikkleson and R. Jourdenais (eds) *The Routledge Handbook of Interpreting*, Abingdon and New York: Routledge.

Palmer, I.P. (2002) 'Psychological Aspects of Medical Humanitarian Aid', in J. Ryan, P.F. Mahoney, I. Greaves and G. Bowyer (eds) *Conflict and Catastrophe Medicine: a practical guide*, London, Berlin, Heidelberg: Springer-Verlag.

Pöllabauer, S. (2004) 'Interpreting in Asylum Hearings: issues of role, responsibility and power', *Interpreting*, 6 (2): 143–80.

Right to Remain, *Toolkit on Evidence and Credibility in Asylum Claims*. Online. Available at: http://righttoremain.org.uk/toolkit/evidence-and-credibility.html#challenging (accessed 5 December 2014).

Rosenblum, M.R. (2015) *Unaccompanied Child Migration to the United States: the tension between protection and prevention*, Washington, DC: Migration Policy Institute.

Splevins, K., Cohen, K., Joseph, S., Murray, C. and Bowley, J. (2010) 'Vicarious Posttraumatic Growth Among Interpreters', *Qualitative Health Research*, 20 (12): 1705–16.

Tipton, R. (2008a) 'Reflexivity and the Social Construction of Identity', *The Translator*, 14 (8): 1–19.

Tipton, R. (2008b) 'Interpreter Neutrality and the Structure/agency Distinction', *Proceedings of the 3rd International Congress on Translation and Interpreting for the Public Services: challenges and alliances in PSIT research and practice*, Madrid: University of Alcalá de Henares.

UNHCR (2001) 'The Wall Behind Which Refugees Can Shelter', *Refugees*, 2 (123): 1–31.

UNHCR (2010a) *United Nations Convention Relating to the Status of Refugees*. Online. Available at: www.unhcr.org/3b66c2aa10.html?_ga=1.172551076.6888478 96.1402914931 (accessed 12 April 2015).

UNHCR (2010b) *Improving Asylum Procedures: comparative analysis and recommendations for law and practice*. Online. Available at: www.unhcr.org/4c7b71039. pdf (accessed 12 April 2015).

UNHCR (2014) *Asylum Trends Report, First Half 2014: levels and trends in industrialized countries*. Online. Available at: www.unhcr.org/5423f9699.html (accessed 12 April 2015).

United Kingdom: Asylum and Immigration Tribunal/Immigration Appellate Authority (2008) *AA (Language Diagnosis: Use of Interpreters) Somalia* v. *Secretary of State for the Home Department* 2008) UKAIT 00029, United Kingdom: Asylum and Immigration Tribunal/Immigration Appellate Authority, 9 April 2008. Online. Available at: www.refworld.org/docid/47fdd8982.html (accessed 25 July 2014). www.nationalarchives.gov.uk/doc/open-government-licence/.

United Kingdom Visas and Immigration (2012) *Considering the Protection Claim (Asylum) and Assessing Credibility*. Online. Available at: www.gov.uk/government/uploads/system/uploads/attachment_data/file/257426/considering-protection-.pdf (accessed 12 April 2015).

United States Citizenship and Immigration Services (2009) *Guidelines for Children's Asylum Claims*. Online. Available at: www.uscis.gov/sites/default/files/USCIS/Humanitarian/Refugees%20%26%20Asylum/Asylum/AOBTC%20Lesson%20Plans/Guidelines-for-Childrens-Asylum-Claims-31aug10.pdf (accessed 17 May 2015).

United States Citizenship and Immigration Services (2010) *Working with an Interpreter*. Online. Available at: www.uscis.gov/sites/default/files/USCIS/Humanitarian/Refugees%20%26%20Asylum/Asylum/AOBTC%20Lesson%20Plans/Interview-Part6-Working-with-an-Interpreter-31aug10.pdf (accessed 12 April 2015).

United States Citizenship and Immigration Services (2013a) *RAIO Directorate – Officer Training. Interviewing – Working with an Interpreter*. Online. Available at: www.uscis.gov/sites/default/files/USCIS/About%20Us/Directorates%20and%20Program%20Offices/RAIO/Interviewing%20-%20Working%20with%20an%20Interpreter%20LP%20(RAIO).pdf (accessed 17 May 2015).

United States Citizenship and Immigration Services (2013b) *Overview of Non-adversarial Asylum Interview*. Online. Available at: www.uscis.gov/sites/default/files/USCIS/About%20Us/Directorates%20and%20Program%20Offices/RAIO/Interviewing%20-%20Intro%20to%20the%20NonAdversarial%20Interview%20LP%20(RAIO).pdf (accessed 12 April 2015).

Valero Garcés, C. (2010) 'The Difficult Task of Gathering Information on PSI&T', *Babel*, 56 (3): 199–218.

Vergara, J.A. and Gardner, D. (2011) 'Stressors and Psychological Wellbeing in Local Humanitarian Workers in Colombia', *Journal of Managerial Psychology*, 26 (6): 500–7.

Warren, R. and York, S. (2014) *How Children Become Failed Asylum Seekers: research report on the experiences of young unaccompanied asylum-seekers in Kent from 2006 to 2013, and how 'corrective remedies' have failed them*, Kent Law Centre: University of Kent. Online. Available at: www.kent.ac.uk/law/clinic/how_children_become_failed_asylum-seekers.pdf (accessed 12 April 2015).

Zwiers, M.L. and Morrisette, P.J. (1999) *Effective Interviewing of Children: a comprehensive guide for counselors and human service workers*, Philadelphia: Accelerated Development.

Recommended reading

Cherubini, F. (2014) *Asylum Law in the European Union*, London and New York: Routledge.

Goodwin-Gill, G.S. and McAdam, J. (2007) *The Refugee in International Law*, 3rd edn, Oxford: Oxford University Press.

4 Healthcare interpreting

I thought the tragic images of the day would stay and haunt me. But in the end it was the smile of the patient and the words 'You are now cancer free' that kept resonating.

(Mariana Rodriguez-Pardy, medical interpreter, USA)

1 Introduction

This chapter discusses the nature and structure of the medical interpreting event, analyses key factors that affect the interpreter's performance in the healthcare setting, and provides an overview of reasons why the professionalization of medical interpreting is a slow process worldwide. Furthermore, this chapter addresses issues such as: who decides when a patient needs an interpreter, different parties' expectations of what the interpreter should do, the boundaries of the interpreter's intervention, and the possible conflicts that arise when those boundaries are not respected. It also focuses on decisions made by primary healthcare stakeholders in regard to providing language services to patients, including attempts by hospital administrations to introduce new interpreting technologies. Additionally this chapter defines selected setting-specific competencies required to become a medical interpreter and presents reasons why healthcare interpreting remains an interpreting domain in which remuneration does not reflect interpreters' level of responsibility and professional preparation.

Given the complexity of the medical setting and multiple possible interpreting scenarios, an overview of interpreting features characteristic of all medical contexts is presented without analysing situations specific to sub-specializations or different types of healthcare institutions. For the sake of clarity, one defined setting is chosen as the main point of reference – a medium-sized hospital[1] (100–300 beds), however, several activities include other less common healthcare-related settings. The discussions draw extensively on experiences in the USA; however, what is being presented is not necessarily endorsed by all interpreting services providers or applicable across different geonational contexts. The recommended reading section indicates where further material on these more specialized or other national contexts can be found.

2 Healthcare communication: settings and modes in medical interpreting

Of all dialogue interpreting settings *healthcare interpreting*, also called *medical interpreting* or sometimes *hospital interpreting*, is the setting with the most variables. It covers interpreting in hospitals of different sizes and types, teaching hospitals, emergency rooms and urgent care units, and private and rural clinics. It also includes specialized contexts such as mental health interpreting, dental interpreting, pediatric interpreting, interpreting for hospice or palliative care, interpreting in physiotherapy sessions, interpreting for health tourism, and interpreting in the mission fields such as field clinics or disaster areas. In addition, along with religious interpreting, it is the field which, as of 2015, still sees the largest variety of *ad hoc interpreters*, ranging from bilingual employees in a given healthcare institution (e.g. nurses, nurses aides, dietitians, data entry personnel, medical students, environmental services and security personnel), to family members, volunteers, friends, other patients and even providers who attempt to use their limited second-language skills to communicate with patients. Some claim that they have taken medical terminology courses in a foreign language and find a patient's visit an appropriate place to practice their foreign language proficiency. Others are convinced that two years of high school second language courses suffice to make them fluent in that particular language. Hence, the need to educate the users seems to be most pronounced in medical settings as compared to other interpreting contexts.

The healthcare setting uses a wide variety of interpreting modes:

a   on-site bilateral interpreting (also called short consecutive which requires note taking);
b   telephone interpreting for less-common languages, in smaller clinics, or in remote rural or mountainous areas;
c   video interpreting, which is also being introduced on many large medical campuses in the United States as the in-house mode;
d   sight translation.

Medicine-related interpreting that occurs during medical or pharmaceutical research congresses and conferences is considered conference, not dialogue, interpreting and thus is not included in this chapter.

3 Healthcare interpreting: scope and nature

At the third Critical Link conference in Montreal, Canada, in 2001, Holly Mikkelson listed medical interpreting as one of two main fields of community interpreting, casting doubt on its status as a separate subdomain. In her article on the nature of different types of interpreting, published on the AIIC website in 2009, she states:

Community interpreters were once considered amateurs and well-meaning but misguided 'do-gooders' ... but nowadays they are increasingly recognized as specialists in their own right. Some writers consider community interpreting an umbrella term that includes court and medical interpreting ..., while others (mainly court interpreters) regard it as a separate category.

(Mikkelson 2009)

In the United States, in addition to the growing body of research on the topic, an increase in data-gathering initiatives has been observed, originally prompted by the results of the US 2000 Census and the attempt to define, map and improve healthcare access for non-societal language speakers. Furthermore, the Joint Commission, a US hospital accreditation body, has developed a new set of standards on Patient-Centered Communication that emphasize the importance of language services, cultural competence and patient-centered care. Hospitals seeking accreditation have been expected to comply with these recommendations since 2012. The role of language barriers and their impact on adverse events is presented in depth in an Executive Summary provided by the Agency for Health Research and Quality (AHRQ), a division of the US Health and Human Services Department, highlighting the fact that adverse events that affect limited English proficient (LEP) patients are more frequently caused by communication problems and more likely to result in serious harm compared to English-speaking patients.[2]

Another large initiative related to cross-cultural communication in US healthcare is the Community Access Monitoring Survey (CAMS). This survey, led by the Access Project,[3] gathered data from over 10,000 uninsured individuals who received care at 58 different healthcare facilities in 18 different states. The survey asked people about their experiences in a wide range of topics, including the facility's openness to the uninsured respondents' difficulties in paying for care, and the availability of interpreters and other materials for respondents with limited English proficiency. On 25 April 2002, the first issue on the national findings, *What a Difference an Interpreter Can Make: healthcare experiences of uninsured with limited English proficiency*, was released. This report describes the impact of having interpreters available for those with limited English proficiency on the respondents' overall experience at the urban hospitals included in the survey.

Another large project focused on the development of two survey instruments with closed- and open-ended questions to examine attitudinal and perceptual consensus and difference between two cohorts of respondents – healthcare interpreter trainers/curriculum developers, and practicing interpreters/interpreters in training – regarding the core competencies essential to a high-quality healthcare interpreting training. Its findings are presented in Section 4.2.3.

Australia, Sweden and Canada have long been known for their efforts in the recognition of community interpreting, but still lack structured regulations specifically for healthcare interpreting. In Europe, the predominant population served by medical interpreters are immigrants or second-generation immigrant residents in the host country in spite of the existence of significant medical tourism needs, in particular dental care tourism from Germany and the UK to Poland and other Central European countries, and sporadic medical emergency events related to student exchange programmes or traditional summer tourism in the Mediterranean. Hence, the countries and regions with the highest immigrant influx have naturally become prominent players in the field of healthcare interpreting practice and research. Since interaction occurs between the dominant (societal) and non-dominant (non-societal) language speakers, this also implies power inequities and adds to medical context issues that can cause a moral dilemma between ethical professional obligations and attitudes of solidarity/hostility, as has been noted in the United States. In many US states, access to emergency rooms has been hindered by uninsured immigrants who visit the Emergency Department for non-life threatening conditions, which could otherwise be ameliorated by a primary care provider. As a result, during the first decade of the twenty-first century emergency room waiting times have increased by 60 per cent in certain areas, negatively affecting English-speaking patients who require emergency treatment for serious and urgent cases.

The countries leading medical interpreting efforts in Europe include the United Kingdom (El Ansari *et al.* 2009) and Spain (Abril Martí 2006). There is also growing interest in places such as Sweden, Switzerland (Bischoff 2006), Ireland (Phelan and Martín 2010), Italy (Baraldi 2009; Farini 2012), the Netherlands and Belgium, and outside of Europe in South Africa (Lesch and Saulse 2014) and the United Arab Emirates (Hikmet Hannouna 2012). In 2004 the European Commission's 'Migrant Friendly Hospitals' project developed a series of 11 recommendations for ensuring quality healthcare for diverse populations.[4] In response to growing demand, training programmes in indigenous languages for several public services settings, including medical, have recently been introduced in Chile (Mapuche) and Mexico (Veracruz region) in addition to Canada (Eskimo-Aleut languages). In Asia, the flow of seasonal unqualified workers from the Southern Continental Asian regions has increased in the last decade in South Korea, thus contributing to work-related accidents and more frequent cases of interpreting in the medical setting.

In 2004, Mara Youdelman, managing attorney of the Washington, D.C. office of the National Health Law Program, an advocacy group for the underserved that has studied the need and effect of medical interpretation services, stated that providing competent interpreting services to everyone who needs them had not yet been accomplished, but 'we've come a long way'. As the US grows increasingly more linguistically and culturally diverse, some safety experts worry that too often healthcare providers are not making professional interpreter and translator services available to patients and families. Instead, they frequently rely on non-professionals, including patients' family members, who are not knowledgeable about medical terminology. This increases the risk of medication errors, incorrect procedures, avoidable readmissions and other adverse events. According to the Agency for Healthcare Research and Quality, nearly 9 per cent of the US population is at risk of an adverse event because of language barriers.

A study by Wasserman *et al.* (2014) published in the *Journal for Healthcare Quality* identifies high-risk clinical situations in which medical errors are most likely to occur among limited English proficiency patients, and investigates tools that can help prevent those situations. Three common causes of medical errors due to insufficient patient language proficiency are identified:

1   Use of family members, friends or non-qualified staff as interpreters.
2   Clinicians with basic foreign language skills who try to communicate without using qualified interpreters.
3   Cultural beliefs and traditions that affect healthcare delivery.[5]

A number of similar systemic studies resulting from growing migration patterns, insurance companies' interest in more-efficient healthcare management, as well as an increasing level of awareness of patients' rights across the globe seem to indicate that medical interpreting will continue to be one of the most developing domains of dialogue interpreting services in the coming decades.

3.1 The structure of an interpreted medical encounter: pre-event, event/interaction time, post-event, in-between events

A definition provided by Angelelli (2014) describes an interpreted event in a medical setting as an interaction that

> occurs among three participants: a speaker of a non-societal language (for example a patient seeking healthcare), a speaker of the societal language (generally the service provider – for example a physician, a nurse, or a hospital administrator), and an interpreter who facilitates the communication in either consecutive or simultaneous mode. These three parties should interact for the encounter to be considered an interpreted communicative event. Interaction can occur face to face or remotely.
>
> (2014: 574)

According to the California HealthCare Interpreting Association, the interpreted event in the medical setting can be divided into three parts: Protocols 1, 2 and 3. In addition to the **pre-event, event/interaction time** and **post-event** stages, we recommend that a fourth stage, **in-between events**, be included in the event structure, as proposed by Zhu (2015) who advocates an organizational approach to the interpreted encounters within the institutional context.

I Pre-event

PROTOCOL 1: PRE-ENCOUNTER, PRE-SESSION OR PRE-INTERVIEW

This protocol outlines the information that interpreters should provide in pre-session introductions to assure confidentiality and gain the cooperation of the patient and providers for a smooth interpreted encounter. The protocol also allows for a pre-encounter briefing of the interpreter or provider as necessary (CHIA 2002).

Issues to be addressed during this stage are:

ASSESSMENT OF NEED

Who decides whether the patient needs an interpreter (see also Section 2.1)? Healthcare literacy is an issue among many monolingual patients. It is a challenge even for patients who speak English, observes the Joint Commission's Dr Ana Pujols-McKee: 'Assessing a patient's ability to communicate effectively with a healthcare professional is an important part of the evaluation' (the Joint Commission website).

PARTIES INVOLVED

Who are the parties? How prepared are they to work with interpreters in general? Is this the interpreter's first interaction with this particular patient and provider?

The briefing session with the provider depends on the level of the interpreter's familiarity with the patient's history, the complexity of the case and the time that the provider expects each visit to last. In general, the briefing session should always include:

- introduction of all medical team members present (providers, interpreter, nurses, physician assistants, medical students);
- overview of the history and condition of the patient;
- purpose of the visit.

▲ COLLABORATIVE DIMENSIONS

Activity 1: Guidelines for providers and patients

Write your own guidelines for providers that would fit on a laminated card that they can place in their pocket. Guidelines should contain less than ten items. Use the guidelines for conference interpreters prepared by AIIC as a model.[6] An example is provided in Appendix 2.

TERMINOLOGY PREPARATION

Moser-Mercer (1992: 289) states that 'software developers targeting the conference interpreting market must provide a tool that meets the specific needs of the interpreters and not just market translation tools'. More recent studies have also examined interpreters' current needs and practices regarding terminology management (Bilgen 2009; Rodríguez and Schnell 2009), and share the same findings: interpreters require specific tools to meet their needs, which are different from those of translators and terminologists.

Resources provided by medical interpreters' associations quickly become outdated or inaccessible due to the rapid disappearance of websites. Many hospitals have their own specialized glossary, but we advise medical interpreters to learn to use terminology tools. While a detailed explanation of terminology software is beyond the scope of this guide, some of the recommended terminology tools include Intragloss, InterpretBank, Intraplex, MultiTerm, Anylexic, Lingo, UniLex and The Interpreter's Wizard (Costa *et al.* 2014). So far these tools have mainly been tested in conference settings for simultaneous interpreting; hence, community interpreters must still evaluate how these tools could assist bilateral interpreting in a medical environment.

II Event/interaction time
PROTOCOL 2: DURING THE ENCOUNTER, SESSION OR INTERVIEW

This section presents interpreting practices to support the patient-provider relationship during the medical encounter. These include encouraging direct patient-provider communication through practices such as positioning, verbal reminders or gesturing in order for the patient and providers to address each other directly, and use of first-person interpreting. This protocol addresses the need to manage the flow of communication and facilitate or seek clarification of messages, as well as how to conduct more active intervention when necessary. Additionally, this section highlights the importance of interpreters clearly identifying when they are intervening and speaking on their own behalf, and describes how this can be done (CHIA 2002).

Issues to be addressed during this stage are:

PHYSICAL VISIBILITY/POSITIONING

Where does one stand/sit? Is it better that I sit or stand? Should the interpreter change her/his position during the event?

The recommended physical placement of the interpreter is to the side of both the patient and the medical provider (also called *triangular situating*), within a distance of approximately 1–1.5 m. In certain settings though, such as in the emergency department, it may be useful to position oneself at the head of the bed (stretcher) in a trauma situation so that all the agents involved can do their job without obstruction, and also so that the patient, who may be experiencing a lot of pain, discomfort or may be coming in and out of consciousness can hear and respond to the questions being asked by providers through the interpreter.

NOTE TAKING

The interpreting mode typically used in the medical setting is bilateral, also called short consecutive. Hence, advanced note-taking strategies are not needed as they would be in a long consecutive interpreting event. Glossaries are helpful but should not be used more than two to three times per session. The use of glossaries is mostly recommended during the terminological preparation (see previous stage, Pre-event).

TRANSPARENCY

According to the glossary provided by the California HealthCare Interpreting Association, the principle of transparency is

> the idea that the interpreter keeps both parties in the interpreting session fully informed of what is happening, who is speaking, and what the interpreter is doing. Whenever interpreters intervene by voicing their own thoughts and not the interpreted words of one of their clients, it is critical that they ensure that a) the message is conveyed to all parties and b) everyone is aware that the message originates from the interpreter.
>
> (CHIA 2002)

■ PERFORMANCE SKILLS

Activity 2: Communicative strategies

A   A pregnant woman came in with her husband; the couple requested an interpreter but the woman does not look at you or listen to you when you interpret for her but instead looks at her husband who, while nodding his head most of the time, sometimes adds to or clarifies your interpretation. You do not doubt the correctness of your interpretation, but feel more and more uncomfortable. In addition, they brought their two small children (three and five years old), who are playing, making noise and asking questions. The mother is trying to keep them quiet while listening to you or her husband. The provider wonders what the husband is saying and looks at you, expecting your interpretation of the husband's remarks.

- How can you ensure that the patient heard what the provider said?
- Do you repeat it each time when the husband's rendition interrupts yours?
- Do you ask the husband to stop rephrasing your words?
- Does then the need for setting ground rules among the parties with regards to who will do the interpreting arise?

B   Do you interpret everything that the leading doctor is explaining to the resident/all the interactions between three or four family members who are discussing the doctor's comments/explanations among themselves?

CULTURAL AND LITERACY BROKERAGE

When does one ask questions to clarify cultural differences or specialized medical terms? How often is the interpreter allowed to ask questions?

Other issues to be considered under cultural competencies (see also Section 5.1) are:

- length of interpreter's interaction with one of the parties so that the other party does not feel excluded;
- need to explain the cultural differences in detail or only give a summary;
- tendency to lower the register or add an explanation when the provider uses a scientific medical term.

■ PERFORMANCE SKILLS

Activity 3: Regional expressions

Interpreters from countries that use the same language may not have problems when understanding accents, but frequently face problems with dialectic idiomatic expressions, particularly in references to medicinal plants, endemic fruits, symptoms, popular names of diseases or folk remedies. It has been found that other than local customs and religious traditions, the most diverse semantic areas are cuisine/food and medical treatments. Prepare a list of ten colloquial terms related to symptoms/treatments in your working language that is spoken in multiple countries/regions and find their equivalences in different countries/regions.

III Post-event

PROTOCOL 3: POST-ENCOUNTER, POST-SESSION OR POST-INTERVIEW

This protocol addresses the steps that interpreters take to provide closure to the interpreted session. This ranges from ensuring that the encounter has ended and no other questions or concerns are outstanding, to facilitating follow-up appointments and scheduling interpreter services as necessary, to debriefing with the provider or interpreter's supervisor as needed (CHIA 2002).

Issues to be addressed during this stage are:

FOLLOW-UP ASSISTANCE

Does the interpreter leave the room right away when the doctor leaves? Does s/he take the patient to the lab? Make sure that the patient has a follow-up appointment?

Several studies, particularly in Europe, have started to explore facilitation/mediation/acculturation in interpreted encounters. These studies attempt to redefine the profession as, among others, interlinguistic mediators in Italy (Baraldi and Gavioli 2007), interlinguistic and intercultural medical mediators in Spain (Grupo CRIT 2014) and enablers in Switzerland (Bischoff and Hudelson 2010). This dimension, considered an extended role, is addressed in Section 4.

SELF-CARE OF THE INTERPRETER

This covers writing reports, clarifying terminology through consultation of terminology databases/corpora or conversations with peer interpreters, dealing with emotional burnout, physical fatigue and compassion fatigue.[7]

 COLLABORATIVE DIMENSIONS

Activity 4: Opportunity versus success

Watch the Opportunity Video, then write down what all three parties could have done differently to improve the interpreted event. Then watch the Success Video and compare it with your notes.[8]

IV In-between events

Interpreting units or departments have become part of the hospital structure in the USA, either as stand-alone language services units or subunits of Patient Experience divisions. A medium-sized (225 beds) hospital in the United States employs on average 5–7 full-time interpreters and contracts freelancers to cover night shifts, weekends or temporary vacancies. In the last five years a small number of studies (e.g. Greenhalgh *et al.* 2007) began looking into organizational behaviour paradigms as a possible way to improve interpreters' performance and better integrate language services into medical institutions.

Greenhalgh *et al.* (2007) identify a number of general properties of the interpreted consultation as an organizational routine, including the wide variation in the form of adoption, and the stability, adaptability and strength of the routine. In addition, they find that this variation can be partly explained by the characteristics of the practice as an organization, particularly whether it was traditional (small, family-run, 'personal' identity, typically multilingual, loose division of labour, relatively insular) or contemporary (large, bureaucratic, 'efficient' identity, typically monolingual, clear division of labour, richly networked). These authors suggest that there is a fruitful research agenda to be explored that links the organizational dimension of interpreting services with studies of clinical care and outcomes.

Zhu (2015) proposes the in-between events stage in addition to the first three stages, and defines it as the time interval between a limited language proficient (LLP) patient's previous healthcare visit and next visit. Some LLP patients may come back for treatment of the same symptom on a regular or frequent basis; some may not return for a long time, or not return at all. These data, such as the length of this interval, reason for doctor visit and the percentage of LLP patients that never show up again, are likely to be important indicators of medical interpreting service quality and patient satisfaction, hence trained interpreters' compliance may increase and readmission rates be reduced.

As full-time employees at a hospital, medical interpreters can also use this interval to established individualized language/culture files for each LLP patient so that they can service these patients in a better way next time. Zhu (ibid.) calls this organization-related role a *data keeper*. He proposes a **process-based role model** integrating all contextual variables (i.e. linguistic, cultural and organizational ones), all roles proposed so far and the important dimension of time. This model helps us gain a deeper understanding of all the situations medical interpreters need to work in and the corresponding roles they need to take on. According to Zhu, this model also has the potential to monitor and improve interpreting performance in healthcare settings. A partial strategy similar to the model proposed by Zhu is used at the Baptist Medical Center in Winston-Salem, NC, USA. In their interpreting team, if one has dealt with a patient that has special needs or a special circumstance, that person communicates this to the rest of the team via email. S/he details the key points of the interaction and next steps as presented by the care team so that the entire team is aware of that patient's situation as it is unknown who will be serving this particular patient the next time an interpreter is requested. Such practice, which has proven useful, may nevertheless raise questions about patient confidentiality.

3.2 Key factors in the medical interpreting setting

3.2.1 Time
Time is a crucial factor in healthcare interpreting; it affects all three parties. Doctors do not want to wait for the interpreter. Interpreters have limited time in which they can perform their services – for example, at Wake Forest Baptist Medical Center interpreters' waiting time limit is ten minutes; after that they check in with the dispatcher, who decides, based on current work load and demand, whether the interpreter should take the next assignment from the dispatcher and leave the area that had requested their services but was not ready to use them, or stay and service the call. Many patients feel that their time with the provider is shorter than that of monolingual patients because the interpretation takes time away from their direct interaction with the provider.

In Sweden, Wiking *et al.* (2013) researched participants' perceptions of and reflections on triangular meetings by means of in-depth interviews with immigrant patients from Chile, Turkey and Iran, interpreters and general practitioners. According to the participants, a successful meeting between the patient and the general practitioner during the consultation requires adapting to the individual patient, a process that they call the *individual tailored approach*. Section 4, which reviews role conflicts, discusses this approach in depth. Other important factors were **consultation time**, the patient's feelings and the role of family members. Cited below are three comments from the aforementioned study, from the interpreter, the patient and the provider respectively, on time constraints affecting the outcome of the interpreted event. The majority of the interpreters felt that the consultation time was never sufficient. They experienced frustration since establishing a relationship with the patient when the provider is stressed is difficult to accomplish properly. One of the interpreters commented:

> Even if the doctor is under stress and does not want to hear everything the patient says in detail, or is not listening the whole time, the interpreter has to do what is needed. The brain is not a factory for transforming words from one language to another. One needs a lot of imagination and undivided presence to convey the intended message in the best way.

Patients also noted that the consultation time was insufficient. The patient has the need to tell the family doctor everything at the first visit, be properly examined and be able to ask questions. In addition more than half of the providers felt that it was desirable to have longer consultation times because the interpretation takes time, as stated by one of the doctors:

> We do not have longer consultations when an interpreter is present. There is also another problem due to the patient's lack of knowledge about how the body works, which may give you an inadequate medical history.... It can take an incredibly long time to find out what it is about.
> (Wiking *et al.* 2013: 4–5)

3.2.2 Trust

Trust is the foundation of the interrelationships in medical encounters. Within those encounters, patients are inherently vulnerable and must be trustful of the institutional entities and trust that individual healthcare providers are competent and will have their best interests in mind while making treatment decisions. In an interpreted event trust must be built in a three-dimensional way: patient-interpreter, provider-interpreter and patient-provider. In order for the patient to feel comfortable with the medical provider, s/he must first be able to trust the interpreter's language abilities so as to feel that their emotions are conveyed accurately to the doctor, and ultimately for them to describe their emotions without reservation. Second, the patient needs to be assured of patient privacy and confidentiality rights and informed of the ethical principles of interpreting. All of this needs to be accomplished in one or two sentences. It is difficult to build a rapport of trust in such circumstances, and even more when the health condition of the patient is serious or even life-threatening.

Since the issue of trust is complex and develops as a result of other conditions that will be discussed in the following sections such as interpreters' competence, shared goals of all participants and professional boundaries (Hsieh *et al.* 2010), cited below is an in-depth study that helps to shed some light on the multilayered nature of trust factors:

Trust was a prominent theme in almost all the narratives. The triadic nature of interpreted consultations creates six linked trust relationships (patient-interpreter, patient-clinician, interpreter-patient, interpreter-clinician, clinician-patient and clinician-interpreter). Three different types of trust are evident in these different relationships – *voluntary trust* (based on either kinship-like bonds and continuity of the interpersonal relationship over time, or on confidence in the institution and professional role that the individual represents), *coercive trust* (where one person effectively has no choice but to trust the other, as when a health problem requires expert knowledge that the patient does not have and cannot get) and *hegemonic trust* (where a person's propensity to trust, and awareness of alternatives, is shaped and constrained by the system so that people trust without knowing there is an alternative).

(Robb and Greenhalgh 2006: 434)

Robb and Greenhalgh conclude that the quality of the interpreted consultation cannot be judged purely in terms of the accuracy of translation. The critical importance of voluntary trust for open and effective communication, and the dependence of the latter on a positive interpersonal relationship and continuity of care, understood as a **shared responsibility** for the interpreted event, should be acknowledged in the design and funding of interpreting services and in the training of clinicians, interpreters and administrative staff.

3.2.3 Control/co-power
The control/co-power issue is closely related to the roles and role confusion that are discussed in detail in Section 4. The two excerpts below illustrate this interrelationship:

a   the provider accepts the transfer of power when the interpreter acts as co-interviewer, from Davidson (2000) 'Interpreter as Institutional Gate-keeper: the social-linguistic roles of interpreters in Spanish–English medical discourse';
b   the provider uses multimodal resources to remain a participant in the conversation and to retain control of the event, from Pasquandrea (2011) 'Managing Multiple Actions through Multimodality: doctors' involvement in interpreter-mediated interactions'.

A THE INTERPRETER AS CO-INTERVIEWER
One common scenario for interpreted medical interviews at the Riverview medical centre in Davidson's study was that the interpreter arrived while the physician was busy elsewhere, and would begin some form of interaction with the patient before the physician arrived. This had two effects. First, from the physician's point of view, the process of elaborating a chief complaint (a named entity in medical practice, usually written in chart notes as the abbreviated 'CC') from the patient was apparently simplified; the interpreter might greet the physician at the door of the examining room with

an announcement of whatever the patient had specified as his or her problem, as in Excerpt 1 in which 69 lines of transcript occur before the physician enters the room. However, the second effect was that the interpreter set the focus of the initial portion of the interview, and would occasionally conduct the initial portions of the interview:

Excerpt 1 (from Visit 30):[3]
(Dr enters the room)
70 Pt Anda, a ver que dice el doctor.
Well, let's see what the doctor says.
71 Dr Hi:!
72 how are you doing?
73 Int Doctor, I was looking for something to put over there because he
74 wants to show you his:
75 (1.5 seconds)
76 foot but I didn't find something.
77 Dr Oh.
78 Let's see:=
79 Int =One of those (xx)s, or.
80 Dr Maybe he: re, no:
81 Int Maybe in the (xx). ((banging noises – searching for a stool))
82 (2 seconds)
83 Dr Wouldn't surprise me.
84 (6 seconds)
85 Int At least we are not (xx).
86 Levante(te?) un poquito la pierna. (louder than previous English) Lift your foot a little bit.
87 Pt Sí, sí, señora.
Yes, yes, ma'am,
88 Ahora bien. Okay now.
89 [x]
90 Int [¿Cuál] es el malo?
[Which] is the bad one?
91 Pt ¿Mande?
Excuse me?
92 Int ¿Cuál es el [enfermo?]
Which is [the 'sick' (bad) one?]
93 Pt [Éste.]
[This one.]
94 Int A ver,
Let's see,
95 quitense el caletín y el [XXX] por favor.
take off your sock and [XXX] please.

96 [(loud banging noise)]
97 Pt Oh, no.
98 (2 seconds)
99 Int He says that, ah,
100 you explained to him the last time then ah...

(Davidson 2000: 388)

B Doctors' interventions in dyadic interactions

Linguistic and extra-linguistic parameters affect significantly an inter-linguistically mediated medical encounter but few studies present empirical data that demonstrate the impact of non-verbal communication on inter-preting in medical settings. Pasquandrea's (2011) study acknowledges that although non-verbal features have been recognized as part of human social interaction as well as important vectors of meaning and coordination, their use by interpreters is still largely uncharted territory. Having to manage mul-tiparty and multitask conversations with patients, with whom no direct com-munication is possible, doctors are forced to rely heavily on multimodality: gaze, gesture, bodily alignment, posture manipulation, spatial arrangement, proximity, object manipulation and talk. In the event cited below between a Chinese patient and an Italian doctor, in which extended dyadic sequences intertwine with triadic interactions, Pasquandrea analyses how the doctor regains power after several minutes of being excluded from the conversation between the patient and the interpreter.

Excerpt 2
(11) Obstetric visit 3: Detecting and fixing a problem during a dyadic sequence

In all of the examples that Pasquandrea examines prior to sequence 11, the doctors never intrude in the dyadic interactions, preferring instead to wait for the conversation to spontaneously come to an end before again taking their turn. Yet there are cases in which the doctor interrupts, tempor-arily or permanently, a sequence of dyadic conversation between the inter-preter and the patient. An example is shown in the excerpt below taken from the initial phase of an obstetric visit. In the first lines of the excerpt the patient is signing the form of informed consent while the doctor is gazing at the computer and using the mouse.

1 PAT: *Isúbiàn qiān Zhōngwén yě kěyǐ ma
   'Is it okay if I sign in Chinese?'
   * DOC>computer screen
   ʃDOC keeps her right hand on the mouse
2 INT: =hm:: Yìdàlìyǔ a
   'Hm ... in Italian!'
3 (0.8)

4   PAT: °>wǒ dōu bùzhīdào zěnme [qiān<°
      'I don't even know how to sign (in Italian).'

5   INT: [o::h.

6   ʃ(0.8)
      ʃINT takes a folded sheet and unfolds it

7   PAT: °>zhègè búshí *wǒde<°
      'This is not mine.'
      *PAT>desk *INT >desk

8   ʃ(0.4)
      ʃINT leans towards the desk

9   INT: ( )°ʃ
      ʃINT extends her right hand

10 (1.0)

11 INT: [°yīl- yǐ:láokā °ʃ
      'The medical card…'
      ʃPAT stretches her right arm towards the desk

12 DOC: [tsk (.)ʃ sì::? Cosa serve?
      'Yes? What do you need?'
      ʃINT puts her right hand on the desk, in front of the doctor

13 INT: il:tesserino sa(h)nitario perché non *sa scrive °ʃ [re bene il nome(h)
      'The … medical card because she can't write her name very well.'
      *DOC . desk *DOC . computer
      ʃDOC takes the card

14 DOC: [è qua
      'Here it is'

15 *ʃ (1.0) *(5.0)
      *DOC>desk/INT *DOC>keyboard
      ʃDOC hands the card to INT

(Pasquandrea 2011: 470)

In line 4, a problem occurs: the patient is not able to write her own name in Latin characters. In lines 6–10, the patient and the interpreter search for the patient's medical card in order to check the correct spelling of the patient's name. This implies a series of body and gaze movements, including opening a folded sheet (line 6), looking on the desk (line 7) and putting the interpreter's hand directly in front of the doctor (lines 9–11). In lines 11–15, the doctor asks for an account of the problem and hands the medical card to the interpreter. The doctor is not gazing at the other two participants, yet she notices the movements. Interestingly, she reacts as soon as the interpreter positions her hand on the desk (line 12). This action can be interpreted as a trespassing of the imaginary line that separates the interpreter's space from the doctor's space and considered co-construction of the event. In this sense, the interpreter's action and the doctor's reaction co-construct the relevance of the space for the ongoing interaction, and allow the doctor to detect such behaviour as indicating a problem of some kind.

3.2.4 Role conflict

Since the 1980s medical interpreters' roles have been studied and proposed, mainly in relation to the role defined for conference interpreters. In 2004, Angelelli introduced the interpreter as a visible agent, and more recently scholars from several European countries, recognizing the multiplicity of tasks and goals to be achieved through the interpreted medical encounter, have emphasized the **fusion approach** in which the language broker also becomes **a cultural mediator, facilitator, negotiator** and, in the United States, **a cultural broker** or **patient navigator**.

One of the approaches to understanding the realities among which the interpreters must move is that they have to confront and then reconcile Habermas's distinction between the concepts of the System and the Lifeworld. The System, which comprises the economy and the state, is characterized by strategic action (oriented toward efficiency and success). The Lifeworld, which comprises the private and public spheres, is characterized by communicative action (oriented toward making collective sense of a situation in order to come to a consensual understanding on the course of action to take). This distinction applied to interpreting contexts in healthcare was used by Brisset et al. (2013) in their systematic review of relational issues concerning interpreters' **co-power** in healthcare settings. In the figure below, Brisset et al. (2013: 136) offer a comprehensive overview of attempts to define the role of the interpreter.

Brisset et al. (2013) state that in their different roles, interpreters oscillate between the Lifeworld and the System. Authors' descriptions of typologies are not static: oscillation is necessary for communication to occur. We find the pendulum metaphor particularly apt for describing these changes in interpreters' positions along the continuum. Interpreters' roles are associated with different relational issues but none of these issues is specific to one type of interpreter.

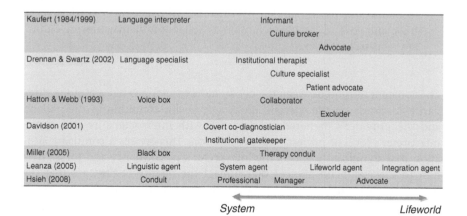

Figure 4.1 Overview of healthcare interpreter role.

These issues are described in terms of **conduit** metaphor (the interpreter must translate the information word for word, like a machine), **neutrality, commitment/loyalty, empathy, intrapersonal conflict, control or power, trust,** and **recognition**. All are connected to the pendulum and its oscillations. It is not surprising, therefore, that interpreters report *conflict* in having to manage their many different roles: this is the result of tensions between *neutrality* and *commitment/loyalty* (to the System or to the Lifeworld). The more committed they are to the patient and the more *empathy* they express, the less *neutral* they will be, and the more practitioners will have a sense of loss of *control* or *power* over the consultation. Building *trust* and *respect* (*recognition*) is a prerequisite to establishing a collaboration that allows all protagonists to find their place in the relational dynamic.

(2013: 136, authors' emphasis)

Tensions and dangers related to misunderstandings about the status of the interpreter and her/his role are also presented in Hseih and Kramer's (2012) analysis that focuses on the utilitarian approach to interpreters' functions. They define the utilitarian approach as one that presumes that the interpreter, while a part of the healthcare process and team, is also somewhat peripheral to the process, playing an auxiliary or supporting role and state that it could result in silencing patients' perspectives or exploiting patients' needs.

When interpreters are viewed as passive instruments, a utilitarian approach may compromise the quality of care by silencing patients' and interpreters' voice, objectifying interpreters' emotional work, and exploiting patients' needs.... However, when interpreters can be viewed as smart technology, a utilitarian approach allows providers to remain in control of medical encounters while taking advantage of interpreters' feedback and recommended parameters. All parties will need to learn from and co-evolve with each other as collaborators in achieving culturally sensitive care.

(2012: 161)

The constant tension between the needs and expectations of each of the three parties depends on the specialization, age, health condition of the patient, and the provider's preparedness to work with interpreters, as well as the interpreter's level of professional preparation. This creates a confusing situation that significantly affects the interpreter's performance and forces her/him to make difficult choices that impact the quality of the care that the patient receives. In Section 4, we take a closer look at the possible sources of role conflict and how to find the best ways to balance the overt and covert expectations of all parties.

3.2.5 Institutional regulations

One of the main issues that makes healthcare regulation difficult is the lack of international or transnational standards, as compared, for example, to international political asylum laws. Until now, in several countries, associations of interpreters, translators or medical interpreters have been established and have published standards of practice for medical interpreting, but in most cases they remain ignored. Due to the limited interest of primary stakeholders and other reasons mentioned above, both professional and public awareness of the legislation in this field is low. The prevailing opinion is that anyone who is bilingual, regardless of their level of proficiency in both languages not to mention the other aspects of the inter-lingual medical communication event, could perform the message-transfer task. Putting aside a lack of understanding of the task of the interpreter in general, regardless of the setting, this perception also concerns the intimacy of the medical encounter, assumed brief conversational exchanges and, as explained before, systemic factors, e.g. time pressure. Work is in progress in various countries to establish and promote more globally accepted standards for non-conference interpreting in different domains. While standardization may not be the most feasible or desirable solution for healthcare interpreting due to different national, or even regional, regulations and different linguistically diverse population profiles, the 2014 ISO standards, along with the validated job profiles that are beginning to be commissioned or researched in the United States and Spain, are intended to become the foundation and reference for more uniform accreditation and hiring regulations worldwide.

In the United States, every state has laws on language access in healthcare settings but only the District of Columbia and 13 states provide direct reimbursement for linguistic and cultural services used by recipients of Medicare and the Children's Health Insurance Program. Reimbursement may not come directly to the provider if the provider is part of a hospital or health system. In that case, the claim for reimbursement is submitted directly to the hospital as the provider is paid a salary from the organization. However, in private practice, the provider may be reimbursed directly. In addition, National Standards for Culturally and Linguistically Appropriate Services (CLAS) in Healthcare were developed in 2013 by the US Department of Health and Human Services Office of Minority Health to help hospitals comply with Title VI of the Civil Rights Act of 1964 and the Americans with Disabilities Act (note that the Department of Health and Human Services treats limited English proficiency as a disability). Despite the fact that the Joint Commission, a body responsible for regulating healthcare policies in the United States and hospital accreditation, stated that communication problems are among the root causes of 59 per cent of serious adverse events reported to the Joint Commission's Sentinel Event Database (The Joint Commission 2012) (which continues to be 58 percent in 2015) and, as of 2012, requires hospitals to provide qualified interpreting and translation services to LEP patients, there is still resistance to applying this in practice. On the other hand, since the Joint Commission included requirements to provide language access to LEP patients as part of their accreditation process, it has resulted in a broader scope of research and publications on the topic, which could be considered a positive beginning.

Several other US organizations have been working on promoting healthcare standards, but their role is only advisory and not regulatory. One of the oldest organizations is the National Council on Interpreting in Healthcare (NCIHC), a multidisciplinary organization whose mission is to promote and enhance language access in healthcare in the United States. In 2005, the NCIHC published the National Standards of Ethics and Standards of Practice, designed to help provide national standards and improve the quality and consistency of interpreting in healthcare. Like clinical protocols for physicians, these new standards provide guidance as to what is expected of healthcare interpreters and what constitutes good practice. The National Code of Ethics and Standards of Practice have been endorsed by an array of organizations such as universities, teaching hospitals and small private clinics, but the number of those bodies is minimal considering the US population and the number of medical institutions serving this population.[9]

Given the above facts, as of 2015 the United States is considered the leader in the promotion of healthcare interpreting regulations; it remains to be seen whether these standardization and legislative efforts will be reflected in the practices of medical institutions.

4 Sources of professional interpreters' role conflicts

The issue of roles and role boundaries, expectations, perceptions and actual action taking in the healthcare setting has been researched thoroughly and still remains an evolving and the most explored theme in the healthcare interpreting field. This section discusses the expectations of all users and of the interpreter her/himself, institutional knowledge and general public understanding of the profession as **sources of role confusion**.

In their overview of research on medical interpreting, Brisset *et al.* (2013: 135) indicate that three themes emerge from the meta-ethnography:

1   interpreters' roles or the behaviors and skills associated with being an interpreter, as expressed by interpreters or expected by institutions, practitioners and patients,
2   difficulties related to working with the interpreter and
3   communication characteristics of interpreted consultations.

All three themes oscillate around control/co-power (see also Section 3.2.3) and are oriented toward evaluating the quality of healthcare received by the patient. In the table below, extracts are provided from Brisset *et al.*'s map of concepts that have been used to describe roles that medical interpreters

Table 4.1 Map of concepts used to describe medical interpreter roles

A brief summary of selected studies on working with interpreters in healthcare ordered chronologically by type of interpreter, within the interpreter's role (*n* = 26).

First author (year), country	Perspective	Principals findings
Type of interpreter: non-specified		
Kaufert (1984) [29], Canada	I; R	Four interpreters' roles: language interpreter, informant, cultural broker, advocate
O'Neil (1989) [41], Canada	I; Pr; Pa	Role of advocate, differences between 'explicit advocacy' and 'implicit advocacy'
Dysart-Gale (2005) [42], USA	I; Pr	Complementarities between the role of conduit (translator) and the role of advocate
Pugh (2009) [38], UK	Pr	Interpreters described as both an obstacle and a facilitator of the empathetic process. Working with an interpreter provides opportunities to foster a broader empathetic understanding of the client
Type of interpreters: professional versus ad hoc		
Greenhalgh (2006) [21], UK	I; Pr; Pa	Seven themes: interpersonal relationships, time pressure, system agent and informative guide to health system, community agent, interprets as an instrument, power and control, role dissonance
Rosenberg (2007) [39], Canada	I; Pr	Professional and ad hoc interpreters must translate the discourse, professional interpreters have to serve as culture brokers, and ad hoc interpreters must fulfil caregiver roles
Rosenberg (2008) [51], Canada	I; R	Professional interpreters create a safe environment for the patient, and mediate between cultures. Ad hoc interpreters ensure diagnosis/treatment, interact with care system and fulfil family role
Hilfinger Messias (2009) [52], USA	I	Three main results: embodying and challenging the conduit role, experiencing role dissonance and conflicting expectation, crossing and expanding role borders
Hadziabdic (2009) [53], Sweden	Pa	Three recurring themes: issue of trust, informative guide to the health system, issue of neutrality

Notes:
I: interpreter; Pr: practitioners; Pa: patients; AS: administrative staff.

perform, as researched over the last three decades. Possible sources of role confusion include therefore:

- use of ad hoc interpreters, selected by chance, and with no awareness of competencies required in this role (i.e. bilingual proficiency assumptions, liabilities not being considered);
- strong sense of assistance and need to help;
- general lack of public and institutional knowledge about the profession;

- inadequacy of role prescription;
- role overload;
- power conflict., e.g. in asymmetrical settings – powerful and powerless.

 COLLABORATIVE DIMENSIONS

Activity 5: Role boundaries: provider/administration perspectives

You work as a freelancer and are hired to substitute for a regular staff interpreter for one eight-hour shift. You are asked to accompany the patient to the lab and explain to the lab worker not only what kind of tests the patient needs as per reference, but also to comment on the patient's current health condition (fasting, low blood pressure). The doctor did not make any written notes assuming that you can convey the information because you heard it all when interpreting. You know this is a part of the staff interpreters' routine in this hospital. However, you do not believe that an interpreter should be stepping outside of her/his boundaries and acting as a facilitator in any kind of setting, and you also know that the hospital does not require this kind of action from subcontracted interpreters due to liability issues. What do you do in this particular instance? What do you do if it keeps occurring during this shift, and then during the next shift that you have been called to cover for?

4.1 Expectations

When entering the field of medical interpreting, one of the most important considerations is to be aware of the impact that users' expectations and interpreters' self-perception has on her/his choices during the interpreting activity. How many different realities does the interpreter move between? What influences her/him? Who defines the boundaries? What is the actual gap between prescribed approaches and real-life actions?

4.1.1 Self-perception

Bischoff *et al.* (2012) examine how interpreters see their work within the context of the integration of immigrants into the host society (Switzerland) in general, and into the local health system in particular. In their findings the interpreters describe four main roles: **word-for-word interpreting, intercultural explanation, building patient–provider relationships** and **accompanying immigrant patients**. An additional cross-cutting theme emerged: interpreters facilitating the integration of immigrants. Only the first of these is generally regarded as their 'official' role. During a consultation the interpreters take on the additional roles as necessary in response to the needs of the patient and the health professionals; however, more and more hospitals in the US are hiring **patient navigators** to do this.

▲ COLLABORATIVE DIMENSIONS

Activity 6: Role boundaries: co-worker perspectives

Compare job announcements for positions of an interpreter and a patient navigator in a US hospital (see Appendix 3). Think whether they present possible conflicts between employees working in these two positions or rather open opportunities for collaboration. Name at least three specific situations for each scenario: conflict or mutual support.

This double-focus approach makes Bischoff *et al.*'s (2012) study one of the first to examine how healthcare interpreters see their work in the context of **promoting integration**. Bischoff makes an important point, which has been an emerging theme in recent studies that deal with interpreters as facilitators or, as he calls them, 'enablers'. Similar findings can be found in a Spanish-language book by Raga Gimeno (2014) (see Recommended Reading), in which a case is made for extending the boundaries of the medical interpreter into integrators or facilitators. This tendency is more present in research conducted in European countries such as Switzerland, Spain or Italy (Farini 2012), probably due to a greater need to adapt to the host country given the lower number of immigrants. This contrasts with Australia, Canada or the United States, which are considered immigrant nations and where integration is less crucial because of large numbers of ethnic populations in which cultural and social identity is more easily maintained and to a larger extent than in most European countries. Bischoff *et al.* (2012: 18) indicate that

> integration is not just about language learning by immigrants (Switzerland's Federal Office for Migration (FOM) 2010), but also about providing interpreting services; integration is not just about providing interpreting services but also about providing interpreters who are **enablers** (with their history, their relationships, their being in the middle); integration is not just about providing interpreters as people, but also about these people being role models for immigrants.
>
> (Author's emphasis)

An interpreter's self-perception does not mean that s/he will act on their beliefs in their work, which calls for a more structured development of self-knowledge and self-critique as proposed in Chapter 1. In her book *Revisiting the Interpreter's Role: a study of conference, court, and medical interpreters in Canada, Mexico, and the United States*, Angelelli (2004) provides an analysis of how self-perception of the performed role is manifested in daily interpreting activities by comparing interpreters' beliefs about their role and their actual actions when interpreting. Similarly, Sleptsova *et al.* (2015) compare interpreters' beliefs and actual actions. In the quantitative part of the study, the interpreters evaluated their role in the clinical encounter through a questionnaire, in the qualitative part the interpreters' role was assessed by analysing videotapes of the clinical encounters. A total of 373 questionnaires and 19 videotapes were collated and analysed. According to the results of the questionnaire interpreters seem to prefer a neutral role (minimal intervention) in the clinical encounter. This was in contrast to what was observed in practice, as seen in the videotapes. In reality, they take an active role while interpreting. Consequently, Sleptsova *et al.* find that it is important that medical professionals and interpreters discuss their roles and expectations before every clinical consultation (see also Section 4.1.2).

 RESEARCH

Activity 7: Beliefs versus practice

Find a Code of Ethics for Medical Interpreters applicable to your geonational context (e.g. International Medical Interpreters Association) and discuss it with a colleague who works as a healthcare interpreter. Can you identify any conflicting views? How could you explain these contradictions to a student intern that you supervise in a hospital?

4.1.2 Users' expectations

By the term 'users' we mean patients and providers and other hospital staff members (chaplains, financial counsellors, registration representatives, pharmacists), but also hospital management exercising its own covert or overt pressure on full-time staff interpreters and healthcare providers. A difference in how providers and interpreters respond to covert users' influence can be noticed when interpreting is done by freelance interpreters hired by the hospital on an as-needed basis, either when their own interpreting staff is unavailable due to sickness or other personal reasons, or with those patients whose languages are not covered by full-time interpreters. The role of a gatekeeper or a co-diagnostician is not part of freelancers' perception of the service that they provide. Therefore, conflicts result more frequently as a result of the set expectations of the providers/hospital administrators who will not know whether this particular interpreter is a subcontracted freelancer or a hospital employee.

However, notwithstanding the uncertainty about an interpreter's contractual situation and acknowledging the fact that hospital policies can play a role in how interpreters and providers interact, evidence-based research demonstrates that in most situations the success of the interpreted medical visit is directly related to the perceptions and needs of patients and providers, and less significantly related to the role promoted by the guidelines established by the hospital management. In addition, few healthcare institutions rely solely on full-time interpreters; in a similar way, interpreters are rarely constrained to working with only one hospital or clinic. We therefore focus here on users understood as patients and providers, and return to the hospital administration's perspectives in Section 4.2.

PATIENTS

A study by Hadziabdic *et al.* (2009) among former Yugoslavians living in Sweden was conducted in order to determine: (1) prerequisites for good interpretation situations; (2) aspects of satisfaction or dissatisfaction in the interpretation situation; and (3) measures to facilitate and improve the interpreter situation. These authors conclude that

> [u]sing an interpreter was perceived as a hindrance, though also needed in communication with healthcare staff and as a guide in the healthcare system. Face-to-face interaction was preferred, with the interpreter as an aid to communication. As part of individual care planning it is important to use interpreters according to the patients' desires.
>
> (Ibid.: 461)

 COLLABORATIVE DIMENSIONS

Activity 8: Role boundaries: the patient's perspective

You and the patient share a migratory experience. You even come from the same ethnic group and the same region, speaking the same dialect. It turns out that the patient's younger brother and your older sister went to the same high school. The patient is asking for advice on whether he should have a particular procedure done or not, since he is scared and does not know very much about this disease and the ways to treat it. In addition, he is asking you – in the room in front of the doctor – whether this doctor is the most competent doctor or whether you would recommend someone else in the area. What would you do?

PROVIDERS

Understanding providers' expectations and needs can help address the source of role confusion. What adds to the complexity of the issue of providers' perspectives on interpreters is that these expectations and views vary depending on the age of the provider, on whether they have received any training on how to work with interpreters, how long that training lasted, whether it was part of the medical school curriculum or just in a lunchtime workshop, and whether they have worked with the interpreters before. It depends on their own cultural and linguistic experience (proficiency in another language, not necessarily the language of the current encounter), on the organization of the interpreters' work and their status in that particular healthcare institution, and also on the medical specialty.

The study by Bischoff and Hudelson (2010) demonstrates that the majority of respondents reported using interpreters, either professional or ad hoc, only a few times a year (66 per cent). The strategies used most frequently to overcome language barriers varied according to the language in question:

> For Portuguese and Spanish, over half of the respondents used bilingual employees most often, while only 5% to 6% used professional interpreters most often. In contrast, over a third of the respondents used professional interpreters most often for Tamil, Albanian, Bosnian Serbian, and Croatian. Between 2 and 18% of respondents used untrained volunteer interpreters most often. At least a quarter of the respondents relied on patients' relatives and friends to interpret for all but Portuguese and Spanish.
>
> (2010: 17)

The study shows that most respondents use interpreters to communicate with their limited French proficient (LFP) patients; however, certain language groups (Turkish, Arabic, Portuguese and Spanish) are at increased risk of ad hoc interpreter use. Bischoff and Hudelson conclude that the choice to use professional versus ad hoc interpreters seems to be influenced by three main factors: availability of bilingual staff, perceptions of interpreting quality, and cost concerns. In some departments, clinical staff were less familiar with how to organize an appointment with an interpreter, and less comfortable working with a non-staff interpreter. In order to address this problem, language services thus need to be integrated into organizational routines.

Hsieh *et al.* (2013) find that providers from different specialty areas vary significantly in regard to their expectations and suggest three components that define providers' views of interpreters: patient ally, healthcare professional and provider proxy. As a conclusion to their study, they propose three research directions to improve collaboration between providers and interpreters:

- reconceptualization of interpreters' performance with special attention to patient ally;
- examination of commonly held attitudes shared by all providers and of potential tensions within these attitudes;
- identification of contextual factors that influence providers' perceptions and choice of interpreters.

The findings indicate that providers' expectations can be categorized in two groups: attitudes shared by all providers, and specialty-specific needs. The attitudes shared by all providers in the study by Hsieh *et al.* (2013) are treating the interpreter as:

a   a professional: desired interpreters' neutrality; need for literal interpretation; desire to only facilitate communication (for example, no need to construct, mediate or negotiate meaning, only a channel for information exchange);

b   a provider proxy: supplementary role in fulfilling providers' goals, including anticipating and actively managing provider-patient interaction (for example, keep patient narrative on track in medical interviews); pursuing the agenda of the provider.

On the other hand, they found that certain specialties, such as nursing, expect interpreters' emotional or advocacy functions while others, such as oncology, do not require it or place much less importance on it than emergency medicine and nursing.

One of Hsieh *et al.*'s (2013) most relevant findings is that it is important to recognize that providers may not be aware of their competing, if not conflicting, expectations of the medical interpreter. For example, if an interpreter were truly a neutral conduit (i.e. professional), s/he would not be able to pursue the provider's agenda (i.e. provider proxy). A crucial concern highlighted by these authors concerns the conflicting desires for providers and interpreters as they negotiate and manage different aspects of care, including therapeutic objectives, interpersonal relationships, education and empathy. Educating providers and interpreters to increase their awareness about their potentially conflicting demands for interpreters' roles and functions can be extremely valuable.

In addition to increasing mutual awareness of possibly **conflicting expectations**, our recommendation to address this recurring and indeed frustrating roadblock of providers' conflicting expectations, even within the same specialty, is to implement a **profiling strategy**. In addition to looking for information in recent scholarship on the providers' perception of interpreters, one possible way to approach this is to have a post-event briefing with the provider, and construct a profile of the providers within each of the specialties or even of each provider with whom the interpreter works on a regular basis. In practice, this means that in the interpreter's folder for each medical specialization next to the terminological resources, there would be a reference sheet that summarizes providers' attitudes, views and needs regarding interpreters, both general and specific to this specialization. The interpreter would be advised to note how conflicting the expectations could be, whether they differ depending on the time point in the visit (beginning, middle, end), on the type of treatment, on the profile of the provider (age, cultural background, training received in medical school, and so on, as stated earlier), and should be updated as experience in this particular area of medicine develops. Profiling can be a possible strategy to address conflicting expectations but this is only feasible in contexts like the US where interpreters work frequently with the same providers. In the UK, for example, the chances of seeing the same medical personnel on assignments are very low.

▲ COLLABORATIVE DIMENSIONS

Activity 9: Users' education

Design a PPT of no more than five slides to educate a group of medical providers (nurses, physicians) during their lunchtime (30 min.). Think about giving examples from your own interpreting experience in different clinics (cardiology, oncology, postnatal care). Specify what they should and should not do in order to facilitate your task and why. Use one slide to educate them about the interpreting profession and what it takes to become an interpreter.

To conclude, based on the discussion in this section, the four most common roles combined using Beltran Avery's categorization are defined. Although proposed at the beginning of the twenty-first century, this categorization still appears to best streamline all the subcategories of medical interpreters' roles, and help interpreters to quickly orient themselves during each medical interpreted event in regard to the expectations of the users and their own perceptions (Beltran Avery 2001). These four approaches are:

1   The interpreter should be **a conduit** between patient and caregiver = **liaison**.
2   The interpreter should be a manager of the cross-cultural/cross-language mediated clinical encounter = **cultural broker**.
3   The interpreter should behave according to **an incremental intervention** model.
4   The interpreter is embedded in her/his cultural-linguistic community = **advocate**.

It is thus recommended that the medical interpreter should use the approach defined by Beltran Avery as **incremental intervention**. The level and the frequency of incrementing and the way it is done should depend on each case. This recommendation is also confirmed by the metaphor that Brisset *et al.* (2013) use in their overview, in which they compare the interpreter's role to a pendulum.

Incremental intervention can also be called **tailored intervention**. A comprehensive narrative review by Sleptsova *et al.* (2014) examines published models of healthcare interpretation and associated roles, expectations and outcomes. Of 34 articles, only two recommend strict adherence to the conduit model. In 32 studies the interpreter's role is defined in broader terms as the role of cultural broker (18), manager or clarifier (22), patient advocate (13) and mediator (six). The study concludes that many recent publications reiterate the early critique against the conduit model as focusing on the linguistic message only, and as disregarding its social and cultural construction.

Since the researchers intended to explore the extent to which a preference for one of these models is based on empirical studies, they conclude that empirical data are lacking and that healthcare interpreters follow many different roles beyond the conduit model. It was also clear that each party in an interaction has different expectations concerning the interpreter's role, as was demonstrated earlier in this chapter. Sleptsova *et al.* (2014) suggest that healthcare providers and interpreters must explicitly clarify their mutual expectations before they begin conducting a healthcare encounter. They also encourage a proactive position for doctors and nurses, and advise them to address any problems with interpretation directly, especially when they have limited understanding of the process of interpretation.

It is also recommended that within the approach of incremental intervention or tailored intervention, the role and some basic rules should be agreed in advance with each service provider. It may not be practical to do this at length before each interpreted event, but clearly stating it in a language form accessible to both providers and patients should be feasible. If the interpreter is keeping a database of profiles of each provider (profiling strategy) with whom s/he works frequently, such briefing will only be needed to provide a clarification/reminder of how s/he will be performing her/his duty. We also suggest that the interpreter have terms that will be keywords and serve for quick communication with the providers to negotiate and define the level of intervention in that particular visit. For example:

> channel – bridge – vehicle
> neutral – helper – advocate
> minimal – medium – maximum.

One word can be said during the pre-event and then used throughout the interaction to ensure that it is the level that the provider prefers, especially in the event that any kind of communication difficulties arises. Having more than three designated terms can be too cumbersome and confusing for the users, but asking the provider to choose one of those three (with definitions provided earlier) will quickly convey to the interpreter how the provider wants her/him to act and help support decisions about her/his role in this particular interaction.

4.2 Institutional knowledge

The term *institutional knowledge* refers to the knowledge about the availability of interpreters, the cost of interpreters and who is responsible for covering that cost; it also includes understanding that the interpreter is part of the professional team providing healthcare (Corsellis 1997; Schapira *et al.* 2008). Rosenberg *et al.* (2008) state that interpreters suffer from lack of respect or recognition. For example, in one US hospital the interpreters received uniforms similar to those of patient services staff, who were mainly volunteers; in another, their uniforms resembled those of medical helpers who transported patients, took patients to the lab or gave directions.

The Institute of Medicine's report *To Err is Human: building a safer health system* (Kohn *et al.* 2000) shocked the US readership by estimating that at least 44,000 and as many as 98,000 people die per year from medical errors that occur in hospitals. In a study mentioned earlier, Wasserman *et al.* (2014) state that although many hospitals identify a direct relationship between patient safety issues and patients' linguistic needs, few monitor their patient safety data by language. In addition, very limited data are available on how healthcare organizations nationwide address issues of LEP patient safety. Therefore, as already mentioned in Section 3, new standards have recently been developed to promote effective, culturally and linguistically appropriate hospital communication with patients (Office of Minority Health 2013; The Joint Commission 2010). AHRQ's new Guide for Hospitals and Team-STEPPS LEP module can help hospitals meet those standards for LEP patients within a patient safety framework.

4.2.1 Assessment of needs and management of assignments
AVAILABILITY OF INTERPRETERS

Marcos Pesquera, Director of the Center on Health Disparities for Adventist HealthCare (Maryland, US) notes that 'If the provider has the perception that accessing the resource is hard they are less likely to use it' (Rice 2014), hence his recommendation is to make interpreters easily accessible, such as by listing them on the hospital's intranet and making them available via video technology.

Maul *et al.* (2012) conducted 25 in-depth, semi-structured telephone interviews with physicians in different practice settings who, while not native speakers, routinely interact with LEP patients using second-language skills. They state that many factors impact on the decision whether to use their own language skills, including levels of patient language proficiency, costs, convenience and clinical risk and suggest that there is a need for practical guidance and training for clinicians on the appropriate use of second-language skills and interpreters in clinical care.

At one of the teaching hospitals in North Carolina, USA, a study was designed where the interpreters' team worked one-on-one with every third year medical student and every second year PA student during their family medicine rotation and did a standardized patient encounter to serve as training for working with interpreters and LLP patients. The activity was accomplished in one day with minimal faculty involvement and a direct cost of less than $700. The activity was positively rated by the students. Reich *et al.* (2012) state that this refined approach improved effective use of interpreters in a simulated clinical setting. Below are presented the study's findings after a two-year trial period:

> Analyses indicated improvement both in students' knowledge and skills following participation in the revised standardized patient activity. Data revealed that students need improvement in these areas:
>
> 1 Giving instructions and expectations to the interpreter at the beginning of the visit
> 2 Checking for patient's understanding
> 3 Remembering to thank the interpreters for their services
>
> (Reich *et al.* 2012)

▲ COLLABORATIVE DIMENSIONS

Activity 10: Assessment of societal language proficiency

Different practices observed in a large hospital in the United States include asking the patient, 'Do you need an interpreter?' Some of the answers were: 'No, my son will do it for me' and 'No, I can understand English quite well'. Prepare a list of answers that you have encountered in your practice, and for each case provide an argumentation that would convince the patient to use a professional interpreter.

PRIORITIZING THE USE OF INTERPRETING RESOURCES

In Section 4, we commented on the role confusion that occurs when interpreters become physician assistants, nurses or administrative assistants. However, the hospital managers' expectations that interpreters should also serve as translators of hospital leaflets, announcements or hospital policies in between their assignments is another common problem. If the interpreting services department also provides translation services to the hospital, there should be a dedicated time in the interpreters' schedule to perform such tasks or a position such as Interpreter/Translator needs to be created with a defined job description and perhaps a salary compensation difference. Asking the interpreter to translate needed documentation in between their assigned encounters adds additional stress and increases the risk of medical errors. When not assigned to a particular encounter, interpreters should work on their terminology, have time to prepare for the next assignment, or have secured time slots to exchange experiences with the rest of the interpreting team, not only in regard to new terminology but also profiling of the providers with different specializations or strategies to educate users.

Bischoff's (2006) survey indicates that simply making professional interpreter services available to healthcare professionals does not appear to guarantee their use for limited French proficiency (LFP) patients. Future efforts should focus on developing procedures for systematically identifying patients needing linguistic assistance, linguistic assistance strategies that are responsive to provider and institutional contexts and constraints, and institutional directives (Bischoff and Hudelson 2010).

4.2.2 Modalities used in healthcare interpreting: in person, telephonic, videoconferencing

One of the most recent trends in large hospital campuses is the intent to change from traditional face-to-face and telephone interpreting to video-interpreting mode. The assumed advantages are primarily time and cost efficiency; the video-interpreting mode is thus promoted mainly by hospital administrators. Previous research on the use of video interpreting in political and diplomatic settings discusses several negative effects, primarily for the interpreter, including unreliable technology, limited view, strain on eyes and neck, and lack of interpersonal cues. In a more comprehensive study on **interpreters' perspectives** on in-person, telephonic and videoconferencing interpretation in medical encounters conducted by Price *et al.* (2012) where 52 interpreters completed a survey on 21 common clinical scenarios in the hospital and ambulatory setting, the researchers concluded that all modalities are equally satisfactory for conveying information. The fact that respondents favoured in-person video-conference medical interpreting (VMI) represents an improvement in communication taking place in clinical scenarios with substantial educational/psychosocial components where telephonic interpretation is often inadequate. In scenarios with substantial educational or psychosocial dimensions, videoconference medical interpreting was preferred to the telephonic mode. Price *et al.* (2012) recommend a mixed use of multiple modalities, depending on the type of clinical scenario. However, the interpreters' perspective on how in-person interpreting compares to one facilitated through the videoconferencing mode is yet to be explored.

Patients' satisfaction with different methods of interpreting was measured in a study by Gany *et al.* (2007) where also remote simultaneous medical interpreting (RSMI) was included to address the language barrier. A total of 1,276 English-, Spanish-, Mandarin- and Cantonese-speaking patients attending the primary care clinic and emergency department of a large New York City municipal hospital were screened for enrolment in a randomized controlled trial. Language-discordant patients were randomized to RSMI or usual and customary (U&C) interpreting: 371 were randomized to RSMI, 167 of whom were exposed to RSMI; and 364 were randomized to U&C, 198 of whom were exposed to U&C. In this randomized controlled trial of RSMI vs U&C interpreting, there were a few areas in which patients in the RSMI group were more satisfied than in the U&C group. Patients felt they were treated with more respect by their physicians and that their privacy was better protected. Gany *et al.* concluded that RSMI may be particularly useful in clinical situations in which sensitive topics are discussed and patient privacy is paramount, for example, the mental health encounter or the evaluation of sexually transmitted diseases.

Gany *et al.*'s (2007) findings suggest that RSMI could not only be an important component of a multipronged approach to improving patient satisfaction in the interpreted encounter by removing one potential barrier (interpreter's physical presence in the room) to patients' willingness to disclose sensitive information, but also that more work needs to be done in the area of users' education (2007: 317). Professional interpreters, physicians and patients need more training on how best to facilitate the interpreted medical encounter. Another important suggestion from this study indicates that there is a need for qualitative data to learn what specifically detracts from patient satisfaction with interpreting in order to develop appropriate interventions to address the dissatisfaction documented in this study.

Finally, **providers' satisfaction** with any of the given modes should also be taken into consideration. Locatis *et al.* (2010) sought feedback from all the participants in the interpreted triangle; 241 Spanish-speaking patient volunteers, 24 health providers and seven interpreters participated in their study. Patients, providers and interpreters each independently completed scales evaluating the quality of clinical encounters and, optionally, made free text comments. Interviews were conducted with three of the providers, the seven interpreters and a subset of 30 patients. Locatis *et al.* (2010) found that

> encounters with in-person interpretation were rated significantly higher by providers and interpreters, while patients rated all methods the same. There were no significant differences in provider and interpreter ratings of remote methods.... Providers and interpreters were exposed to all three methods, were more critical of remote methods, and preferred videoconferencing to the telephone as a remote method. The significantly shorter phone interviews raise questions about the prospects of miscommunication in telephonic interpretation, given the absence of a visual channel, but other factors might have affected time results.
>
> (2010: 345)

Trials of new possibilities are on the rise, supported heavily by hospital administrators and technology companies that see a big market for their remote interpreting applications and equipment. The direct users differ in their opinions. As seen above, and again stated by Locatis *et al.* (2011: 809) who tested the feasibility of using cell phone technology to provide video medical interpretation services at a distance, 'patients appreciate the interpretation service no matter how it is provided, while health providers and interpreters prefer video' when only given a choice between the two remote options. Still, it may not be a preferred method of communication for all Deaf and LEP patients; for example, a language services manager at Presence Health (Chicago, Illinois, USA) reports that many patients refuse remote and only accept in-person. Ultimately, their first choice is in-person interpreting.

COLLABORATIVE DIMENSIONS

Activity 11: Modes of interpreting and cost

Hospital administrators are considering cutting the costs of interpreting services once again and this time they ask for your input. During the discussion, you will have only five minutes to inform them of recent developments in the area of video interpreting. List its advantages and disadvantages as if you were to defend both positions.

4.2.3 Implementation of interpreting polices

According to a report published in the *Journal for Healthcare Quality*, physicians and hospital staff frequently ignore policies covering professional interpreting services because they feel the wait for a qualified medical interpreter would delay patient care. The report details a study that found that many healthcare providers are unfamiliar with the availability of interpreters or consider the procedure to arrange for interpreting services too complicated. Dr Elizabeth Jacobs, associate vice chair for health services research at the University of Wisconsin, says these issues discourage physicians from asking for an interpreter knowledgeable in medical terminology. 'They go with the easiest thing to do at the moment – their own limited language skills, a family member, or whoever happens to be accessible', Jacobs says. They 'don't readily recognize the impact it can have'.

A study by the National Health Law Program (NHeLP) analysed 35 language-related claims filed against one liability insurer in four states between January 2005 and May 2009. NHeLP reported that the insurer paid $2.3 million in damages or settlements and $2.8 million in legal fees for cases where the provider failed to offer a professional interpreter. Given the numbers, advocates of language access are concerned about healthcare facilities' failure to consistently report language-related errors. Contributing to the problem is research showing that patients with limited English fluency are less likely than US-born English speakers to point out errors in their care. Without reliable statistics, researchers say, it is difficult to know how well the healthcare system is doing in lowering the incidence of language-related clinical errors (*Modern Healthcare (IL)*).[10]

Another issue that researchers have been attempting to address over the last decade is how to convince hospital management and providers that interpreters constitute an added value to the hospital administration. Several studies were undertaken to document **health dangers** and **inefficient use of resources** resulting from the lack of using professional interpreters. According to the literature review conducted by Wasserman *et al.* (2014), one study found that LEP patients are safer with a professional medical interpreter. Despite this evidence, healthcare professionals frequently try to get by without an interpreter. While Wasserman *et al.*'s review is limited because it only includes findings from PubMed and Google scholar, as well as some grey literature, it confirms results obtained by interpreting studies scholars. It also demonstrates that a closer collaboration and cross-pollination between different disciplines concerned with patient safety and cultural competencies is desirable. This also serves as a reminder that when looking for answers, interpreters should explore databases from the sciences outside of linguistics or translation and communication studies.

While many US medical institutions identify a direct relationship between healthcare quality and patient proficiency in English, few have instruments in place that record and analyse their particular situation. Therefore, in order to establish credible databases the approach taken by Wasserman *et al.* (2014) seems promising. They developed a tool that aims to help providers and hospital managers gather their own data and thus more easily identify the needs of their own institutions. The following are actual patient-safety reports from one hospital in Wasserman *et al.*'s study that illustrate key issues related to language assistance categorized by types:

a   delays
 •   Patient arrived in hemodialysis unit to do stat chest X-ray; patient had no identification wristband and could not verify because he did not speak English.
 •   Patient did not have a stress test because a Spanish interpreter was not available. This delayed discharge for at least twenty-four hours.
b   medical errors
 •   Patient is Ethiopian speaking. On multiple occasions, there had been a failure to provide an interpreter. She has been using family members to translate, and they are not always available. This is unacceptable, as we have had issues with medications (i.e. which to take, when) and I believe her worsening diabetes is a direct result of my inability to have effective clinical meetings with her.
 •   LEP patient arrived in the step-down unit s/p thoracic surgery. Hypertension in OR and upon arrival to recovery room, 205/97. Patient with history of CVA in past month, no past medical history or medication list available. Anaesthesia unable to give proper report or orders for hypertension management due to lack of information.

For more examples on patient-safety reports related to linguistic or cultural factors, please see the Routledge Translation Studies Portal.

The *Improving Patient Safety Systems for Patients With Limited English Proficiency: a guide for hospitals*, a tool developed by Wasserman *et al.* (2014), outlines five key recommendations that aim to both improve detection of medical errors across diverse populations and prevent high-risk scenarios from becoming safety events:

 •   foster a supportive **culture** for safety of diverse patient populations;
 •   adapt current systems to better **identify** medical errors in LEP patients;
 •   develop institutional strategies to empower frontline staff and interpreters to **report** medical errors;
 •   develop systems to **monitor** patient safety among LEP patients routinely, as well as processes to analyse medical errors and near misses that occur among these populations;
 •   develop strategies and systems to **prevent** medical errors among LEP patients. These include strengthening interpreter services, improving coordination of clinical services, providing translated materials, and developing training for healthcare providers and staff on team communication, interpreter use, cultural competency and advocacy.[11]

The objective of the second tool developed by Wasserman *et al.* (2014), *TeamSTEPPS Enhancing Safety for Patients with Limited English Proficiency*, is to help the provider view the interpreter as part of the professional team. This tool addresses the following issues:

- understanding the safety risk to patients with limited English proficiency;
- knowing the process for assembling the most appropriate and effective care team;
- identifying and raising patient communication issues.

Wasserman *et al.* (2014: 14) recommend that

> hospitals consider implementing *Improving Patient Safety Systems for Patients With Limited English Proficiency: A Guide for Hospitals* and the *TeamSTEPPS Enhancing Safety for Patients with Limited English Proficiency Module* as part of their strategy to meet the new standards. These tools provide a case for why this field is important, and the basic strategies necessary to build safety systems that truly protect all patients.

On the other hand, healthcare institutions' resistance to providing interpreting services can be explained by high costs, for which coverage has not yet been regulated. The Office of Management and Budget in 2002 estimated that US hospitals' annual costs for providing interpreter services was $78 million for inpatient visits, $12 million for outpatient visits and $8.6 million for emergency department visits. An American Medical Association survey found that costs of $150 or more for interpreter services often exceeded a physician's payment for the visit, presenting what the AMA called a 'significant hardship' for practices (Rice 2014).

Jacobs *et al.* (2004) assess the impact of interpreter services on the cost and utilization of healthcare services among patients with LEP. Compared to English-speaking patients, patients who used interpreter services received significantly more recommended preventive services, made more office visits, and had more prescriptions written and filled. The estimated cost of providing interpreter services was $279 per person per year.

With an aim of providing a better foundation for hospital-management decisions in regard to the systemic integration of trained healthcare community interpreters into the healthcare system, the Abraham and Fiola (2006) study, carried out at healthcare institutions in the three largest Canadian cities, looks at the risks involved when working with untrained interpreters, the resistance to working with professional interpreters, and a paradigm shift. They conclude that

> the structural and institutional resistance, as well as attitudinal barriers to the healthcare access, is embedded in policies and regulations in the

public and institutional sectors, as well as in the attitudes of those service providers who are ill-prepared to consider the effects of miscommunication on the quality of healthcare delivered to those patients who have a limited proficiency in Canada's official languages.

(Ibid.: 200)

The study also suggests that considering language barriers from a risk-management perspective instead of a human-rights position could possibly indicate a paradigm shift in Canada.

Once the issue of convincing healthcare institutions to use interpreters is resolved by providing data on how linguistic errors affect patient safety, the next step is to organize interpreting services within the hospital structure, and to decide on the distribution of responsibilities related to the management of interpreters. While discussing the management of interpreting services is beyond the scope of this guide, it is important to realize that each healthcare institution, even within the same county or region, can have very different interpreting hiring regulations, expectations and policies.

The importance of quality and safety in healthcare related to linguistic limitations of patients is demonstrated by the number of articles on this subject published between 2005 and 2015 (486), as compared to the number published between 1995 and 2004 (197) in strictly medical care-oriented journals (PubMed) rather than those specializing in language and culture communication-related issues. Karliner et al. (2007) conducted a systematic literature search,[12] to determine the extent to which professional medical interpreters have a positive impact on clinical care for LEP patients and concluded that published studies report positive benefits of professional interpreters on communication (errors and comprehension), utilization, clinical outcomes and satisfaction with care.

As demonstrated above, hospital administrators, as decision makers, are important stakeholders in the process, not only in improving healthcare access for LLP patients but also in the professionalization of medical interpreters. It remains to be seen whether healthcare institutions will be more inclined to base their decisions regarding usage of interpreters on the aspects discussed in this section after seeing the impact they have.

4.3 General public understanding of the medical interpreting profession

The lack of public understanding of the medical interpreting profession can be seen at two levels: its importance and its complexity. The first dimension refers to increasing public **awareness of the importance of** professional interpreting. Making materials on interpreting, and what it involves, publicly available, has become, in addition to studying the cost coverage options for medical interpreting services, the course of action in many countries, primarily in the United States. The US Commonwealth Fund provides guidelines on how to become an effective advocate for language services for the underserved. The materials are published as an *Action Kit* and include sections on:

- federal laws and policies requiring access to services in healthcare settings for people with Limited English Proficiency;
- paying for language services and reimbursement models;
- consequences of not providing language services: some facts and personal stories;
- what is available and why we need it.

 RESEARCH

Activity 12: Local regulations

A   Using this *Action Kit*[13] as a model, update each section with the information you can find on the regulations in your own country.
B   Prepare a similar action kit for your possible local clients.

The second dimension involves **awareness of the complexity** of interpreting and is closely connected with the level and depth of the education required to become a well-prepared interpreter.

 RESEARCH

Activity 13: Contributions of various disciplines

For each of the following disciplines write down the ways that findings from that discipline can contribute to the understanding of the field of medical interpreting. If you do not know the scope of the discipline, find its definition first. Try to use one source other than Wikipedia.

- cognitive sciences
- neurolinguistics
- psychology
- sociology
- pragmatics
- discourse studies
- communication studies
- bilingualism
- applied linguistics
- ethnographic studies and anthropology
- literary criticism
- law
- psychotherapy
- public health
- history.

As awareness of the complexity of interpreting tasks develops in the society at large, healthcare administrators and providers' choice to use interpreters may go beyond cost concerns. It will likely depend on whether they consider it a priority and how easily they can access interpreters, but also on the level of importance they place on it, which is related to public knowledge and understanding of the interpreting process and, consequently, the public's ability to view it as a profession rather than a voluntary activity.

5 Professionalization of medical interpreting

AIIC has published its own code of ethics and professional standards that apply to conference interpreting; however, there is no clear definition or distinction between codes of ethics, codes of conduct, standards of practice, and career guidelines regarding non-conference interpreting services. As a result, requirements or recommendations under various names in other fields of interpreting developed throughout the second half of the twentieth century at different speeds. In general, they address confidentiality; ethical issues; impartiality; transparency; the role of the interpreter; cultural competency; intervention boundaries; and sometimes specific procedures in relation to the particular interpreting context such as medical, legal, educational or military (Furmanek 2012). The multiplication of associations, competing or redundant standards, lack of coordinated efforts to increase public awareness about the work of the interpreter, and short-term research funding aimed at providing temporary solutions in countries with high migration indexes add to the continual delay in the professionalization of the interpreting profession. On the other hand, new, solid research is emerging, interpreters' self-awareness as professionals is higher than ever, and professional organizations are attempting to improve their communication in order to join their efforts to ensure legislative support worldwide. For example, Youdelman (2013) describes the current stage of US medical interpreters' certifications efforts in her article 'The Development of Certification for Healthcare Interpreters in the United States' (see Recommended Reading).

5.1 Competencies and job profile

Competencies

The two essential aptitudes for interpreting that appear in the literature under different names are *linguistic competency* and *cultural competency*. Other aptitudes for interpreters generally considered crucial are *general knowledge, comprehension and production competency, memory skills, public speaking skill, subject area/background knowledge, curiosity about the world* and *stress tolerance*. One of the challenges that researchers face is the categorization of these skills and aptitudes (see also Introduction, Section 3).

In 2006, Abril Martí from Spain presented a list of types of competency narrowed to those needed when interpreting in public services, and organized into the following subcategories:

- communicative and textual competency in at least two languages and cultures: understanding the active and passive phases of communication, such as the different textual or literal conventions of the two cultures;
- cultural and intercultural competency: knowledge of the associated social and cultural background of the language in which the interpreter is working, which goes beyond knowledge of the institutions, history and geography of a particular culture to include perceptions, beliefs, values and so on;
- thematic competency: specific understanding of the field in which the interpreter will be practicing, especially those competencies that allow them to have a better understanding of the situation they will be interpreting;
- instrumental professional competency: use of documentary sources and tools of investigation and management terminology, and the management of the most useful informational applications for the practice of the profession; this includes basic knowledge for managing professional work (contracts, fiscal obligations, budgets, invoices and so on) such as of ethics and the formation of professional organizations;
- psychophysiological competency: interpreter's self-understanding, such as their psychophysiological qualities and aptitudes including their attention span, concentration and memory;
- interpersonal competency: capacity to work in a team professionally and interrelate in a professional manner with the distinct players that play a role in interpretation (colleagues, inspectors, documentarists, clients, users, experts and so on);
- strategic competency: encompasses all the processes that apply to planning, organization and execution of the work, to the identification and resolution of problems, and auto-evaluation and revision; it directs the facilitation of the other competencies.

(Abril Martí 2006: 667–9; Monica Weber's translation)

In 2013, Refki *et al.* in the USA published a preliminary list of competencies specifically needed for medical interpreting that 'was informed by an extensive consultation of literature, a review of healthcare interpreter training curricula, and solicitation of the perspectives of curricular developers, interpreters, policy makers, administrators and providers' (ibid.: 72). The investigators organized healthcare competencies in categories (that they call *domains*):

- context of healthcare interpreting: general, regulatory and legal requirements;
- healthcare interpreting profession: interpreters' roles and responsibilities and interpreters' standards and boundaries;
- medical terminology and understanding the human body;

- intersection of health and culture;
- linguistics technique.

For details of the lists by Abril Martí (2006) and Refki *et al.* (2013) see the information on the Routledge Translation Studies Portal.

 RESEARCH

Activity 14: Identifying competencies for the healthcare setting

Compare Abril Martí's (2006) general community interpreter's competencies with the compilation proposed by Refki *et al.* (2013). Using Abril Martí's list as a model, provide the table of competencies for the healthcare interpreting setting in your native language. Decide which ones are most needed and then rank them for yourself, stating which ones you have developed adequately and which still need to be improved.

MY COMPETENCIES FOR HEALTHCARE INTERPRETING
1   Communicative and textual
2   Cultural and intercultural
3   Thematic
4   Instrumental professional
5   Psychophysiological
6   Interpersonal
7   Strategic

Job profile

One of the obstacles to standardization is that no single generally accepted profile exists for the job of healthcare interpreter. There are many research sources that list characteristics related to the job and to the people who hold it (research reports, hiring protocols from health agencies, government documents and occupational websites), but these resources are not well integrated. As discussed previously, 2014 ISO 9001 standards for non-conference interpreting along with the validated job profiles that are beginning to be commissioned or researched (e.g. United States and Spain), are intended to become the foundation and reference for accreditation and hiring regulations worldwide.

Research on the personality traits of current healthcare interpreters indicates that the following traits are considered important for succeeding in this career: an interpreter should be ethical and dependable, have a concern for quality that makes them monitor their own work, and have good time-management skills. They should also be able to maintain a professional presence, and be able to remain professionally detached when working in a medical situation involving highly personal matters. Finally, being open-minded and flexible is very important.

The occupation of healthcare interpreter involves working with people; thus a number of social traits are also necessary. Foremost, of course, is that the interpreter should enjoy working with people and have a concern for others. A positive attitude and self-confidence are also good traits to have. An interpreter should be self-aware, understanding her/his own characteristics and how they impact the situation. The interpreter also needs to be socially perceptive and sensitive to both verbal and non-verbal information from others. They will be working in groups, so the ability to cooperate and coordinate with others is important. Since this career relies on oral translation, an interpreter needs to be verbally skilful and able to manage complex conversations. They should be tactful and sensitive to the issues and people involved. On occasion the job of healthcare interpreter can place an interpreter in a difficult social situation, thus the ability to handle stress, maintain composure and keep emotions in check are also important traits for a healthcare interpreter.

A project funded by the US Department of Labor and led by Furmanek *et al.* (2010) in a professional medical community in central North Carolina (USA) researched the **socio-psychological job profile** of the healthcare interpreter. The final sample totalled 25 interpreters, ten male and 15 female. This group presented a wide range of backgrounds and experience. These interpreters completed a series of commonly used self-report psychological measures. One of the measures was the Holland Self-Directed Search, a reliable and validated measure of career interest that is used extensively in career counselling. The six career interests are: artistic, conventional, entrepreneurial, investigative, realistic and social. A brief description of each taken from the *Dictionary of Holland Occupational Codes* follows:

> Artistic (A) indicates a preference for literary, musical, or artistic activities.
> Conventional (C) indicates a preference for establishing or maintaining orderly routines and the application of standards.
> Entrepreneurial (E) indicates a preference for persuading, manipulating or directing others.
> Investigative (I) indicates a preference for exploration, understanding, and prediction or control of natural and social phenomena.
> Realistic (R) indicates a preference for manipulation of machines, tools and things.
> Social (S) indicates a preference for helping, teaching, treating, counselling or serving others through personal interaction.

In addition, each occupation can be characterized by its relevant career interests. Using this system, on the US government job website, the Holland code that was assigned for **interpreters was AS**. Using the same system of assigning codes, in the *Dictionary of Holland Occupational Codes* the code for **professional interpreter was ESA**. The book also lists a separate code for a

sign interpreter, **SCE**. Thus it appears that the code being used in the US database is basically that of a conference interpreter. However, the occupation of healthcare interpreter is probably more similar to a sign language interpreter than a conference interpreter. Thus the appropriate career interest pattern for a healthcare interpreter should probably include S, C and E. To validate this suggested pattern of career interests, the 25 participants in the current study were asked to read brief descriptions of each of the six career interests and indicate their importance for being an effective healthcare interpreter on a scale from one (not at all important) to seven (very). The results from highest to lowest were: **S (5.7)**, **I (5.4)**, **C (4.9)**, A (3.0), E (2.9) and R (2.7). From this it can be seen that **S and C** are again prominent in the description of the job of healthcare interpreter.

The final question was to determine the actual career interests of the interpreters. As noted above, the average was taken across the 25 interpreters for each career interest. The results from highest to lowest were as follows: **S (34.8)**, **E (27.8)**, **C (27.7)**, A (26.5), R (24.3) and I (23.4). The three highest were **SEC**, which is basically the career interest pattern indicated by the interpreters when they were describing the occupation and also matches the pattern provided in the *Dictionary of Holland Occupational Codes* for sign interpreters. It should be noted that since the E and C have very similar averages, their relative order could reasonably be reversed to **SCE**.

This pattern of career interests can be used for advising those who are considering entering a healthcare interpreter programme, and applicants to healthcare interpreting positions could be encouraged to take this measure to see if their career interests match those of people already within the profession and the career itself. As a side point, the **SEC** pattern also characterizes the occupations of social worker, teacher assistant, child care worker and elder care worker.

5.2 Non-professional (ad hoc) interpreters: bilingual hospital employees versus family interpreters

The field of medical interpreting sees the most usage of non-professional interpreters, also called *ad hoc interpreters* or *lay interpreters*. Most often these are bilingual hospital employees or the patient's family members. Angelelli defines **ad hoc interpreter** in the healthcare setting as an individual who

> does not hold a degree in interpreting, nor have any other qualifications or credentials, and may or may not have any experience in performing the task at hand, and may or may not observe any code of ethics, although this person may exhibit the ability to speak both the source and target languages and volunteer to perform the role of an interpreter, or be directed to do it by the pertaining authority (e.g., the case of bilingual employees in hospitals). Speakers of the non-societal language cannot

always access services through interpreters, mostly due to lack of availability. Therefore, in the absence of quality interpreting, users of non-
societal languages often resort to ad-hoc interpreters to communicate
with speakers of societal languages. These include bilingual service providers (e.g., teaching assistants, laboratory technicians, receptionists) as
well as family members (including minors) or friends who are asked to
step in and to help broker communication with various degrees of
success. This may lead to serious consequences that undermine equal
access to services.

(Angelelli 2014: 574)

Most interpreters' associations and regulatory agencies advise against the use
of a patient's family or friends, who can potentially do more harm than good.
Bilingual clinical employees are also discouraged from stepping in if they
have not been certified as medical interpreters. However, physicians and hospital staff often ignore these policies, typically because of time pressures, lack
of knowledge about the availability of professional interpreters, or procedural difficulties in arranging for interpreters. This occurs in spite of the fact
that a 2002 study funded by the Commonwealth Fund found 31 mistakes on
average in each encounter of medical interpreting in 13 sessions reviewed.
Mistakes were most likely to occur when an ad hoc interpreter was used,
such as a family member or hospital employee with limited medical
background.

Schenker *et al.* (2011: 712) discovered that 'professional interpreters were
rarely used; with physicians, use of ad hoc interpreters such as family or
friends was most common; with nurses, patients often reported "getting by"
without an interpreter or barely speaking at all'. Leanza *et al.* (2010) identify
the specific risks involved when communicating through family members as
interpreters: imposing their own agenda vs that of the patient (biased interpreting), and controlling the consultation process, which is manifested
through interruptions or changes in meaning. In addition, trained interpreters are more likely to transmit the patient's resistance when physicians ignore
their contextually grounded experience.

Flores *et al.*'s (2012) article presents findings of a comparison of professional, ad hoc and no interpreters during emergency department visits. The
proportion of errors with potential consequences was significantly lower (12
per cent) for professional interpreters compared to ad hoc (22 per cent) and
no interpreters (20 per cent). Among professional interpreters, previous
hours of interpreter training but not years of experience were significantly
associated with error numbers, types and potential consequences. Flores *et
al.* also provide a practice recommendation that can serve as a benchmark to
differentiate between well-trained and insufficiently trained interpreters,
stating that 'requiring at least 100 hours of training for interpreters
might have a major impact on reducing interpreter errors and their consequences in healthcare while improving quality and patient safety' (2012:

552). A model similar to the one recommended by Flores *et al.* (2012) has been in place since 2010 at a teaching hospital in North Carolina. New interpreters are asked to shadow without interpreting for the first month after they start working (160 hours). Then, they are shadowed by their mentor for the next month (160 hours), and then they are allowed to interpret on their own with weekly check-ins and unannounced shadowing for the next month; this constitutes a probationary period of 90 days.

Researchers present various views in regard to using family members as interpreters, finding some advantages to their use as compared to bilingual hospital employees. Hadziabdic *et al.* (2014) suggest that:

> when family members acted as interpreters, their role was to give both practical and emotional support, and this led to both positive and negative emotions. Use of simple language, better collaboration in the health-care organization and developing the interpreters' professional attitude could improve the use of professional interpreters. The type of interpreter, mode of interpretation and patient's preferences should be considered in the interpretation situation. In order to achieve high-quality healthcare, health-care professionals need to organize a good interpretation situation case-by-case, choose the appropriate interpreters with the patient in focus and cooperate with members of the patient's social network.
>
> (2014: 156)

Similarly, in another study Rosenberg *et al.* (2008) looked at self-perception in regard to its role for both family and professional interpreters. The data were obtained through videotaping encounters between 19 physicians and 24 patients accompanied by six professional and nine family interpreters, and then eliciting interpreters' perceptions by stimulated recall. Rosenberg *et al.* comment that 'family members did not describe the tension between roles reported by professionals as they did not perceive themselves as system agents at all' (2008: 88). Comparing the roles of professional, hospital workers and family interpreters, Rosenberg *et al.* conclude:

> **Family interpreters** represent a distinct sub-group of 'ad hoc' or lay interpreters. They have privileged access to patient information. As such they can be **invaluable healthcare partners** and they are less likely to commit translation [interpreting] errors made by untrained hospital volunteers.
>
> (Ibid.: 92, author's emphasis)

As a consequence Rosenberg *et al.* state that the prevalent understanding of the advantage of using a professional interpreter is even higher when the physician invites the interpreter to act as advocate for the patient and a cultural broker. In addition, they emphasize that a family member can also be a valuable participant in the interpreting process because s/he may be 'an advocate who can continue physician-to-patient information transfer after the encounter and ensure patient care' (ibid.: 92), which is an important element in the care of chronically ill and/or elderly migrant patients.

On the other end of the spectrum, some studies explore the possibility of training bilingual hospital staff as interpreters in order to use them on an ad hoc basis in emergency situations. An initiative following the recommendations from New Jersey Hospital Association's (NJHA) Interpreter/Translation Task Force and the New Jersey Office of Minority and Multicultural Health to address language barriers in healthcare settings provides training to bilingual staff as dual-role medical interpreters. The programme was developed to advance workforce competency and create an alternative pool of trained interpreters to provide timely access to communication services. An eight-hour workshop provides bilingual employees with the foundations, skills and knowledge they need to bridge the communication gaps between providers and patients. Findings from the training assessments showed significant improvement, as reflected in the mean score of participants that increased pre- and post-assessment by about 40 per cent. While a temporary solution, this could still be a better option than using ad hoc interpreters with no preparation at all; however, a more appropriate model would last at least 60 hours and address a broader range of competencies (see Section 5.1) even if only in a limited way, for example A Dual Role Interpreter Training for bilingual employees at Presence Health in Chicago, USA is 100 hours.

The majority of findings confirm that an experienced, trained medical interpreter is the best option for patient care but this is not always feasible. The Royal Australian College of General Practitioners states their standards for general practices in the Interpretive Guide for Aboriginal and Torres Strait Islander health services in regard to using non-professional interpreters. They seem to offer the most optimal solution when considering an ad hoc language broker:

Friends and relatives as interpreters
Qualified medical interpreters should be the interpretation medium of choice.

The use of patients' relatives and friends as interpreters is common. This is acceptable if it is an expressed wish of the patient and the problem is minor. However, further consideration should be given to the following:

- whether friends and relatives will put their own interpretation into the translated communication;
- the use of friends and relatives in sensitive clinical situations or where serious decisions have to be made may be hazardous;
- the use of children as interpreters is not encouraged.[14]

6 Conclusion

Healthcare interpreting is the fastest growing field in community interpreting and one with significant impact on a person's well-being. It still remains one of the least recognized and remunerated subfields of interpreting. Parallel careers, such as **medical facilitators, cultural navigators** or **managers of intercultural services in healthcare** are on the rise in the United States and in parts of Europe. It seems probable that, as a result, the profession of healthcare language brokers may become a hybrid career. The discussion on providing meaningful access to healthcare to limited language proficiency patients will continue to impact an increasing number of stakeholders as healthcare access and healthcare literacy gain importance in countries with ageing populations in the Northern Hemisphere and in the developing parts of the world where medical care is rapidly improving.

In many countries medical interpreting is an interpreting domain in which full-time employment is becoming more common. Interpreters who are fully employed as part of hospital staff are marking the trend for the coming decades. For those entering into or progressing in the profession of healthcare interpreting, it is important to remember that in addition to level of experience and previous medical background, familiarity with the most recent research findings in a variety of cross-related fields such as public health, communication studies, patient-provider relationship, insurance regulations, bilingual policies and sociolinguistics can significantly inform reflection on performance dimensions of the interpreter in the medical setting. As literature reviews and surveys indicate, it is a domain in which interpreters will be able increasingly to find research-supported answers to their everyday dilemmas regarding their role, involvement, responsibilities and competencies.

When choosing continuing education options, caution needs to be exercised with regard to commercial companies that offer basic ethics and terminology courses. For both the novice and the seasoned interpreter, reliable open-access databases that provide scholarly articles, views from public health specialists, and white papers on the interests of hospital administrators and insurance companies are recommended.

Finally, the ISO standards provide best practices recommendations that will be especially useful as a reference for language service providers. However, as can be observed around the world, international standardization for medical interpreting is unlikely to happen in the near future. In our opinion, standardization is not the most viable option, due to the variety of healthcare systems in different countries and to different models and structures promoted by both medical providers and administrators that depend on multiple factors, such as the size of the healthcare unit, the ethno-demographic population they serve, and the level of awareness of the need for linguistic and cultural brokerage of all users. The **incremental intervention/tailored approach** that has been emphasized throughout this chapter, therefore, applies not only to the interpreted event per se, but also to the overall professional choices that are made in this challenging but still rewarding domain of dialogue interpreting.

Notes

1 www.beckershospitalreview.com/hospital-management-administration/50-things-to-know-about-the-hospital-industry.html (accessed 10 April 2015).
2 For more extensive information see AHRQ Executive Summary at www.ahrq. gov/professionals/systems/hospital/lepguide/lepguidesumm.html (accessed 9 April 2015).
3 www.accessproject.org/new/pages/index.php (accessed 15 April 2015).
4 www.mfh-eu.net/public/home.htm (accessed 9 April 2015).
5 www.beckershospitalreview.com/quality/study-3-causes-of-medical-errors-due-to-language-barriers.html (accessed 10 April 2015).
6 http://aiic.net/page/29/guidelines-for-speakers/lang/1 (accessed 10 May 2015).
7 For more on compassion fatigue see Chapter 3.
8 www.ahrq.gov/professionals/education/curriculum-tools/teamstepps/lep/videos/ index.html (accessed 11 April 2015).
9 www.ncihc.org/assets/documents/publications/National_Standards_5–09–11.pdf (accessed 15 April 2015).
10 www.modernhealthcare.com/article/20140830/MAGAZINE/308309945 (accessed 10 May 2015).
11 *The Guide* is available online at no cost. See AHRQ (2012).
12 The search was limited to the English language, in PubMed and PsycINFO for publications between 1966 and September 2005, as well as a search of the Cochrane Library.
13 www.commonwealthfund.org/usr_doc/LEP_actionkit_0204.pdf?section=4057% 20vvv (accessed 10 May 2015).
14 www.racgp.org.au/your-practice/standards/standards4thedition/practice-services/ 1–2/interpreter-and-other-communication-services/ (accessed 11 May 2015).

References

Abraham, D. and Fiola, M.A. (2006) 'Making the Case for Community Interpreting in Health Care: from needs assessment to risk management', *Linguistica Antverpiensia*, 5: 189–202.

Abril Martí, M. (2006) *La Interpretación en los Servicios Públicos: caracterización como género, contextualización y modelos de formación. Hacia unas bases para el diseño curricular*. PhD thesis, University of Granada, Granada.

AHRQ (2012) 'Improving Patient Safety Systems for Patients with Limited English Proficiency: a guide for hospitals'. Online. Available at: www.ahrq.gov/professionals/education/curriculum-tools/teamstepps/lep/hospitalguide/lephospitalguide.html (accessed 3 February 2014).

Angelelli, C. (2004) *Revisiting the Interpreter's Role: a study of conference, court, and medical interpreters in Canada, Mexico, and the United States*, Amsterdam/Philadelphia: John Benjamins.

Angelelli, C. (2014) 'Interpreting in the Healthcare Setting: access in crosslingustic communication', in H. Hamilton and W.-y.S. Chou (eds) *The Routledge Handbook of Language and Health Communication*, Hoboken, NJ: Taylor & Francis.

Baraldi, C. (2009) 'Forms of Mediation: the case of interpreter-mediated interactions in medical systems', *Language and Intercultural Communication*, 9 (2): 120–37.

Baraldi, C. and Gavioli, L. (2007) 'Dialogue Interpreting as Intercultural Mediation: an analysis in health care multicultural settings', in M. Grein and E. Weigand (eds) *Dialogue and Culture*, Amsterdam: John Benjamins.

Beltran Avery, M.P. (2001) 'The Role of the Health Care Interpreter', *National Council on Interpreting in Health Care*. Online. Available at: www.ncihc.org/workingpapers.htm (accessed 23 July 2015).

Bilgen, B. (2009) *Investigating Terminology Management for Conference Interpreters*. Unpublished MA dissertation. University of Ottawa, Ottawa, Canada.

Bischoff, A. (2006) 'Measuring Quality and Patient Satisfaction in Healthcare Communication with Foreign-Language Speakers', *Linguistica Antverpiensia*, 5: 177–87.

Bischoff, A., and Hudelson, P. (2010) 'Communicating with Foreign Language-Speaking Patients: is access to professional interpreters enough?' *Journal of Travel Medicine*, 17 (1): 15–20.

Bischoff, A., Kurth, E. and Henley, A. (2012) 'Staying in the Middle: a qualitative study of health care interpreters' perceptions of their work', *Interpreting: International Journal of Research and Practice in Interpreting*, 14 (1): 1–22.

Brisset, C., Leanza, Y. and Laforest, K. (2013) 'Working with Interpreters in Health Care: a systematic review and meta-ethnography of qualitative studies', *Patient Education and Counseling*, 91 (2): 131–40.

CHIA (2002) *California Standards for Healthcare Interpreters: proposed ethical principles, protocols and guidance on interpreter interventions and roles*. Online. Available at: www.calendow.org/uploadedFiles/ca_standards_healthcare_interpreters.pdf (accessed 20 July 2015).

Corsellis, A. (1997) 'Training Needs of Public Personnel Working with Interpreters', in S. Carr, R.P. Roberts, A. Dufour and D. Steyn (eds) *The Critical Link: interpreters in the community*, Amsterdam/Philadelphia: John Benjamins.

Costa, H., Pastor, G.C. and Durán-Muñoz, I. (2014) 'A Comparative User Evaluation of Terminology Management Tools for Interpreters', Paper presented at the 4th Int. Workshop on Computational Terminology (CompuTerm'14), Dublin, Ireland.

Davidson, B. (2000) 'The Interpreter as Institutional Gatekeeper: the social-linguistic role of interpreters in Spanish–English medical discourse', *Journal of Sociolinguistics*, 4 (3): 379–405.

El Ansari, W., Newbigging, K., Roth, C. and Malik, F. (2009) 'The Role of Advocacy and Interpretation Services in the Delivery of Quality Healthcare to Diverse Minority Communities in London, United Kingdom', *Health Soc Care Community*, 17 (6): 636–46.

Farini, F. (2012) 'The Role of Interpreter in Healthcare Relationships: translator or moral interpreter?' *Etnografia e ricerca qualitativa*, 5 (1): 59–82.

Flores, G., Abreu, M., Barone, C.P., Bachur, R. and Lin, H. (2012) 'Errors of Medical Interpretation and their Potential Clinical Consequences: a comparison of professional versus ad hoc versus no interpreters', *Annals of Emergency Medicine*, 60 (5): 545–53.

Furmanek, O. (2012) 'Professionalization of Interpreters', *The Encyclopedia of Applied Linguistics*, Oxford: Blackwell Publishing Ltd.

Furmanek, O., Gonzalez, L., Solano, C., Calles, J. and Batiz, L. (2010) *WIRED Healthcare Training and Education*, Winston-Salem, NC: Piedmont Triad Partnership, US Department of Labor.

Gany, F., Leng, J., Shapiro, E., Abramson, D., Motola, I., Shield, D.C. and Changrani, J. (2007) 'Patient Satisfaction with Different Interpreting Methods: a randomized controlled trial', *Journal of General Internal Medicine*, 22 (Suppl 2): 312–18.

Greenhalgh, T., Voisey, C. and Robb, N. (2007) 'Interpreted Consultations as "Business as Usual"? An analysis of organisational routines in general practices', *Sociology of Health and Illness*, 29 (6): 931–54.

Grupo CRIT (2014) *La práctica de la mediación interlingüística e intercultural en el ámbito sanitario*, Granada: Editorial Comares.

Hadziabdic, E., Albin, B., Heikkila, K. and Hjelm, K. (2014) 'Family Members' Experiences of the use of Interpreters in Healthcare', *Primary Health Care Research and Development*, 15 (2): 156–69.

Hadziabdic, E., Heikkilae, K., Albin, B. and Hjelm, K. (2009) 'Migrants' Perceptions of Using Interpreters in Health Care', *International Nursing Review*, 56 (4): 461–69.

Hikmet Hannouna, Y. (2012) 'The Need for Adequate Community Interpreting Services in Healthcare Multilingual Settings: a case study in Al-Ain, UAE', *Translation and Interpreting Studies*, 7 (1): 72–95.

Hsieh, E. and Kramer, E.M. (2012) 'Medical Interpreters as Tools: dangers and challenges in the utilitarian approach to interpreters' roles and functions', *Patient Education and Counseling*, 89 (1): 158–62.

Hsieh, E., Ju, H. and Kong, H. (2010) 'Dimensions of Trust: the tensions and challenges in provider-interpreter trust', *Qualitative Health Research*, 20 (2): 170–81.

Hsieh, E., Pitaloka, D. and Johnson, A.J. (2013) 'Bilingual Health Communication: distinctive needs of providers from five specialties', *Health Communication*, 28 (6): 557–67.

Jacobs, E.A., Shepard, D.S., Suaya, J.A. and Stone, E.L. (2004) 'Overcoming Language Barriers in Health Care: costs and benefits of interpreter services', *American Journal of Public Health*, 94 (5): 866–9.

Karliner, L.S., Jacobs, E.A., Chen, A.H. and Mutha, S. (2007) 'Do Professional Interpreters Improve Clinical Care for Patients with Limited English Proficiency? A systematic review of the literature', *Health Services Research*, 42 (2): 727–54.

Kohn, L.T., Corrigan, J.M. and Donaldson, M.S. (eds) (2000) *To Err is Human: building a safer health system*, Washington, DC: National Academy Press.

Leanza, Y., Boivin, I. and Rosenberg, E. (2010) 'Interruptions and Resistance: a comparison of medical consultations with family and trained interpreters', *Social Science and Medicine*, 70 (12): 1888–95.

Lesch, H.M. and Saulse, B. (2014) 'Revisiting the Interpreting Service in the Healthcare Sector: a descriptive overview', *Perspectives: Studies in Translatology*, 22 (3): 332–48.

Locatis, C., Williamson, D., Gould-Kabler, C., Zone-Smith, L., Detzler, I., Roberson, J. and Ackerman, M. (2010) 'Comparing In-person, Video, and Telephonic Medical Interpretation', *Journal of General Internal Medicine*, 25 (4): 345–50.

Locatis, C., Williamson, D., Sterrett, J., Detzler, I. and Ackerman, M. (2011) 'Video Medical Interpretation over 3G Cellular Networks: a feasibility study', *Telemedicine Journal and E-Health*, 17 (10): 809–13.

Maul, L., Regenstein, M., Andres, E. and Wynia, M.K. (2012) 'Using a Risk Assessment Approach to Determine which Factors Influence whether Partially Bilingual Physicians Rely on their Non-English Language Skills or Call an Interpreter', *Joint Commission Journal of Resources for Patient Safety*, 38 (7): 328–36.

Moser-Mercer, B. (1992) 'Terminology Documentation in Conference Interpretation', *Terminologie et Traduction*, 2 (3): 285–303.

Mikkelson, H. (2009) 'Interpreting is Interpreting – or is it?', The AIIC Webzine, Winter 2010. Online. Available at: http://aiic.net/page/3356/interpreting-is-interpreting-or-is-it/lang/1 (accessed 23 July 2015).

Office of Minority Health (2013) Online. Available at: www.thinkculturalhealth.hhs.gov/content/clas.asp (accessed 15 October 2015).

Pasquandrea, S. (2011) 'Managing Multiple Actions through Multimodality: doctors' involvement in interpreter-mediated interactions', *Language in Society*, 40 (4): 455–81.

Phelan, M. and Martín, M. (2010) 'Interpreters and Cultural Mediators – Different but Complementary Roles', *Translocations*, 6 (1). Online.

Price, E.L., Pérez-Stable, E.J., Nickleach, D., López, M. and Karliner, L.S. (2012) 'Interpreter Perspectives of In-person, Telephonic, and Videoconferencing Medical Interpretation in Clinical Encounters', *Patient Education and Counseling*, 87 (2): 226–32.

Refki, D., Paz Avery, M. and Dalton, A. (2013) 'Core Competencies for Healthcare Interpreters', *International Journal of Humanities and Social Science*, 3 (2): 72–83.

Reich, S., Crandall S., Dorton, L.B. and Hildebrandt, C.A. (2012) 'Physician Assistant Training in Effective Use of Medical Interpreters'. Unpublished work.

Rice, S. (2014) 'Language Liabilities: to avoid errors, hospitals urged to use qualified interpreters for patients with limited English', *Modern Healthcare*, 44 (35): 16–20.

Robb, N. and Greenhalgh, T. (2006) '"You Have to Cover up the Words of the Doctor"', *Journal of Health Organization and Management*, 20 (5): 434–55.

Rodríguez, N. and Schnell, B. (2009) 'A Look at Terminology Adapted to the Requirements of Interpretation', *Language Update*, 6 (1): 21–7.

Rosenberg, E., Seller, R. and Leanza, Y. (2008) 'Through Interpreters' Eyes: comparing roles of professional and family interpreters', *Patient Education and Counseling*, 70 (1): 87–93.

Schapira, L., Vargas, E., Hidalgo, R., Brier, M., Sanchez, L., Hobrecker, K., Lynch, T. and Chabner, B. (2008) 'Lost in Translation: integrating medical interpreters into the multidisciplinary team', *Oncologist*, 13 (5): 586–92.

Schenker, Y., Perez-Stable, E.J., Nickleach, D. and Karliner, L.S. (2011) 'Patterns of Interpreter use for Hospitalized Patients with Limited English Proficiency', *Journal of General Internal Medicine*, 26 (7): 712–17.

Sleptsova, M., Hofer, G., Marcel, E., Grossman, P., Morina, N., Schick, M., Daly, M.L., Weber, I., Kocagöncü, O. and Langewitz, W.A. (2015) 'What do Interpreters Understand as their Role in a Medical Consultation and How do they Carry it out in Reality?' *Psychotherapie, Psychosomatik, Medizinische Psychologie*. Epub ahead of print.

Sleptsova, M., Hofer, G., Morina, N. and Langewitz, W. (2014) 'The Role of the Health Care Interpreter in a Clinical Setting – A Narrative Review', *Journal of Community Health Nursing*, 31 (3): 167–84.

The Joint Commission (2010) 'A Crosswalk of the *National Standards for Culturally and Linguistically Appropriate Services (CLAS) in Health and Health Care* to The Joint Commission *Hospital Accreditation Standards*'. Online. Available at: www.jointcommission.org/assets/1/6/Crosswalk-_CLAS_-20140718.pdf (accessed 15 October 2015).

The Joint Commission (2012) 'Sentinel Event Data: Root causes by type'. Online. Available at: www.jointcommission.org/Sentinel_Event_Statistics (accessed 10 June 2012).

The Joint Commission (2015) 'Sentinel Event Database'. Online. Available at: www.jointcommission.org/assets/1/18/Root_Causes_Event_Type_2004-2Q_2015.pdf (accessed 15 October 2015).

Wasserman, M., Renfrew, M.R., Green, A.R., Lopez, L., Tan-McGrory, A., Brach, C. and Betancourt, J.R. (2014) 'Identifying and Preventing Medical Errors in Patients with Limited English Proficiency: key findings and tools for the field', *Journal of Healthcare Quality*, 36 (3): 5–16.

Wiking, E., Sundquist, J. and Saleh-Stattin, N.R. (2013) 'Consultations between Immigrant Patients, their Interpreters, and their General Practitioners: are they real meetings or just encounters? a qualitative study in primary health care', *International Journal of Family Medicine*, Article ID 794937, 10 pages, http://dx.doi.org/10.1155/2013/794937.

Youdelman, M. (2013) 'The Development of Certification for Healthcare Interpreters in the United States', *Translation & Interpreting*, 5 (1): 114–26.

Zhu, C. (2015) *Organization-related Roles Overlooked? A new process-based integrated role model for the study of medical interpreters*. Unpublished work.

Recommended reading

Crossman, K.L., Wiener, E., Roosevelt, G., Bajaj, L. and Hampers, L.C. (2010) 'Interpreters: telephonic, in-person interpretation and bilingual providers', *Pediatrics*, 125 (3): 631–38.

Edwards, R., Alexander, C. and Temple, B. (2006) 'Interpreting Trust: abstract and personal trust for people who need interpreters to access services', *Sociological Research Online*, 11 (1).

Hsieh, E. (2015) *Provider-Patient Communication in Bilingual Health Care: medical interpreting as a coordinated communicative activity*, London/New York: Routledge.

Lesch, H.M. and Saulse, B. (2014) 'Revisiting the Interpreting Service in the Healthcare Sector: a descriptive overview', *Perspectives: Studies in Translatology*, 22 (3): 332–48.

Youdelman, M. (2013) 'The Development of Certification for Healthcare Interpreters in the United States', *Translation & Interpreting*, 5 (1): 114–26.

5   Educational interpreting

We want our children to have immigrant hearts and global minds. All
parents, whether they need interpreters or not, want the best for their
children.

(English Learner parent during parent-teacher conference, USA)

1 Introduction

Interpreter mediation in educational settings may be understood as the facilitation of communication in 'any and all settings where learning takes place'
(Conrad and Stegenga 2005: 294) and includes formal educational and non-
credit bearing courses. However, in practice, interpreting for spoken languages is much less likely to be provided across the spectrum of educational
events that sign language interpreting provision covers, raising questions as to
the nature and scope of dialogue interpreting in these settings. This chapter
describes the complexities of education-related communication with refugee,
displaced and immigrant children and their families, and the range of language support mechanisms available. Attention is given to interpreted parent-
teacher communication, special educational needs assessments and interpreter
recruitment processes. Since the emphasis is placed on early years and high
school settings, the needs of tertiary education are only briefly mentioned.
Furthermore, it is beyond the scope of this guide to address so-called grey-
zone subsettings of educational interpreting (e.g. interpreting for and contributing to research grant proposals involving multilingual research teams) or
scholary research projects (i.e. surveys, questionnaires, interviews, etc.).

Ethical questions are discussed with specific reference to research findings
that illuminate interpreter self-perception in educational settings. These are
contrasted with policy developments in certain geonational contexts, which
together invite approaches to the interpreter's co-power and impartiality to
be revisited. Activities are designed to develop knowledge of local policies,
needs assessment procedures, sight translation, negotiation and planning
skills, and collaborative approaches to users' education.

Two case studies are presented. One introduces an initiative for young
interpreters in England, UK and highlights the ways in which young people

can engage with the profession and develop intercultural communication skills in a safe and structured environment. The second, a case study from Colorado, USA provides insight into best practice for interpreting in schools.

2 Educational interpreting: scope and nature

In educational settings the provision of spoken language interpreting for students from indigenous and migrant backgrounds with limited proficiency in the language of instruction needs to be viewed as part of a wider range of available learning support mechanisms. Currently there is little consensus as to what constitutes best practices within and across national contexts. Despite growing attention to this domain in policy terms (see Section 6), it is important to note that it is one of the most neglected in terms of interpreting studies research and frameworks for competencies development in spoken language interpreting, at least when compared to sign language interpreting.

In educational settings, the development of interpreting is richly informed by research and practice in **bilingual education** since a more holistic understanding of the interpreter's role and responsibility in these settings depends on the ability to make connections between language learning, social experience, peer influences, and the ethos of a particular establishment or education system. In these settings, therefore, 'role-space' (Llewellyn-Jones and Lee 2014) is a particularly helpful descriptive tool for evaluating interpreter performance dimensions, not least because the 'presentation of self' and reduction of social distance between the interpreter and young interlocutor is of particular importance in the learning process.

2.1 Synergies with research on sign language interpreting

To date, the term 'educational interpreter' has been chiefly used in reference to sign language interpreters and there is little research available on spoken language interpreting in educational settings. However, the sizeable body of literature on sign language interpreting serves as a valuable point of reference and contrast. It is important to note that while spoken language educational interpreting can benefit from insights from research and work practices of sign language interpreters in school settings, sign language interpreters work primarily for deaf and hearing impaired students and accompany students throughout the school day whereas spoken language interpreters mainly assist parents or other student family members, only occasionally facilitating communication for students. These distinctions thus open a different direction for the development and understanding of spoken language interpreting in educational systems.

The extensive amount of student-focused interpreting carried out by sign language interpreters in the classroom means that role is considered in particularly expansive terms. Labels such as interpreter-tutor, classroom aide and liaison officer have all variously been applied to sign language interpreters.

This is demonstrated in job profiles (Conrad and Stegenga 2005), which are indicative of the variability of perceptions about what interpreters can and should be doing in these settings (see also Napier 2002). Furthermore, Conrad and Stegenga raise questions as to the level of education-specific training interpreters receive in order to undertake a multirole function, and even whether precedence is given to viewing individuals as (para-)professional educational assistants as opposed to interpreters with a distinctive professional profile.

A child's age and stage of cognitive development are important factors to consider when appraising the nature and scope of interpreting in educational settings, not least because they impact on the way in which children perceive and interact with interpreters. For example, Humphrey and Alcorn (1995: 299) observe that the ability of a young child to distinguish between the interpreter and a teacher is limited since all s/he sees is a 'big person'. In such settings the sign language interpreter is positioned first and foremost as a responsible adult; s/he cannot ignore a child who approaches them about issues of bullying or who might have fallen during play, for instance. However, Conrad and Stegenga (2005) draw attention to the risk of ill-managed teacher-interpreter relations that could lead a child to perceive instructional messages as coming from the interpreter and not the class teacher, with the potential for over-dependency on the interpreter that has implications for learner independence. Of note, however, is an experimental study on spoken language interpreting by Nilsen (2013) involving four events each with a Norwegian-speaking child, a woman speaking only in English and an interpreter. The findings from the study indicate that a child as young as three has sufficient communicative competence to participate successfully in an interpreted event.

Evidence from research and practice strongly suggests that sign language interpreters are likely to be viewed as part of the wider educational team. In fact, in some contexts such a role is made explicit (e.g. through federal law and certification requirements), as a result of which the interpreter is positioned as having direct responsibility for supporting a student's individualized learning plan and educational progress.[1] For spoken language interpreters who are used to working in other domains in which their role is more narrowly circumscribed, this additional level of responsibility and accountability means taking a very different view of neutrality and intervention than might be adopted elsewhere.

However, there are other educational contexts that also challenge traditional views of interpreter performance dimensions (see Chapter 1, Section 6) that are premised on the interpreter's lack of vested interest in the outcome of the interpreted event. For example, research on the South African context shows that spoken language interpreters employed in the tertiary education system view their work as being motivated by a sense of social responsibility toward their end users (Verhhoef and Blaauw 2009). This suggests that interpreters view themselves and act explicitly as stakeholders in the understanding that unfolds from the interpretation process in ways that invite new approaches to professional ethics and accountability.

As mentioned above, the main difference between spoken and sign language interpreting in educational settings concerns the extent of the interpreter's involvement and interaction; at the same time, important distinctions are identified at the level of interpreting practice. For example, word contractions and omission errors all point to the lack of parallelism between spoken and sign interpretation in educational settings. The preference for immersive education and ad hoc support interventions means that it is very unlikely that a spoken language interpreter will be employed on a full-time basis. In sum, while spoken language interpreters are unlikely to face the range of multirole demands placed on sign language interpreters, the literature nevertheless provides useful insights into educational environments and sheds important light on the ways in which the interpreter's role can be understood.

2.2 Nature of the limited language proficiency student body and interpreter provision

Dialogue interpreting in educational settings brings interpreters into contact with students from a range of migrant, refugee and minority indigenous backgrounds. The diversity of the student body raises questions with regard to the level of students' preparedness for participation in mainstream education based on previous experiences, the capacity to take instruction following serious trauma, and the consistency and stability of access to educational settings (see Section 3.1 for a discussion on entry assessment of language proficiency). Important questions are also raised with regard to institutional capacity to accommodate the needs of students from these backgrounds; in some contexts, for example, schools serving children from low socio-economic and migrant backgrounds are characterized by distrust and low expectations, among others (see Súarez-Orozco and Súarez-Orozco 2001). In these settings interpreters can therefore serve as important role models, helping to enhance social and economic aspirations.

Access to educational provision can be particularly problematic for migrant families who depend on income from agricultural and seasonal work and who regularly move from location to location as a result. Fluctuations in earnings can also mean children go hungry and are unlikely to have money for books and clothing. Charitable organizations dedicated to supporting children in such circumstances have emerged and a number of innovative programmes involving educational technologies are being tested in the United States (Daniels Brown 2008).

For asylum seeker and refugee children, social and economic disadvantages are often barriers to their ability to participate fully in schooling, especially if living accommodation is substandard and subject to change due to dispersal policies (see Arnot and Pinson 2005).[2] In some cases this leads to poor educational achievement and behavioural problems. In many countries local educational authorities are required by law to educate all students in their area regardless of legal status. However, in the United States, unaccompanied minors who are temporarily housed in shelters provided by the Department of Health and Human Services are usually not enrolled in local schools until they have been placed in the care of an appropriate sponsor or foster family; instead, educational services are provided in the shelters.

With regard to interpreting provision for indigenous languages in education systems, South Africa merits particular attention. Simultaneous interpreting has been implemented in a number of higher education institutions to support the goals of the Language Policy for Higher Education (2002) (see Beukes and Pienaar 2009), as an alternative to *parallel medium teaching*. Research has shown that interpreting in such settings varies between more formal lectures requiring interpreters to perform according to conventions established in conference interpreting, and approaches to learning that warrant the use of conventions usually associated with community interpreting (Verhoef and Bothma 2008). The viability and practicalities of implementing simultaneous interpreting in situations of 'extreme linguistic diversity' (Beukes and Pienaar 2009) are topics of ongoing review at the local level as a reflection of changing attitudes toward language among the student body. As these authors assert, language attitudes and beliefs can 'hamper the applicability of a service if only a small number of students benefit' (ibid.: 238); however, wider questions of purpose and ideology with regard to the protection and promotion of minority languages impact policy development, and make it difficult to predict both the roll out and take-up of provision in the short-medium term.

In other contexts, such as Australia, the National Indigenous Language Policy is currently establishing a framework for the training and use of interpreters and translators to support indigenous language and culture within communities through accreditation schemes leading to expertise in particular subject areas.[3] Finally, despite formal recognition of indigenous populations' rights with regard to language (e.g. General Law on Linguistic Rights of the Indigenous Peoples, in effect from 2003), in Mexico provision for interpreters in formal terms seems limited to the judicial system, and the educational needs of a diverse linguistic population continue to present challenges (Schmelkes 2013). However, interpreter education programmes for speakers of indigenous languages are emerging as a means of supporting access to education and other public services (e.g. at the University of Veracruz).

3 Educational interpreting: settings and types of situations

When considering the settings and types of events to which interpreters are assigned, it is helpful to differentiate between levels and end user profiles;

here again it is useful to compare sign and spoken language provision. At the primary and secondary levels the following situations are listed in Standards of Interpreting released by the Registry of Interpreters for the Deaf in the United States: 'The interpreter may perform this responsibility in a variety of settings, in and outside of the classroom including: instructional activities, field trips, club meetings, assemblies, counseling sessions and athletic competitions.' Other issues that may need interpreting for deaf-impaired students concern equipment, particularly for swimming, food/dietary, non-uniform, behaviour/bullying and health. The document also states that in some schools interpreters may also interpret for deaf parents, deaf teachers and other deaf employees.

By contrast, the California educational interpreting guidelines (California State Dept. of Education 2006) list scenarios for spoken language interpreting in which the primary user of the interpreting services is the parent. Typical interpreting scenarios include but are not limited to:

- teacher to student;
- teacher to parent;
- paraprofessional to parent;
- administrator to student;
- administrator to parent;
- classified personnel to student;
- pupil services personnel (e.g. nurses, counsellors) to student or parent;
- local or state educational agency board meetings with parents of English learners who testify or offer public comment.

At the tertiary level examples taken from data from Rand Afrikaans University and the University of Johannesburg (Beukes and Pienaar 2009) show that spoken language interpreter mediation was used in the following types of situation in the academic year 2004–5. These are very specific to the multilingual context of South Africa and are not necessarily reflected in other contexts where immigration is the main driver behind interpreting provision but might be useful to consider when implementing interpreting for indigenous populations:

- council meetings;
- institutional forum meetings;
- senate meetings;
- faculty board meetings;
- management committee meetings;
- memorial lectures;
- subject-specific lectures (a limited range);
- student service centre;
- disciplinary hearings;
- welcome meetings.

3.1 Policy: assessment of limited language proficiency children[4] and immersion programmes

The level of language proficiency as a determining factor of readiness for integrating into the school environment is assessed with or without inter- preter mediation (Rhodes 1996). Schools adopt various approaches to the assessment of language competence on entry and students are not only assessed for their language proficiency but also for programmes for excep- tional children, individualized education programmes, disability and special educational needs (Hardin *et al.* 2009; More *et al.* 2013) and psychological needs (O'Bryon and Rogers 2010). Diedrich (2013) discusses the role of the interpreter in validating the prior learning of a recently arrived immigrant in Sweden. In line with the most recent views of the interpreter as a **co- constructor** of the interpreted event, i.e. the knowledge generated during the event and its real-life implications, he shows that the interpreter is pro- foundly involved in the construction of that knowledge rather than simply being the conduit for the conversation between the immigrant and the assessor.

Conducting specialized assessments are a particular challenge for school employees working with the interpreter and for the interpreter her/himself. For example, there is a fine line between still learning a language and becom- ing eligible for speech and language services or learning disability services, which fall under special education. Research by Collins *et al.*, for example, emphasizes the importance of creating a dual profile of language compet- ency, in Language 1 (L1) and Language 2 (L2) as a means of understanding 'normal and delayed dual language development' (2014: 582). Very often, as these authors observe, only the language of the receiving country is assessed, making it difficult to 'differentiate children who, due to impairments, may not make significant gains in either language from those who have not yet had the opportunity or time to learn' (ibid.), in this case, English.

Some schools rely on self-reporting techniques by families; for example, through pro forma procedures families could be asked to reflect on the type and extent of previous educational experience, age when schooling started, and length of disruption in the event a family has had to flee a conflict situ- ation, although these can be unreliable due to poor memory and ability to present information that makes sense in relation to the new context. Assess- ments can also involve the student completing a short test. For example, in Catalonia, Chinese students entering the school system may be asked to complete an L1 profile exercise that involves matching pictures with their Chinese characters and reading short texts, with answers provided if an *inter- cultural mediator* is unable to facilitate the exercise (Vargas-Urpi 2009).

Current policy in Britain favours full immersion with support often being provided outside of the school by the community.[5] Some argue that those who learn a second language should be learning it as 'an additional tool and **never to replace the first or home languages**' (Smidt 2008: 22, citing Datta

2000, emphasis in original), due to the risk of 'subtractive bilingualism' (i.e. the gap between meanings and repeated patterns of behaviour and the self-image and confidence of the learner) (Smidt 2008: 23). Research shows there is a positive relation between basic thinking skills (e.g. problem solving) and being a proficient bilingual who continues to use both languages (Bialystok 2001), although different degrees of bilingualism need to be acknowledged as a result of different factors (environmental, social, age-related) impacting acquisition and use. This supports approaches that establish both L1 and L2 profiles on entry and research that emphasizes the importance of using the first language to enhance second language learning, often described as 'additive bilingualism' (e.g. May 2011).

3.1.1 Special educational needs

As mentioned earlier, interpreters can be involved in assessments of language competence and other learning needs. However, they are not usually employed to help deliver support plans based on such assessments; instead in the UK, this role is likely to be filled by a dedicated educational assistant who may have bilingual skills. In the United States only a licensed certified professional can perform an assessment, but s/he may not be bilingually proficient. In addition, the area of special education is often a taboo subject in many cultures, leading to the need for clarification of what special education is or is not, and highlighting the difference between special education in the host or receiving country and in the country of origin, thus requiring bicultural proficiency as well.

In terms of learning needs other than language, assessments concern issues such as dyslexia, dyspraxia, hyperactivity, attention deficit disorder, physical care needs, autistic spectrum disorder, depression, cerebral palsy, moderate-profound/multiple learning difficulties, speech difficulties, visual/hearing impairment. They also encompass assessments for supporting exceptionally gifted and talented children. In many cases language proficiency problems are not considered grounds for a statement of special educational needs, as is the case in England (Lindsay and Shah 2009). However, it can take time for special needs to be identified in students who are developing their L2 language proficiency; it is not always clear whether slow progress is due to a lack of proficiency in L2 use or other learning difficulties. The lack of available specialized training is particularly of concern for those interpreters involved in psychoeducational evaluations and speech/language evaluations. An untrained interpreter who assists with these types of evaluations can contribute to a school qualifying a child for special education services when none are needed.

In one of the earliest publications on assessing immigrant children in the United States, Rhodes (1996) identifies one of the long-standing challenges for special education personnel as how to appropriately involve (Spanish-dominant) migrant parents in the Individualized Education Program (IEP) process, especially in rural and agriculturally based school districts. In this publication 12 recommendations for the IEP process are presented that relate to parent rights, parent orientation to school procedures, comfortable atmosphere, interpreters, transportation and childcare.

A more recent study by Hardin *et al.* (2009) reveals a number of factors contributing to the disproportionate number of young English language learner children in special services, including inconsistent screening and evaluation methods; an insufficient number of bilingual professionals and trained interpreters; communication barriers and contradictory procedures that undermine meaningful partnerships with parents of these learners; the need for professional development on the purposes and administration procedures of screening and evaluation tools; and a need for policy and regulation changes pertaining to such children, such as the timing of screenings and evaluations.[6] Interpreters must take into account the empowerment of parents in the assessment and support of children with special educational needs. Special attention to non-verbal communication in fostering such empowerment is an important consideration in professional development.

 RESEARCH

Activity 1: Understanding the challenges in special education evaluation

Using the list in Section 3.1.1, research each of the listed needs to understand their key features and the impact they can have on a child's academic performance and behaviour in school.

3.2 Parent-oriented issues: home-school communication

3.2.1 Expectation management and communicative goals
Although dialogue interpreting is chiefly provided to support parent-teacher communications, the nature of such communications is often wide ranging and implies some interchangeability between translator and interpreter roles, e.g. if letters and notifications need to be sent home (see Section 5.4). Furthermore, bilingual community interpreting carried out by dedicated liaison workers, especially with larger communities who have the same language, helps to provide continuity of support in ways that go beyond linguistic mediation (see Section 5.3). Identifying the range of communicative goals in parent-teacher meetings is an important part of interpreter development in these settings since it is easy to assume they only concern progress reports delivered at parents' evenings in which parents play a fairly passive role as information receivers. The fact that schools might use a range of mechanisms for communicating information about learning activities to parents with different cultural backgrounds, such as videos, booklets with examples and invitations to spend time in the classroom with the children (Smidt 2008: 9), shows that the communicative goals of parent-teacher interaction cannot be

viewed solely in terms of periodic contact. This is why considering an in-between stage approach similar to the one proposed for healthcare interpreters and based on organizational behaviour paradigms may be useful (see Chapter 4, Section 3.1). At a broader level, parent-teacher communication also concerns the communicative goals of encouraging parental engagement in the child's learning and the school's wider activities and ethos. Such communications may also involve other agencies, especially if the child has been identified as at risk of academic failure (see Chapter 6). This emphasizes the importance of pre-meeting briefings prior to such events (pre-event stage) since this will help interpreters anticipate the nature and level of intercultural knowledge gaps they are likely to encounter and the expectations of all parties.

Guo (2010) reports on a study of a parent night involving Chinese immigrant parents in Canada and the specific issue of the delivery and scheduling of language support classes; the differences in expectations of parental involvement in school life and the importance attached to parent night events are highlighted. In this study the use of bilingual staff members proved instrumental in persuading parents to attend and facilitating the evening's events, which ranged from large-scale presentations in an auditorium to smaller group discussions. In this event the bilingual staff member performed three interrelated roles: *language interpreter* (explaining educational jargon), *cultural interpreter* (explaining Canadian school culture) and *go-between* (helping parents to participate) (see Guo 2010: 125, 133–4).

▪ PERFORMANCE SKILLS

Activity 2: Preparing for parent-teacher events

Prepare for the following parent-teacher scenarios paying special attention to the nature of the school system in your area and the different performance dimensions discussed in Chapter 1. Consider each scenario from the perspective of each interlocutor, and primary and secondary level education:

A   A meeting between the head teacher of a school and parents (with refugee status) about their child's disruptive behaviour in class.
Consider the possible reasons for the behaviour (cultural, linguistic and/or psychological), and the local frameworks and policies in your area for dealing with poor behaviour in schools.

B   A meeting between a class teacher and parents about ways to support their five-year-old child's motor skills (ability to coordinate movements, handle objects like a pencil with confidence) at home.

C   A meeting between parents and a class teacher in which the parents think that their child (aged six) is playing too much in school.

D   A meeting between parents and a class teacher about concerns over mixed sex physical education classes and the type of clothing worn by girls.

E   A meeting between a head teacher, social worker and parents about the support mechanisms proposed to help a child that has been identified as at risk of educational failure.

F   A meeting between a head teacher, a group of parents who share the same language background and a representative of a complementary community school that provides language learning support to discuss ways that the two institutions can work together effectively to enhance achievement levels. Consider the issues involved in working in situations where speech is likely to be overlapping.

3.2.2 Interpreter performance in parent-teacher meetings

There are few studies involving authentic interpreted parent-teacher interactions. Notable among those available are Davitti (2012, 2013) and Vargas-Urpi and Arumí Ribas (2014). Davitti's study examines parent-teacher meetings in Italian and British pedagogical settings in 2008–9, to explore 'whether and how interpreters contribute to the establishment of co-operation, empathy and social solidarity' (2012: 13), elements that she identifies as present in monolingual events. In addition to evaluating verbal exchanges in such meetings, Davitti places emphasis on non-verbal elements, specifically gaze and the impact this has on the unfolding conversation. This research found that teachers in the study tended to look only at the interpreters and parents rarely intervened to ask a question or explanation, suggesting a lack of attention to fostering an inclusive environment. This shows the importance of the interpreter's attention to non-verbal communication in the mediated event, and thus her/his role as a **co-constructor** of the event, especially since Davitti's findings suggest that interpreters who hold gaze with participants can help to reassure parents and enhance the sense of inclusiveness in meetings.

Vargas-Urpi and Arumí Ribas (2014) analyse a recording of authentic interpreter mediated interaction from 2010 between a Chinese-speaking mother and a secondary school teacher in the metropolitan area of Barcelona. The interpreter was of Chinese origin and spoke a different dialect from the mother. Of note is the fact that the interpreter, whose training and qualifications are not known, explicitly positions herself as an intercultural mediator and not an interpreter, a distinction particular to educational settings in Spain (see also Foulquié Rubio and Abril Martí 2013). The study highlights several features of the interpreter's performance such as a tendency to use the third person over the first person, which in this case seems to allow the interpreter to observe politeness norms particular to the Chinese culture. Also of note is the influence on the interpreter of the mother's perceived lower socioeconomic status that appears to impact register and the number of self-initiated interventions and are largely attributed to the interpreter 'anticipating possible doubt on the mother's part' (authors' translation).

A number of the interpreter's self-initiated interventions seem to tie into power management strategies (following Merlini and Favaron 2003) in which the interpreter, as Vargas-Urpí and Arumí Ribas observe, appears to adopt a quasi-pedagogical approach toward the service user (see Extracts 1 and 2 below).

Extract 1

(57) T Que pot passar que ell vulgui un cicle que no el fan aquí, haurà d'anar a Barcelona. *Que quizás puede pasar que él quiera un ciclo que no hacen aquí, entonces tendrá que ir a Barcelona.*

[It is possible that he might want to do a programme that they don't offer here, in which case he will need to go to Barcelona.]

I 唯一的就是，比如说孩子他喜欢一个专业，是吧？然后到这边 [城市]，让孩子就是跑到Barcelona去学，这是唯一的，因为他 们镍中专和高中就是随便你们自己选的，你们选择这边还是别 的城市。

Lo único es que, por ejemplo, al niño le gusta una especialidad, ¿no? Entonces si aquí en [ciudad] no hay, tendrá que ir a estudiar a Barcelona, esto es lo único. Porque los ciclos de grado medio y de grado superior los podéis escoger vosotros, podéis escogerlos aquí o en otra ciudad.

[The only thing is that, for example, imagine the boy is interested in a specialism. In that case, if here in [city] no such programme of study is offered, he will need to go and study in Barcelona, that is the only thing. This is because you can choose intermediate- or higher-level programmes of study, you can select them here or in another city.]

Extract 2

(57) T I a part, els tutors, tots, tenim una entrevista individual amb cada nen I el orientem, és a dir, si està desviat, el::: *Y, aparte, los tutores, todos, tenemos una entrevista individual con cada niño y lo orientamos, es decir, si está desviado lo:::*

[And furthermore, all of the teachers hold individual meetings with students to provide advice, that is, if they need it, he:::]

I 不用担心，老师她会跟每个孩子单独的谈，就是看看孩子到底 适合读哪个专业。

No te preocupes, porque la profesora hablará con cada niño por separado, para ver qué especialización le puede ir mejor a cada niño.

[Don't worry because the teacher will speak to each student separately to see which specialism will suit best.]

4 Key concepts

4.1 Educational setting-specific competencies

In some educational settings sight translation is a common mode of delivery. When done without preparation, it can significantly hinder parents' full comprehension of school-system decisions and their repercussions. For example, in the United States an Individual Education Program (IEP) is a legally binding document that parents must sign, and as such it must be explained fully and completely. Student disciplinary hearings, which are technically legal proceedings for the student in the IEP, are another situation in which the interpreter should not only be well versed in educational terminology/abbreviations, but must also be knowledgeable of legal proceedings and be able to sight translate students' and witnesses' statements; be comfortable with simultaneous interpretation techniques, often without equipment; and familiar with teenage slang, colloquialisms and expressions.

 PERFORMANCE SKILLS

Activity 3: Sight translation in parent-teacher meetings

You have been asked to sight translate the following report at a parent-teacher meeting for a child aged seven. Working with a partner who understands your working languages, perform the task several times pausing in between to evaluate fluency, terminological choice and choice of expression. Ask your partner for feedback on her/his experience as a service user.

Reading
Louis has made good progress in reading this year. He can recognize fiction and non-fiction texts. He reads with expression but needs work on his fluency when reading out loud. Louis shows understanding of the main points by recalling and finding information in the texts and can often use examples from the text to support his answers when discussing what he has read. He makes thoughtful links to real life and to other books he has read when discussing a text. Louis needs to make sure his library book, and his own choice of book from home if he likes, are brought into class every day so he can benefit from opportunities to read during the day.

An important subset of competencies in the school setting concerns thematic competencies that extend beyond domain – specific language use and educational terminology and also refer to school systems (see also Introduction, Section 3). Caution should be particularly applied when transferring concepts and terms between countries where the same language is spoken, for example school systems are different in Spain and Mexico, or in Chile and Nicaragua. In addition, understanding of education availability, literacy rates, grading scales and end-of-high-school exams are part of socio-institutional knowledge rather than cultural knowledge and should be addressed as a separate subset of domain-specific competencies. Abbreviations used abundantly by educational practitioners in most countries present another challenge that might affect the interpreter's confidence, and thus her/his interpreting strategies (by over-using omissions, simplifications and incorrect equivalences) and, as a result, the outcome of the meeting.

■ PERFORMANCE SKILLS

Activity 4: Abbreviations

A   Look up the definitions of acronym versus abbreviation. Choose ten acronyms from this list provided by the Illinois State Board of Education (www.isbe.net/Glossary.htm), then translate the terms into your working language/s. Try to come up with an acronym that would make sense. Once you have a list of equivalences of both the full name and the acronyms, consult with a colleague on the following issue: when communicating with the parents should an acronym be used only in the source language, or only in the target language, or both? Why?

B   During your next assignment in a local school ask for a list of the acronyms most commonly used in the system, define the concepts they refer to, translate them literally into your working language/s, and search for equivalences in those languages. Prepare a list of these equivalences and their abbreviations. Certain cultures do not use abbreviations as abundantly as others, so while concepts and even terms may be equivalent there may be no abbreviations in the target language. Remember that for languages spoken in various countries (Spanish, French, English) each national educational system can have different terms for the same concept.

See also: www.acronymfinder.com/.

4.2 Parents' expectations: cultural aspects and legal implications

The concept of 'parent involvement' differs according to country. In many cases, **culturally and/or linguistically diverse** (CLD) parents may feel that they are 'involved' if they feed their children before school and provide them with school supplies. In other cases, some adjustment to local norms is required; for example, in some countries students go to school on Saturdays or half a day, they may not engage in cooperative learning or team projects, textbooks may need to be purchased by parents, and a school bus service might not exist.

The issue of parent involvement and expectations is complex since it is closely related to the number of the years spent in the receiving country and the experience gained with every subsequent child entering the receiving country school system. This means that if the school administration is not aware of these factors, it would be the interpreter's role to clarify the situation. When looking at this issue chronologically, the parent involvement pendulum tends to move from apprehension, or even fear, lack of engagement, and lack of willingness to follow the receiving country's educational customs and child-rearing practices, all the way to legal action taken when parents are denied access to information about their children's academic performance and progress due to the lack of interpreters. The ability to adequately assess these stages in the local educational institution can greatly contribute to proper usage of trained and qualified interpreters and decision making in regard to the interpreter's role and task of co-constructing the interpreted event.

As the family's number of years of residence in the receiving country increases, parents may still be unable to speak the societal language but can better understand how the school system works, what they can expect from the school and what they can demand. One of the factors that indicates the increasing importance of providing structured and professional interpreting in school settings is growing parental awareness and parents' subsequent actions supported by immigration coalitions and other 'right to education' organizations. This is particularly clear in countries with a significant immigrant population whose average age is 15–35, and with strong procreative traditions, such as Hispanics in the United States. In many areas of the United States parents have been identified as the primary users of interpreting services, and documents specify the actions that need to be taken on school campuses in order to address their needs: identification of CLD parents and appropriate location for registration of CLD parents, provision of information to LLP parents, appropriate identification of the language needs of CLD parents, availability of trained and qualified interpreters/translators and written translations, and staff training for CLD services. In spite of this, interpreters may still not be provided at all, access to interpreting services may be difficult, or interpreters present at meetings do such a poor job that the parent is left confused. Parents have also become more conscious of their rights. Two initiatives reflecting this increased awareness occurred in the United States at the beginning of 2015. In January 2015 when a complaint was filed against the Ohio Department of Education by the Latino Alliance of Northwest Ohio:

> This Complaint is submitted on behalf of parents and children who have a limited understanding of English against seven school districts in Ohio and the Ohio Department of Education (ODE) and its Office for Exceptional Children. Complainants allege that ODE and the school districts have discriminated against them on the basis of national origin and have engaged in discriminatory practices.... The discriminatory practices include failing to provide parents and children who have a limited English proficiency (LEP) with qualified interpreters at meetings with school officials, teachers, and other educational providers. The school districts have also failed to provide translated documents that are regularly and routinely a part of both general education and special

education. ODE has similarly failed to provide important documents (e.g., complaint forms and information about due process) in the parents' native language and has failed to have an effective means of communicating with parents who call ODE for assistance. Further, ODE has failed to bring the named, as well as all other school districts in Ohio, into compliance with the requirements of the law. In this case, ODE has failed to ensure that LEP parents and students are provided with translation and interpretation services to access the education programs.[7]

In February 2015 a consortium of immigrants' rights advocacy groups in New York appealed to the Department of Education for better translation services for parents. Specifically, they requested a staff member be in charge of translation and interpreting services in each superintendent's office, which would expand as part of a reorganization of the school system. The consortium claimed that these offices – or the new borough centres – would be in the best position to help schools struggling to provide materials to parents in their native languages. Parents stated that help was still sorely needed, telling stories of student report cards and progress reports not being sent home in a parent's native language, flyers informing parents about their right to translation services printed in English, and parent-teacher conferences and school workshops held without translation services. Earlier that year middle school guides were provided in English, but translations were not available for several weeks. City officers responded favourably stating that each superintendent's office would have two 'family engagement officers'.[8]

4.3 Authority shifts

Power and authority shifts occur both when interpreting for one's own parents as well as for one's friends and school peers as discussed by Vera (2002). This underlines the dangers of using interpreters that affect family structure and interfamilial relationships:

> Social workers estimate that three out of four immigrant children learn English after two years in the U.S. but that many parents never learn the language at all. As a result, children as young as seven are increasingly being pushed into managing interpreter responsibilities. Social workers and teachers say these children are called upon to handle issues including family financial concerns; medical, mental health, and social service intake screenings; settling housing disputes with landlords and neighbors; fielding telephone calls from companies; and accompanying their parents to the police department to pay tickets.
>
> (*Philadelphia Inquirer*, 15 July 1997, in Vera 2002: 3)

As children become increasingly involved in the financial, legal, medical and social concerns of the family (which can be of a highly sensitive nature such as terminal illness, domestic violence, rape, war crimes or sexually trans-mitted diseases), the traditional parent-child relationship changes, often leading to role conflicts among family members. Even worse is the role reversal that can occur where the adult becomes the child relying on the child, and the child becomes the adult assuming the responsibility of ensur-ing that the parent's needs are being met. Consequently, parents can feel inferior and lose the authority to discipline their children whereas children are placed in the position of carrying a load of adult responsibility on their small shoulders.

4.4 Assessment of the outcome of the interpreted event

In school districts that have staff interpreters, quality assurance is evaluated in general terms (e.g. as part of an employee's general job duties but not interpreting specifically). If the district uses contract interpreters, the inter-preter agency may offer to do spot checks and report findings back to the district. Across national contexts, there is very little information in terms of interpreters' impact on the education system. One of the few studies that explores the quality of interpreting services and the professional preparation of school interpreters was conducted by López (2000) and focuses on school psychological evaluations. Five cases were referred for consultation services because these students exhibited slower patterns of English language acquisi-tion compared to other students with similar CLD backgrounds. All five stu-dents were males. The students' languages were Arabic, Amharic, Farsi, Polish and Mandarin. The parents had all been born in the students' native countries, had been in the United States for less than four years, and could not communicate effectively in English. Five consultees – three teachers and two guidance counsellors – directly interacted with the interpreters. Although all of the consultees had worked with school interpreters on previous occasions to communicate with LEP students and parents, none of the consultees had been trained in working with interpreters. The roles of the consultees were to work with the consultants and interpreters during inter-views and meetings with students and parents to obtain background information, share problem identification data, discuss intervention strat-egies and evaluation data. The data indicated that the use of interpreters influenced:

a   the pace of the instructional consultation process;
b   the clarity of the communication between consultation participants;
c   the establishment of rapport and trust in instructional consultation.

The impact of those factors was noted throughout all the stages of the instructional consultation process.

López (2000) observes that four variables had a direct influence on the pace of the instructional consultation process. First, initial delays were experienced because trained school interpreters had not been located after several weeks of contacting local school districts and interpreters' organizations. Second, because the interpreters who worked with the consultants had other major responsibilities to fulfil within or outside the high school, all translation sessions were scheduled based on their availability. This issue of semi-professional interpreters is addressed in Section 5. The third variable that slowed the pace of the instructional consultation process was the lack of training of interpreters and consultees:

> Because none of the six interpreters had prior training in instructional consultation or translation, the consultants met with each interpreter individually prior to starting the consultation process for single sessions ranging between one to three hours to discuss the process of instructional consultation and his or her role as an interpreter. Among the issues discussed were the stages of instructional consultation, the skills needed to conduct instructional consultation, issues of confidentiality, and the process of translation during instructional consultation activities. Additional sessions were conducted with the interpreters to discuss the assessment tools used in instructional consultation to assess the clients' academic and language skills (e.g., informal reading inventories, informal language samples).
>
> (López 2000: 382)

The consultees noted that the use of interpreters influenced the communication between the consultation participants in positive and negative ways but overall the use of interpreters had been helpful in learning about the students' cultural backgrounds. In all five cases, the interpreters also helped the consultants and consultees understand that the students' schooling experiences in their native countries were very different and sometimes at odds with their experiences in US schools. López's (2000) findings confirm the role of educational interpreter, as compared to other settings, as a highly involved linguistic mediator for both parties and is currently being proposed as the most suitable model in European countries such as Italy, Spain and Germany (see Amato and Garwood 2014; Foulquié Rubio and Abril Martí 2013).

Another approach concerns placing the responsibility for the outcome of the communicative event with all parties. More et al. (2013), for example, suggest a proactive role for teachers when working with interpreters, particularly in special education. Specifically, they recommend that teachers take a leadership role when working with interpreters to ensure that families from diverse backgrounds are collaborative members of individualized education programme teams. Using the framework of collaborative family school partnerships, these authors describe practical strategies for special educators when working with interpreters during IEP meetings with families.

▲ COLLABORATIVE DIMENSIONS

Activity 5: Assessment of interpretation quality

Read the following excerpt from Colorado Department of Education guidelines on:

How will the school professional know if the interpreter is making errors?

The interpreter should be honest and request that the school professional either repeat or rephrase what s/he had said to allow for better interpreting, when s/he is not sure what has been said. As the school professional becomes more experienced in working with the I/T, s/he should become more perceptive in picking up clues that indicate difficulty (e.g. body language, obvious use of excessive words in proportion to what was said, or an interpreted response from the parent that does not coincide with the original question or statement).

In your opinion, given the linguistic limitations of the users, are these strategies sufficient to identify interpreting errors? What might you add to this summary?

4.5 Hiring of interpreters and management of assignments

In most national contexts, there is currently no clear definition of what the school interpreter is responsible for or what her/his role boundaries are. There is also no distinction in terms of proficiency levels, which often leads to an ad hoc and untrained interpreter that helps with a parent-teacher conference (considered basic-level interpreting) being thrown into an individualized education plan meeting (high-level skills) when they are not ready. Possible initial solutions would include establishing levels of proficiency that school administrators can use as a guide, explaining the consequences of using untrained interpreters through case studies, and reaching out to professional interpreting bodies in other domains of interpreting (medical, legal and sign language) to use their professional paradigms as a model. This section presents some successful implementations of mechanisms for hiring interpreters and assignment management, either partial or systematic.

In the document *Quality Indicators for Translation and Interpretation in Kindergarten Through Grade Twelve Educational Settings: guidelines and resources for educators*, the California State Dept. of Education (2006) lists specific questions to be asked when commissioning linguistic and cultural services for schools. The document recognizes that recruiting and educating translators and interpreters present a challenge for many schools and districts with scarce resources and time. Creating partnerships with stakeholders can lead to new ideas and solutions. Questions that arise as the process begins include:

- How can a district find and recruit multilingual, literate candidates?
- How will the district assess their skills?
- What kinds of professional development can be provided?
- Are monetary or other incentives offered?
- How can the talent and expertise of a diverse, multilingual community be used to improve communications with families of English learners?
- What resources from higher education institutions can be utilized?
- What community-based organizations might assist?

The document also provides resources relying heavily on professional associations and interpreting agencies that specialize in court or healthcare interpreting. Only a few agencies that assist school interpreters are on the list but those that are listed offer such resources as guidelines for school interpreters, guidelines to communicate through an interpreter and interpreter-friendly presentation guidelines.[9]

The New York Department of Education in the US has a translation and interpreting unit that serves the need of non-English-speaking parents and children. The leaflet *Parent-Teacher Conferences 2014–15: maximizing potential to improve student progress* (Farina 2014) states:

> Teachers should use the translation and interpretation resources and services as needed to better communicate with limited- or non-English-speaking parent. School-based personnel should call the DOE translation unit at 718-752-7373 ext. 4 for over-the-phone interpretation services during afternoon and evening parent-teacher conferences. These services will be available until 8:30 pm on the evening conference dates. Translate any relevant flyers and signs into appropriate languages. In addition, translated versions of many commonly-used letters, forms, and applications are available on the Translated Documents Intranet page, including the parent-teacher conference notification letter, student report card templates, 'blue emergency cards' used for collecting family contact information, field trip notifications, health forms, and translated signs.

In the New York Metropolitan area there are also language assessment agencies that provide services, available by subscription to school districts, that facilitate communication with bilingual students and their families. These interpreters are trained to provide interpretation during intake, psychological evaluation meetings, parent/teacher conferences and testing.

In Colorado where the Department of Education serves a population of students speaking 141 languages, among them refugees from Afghanistan, Iran, Syria and Somalia, there is no lead agency involved in testing and assessment of an interpreter employed by the school system; however, independent private agencies are contacted to perform those assessments. The Colorado Department of Education has thus developed a different system where extensive technical assistance and resources are offered to guide the development of best practices when using interpreters and translators in their school districts. In addition to interpreters/translators, a position of a **cultural mediator** or **cultural liaison** has been created in some school districts. The responsibilities of a person holding such a position that requires higher level skills than interpreters/translators screened in language and cultural competencies by an independent agency include training for the educators in particular cultures and helping the CLD community understand the US school culture.

 COLLABORATIVE DIMENSIONS

Activity 6: Needs assessment for interpreting

If you were a school administrative manager, how would you arrange to hire an interpreter for a non-major language (such as Macedonian, Mongolian or Mapuche – choose one depending on your geographic location)? Develop an action plan for three of the following events.

INTERPRETATION NEEDED FOR:
- family meeting
- psychological evaluation
- educational evaluation
- social history
- speech/language evaluation
- superintendent's hearing
- disciplinary meeting
- parent/teacher conference
- employee meeting
- graduation
- new entrant/kindergarten screening
- large group meeting (PTA, community forum, informational, etc.).

The above options recommended by the respective bodies of educational systems to hire interpreters, either directly through the official education system or through professional agencies that are prepared to offer interlingual brokerage in school settings, and their variants should be considered first. However, in regions or metropolitan areas with smaller LLP ethnic populations, in rural areas, for less-common languages or in emergency situations an ad hoc interpreter can be a viable option under certain conditions, as explained in the next section.

5 Profiles of ad hoc school interpreters

The current common practices of using untrained interpreters are reminiscent of the situation widely encountered in healthcare interpreting in the 1980s and 1990s: anyone in a school with any level of bilingual skills could be used as an ad hoc interpreter. This includes front office staff, custodians, health workers, cafeteria workers and so on. These individuals may or may not have sufficient language skills to interpret, but are seldom compensated for their extra efforts and are expected to stop their daily duties to assist with unannounced family visits and phone calls. While solutions proven in other community interpreting contexts can also be applied to educational interpreting, in this part we focus on ad hoc interpreters that are rarely available and used in other subsettings – language teachers, peer interpreters and semi-professional interpreters. Based on these discussions, approaches that are tailored specifically for interpreting in schools are recommended.

5.1 The dual role of foreign language teachers

A frequently observed practice across the USA is the reliance on foreign language teachers as language brokers since language teachers are often the most accessible speakers on school campuses. Colomer's (2010) study focuses on how Spanish-speaking educators in new Latino diaspora communities bear an especially heavy burden as dual role interpreters and unofficial school representatives. Drawing from the semi-structured interview data of 26 north Georgia educators, she demonstrates that some Spanish teachers struggle to understand and interpret both the variety of Spanish spoken by Spanish-dominant parents and the technical language of the academic domain. While teachers employ strategies to prevent communication breakdowns, the meaning is not always conveyed as discussed in a study by Colomer and Harklau (2009).

COLLABORATIVE DIMENSIONS

Activity 7: Users' education

Prepare a ten-minute presentation to inform school administration/teachers about when a foreign language teacher can be used as an ad hoc interpreter and what kind of preparation you would recommend for them; no more than three to five PowerPoint slides.

5.2 Peer interpreters

Interpreting by peers has been a controversial issue since the 1990s. In his work on natural interpreters Harris (1976) lists interpreting in schools as one setting where such interpreters can be used. Angelelli (2010) also considers teenage peer interpreting as valid in her article on circumstantial bilingualism versus elective/learned bilingualism. She claims that

> while interpreting for their families, young interpreters develop a sense of how to be linguistic advocates between speakers of minority languages and a society that struggles to accommodate the communicative needs of

its members. In multilingual and diverse societies, it is imperative that the linguistic talents of young bilinguals be fostered and enhanced.

(2010: 94)

 RESEARCH

Activity 8: Natural interpreters in schools

Read Angelelli's article: 'A Professional Ideology in the Making: bilingual youngsters interpreting for their communities and the notion of (no) choice' (2010), as well as this blog entry:

> http://unprofessionaltranslation.blogspot.com/2014/12/young-interpreters-terminology-proposal.html

Organize a group discussion with your colleagues or other professionals to hear their points of view on this subject and defend yours.

One situation in which teachers are forced to use student interpreters is when they need to quickly comply with policy requirements without structural support or previous preparation. A study in Texas by Crockett (2010) presents the collaborative social integration model as a way of meeting the policy requirements for the English Proficiency Standards for oral English acquisition. The study demonstrates that teachers themselves impacted the creation of an ideal interactive learning environment through their lack of formal training in LEP instructional strategies and through an uneven access to informal networks of support. Crockett finds that teachers tend to group students together by native language and use interpreters as a conduit for content. In the United States this happens especially with languages other than Spanish since resources are scarce and contract interpreters in languages other than Spanish tend to be more expensive.

As indicated in Section 4.3, a dangerous authority shift occurs when a student serves as her/his family's interpreter. The generational boundaries are weakened and the child becomes the parent in the household, as Brown (2012) describes in his study of an immigrant mother, Maria, learning English in the south-western United States. The role played by Maria's teenage daughter, Rosa, in mediating her mother's second-language identity construction and in providing psychological access to productive communities of practice appeared to outweigh her role as interpreter. On the other hand, giving bilingual teens an opportunity to learn about the field of interpreting can help contribute to a positive cultural identity and open their horizons in terms of career choices. Perhaps training them to handle a basic conference in a different school to their own could encourage their bilingualism and serve as a foretaste of a career in professional interpreting. This model is currently being tested in the Glenbard High School District (Illinois, United States) for parent-teacher conferences using final year students, following basic training.

▲ COLLABORATIVE DIMENSIONS

Activity 9: Damage control

It often happens that interpreting services are provided in most schools for major languages such as Spanish in the United States but for others, e.g. Urdu, Korean or Serbian they are not. In the UK, by contrast, there does not appear to be any discrimination in terms of language support. According to Hampshire Council, isolated cases of language need are referred to them on a case-by-case basis; where larger clusters occur a bilingual assistant is often provided.

Watch these excerpts from *Childhood in Translation*:

> www.youtube.com/watch?v=3sYYAfBgs7o and https://vimeo.com/1147 10420 or the full movie if possible, or any other similar documentary on children's trauma related to serving as interpreters in schools.

During your next assignment in an educational setting find out whether children are used as interpreters for their own families in that school and for what languages; prepare a plan of action on what to do if this does happen.

The majority of the still quite-limited number of studies available on the topic of peer interpreters does seem to allow, and in some situations encourages, the possibility of using student interpreters, based on the fact that it has the least conflict of interest compared to using family members or teachers of foreign languages. The authority shift remains an issue to be addressed, but is potentially less damaging in these situations than in the case of interpreting for one's own parents. In addition, peer interpreting has been presented as an early introduction to the career of professional interpreting. Other positive side effects of peer interpreting include stronger self-identification with the ethnic group and thus higher self-esteem and pride, appreciation of advanced bilingualism and recognition of possessing non-societal language skills as an asset rather than an obstacle to integration.

RESEARCH

Activity 10: Peer interpreters' reach-out

Design a bilingual poster/leaflet announcing a meeting that would explain the role of peer interpreters and talk about the interpreting profession in general for high school juniors (17–18 years old). How can you attract their attention? How can you encourage them to attend?

Borrero's (2011) study, framed within the growing population of English language learners (ELLs) in urban schools, examines the learning experiences of bilingual Latino/a students who were taught to serve as on-site interpreters at their inner-city K-8 school in California under the programme Young

Interpreters. Participants in the Young Interpreters Program had significantly higher scores in reading comprehension and paraphrasing at post-test in comparison with their classmates. In addition, interview data revealed students' increased efficacy in their overall abilities as interpreters and students. A similar project, called Young Interpreter Scheme in Hampshire, UK is presented as a case study in Section 7.1. Please also refer to the Routledge Translation Studies Portal for more details on peer interpreting models.

5.3 Semi-professional interpreters

Section 4.4 presented recommended models for hiring and assessing interpreting services but temporary solutions are still needed in multiple national and regional contexts. In the Cobb County School District of Georgia, an intervention project was carried out in 2005. The schools in that district were serving a student population representing 131 countries and speaking 81 major languages and professional interpreters were not available in that area for all those languages. A coordinator of the project describes the process of recruiting, screening and training a multilingual staff of interpreters who could be called **semi-professional interpreters** (see also Chapter 7, Section 5). The process had three steps as described by Avila (2005: 48).

> First, each applicant was asked to translate two school documents from English to the language of his or her choice. A professor skilled in the applicant's language checked the translations and graded them using a rubric. Second, the top three candidates were invited for each language to an interview. The first part of the interview challenged the candidate to act as an interpreter during the simulation of an individualized education programme meeting. Then the candidate was asked to read a general magazine article and discuss it with us in the target language. These discussions were recorded and reviewed in detail using a rubric to ensure quality interpretation. The seven applicants we hired came from all walks of life and included clergy, teachers, business people and recent college graduates. Although they had demonstrated their mastery of the target language during the selection process, all were required to pass the American Council of the Teaching of Foreign Languages Oral Proficiency Interview as well. The interpreters attended training sessions on various aspects of school culture, procedures and issues of confidentiality, as well as reportable issues such as child abuse and neglect.

5.4 Recommended approaches

The three most frequent scenarios occurring during ad hoc, in person, on site interpreting, using either foreign language teachers, peer interpreters or semi-professional interpreters, have been described in the section above. Telephone/video interpreting has scarcely been used in school settings and its usefulness and impact on educational interpreting are still to be explored. As of 2015, educational interpreting is still a very new field, especially for limited-diffusion languages; members of the local ethnic community may continue to be hired for several years through the processes described by Avila (2005) and López (2000) in which individuals were prepared to act as **semi-professional interpreters** in order to handle the specific and immediate linguistic needs of a particular educational institution. Therefore, the use of semi-professional interpreters can be recommended as one option in such situations. While such linguistic mediation would be preferred over the use of a child involved in the case or a family member/sibling as interpreter, the issue of confidentiality still remains a problem and needs to be emphasized during the preparatory stages of these semi-professional interpreters' education as confirmed by Vera:

> Individuals serving as interpreters must have an understanding of these requirements and must be informed of the extent and limitations of confidentiality. In small language communities it is not uncommon for many members of this community to know each other and/or their families. Therefore, it becomes crucial for those acting as interpreters to understand well why confidentiality is so important and the kind of damage that can be done when private information is divulged to others.
> (Vera 2002: 7)

Second, given the most recent demographic statistics (e.g. in the 2011 Census in England and Wales 4.2 million people, 7.7 per cent of the population, reported having a language other than English as their main language), in our opinion the **peer interpreting** solution, if considered and planned well (e.g. not in the interpreter's own school or grade), may be the most promising option to be explored rather than using local foreign language teachers as interpreters. In the USA:

> Los Angeles is home to one of the largest group of multi-ethnic millennials. According to the U.S. Census Bureau, more than half of the adults in the Los Angeles area between 18 and 34 speak a language other than English at home – compared to 25% nationwide. Raul Hinojosa, a professor at the University of California Los Angeles, attributes this to the fact that many immigrant parents are passing their native language on to their American-born children. Hinojosa says that, historically, the children and grandchildren of immigrants would stop speaking the parents' native language, but now the opposite is true. The next generation is encouraged to maintain the language of their parents. 'That was unexpected historically and I think it's going to have a huge impact both obviously in terms of the Latino population going forward, but probably other demographic groups that are now also making the choice not to eliminate the original language', Hinojosa says. 'Mandarin is going to be

encouraged. Japanese is going to be encouraged. Vietnamese is going to be encouraged.' Los Angeles may be seeing this change now, but Hinojosa says as the number of minorities continues to grow in the U.S., bilingualism will spread to the rest of the country. Hinojosa predicts this trend will spur a growing interest in learning multiple languages.

(Lee 2015)

5.5 Interchangeable duties of translators and interpreters

In the educational setting the differences between the roles of translators and interpreters are not always clear. In reality, schools may expect a good interpreter to also be a good translator when in fact that may not be the case. Many bilingual people, especially heritage speakers who have learned to speak the language fluently, are not able to read or write it properly. Even undergoing preparation to become a semi-professional interpreter will not qualify them to translate documents, forms or even leaflets. School staff should be made aware that there are significant differences between the competencies required to be a translator and an interpreter, emphasizing the limitations of interpreters in regard to providing written language services. On the other hand, for the sake of professional trust, staff working with interpreters should be clearly informed that they are able to communicate a spoken message accurately, create and strengthen cultural bridges between families and schools, and assume the role of an advocate and clarifier of information during oral communications.

 RESEARCH

Activity 11: Comparing interpreting and translating competencies for users

After reading Kermis' (2008) chart (see Appendix 4), prepare real-life examples of situations in which an individual who has developed only interpreting skills would struggle in performing a translation task. Prepare interlingual samples of paraphrasing: an exercise such as changing older forms of English (or your working languages) into contemporary forms, bringing up the register of a rock song with a lot of slang to a high academic register, turning a nationally known dialect such as that of mountaineers or of a specific metropolitan area into your regional standard language.

6 Institutional factors: national regulations in different countries

Recent policy developments in this domain highlight the increasing attention being given to the educational needs of migrant populations, although implementation appears to vary at the local level. The findings inter alia of a

Department for Education report in England (2012: 9) show that students with English as an additional language tend to have lower attainment levels. The findings also echoed in other national contexts and in the education of hearing impaired and deaf students (e.g. Marschark *et al.* 2006).

In the European context, a report by the Education, Audiovisual and Culture Executive Agency (EACEA), in the Eurydice Network (2009) outlines policies on interpreter mediation in schools in Member States of the European Union. It finds that in six countries access to interpretation is a statutory right for certain categories of migrant family or in 'specific situations requiring contact between immigrant families and schools' (2009: 12); the countries are Estonia, Lithuania, Hungary, Finland, Sweden and Norway. In other countries, the report finds that the use of interpreters is recommended but not compulsory, and interpreter mediation may be supplemented by resource persons to facilitate liaison between families and schools. In some countries where interpreter mediation is recommended, national or regional public bodies provide services as happens, for example, in the French Community of Belgium, Greece, Spain, Luxembourg and Cyprus. However, in others, schools are responsible for funding interpreting provision, which has led to greater reliance on volunteers provided, for example, through charitable organizations (e.g. German Community of Belgium), NGOs (Ireland), teachers at the school who speak other languages (Austria) and bilingual members of the school's support staff (UK) (2009: 13).

Under the Elementary and Secondary Education Act in the United States of America, for example, schools are required to provide information to parents in a language they can understand. In addition to this requirement, Executive Order 13166 makes clear the responsibility of all federally funded programmes to uphold Title VI of the Civil Rights Act of 1964 by ensuring meaningful access to programmes and services for individuals regardless of their English proficiency. Additional laws define access rights to special education such as the Individuals with Disabilities Education Act (IDEA) 2004 stating that

> assessments and other evaluation materials used to assess a child under this part are provided and administered in the child's native language or other mode of communication and in the form most likely to yield accurate information on what the child knows and can do academically, developmentally, and functionally, unless it is clearly not feasible.
>
> (§300.304 (1)(ii))

In Australia, policy on spoken language interpreting for recently arrived migrants in schools is determined at state level and examples of policy in New South Wales and Queensland suggest current provision echoes practice in other countries where interpreting is provided chiefly to support administrative processes and progress meetings with parents.[10]

7 Case studies

7.1 Young Interpreter Scheme*, Hampshire, UK

The Ethnic Minority and Traveller Achievement Service (EMTAS),[11] Hampshire County Council (UK), has developed an award-winning peer interpreter scheme to support new arrivals with limited language proficiency in the school system (Key Stages 1–4 in the British education system). The scheme is designed to help break down barriers and remove inequalities in achievement and forms part of a range of support mechanisms available to schools including bilingual classroom assistants and professional interpreters.

The scheme emerged as a response to observations that bilingual children have the potential to contribute significantly to the life of a school with a diverse student body, but the ways in which this could be achieved and recognized had never been fully addressed. EMTAS discovered, for example, that it was not uncommon for teachers to assume that bilingual children automatically knew how to put their skills and knowledge at the service of others, which is why the scheme seeks to develop and raise awareness of the specific skills associated with cross-cultural communication.

The scheme was piloted in four schools following the accession of ten new Member States to the European Union in 2004 and involved the input of teachers who were specialists in English as an Additional Language (EAL) in the initial development of training sessions out of which grew a research-informed approach to planning and good practice (Gouwy 2014). The findings suggest, among others, that child interpreters often academically outperform their non-interpreter peers and display more sophisticated social interactions with others (Pimentel and Sevin 2009); interpreting has an impact on children's language and literacy development through exposure to a wide range of genres and registers (Orellana 2009); children can confidently interpret for routine classroom instructions because they involve everyday language but they can struggle to translate for new academic content which is unfamiliar to them and which involves more complex concepts and subject-specific vocabulary (Bayley *et al.* 2005); and finally children can find interpreting stressful (Tse 1994).

Role

Although the scheme is titled 'Young Interpreters', in practice pupils do not necessarily engage in interlingual communication on a regular basis. Instead, the scheme is designed as a support for the well-being of new arrivals in the school environment and non-bilinguals are encouraged to be involved, thereby placing emphasis on skills of friendship and empathy first and foremost. Training typically involves age-appropriate exercises in empathy development through discussion and role play, and awareness raising, all of which encourage reflection about how others might feel on arrival and how the Young Interpreter might help practically (e.g. showing a new arrival around the school, involving her/him in play activities and friendship groups). Two publications support the initiative at primary and secondary levels (Hampshire EMTAS 2014a, 2014b).

A number of misconceptions emerged about what the interpreters could and should do, which the scheme addressed in the very early stages of its development. Guidance was developed, for example, to make it clear that children should not be involved in interpreting subject-specific information or in interpreting for assessments or formal events such as parent-teacher meetings. Inter-lingual interpreting, where it does occur, is strictly limited to routine situations and not those that concern sensitive information or new conceptual information that the Young Interpreter might not yet have intellectually assimilated.

All schools who implement the scheme do so through the assistance of a lead coordinator who is a member of the school's staff. This person plays a role in helping to ensure children in the scheme are safeguarded; this might entail making the Young Interpreters aware that if sensitive information is disclosed to them by a peer, they should encourage her/him to speak to their teacher or other responsible adult in the school. The Young Interpreter is also encouraged to speak to an adult or their coordinator if they are worried.

Older children involved in the scheme have an opportunity to take part in a follow-up programme in which they reflect on the social backgrounds of asylum seeker and refugee populations, and Gypsy, Roma and Travellers, and the feelings and experiences these students might bring to the school environment. Through such follow-up sessions the Young Interpreters are more aware of sensitive situations and the nature and type of work a professional interpreter might undertake, although they are not expected to be involved directly. The sessions (available face-to-face and supported by social media activities) also provide an insight into how it might lead to a career in interpreting.

Benefits for the children

In addition to awareness raising about intercultural communication and the experiences of people from different backgrounds, the pupils gain a strong sense of identity through the training and award of certificates and badges that celebrate the achievements and contributions made to the school. EMTAS also coordinates a regular newsletter that allows schools in the scheme to share ideas and successes. The scheme has attracted praise through the Office for Standards in Education, Children's Services and Skills (Ofsted) in England, which commented: 'Inspectors saw some excellent examples of student leadership, including the Young Interpreter group, who give very good support to those students who are learning English as an additional language' (Ofsted, March 2013, Aldworth School, Hampshire, EMTAS website).

▲ COLLABORATIVE DIMENSIONS

Activity 12: Interacting with the next generation of interpreters

Imagine being involved in training sessions for two groups of Young Interpreters: one ages 8–9 and one ages 13–14.

A Age group 1: what advice might you give to the Young Interpreter Coordinator in the school to help the children maintain boundaries within the school environment and outside?

B Age group 2: prepare a talk about your work as an interpreter to highlight the differences between the professional world and the Young Interpreter Scheme.

C Read the guidelines for good practice on the website and reflect on your local context and language needs, making suggestions for adjustment as appropriate. Access to the guidelines on good practice are available here: http://www3.hants.gov.uk/education/emtas/goodpractice.htm.

7.2 Colorado Department of Education, USA

Best practices for effective interpreting at school meetings are also provided by the Colorado Department of Education, as shown in the excerpts below:

Effective Interpretation at School Meetings

BRIEFING

The school personnel and the interpreter should meet prior to the meeting.

The time required for this meeting will decrease as the interpreter and the school personnel work together regularly. Practice and familiarity with expectations will expedite the process. Clarity of expectations promotes positive outcomes.

INTERACTION

The following points should be considered during the actual meeting.

- The educator and the interpreter should make the meeting site comfortable and non-threatening. The conference should be kept to a small group, whenever possible. The interpreter may be able to offer suggestions for promoting a non-threatening environment if familiar with the cultural group. Ways of promoting comfort and decreasing tension vary with cultures.
- The educator, through the interpreter, should introduce the family to everyone at the meeting. Those in attendance should state their names, positions, and specific roles in relation to the student.

- The educator and interpreter should arrange the seating so that the parent is not isolated and can see both the interpreter and the speaker.
- School personnel, through the interpreter, should explain the purpose of the meeting. A suggested estimate of how long the meeting will last may be helpful.
- If the school personnel desire, the interpreter can request that the family summarize the exchange. This is helpful to ensure that the family has understood what was communicated.
- School personnel, including the interpreter, should present themselves as a united team.
- One way that the interpreter can keep teachers and other personnel informed in a parent-teacher conference is through the use of an agenda. The interpreter can indicate when each point in the agenda is being covered, while the teacher observes the interaction. At planned intervals, the interpreter should stop and summarize for the teacher the information that has been communicated. The agenda also serves as an advanced organizer that informs everyone of what is planned for the meeting.

DEBRIEFING

Following the conference, the professional and the interpreter should meet to:

- discuss the information collected;
- discuss any problems relative to the conference itself;
- discuss any problems with the interpreting process; and
- discuss cultural information that can assist in contextualizing and clarifying future communications.[12]

While briefing has been advocated in other settings, the emphasis on de-briefing indicates an organizational behaviour approach that has been introduced as data keeping or profiling in healthcare interpreting settings (see Chapter 4, Section 3.1). Examples of meaningful and important debriefing include clarification in regards to linguistic issues, e.g. Vietnamese children not pronouncing the final consonants in English as result of phonological transferences from their native language or cultural, e.g. Guatemalan parents not looking at the teacher because they do not want to challenge her/his authority.

▲ COLLABORATIVE DIMENSIONS

Activity 13: Anticipating problematic situations

What do I do when…?

The following are situations that you may find yourself in when you are working as a school interpreter. Think about and determine what would be 'best practice' in each scenario. Brainstorm with 2–3 colleagues over social media for a specific period of time (15–30 minutes) and then organize a meeting in person or over Skype to share the key points from your small group's discussion with the larger group.

A What do I do when I am interpreting for a parent at an IEP meeting and various staff members begin to have sidebar conversations?

B What do I do when service providers do not agree with the evaluation results? How do I explain this to the parents?

C What do I do when one of the parents speaks English and they tell me that they do not need my interpretation services?

D What do I do when the terminology used at a meeting is too difficult or technical and I do not know how to interpret it to the parents?

E What do I do when the meeting becomes very emotional for the parent(s)? How do I handle my emotions as I interpret the information for them?[13]

Additional materials on preparation for effective interpreting in school settings can be found on the Routledge Translation Studies Portal.

8 Conclusion

Educational interpreting is one domain of dialogue interpreting in which defining the boundaries can be difficult. It is also a domain in which the level of the interpreter's intervention and the degree of **co-power** and **shared responsibility** for the interpreted event may be placed at the higher end of the spectrum, either as a result of an interpreter's intrinsic interest in helping to shape the educational achievement of their clients and/or due to compliance with a particular legal framework.

In the first decades of the twenty-first century increasing awareness among school administrations in relation to the impact that bilingual personnel can have on parental involvement and engagement has opened possibilities for structural and structured support. As parents become better aware of their rights, the consistency and quality of language services is coming under closer scrutiny, especially in countries experiencing a demographic shift in which immigrant groups become the major users of primary and secondary educational services.

Case studies from the field of educational interpreting highlight the need for improvement and development in terms of quality assurance, interpreter education, standards of practice and users' education at both ends of home-school communication. A growing number of international scholarly publications is beginning to address topics specific to interpreting in schools, thus differentiating this domain from others. This research has led us to reconsider such concepts as **semi-professional interpreters** and **peer interpreters** that challenge highly normative approaches to the professionalization of interpreting while offering a viable option of educational intercultural mediation. Consequently, this domain of interpreting is one of the most promising areas for growth in both research and practical applications in dialogue interpreting for the near future.

Notes

1 The interpreter's role in this regard is made explicit in the United States online at: www.classroominterpreting.org/Interpreters/index.asp (accessed 9 May 2015).
2 'Dispersal' concerns the practice of moving newly arrived migrants to a range of locations to avoid overconcentrations in certain areas.
3 http://arts.gov.au/indigenous/languages (accessed 20 July 2015).
4 The authors recognize the complexities of the assessment levels of bilingualism levels and its definitions but the discussion on such categorization and labelling is beyond the scope of this guide. For simplicity, the terms L1 and L2 are used when referring to first language/native language and second language/non-native language respectively. Readers are encouraged to refer to Second Language Acquisition and Bilingual/Multilingual Education publications.
5 See for example recent research on supplementary schools in Greater Manchester, UK (Gaiser and Hughes 2015).
6 Caution should be exercised as such screening and testing can be invalid due to norming population size of students speaking a minority language.
7 www.laprensatoledo.com/Stories/2015/022015/tps.htm (accessed 20 July 2015).
8 http://ny.chalkbeat.org/2015/02/17/immigrant-groups-see-chance-to-improve-language-services-in-chancellors-reorganization/ (accessed 20 July 2015).
9 http://holalang.com/ (accessed 20 July 2015).
10 See www.schools.nsw.edu.au/gotoschool/a-z/interpretserv.php and http://education.qld.gov.au/schools/inclusive/interpreters-schools.html (accessed 20 July 2015).
11 EMTAS www3.hants.gov.uk/education/emtas/goodpractice/ema-hyis/ema-pupil-interpreters.htm (accessed 25 April 2015).
12 Colorado Department of Education.
13 This activity, slightly modified, is a courtesy of Fran Hernandez-Herbert, of the Division of Results Driven Accountability Continuous Improvement Process, Exceptional Student Services at the Colorado Department of Education, USA.

References

Amato, A. and Garwood, C. (2014) 'Cultural Mediators in Italy: a new breed of linguists', *InTRAlinea*, 16. Online translation journal. Available at: www.intralinea.org/archive/article/Cultural_mediators_in_Italy_a_new_breed_of_linguists (accessed 21 April 2015).

Angelelli, C.V. (2010) 'A Professional Ideology in the Making: bilingual youngsters interpreting for their communities and the notion of (no) choice', *Translation &*

Interpreting Studies: The Journal of the American Translation & Interpreting Studies Association, 5 (1): 94–108.

Arnot, M. and Pinson, H. (2005) 'The Education of Asylum Seeker and Refugee Children: a study of LEA and school values, policies and practices. A report developed for the Research Consortium on the Education of Asylum-Seeker and Refugee Children', Faculty of Education, University of Cambridge.

Avila, V.N. (2005) 'School-Home Communication in Multiple Languages', *School Administrator*, 62 (9): 48–50.

Bayley, R., Hansen-Thomas, H. and Langman, J. (2005) 'Language Brokering in a Middle School Science Class', in J. Cohen, K.T. McAlister, K. Rolstad and J. MacSwan (eds) *ISB4: proceedings of the 4th International Symposium on Bilingualism*, Somerville, MA: Cascadilla Press.

Bialystok, E. (2001). *Bilingualism in Development: language, literacy, and cognition*, New York: Cambridge University Press.

Beukes, A.M. and Pienaar, M. (2009) 'Simultaneous Interpreting: implementing multilingual teaching in a South African classroom', in J. Inggs and L. Meintjes (eds) *Translation Studies in Africa: central issues in interpreting and literary and media translation*, New York: Continuum.

Borrero, N. (2011) 'Nurturing Students' Strengths: the impact of a school-based student interpreter program on Latino/a students' reading comprehension and English language development', *Urban Education*, 46 (4): 663–88.

Brown, A.V. (2012) 'Learning English on Her Own-Almost: the facilitative role of one immigrant's daughter', *Journal of Latinos and Education*, 11 (4): 218–31.

California State Dept. of Education (2006) *Quality Indicators for Translation and Interpretation in Kindergarten Through Grade Twelve Educational Settings*, Sacramento: Guidelines and Resources for Educators.

Collins, B.A., O'Connor, E.E., Suárez-Orozco, C., Nieto-Castañon, A. and Toppleberg, C.O. (2014) 'Dual Language Profiles of Latino Children of Immigrations: stability and change over the early school years', *Applied Psycholinguistics*, 35 (3): 581–620.

Colomer, S.E. (2010) 'Dual Role Interpreters: Spanish teachers in new Latino communities', *Hispania*, 93 (3): 490–503.

Colomer, S.E. and Harklau, L. (2009) 'Spanish Teachers as Impromptu Translators and Liaisons in New Latino Communities', *Foreign Language Annals*, 42 (4): 658–72.

Conrad, P. and Stegenga, S. (2005) 'Case Studies in Education: practical application of ethics and role', in T. Janzen (ed.) *Topics in Signed Language Interpreting*, Amsterdam/Philadelphia: John Benjamins.

Crockett, K.E. (2010) 'Implementing Oral English Language Acquisition Policy in Career and Technical Education Classes: changing to a social pedagogy paradigm', PhD thesis, University of Texas at Arlington.

Daniels Brown, M. (2008) 'Using Technology to Meet the Challenges of Educating Migrant Students'. Online. Available at: www.educationworld.com/a_tech/tech085.shtml (accessed 2 April 2015).

Datta, M. (ed.) (2000) *Bilinguality and Literacy: principles and practice*, London and New York: Continuum.

Davitti, E. (2012) 'Dialogue Interpreting as Intercultural Mediation: integrating talk and gaze in the analysis of parent-teacher meetings', PhD thesis, University of Manchester.

Davitti, E. (2013) 'Dialogue Interpreting as Intercultural Mediation: interpreters' use of upgrading moves in parent–teacher meetings', *Interpreting*, 15 (2): 168–99.

Department for Education (DfE) (2012) *A Brief Summary of Government Policy in Relation to EAL Learners*. Online. Available at: www.naldic.org.uk/Resources/ NALDIC/Research%20and%20Information/Documents/Brief_summary_of_ Government_policy_for_EAL_Learners.pdf (accessed 9 May 2015).

Diedrich, A. (2013) ' "Who's Giving Us the Answers?": interpreters and the validation of prior foreign learning', *International Journal of Lifelong Education*, 32 (2): 230–46.

Eurydice Network (2009) *Integrating Immigrant Children into Schools in Europe: measures to foster communication with immigrant families and heritage language teaching for immigrant children*. Online. Available at: http://eacea.ec.europa.eu/ education/eurydice/documents/thematic_reports/101EN.pdf (accessed 21 April 2015).

Farina, C. (2014) 'Parent-Teacher Conferences 2014–15: maximizing potential to improve student progress', New York Department of Education.

Foulquié Rubio, A.I. and Abril Martí, I. (2013) 'The Role of the Interpreter in Educational Settings: interpreter, cultural mediator or both?' in C. Schaeffner, K. Kredens and Y. Fowler (eds) *Interpreting in a Changing Landscape: selected papers from Critical Link 6*, Amsterdam: John Benjamins.

Gaiser, L. and Hughes, P. (2015) *Language Provisions in Manchester's Supplementary Schools*. University of Manchester. Online. Available at: http://mlm.humanities. manchester.ac.uk/wp-content/uploads/2015/05/Language-provisions-in-Manchester-supplementary-schools.pdf (accessed 21 July 2015).

Gouwy, A. (2014) *The Hampshire Young Interpreters' Perspective – a case study*, MA Dissertation, The University of Winchester, UK.

Guo, Y. (2010) 'Meetings without Dialogue: a study of ESL parent-teacher interactions at secondary school parents' nights', *The School Community Journal*, 20 (1): 121–40.

Hampshire EMTAS (2014a) *Young Interpreter Scheme, Primary Guidance Pack*, Hampshire: EMTAS publications.

Hampshire EMTAS (2014b) *Young Interpreter Scheme, Secondary Guidance Pack*, Hampshire: EMTAS publications.

Hardin, B.J., Mereoiu, M., Hung, H.-F. and Roach-Scott, M. (2009) 'Investigating Parent and Professional Perspectives Concerning Special Education Services for Preschool Latino Children', *Early Childhood Education Journal*, 37 (2): 93–102.

Harris, B. (1976) 'The Importance of Natural Translation', *Working Papers in Bilingualism*, 12: 96–114.

Humphrey, J.H. and Alcorn, B.J. (1995) *So You Want To Be An Interpreter? An introduction to sign language interpreting*, 2nd edn, Texas: H & H Publishers.

Kermis, M. (2008) 'Translators and Interpreters: comparing competences', PhD thesis, University of Utrecht.

Lee, E. (2015) 'More Than Half of Millennials in Los Angeles Bilingual', *Voice of America News (DC)*.

Lindsay, G.A. and Shah, S. (2009) *Special Educational Needs and Immigration/ ethnicity: the English experience*, European Agency for Development in Special Needs Education: Multicultural diversity and SNE. Online. Available at: www. european-agency.org/agency-projects/multicultural-diversity-and-special-needs-education/multicultural-diversity-and-special-needs-education-national-local-reports (accessed 20 July 2015).

Llewelyn-Jones, P. and Lee, R.G. (2014) *Redefining the Role of the Community Interpreter: the concept of role-space*, Carlton-le-Moorland: SLI Press.

López, E.C. (2000) 'Conducting Instructional Consultation through Interpreters', *School Psychology Review*, 29: 378–88.

Marschark, M., Leigh, G., Sapere, P., Burnham, D., Convertino, C., Stinson, M., Knoors, H., Vervloed, M.P.J. and Nobel, W. (2006) 'Benefits of Sign Language Interpreting and Text Alternatives for Deaf Students' Classroom Learning', *The Journal of Deaf Studies and Deaf Education*, 11 (4): 421–37.

May, S. (2011) 'The Disciplinary Constraints of SLA and TESOL: additive bilingualism and second language acquisition, teaching and learning', *Linguistics and Education*, 22 (3): 233–47.

Merlini, R. and Favaron, R. (2003) 'Community Interpreting: re-conciliation through power management', *Interpreter's Newsletter*, 12: 205–29.

More, C.M., Hart, J.E. and Cheatham, G.A. (2013) 'Language Interpretation for Diverse Families: considerations for special education teachers', *Intervention in School and Clinic*, 49 (2): 113–20.

Napier, J. (2002) 'University Interpreting: linguistic issues for consideration', *Journal of Deaf Studies and Deaf Education*, 7 (4): 281–301.

Nilsen, A. (2013) 'Exploring Interpreting for Young Children', *Translation & Interpreting*, 5 (2): 14–29.

O'Bryon, E.C. and Rogers, M.R. (2010) 'Bilingual School Psychologists' Assessment Practices with English Language Learners', *Psychology in the Schools*, 47 (10): 1018–34.

Orellana, M.F. (2009) *Translating Childhoods: immigrant youth, language, and culture*, New Brunswick: Rutgers University Press.

Pimentel, C. and Sevin, T. (2009) 'The Profits of Language Brokering', *The Journal of Communication and Education Language Magazine*, pp. 16–18.

Rhodes, R.L. (1996) 'Beyond Our Borders: Spanish-dominant migrant parents and the IEP process', *Rural Special Education Quarterly*, 15 (2): 19–22.

Schmelkes, S. (2013) 'Educación y pueblos indígenas: problemas de mediación', *Reality, Data and Space, International Journal of Statistics and Geography*, 4(1). Online.

Smidt, S. (2008) *Supporting Multilingual Learners in the Early Years: many languages – many children*, London and New York: Routledge.

Súarez-Orozco, C. and Súarez-Orozco, M.M. (2001) *Children of Immigration*, Cambridge, MA: Harvard University Press.

Tse, L. (1994) 'Language Brokering in Linguistic Minority Communities: the case of Chinese- and Vietnamese-American students', *The Bilingual Research Journal*, 20 (3 & 4): 485–98.

Vargas-Urpi, M. (2009) 'La mediación lingüístico-cultural en las escuelas catalanas. Cómo ayudar en la comunicación entre padres y madres chinos y educadores catalanes'. Unpublished MA Dissertation. Universidad Autónoma de Barcelona. Online. Available at: http://grupsderecerca.uab.cat/txicc/sites/grupsderecerca.uab. cat.txicc/files/vargas_mireia_la_mediacion_linguisticocultural_en_las_escuelas_ catalanas.pdf (accessed 9 May 2015).

Vargas-Urpi, M. and Arumí Ribas, M. (2014) 'Estrategias de interpretación en los servicios públicos en el ámbito educativo', *inTRAlinea*, 16. Online translation journal. Available at: www.intralinea.org/archive/article/2040 (accessed 21 April 2015).

Vera, M. (2002) 'Chapter 6: Interpreters in the School Setting', in R. Brusca-Vega (ed.) *Serving English Language Learners with Disabilities: a resource manual for Illinois educators*, Springfield: Illinois State Board of Education.

Verhoef, M. and Blaauw, J.W.H. (2009) 'Towards Comprehending Spoken-language Educational Interpreting as Rendered at a South African University', in J. Inggs and L. Meintjes (eds) *Translation Studies in Africa*, London/New York: Continuum.

Verhoef, M. and Bothma, R. (2008) 'Assessing the Role of the Interpreter in Facilitating Classroom Communication', in M. Verhoef and T. Du Plessis (eds) *Multilingualism and Educational Interpreting – innovation and delivery*, Pretoria: Van Schaik.

Recommended reading

Armon-Lotem, S., Jong, J.D., Meir, N. and Ebooks, C. (2015) *Assessing Multilingual Children: disentangling bilingualism from language impairment*, Bristol: Multilingual Matters.

Langdon, H.W. (1994) *The Interpreter Translator Process in the Educational Setting: a resource manual, revised*, California State Dept. of Education, Sacramento Div. of Special Education.

Ohtake, Y., Fowler, S.A. and Santos, R.M. (2001) *Working with Interpreters to Plan Early Childhood Services with Limited-English-Proficient Families, Technical Report*, Illinois: Illinois University, Urbana Early Childhood Research Institute on Culturally Linguistically Appropriate Services.

Ohtake, Y., Santos, R.M. and Fowler, S.A. (2000) 'It's a Three-Way Conversation: families, service providers, and interpreters working together', *Young Exceptional Children*, 4 (1): 12–18.

Orellana, M.F. (2009) *Translating Childhoods: immigrant youth, language, and culture*, New Brunswick: Rutgers University Press.

6　Social care interpreting

I don't think interpreters understand what we are doing.

(Social worker, UK)

1　Introduction

This chapter explores interpreting in social care-related settings in the statutory, non-profit and voluntary sectors. It reflects the growing demand for cross-cultural social care and, in so doing, draws attention to the lack of emphasis on this domain in initial interpreter education and the impact on the quality and consistency of interpreting provision in different receiving countries. For reasons of space the chapter does not explore social care interpreting relating to military interventions involving internal minority populations but recognizes that it is a neglected area of research in dialogue interpreting.

Although many interpreting skills are transferable between domains, social care presents specific challenges for interpreters and their institutional interlocutors, not least because of the level of risk experienced by Limited Language Proficiency (LLP) service users and the ethical implications of the interpreter's involvement in systems designed to protect people's welfare and social functioning. Particular attention, therefore, is given to interpreter mediation in events involving victims and suspected victims of child abuse to support expectation and performance management.

The chapter also discusses social care-related services in the voluntary and non-profit sectors and the structural and ideological developments that are shaping approaches to public service interpreting and translation (PSIT) organization and delivery. The aim is to help interpreters better identify the nature and range of opportunities in these sectors and understand the operational requirements and pressures on different types of organizations serving increasingly culturally and linguistically diverse (CLD) service user bases. A case study on the UK-based organization Freedom from Torture provides insight into the workings of a charitable organization and its approach to interpreter recruitment, training and interpreter mediation with LLP service users.

Activities are designed to develop domain-specific competencies in relation to knowledge of relevant legislation concerning social care for vulnerable adults and children, and awareness of issues in cross-cultural social care and the statutory and non-statutory structures available to address them. The activities also develop a structured approach to the handling of interpersonal communication problems in cross-cultural events that deal with abuse and neglect, and communication management strategies with institutional service providers in human services.

2 Interpreting in statutory, non-profit and voluntary care services: settings and modes

Social work services typically emerge in response to rapid social change and social breakdown in circumstances where traditional family and kinship ties are unable to support individuals in coping with change, and where the state and other agencies are able to take on some of the responsibility to provide assistance (Parton and Kirk 2009).

Statutory services are both clinical and non-clinical in nature, and range from support for the elderly and children in troubled families, adoption and fostering, to work in hospitals and other institutional settings. In fact, of the domains discussed in this guide, interpreted social work events arguably encompass the broadest range of interactional settings, making it a particularly challenging domain in terms of professional development planning. This chapter does not address interpreted events concerning wider welfare matters such as housing and access to government financial support but it is of note that interpreters are often needed in such events. Examples of social work in statutory services include:

Educational settings:
- family, school and community liaison work in the form of scheduled meetings and crisis intervention;
- counselling and other therapeutic services when a child is identified as at risk for educational failure;
- risk assessments;
- coordination with other agencies in cases where child abuse or neglect is suspected.

Healthcare settings:
- support for vulnerable patients and families to come to terms with the impact of illness and treatment;
- advocacy work;
- patient and family education;
- facilitation of discharge and transition to home life in cases where a health condition requires changes to the individual's lifestyle and living arrangements.

Detention and correctional settings:

- support for children and families of incarcerated persons;
- reports to parole boards;
- individual/group work to help offenders address offending behaviour;
- risk assessments;
- support for certain categories of offenders leaving prison;
- support for prisoners with substance abuse, housing and employment issues.

Not all service users seek support directly and may instead be referred to a service. This means that the level of engagement and acceptance of support can vary in both mono- and cross-cultural encounters. Social workers have a responsibility to respect the rights of individuals who are capable of refusing or accepting assistance but they must make sure that the risks are communicated, even if such risks concern 'significant or immediate risk to life' (Health and Care Professions Council 2012: 12). Interpreters therefore need to be prepared for potentially high levels of emotional stress in this domain in which access to support is often limited and where service user responses can appear to run counter to their well-being.

Some statutory social work takes the form of casework[1] with a particular individual, family or community group over long periods of time. However, it is worth noting that the same interpreter may not necessarily be involved in a case for its duration, either deliberately or for other operational reasons. This raises questions of service user trust, confidence and continuity, which are examined later in this chapter. In non-profit and voluntary social care settings social workers provide a similarly broad range of services but often operate within different administrative and financial constraints.

The modes of interpreting used in these settings are primarily face-to-face bilateral interpreting, sight translation and remote interpreting (telephone and Web based). In this chapter we focus on the face-to-face bilateral mode.

3   Interpreting in statutory social work: scope and nature

3.1 Social work values and principles

The occupation of *social worker* can mean different things in different countries; for example, care workers in residential child care may be regarded as falling under social workers in one country and under a different professional group in another (Parton and Kirk 2009). Understanding the occupational status of individuals within a particular care system is therefore an important first stage in coming to understand the values and principles that underpin service delivery at the local level and frame the interpreted event.

Social work has been described as a largely Western phenomenon with values that are influenced heavily by its roots in Anglo-American cultures

(Miu 2008). This explains the emphasis on person-centred approaches in many contemporary contexts of practice. Many argue that the domain has evolved toward more managerial and procedural approaches with less emphasis on relationship building, which has impacted frontline work in the form of increased paperwork, emphasis on measuring outcomes and less overall autonomy (Miu 2008). However, such claims need to be judged against local contexts of practice and related legal and regulatory frameworks.

In the European context, social work principles are articulated as 'respect for the worth and dignity of human beings, doing no harm, respect for diversity and upholding human rights and justice' (European Association of Schools of Social Work website). However, the Association acknowledges that tensions sometimes arise as a result of 'conflicting and competing values' between service users and service providers, and asserts that social workers are not obliged to agree with a service user's interpretation of a problem and may engage in 'constructive confrontation' (ibid.). Such practices may seem unexpected and even unwarranted to interpreters, and there is a risk that they might seek to influence events in ways that seem more supportive of the service user's viewpoint. This underscores the importance of developing knowledge of social work that goes beyond understanding language practices and service protocols, and takes account of the complex political and socio-professional frameworks and principles that guide local service delivery.

3.2 Occupational standards and interpreting

Social work training is increasingly shaped by national occupational standards, which also provide guidance on the anticipated capabilities of social workers as they progress through their career; the National Occupational Standards for Social Work developed in the UK in 2004 are one example. These standards have recently been revised and the 2011 revised standards apply in Wales, Scotland and Northern Ireland, whereas a new Professional Capabilities Framework developed in close synergy with the revised standards now applies in England. Table 6.1 provides an outline of social worker roles and standards taken from the revised (2011) National Occupational Standards.

Although occupational standards are not intended to provide a detailed guide to social work practice at the face-to-face level, they can help interpreters understand key social work roles and associated knowledge bases. They also emphasize that, like healthcare, social care is not only concerned with simple information exchange and transactions but also involves complex decision making, often in partnership with other services. The standards above are indicative of a context in which person-centred approaches are promoted. Furthermore, joint planning and goal setting with service users is often a feature of service delivery in person-centred approaches but this cannot be considered as representative of approaches in the domain internationally.

Table 6.1 Social worker roles and standards

Role	Standards
Maintain professional accountability	• maintain an up-to-date knowledge and evidence base for social work practice • develop social work practice through supervision and reflection
Practise professional social work	• manage your role as a professional social worker • exercise professional judgement in social work • manage ethical issues, dilemmas and conflicts • practise social work in multidisciplinary contexts • prepare professional reports and records relating to people
Promote engagement and participation	• prepare for social work involvement • engage people in social work practice • support people in participating in decision-making processes • advocate on behalf of people
Assess needs, risks and circumstances	• assess needs, risks and circumstances in partnership with those involved • investigate harm or abuse
Plan for person-centred outcomes	• plan in partnership to address short- and long-term issues • agree to risk management plans that promote independence and responsibility • agree to plans where there is risk of harm or abuse
Take actions to achieve change	• apply methods and models of social work intervention to promote change • access resources to support person-centred solutions • evaluate outcomes of social work practice • disengage at the end of social work involvement

Source: Sector Skills Council, *Skills for Care and Development*.

National occupational standards are also beginning to reflect the growth of cross-cultural practice around the world. For example, interpreter mediation is mentioned in the National Association of Social Workers (NASW) Cultural Standards Indicators in the United States of America (2007: 27), which guide social workers on communicating effectively with CLD clients through language acquisition, proper use of interpreters, verbal and non-verbal skills, and culturally appropriate protocols. It also advocates for the use of interpreters who are both linguistically and culturally competent and prepared to work in the social services environment.

These extracts provide little guidance on specific approaches to service delivery in interpreted events, such as how to judge what constitutes a 'proper use' of interpreters. This suggests that the document is intended as a general point of reference to be supplemented through dedicated training.

However, the extent to which training is provided in practice is unclear, as Tipton's (2012) study suggests. In this small study, only two respondents from focus groups and individual interviews involving over 50 people in Greater Manchester, UK confirmed that interpreter mediation formed part of their social work training. In both cases training took the form of a short introductory session with no hands-on practice or insight into the development of the profession and relevant standards.

Although further research is needed to establish a fuller picture at the national level and in other geographical areas, the fact that in later one-on-one interviews in Tipton's study respondents expressed uncertainty with regard to the management of interpreted events suggests that the operationalization of occupational standards in relation to the use of interpreters requires additional interprofessional dialogue and support.

 RESEARCH

Activity 1: Developing knowledge about statutory services and interpreter training

I Social work
A   Research social work education in your local context of practice and familiarize yourself with current curricula in this domain. Using university websites will be a useful starting point.
B   Drawing on publicly available information, research the structure of statutory support services for adults and children in your area and identify local services where interpreting may be needed.
C   Identify the ways in which interpreting services are procured, managed and remunerated in your area. Find out how remuneration in this domain compares to other domains.

II Interpreter training
A   Research the availability of specialized interpreter education for social work settings in your area.
B   With a partner, discuss the extent to which you think your interpreter education to date has prepared you to work in the settings listed in Section 2 and identify core, developmental and domain-specific competencies (see Introduction, Section 3) that you think you need to address. Review your list once you have finished reading this chapter.
C   If little or no interpreter education exists in relation to this domain, discuss what practical steps you could take to address the situation.

4 Issues in cross-cultural social work

4.1 Social workers and cross-cultural social work

Although interpreted social work events chiefly entail a focus on the cultural and linguistic barriers facing service users, expectation management needs to also take account of service providers from different cultural backgrounds. For instance, social workers from a different cultural background than the country in which they practice can experience tension in reconciling their own value systems with those of the organizational culture in which they work (Potocky-Tripodi 2002), which may impact on attitudes displayed in interpreted events. At the same time, social workers from the indigenous population can find it difficult to reconcile cultural differences and understandings of otherness, leading them to perform in ways that risk supporting institutional practices that are considered oppressive (Humphries 2006).

Several studies on cultural competence in social work (e.g. Ben-Ari and Strier 2010; Bulcaen and Blommaert 1997) have found a tendency among social workers from indigenous populations to adopt fairly fixed approaches to culture in their practice, as a result of which culture is used as both a descriptive category (to describe the service user's context) and an explanatory category, i.e. as an 'all-determining factor and explanation of the client's problem' (van der Haar 2007: 22). Some of these approaches are reflected in research that examines cultural understandings of what constitutes ideal attachment in child rearing. For instance, social workers from certain cultural backgrounds might consider children who display anxious or resistant behaviours when they are temporarily separated from a parent as 'clingy', whereas parents from another country context might consider such behaviour as 'bonded' (Robinson 2007: 31). Robinson highlights the possibility that social workers could mistakenly equate cultural characteristics with deficiencies as opposed to cultural difference, leading to decisions that are not reflective of the wider cultural issues in question.

These observations do not suggest that interpreters have a part to play in unravelling such matters. However, having some understanding of variability in the cultural positioning and cultural sensitivity of service providers can support an interpreter's understanding of approaches to interventions in this domain. Furthermore, despite the increasing emphasis on the development of cultural competencies in social work training that includes developing in-depth knowledge about the cultural and social background of service users, in practice the pressures of time and casework volume may be such that reliance on an interpreter can be seen as a means to compensate for the social worker's lack of research time.

Social workers are increasingly encouraged to develop reflexive approaches to practice, i.e. self-critical approaches that 'question how knowledge about clients is generated' (D'Cruz et al. 2007), that have the potential to support cross-cultural practice effectively and avoid overreliance on interpreters.

However, such approaches risk being undermined due to the distance generated through interpreter mediation in the form of gaps in turn taking and the
lack of spontaneous exchange (Tipton 2014). Social workers can find that the
effort needed to manage the conversation in interpreted events can lead them
to overlook aspects of the service user's responses, especially if they are trying
to take notes at the same time. In one office in England a social worker
reported on the introduction of a note taker (i.e. a fellow social worker) to
support cross-cultural events as an example of how the problem of reflexivity
could be mitigated (Tipton 2012).

4.2 Limited proficiency speakers and cross-cultural social work

Access to services for users with limited proficiency speaking is problematic
for reasons of policy, ideology and trust, and not solely as a result of language
barriers. For instance, in dealing with issues of abuse involving migrant populations, some services have indicated a preference for matters to be
addressed within particular community structures and not by statutory services, as has been documented in relation to Norway (e.g. Wilkan 2002).
With regard to issues of trust, research in the United States has found that
limited language proficient (LLP) migrants are less likely than those with
English proficiency and the indigenous population to use services and take
up support for fear it could potentially impact decisions on their immigration status (Potocky-Tripodi 2002). This again shows that take-up of services
does not solely depend on the availability of linguistic and cultural services.

At the level of interaction, cross-cultural social work often brings service
users into contact with different attitudes and approaches to issues such as
time and child-rearing practices (see Section 4.1). Individuals and families
can find it difficult to understand the nature of a social worker's schedule,
caseload and the timing of and time available for meetings (Cox 2011: 351);
as a result, appointments can appear rushed. A related issue concerns the
ability of social workers to keep in touch with LLP service users between
appointments to provide short updates or arrange a follow-up appointment.
Tipton's (2012) study found that interpreters were often willing to bridge
communicative gaps on a self-initiated and ad hoc basis in order to establish
continuity and to try to secure the next assignment with the service user, thus
participating strongly in the **co-construction** of the interpreted event.
However, social workers may decide that it is not in the service user's interests to work with the same interpreter over a long period of time, especially if
undue alliances with the interpreter develop. Interpreters who are involved
in the same case can adopt advocatory positions over time without realizing
it, thereby increasing their level of **co-power** and possibly distorting the
relation between service user and service provider. The amount of time and
trust gained through the interpreter's enhanced ability to contextualize
conversational exchanges as a result of continuity of involvement may therefore be legitimately sacrificed if a social worker believes that the outcomes for

the service user would be compromised if s/he continued with the same interpreter.

With regard to child rearing, Cox observes that 'older children who have been soldiers or involved in combat may have different perceptions of physical chastisement from parents or carers than those in receiving communities, or workers investigating allegations of abuse' (2011: 351). Differences also arise regarding the age at which a child may be left unsupervised or left responsible for other children in the household (Thoburn *et al.* 2000) and regarding expectations of adults' engagement in one-on-one play with children (Burke and Paxman 2008). These examples highlight the extent to which the circumstances that contribute to the formation of perceptions are specific to each individual and family experience, thereby drawing attention to the risk of asking interpreters to comment on patterns of behaviour and attitudes at the general cultural level.

 PERFORMANCE SKILLS

Activity 2: Handling cultural bias

A   With a partner or peer discuss your views on punishment in the family in relation to the prevailing social norms in your country of practice.

B   Discuss the circumstances in which you think it could be appropriate to provide the social worker with cultural information on such matters.

5 Interpreting in social work: key issues

Interpreters who are unfamiliar with the scope and nature of social work might mistakenly regard it as an occupation in which common sense is more prevalent than technical expertise, and therefore underestimate the nature and scope of relevant professional development planning. Even in routine events goals may appear opaque and LLP service user responses may be unexpected, possibly leading to the continuation of a difficult situation as opposed to its alleviation.

Interpreters who enter a social work intervention partway through its course inevitably encounter limits in their ability to contextualize discussions, especially in cases where the social worker feels it is inappropriate to provide background details for reasons of confidentiality. In the absence of detail, the interpreter's main resources are flexibility and domain-specific awareness, e.g. about social worker decision making and its possible sequences, and the ways in which a social worker might handle problems of limited proficiency speaker choice and capacity for decision making. In simple terms, this involves developing familiarity with:

- the standards and values that underpin social work practice in the local context of practice;

- relevant legislation in relation to mental health, disability, child protection, discrimination, equality and human rights, and relevant regulatory frameworks;
- the qualifications and training of social workers, for example by reviewing local curricula to see the extent to which cross-cultural communication and cultural competency is featured and in what respects.

5.1 Assessing need and risk in interpreted social care events

At the level of face-to-face interaction, interpreters' understanding of social work can be enhanced by reflecting on the sequence of stages common in social work interventions, each of which involves particular communication skills and techniques. Potocky-Tripodi (2002: 152) describes the main sequences as: engagement, problem identification and assessment, goal setting and contracting, intervention implementation and monitoring, termination and evaluation, and follow-up. This section discusses the **assessment of need and risk** in relation to interpreted events.

Assessing need in social work is rarely a one-off process and in some areas (e.g. child abuse) decisions are made on the basis of imperfect knowledge (Munro 1996). Assessments in statutory social work are often categorized as either needs-led or resource-led. Even if a needs-led assessment leads to support being provided, changes in resource availability over time can require a reassessment, as a result of which a service user may no longer be considered eligible for a service. The outcome for individuals in this situation may be a referral to an organization in the voluntary sector, which can produce high levels of stress and anxiety.

The assessment of risk plays a central role in broader assessment processes and is something that presents particular challenges in interpreted events. Risk takes on different meanings in social work depending on the social group concerned; for example, it is often understood in terms of 'vulnerability' in relation to older people and those with learning disabilities; as 'dangerousness' in relation to offenders and some users of mental health services; and as 'significant harm' in relation to children (Stalker 2003, in Loxton *et al.* 2010).

Assessing risk in interpreted events raises important questions with regard to interpreter positioning (as ethical agents), accountability and ethical decision making. In most domains, interpreters – especially freelancers – are accustomed to being positioned outside of the ethical relation between institutions and service users since they have no vested interest in the outcome of the event. However, in cases where serious issues of personal welfare and well-being arise, the interpreter has a responsibility to comply with institutional policy (where such policy exists), and consider an individual's welfare to be a **shared responsibility** (see Chapter 3, Section 4.2).

In practice, this may mean disclosing to the primary service provider any information an LLP service user provides, such as an aside, that suggests they may be putting themselves or others at risk of harm. For interpreters who view their neutral status to be supported by professional codes of conduct in which comments on substantive matters are often proscribed, such practice entails an adjustment in understanding the importance of the setting-specific statutory requirements to protect vulnerable individuals. It also places responsibility on the institutional care team to ensure that interpreters are suitably empowered to take action when appropriate, and understand the nature of the shared responsibility to protect.

Both risk assessment and problem identification depend on the skills of the social worker in encouraging service users to open up, which can be especially difficult in cross-cultural encounters in which a service user is from a culture in which such disclosure outside of the family home is discouraged. Social workers may seek to determine the nature of a problem by adopting a line of questioning that foregrounds the problem in relation to specific feelings, thoughts, behaviours or events; the place and time that they occur; and the frequency, duration or scale (see Bloom *et al.* 1999). They may even use self-disclosure strategies to establish some common ground with the service user and demonstrate empathy that can take both verbal and non-verbal forms of expression.

Social workers have reported feeling frustrated by the lack of success in encouraging service users to open up, even over the course of several interpreted events; in some cases interpreters have reported that they were asked to take over the process on their own (Tipton 2012). Approaches that are seen to invoke trustworthiness in cross-cultural counselling relationships include topic consistency, accurate paraphrasing, interest and mood consistency, confidentiality and affirmation of sincere interest through behaviour follow-up (LaFromboise and Dixon 1981). Mood consistency can be jeopardized if there is a change in interpreter and particularly if there is a change in the gender of the interpreter that the service user finds unsettling.

When interpreters are assigned to an event where there is an established relation between the service provider and LLP service user, they will be unaware of the level of rapport that has been established and may feel personal responsibility to encourage disclosure if their interpretations are initially met with a muted response. They should guard against reformulating questions too quickly, however, since creating a space for reflection and listening is emphasized as an important aspect of interviewing techniques in social work (e.g. Allen and Langford 2008), and reformulation in the form of paraphrasing can be construed as undermining and offensive by some (Trevithick 2000: 94).

■ PERFORMANCE SKILLS

Activity 3: Supervised intervention

The problem of encouraging others to open up in social work encounters has led practitioners in Britain to try a range of approaches to mitigate the problem. Read the following descriptions and discussion points below.

1   Social workers worked in pairs in interpreted events to allow one to work as a note taker and the other to focus on the interview process and establish open body language, eye contact and so on.
2   The (female) social worker guided the (male) interpreter to speak directly to the (elderly male) service user to encourage the service user to open up after several meetings in which the service user had been very unresponsive. Through this process the interpreter disclosed information about his background, leading the service user to feel a sense of shared background and understanding. As a result of the approach, the service user made a decision to return to his home country and clearly stated he understood the consequences of that decision.

Discuss the following points with your colleague/s:

A   In what settings and types of social work setting do you think each approach may be advised/ill-advised?
B   To what extent do you think the gender of the interpreter in the second approach impacted the perceived success of the intervention?
C   What risks (ethical/professional), if any, do you think the social worker, interpreter and limited proficiency speaker may have been exposed to in the second approach?

5.2 Multi-agency case conferences

Multi-agency case conferences, or family group conferences as they are also known, are a feature of decision making in review and welfare procedures for vulnerable adults and children in contexts where a coordinated approach to service delivery exists.[2] The parties invited to take part are usually required to submit relevant documentation in advance, which forms the basis for discussions. It is uncommon for interpreters (at least in England) to be granted any advance access to materials.

Invited participants can include social workers, police officers, teachers, family doctors, parents and representatives of other agencies; children may also be invited to attend if appropriate. According to Cox (2011: 351), in interpreted case conferences the chairperson plays a key role in managing the conversation, seeking to ensure that 'everything gets translated in all directions'. Ideally, it is the chairperson who briefs the interpreter prior to the conference and sets out the goals and expectations. During such conferences the level of risk or harm is determined and, where appropriate, a plan established for protection, tasks allocated to specific agencies, and a timeline for action and review is set.

▪ PERFORMANCE SKILLS

Activity 4: Preparing for multi-agency case conferences

You have been asked to interpret at a multi-agency case conference. The conference concerns a five-year-old child (male) with limited language proficiency who has been living in the country for two years with his family. Concerns about the child have been raised, leading to a case conference. Key issues identified: poor school attendance (86 per cent absence), lack of engagement with other schoolchildren, poor housing, mother lacks boundary-setting abilities, child has witnessed domestic violence between parents, financial problems in the family, new sibling about to arrive.

Agencies present at the meeting: special educational needs coordinator from the child's school, the child's headteacher, a social worker who has previously worked with the family, housing repair service from local council, and representatives from the department of employment and a local job centre.

The parents are present at the meeting, but not the child.

In preparing for this assignment, consider:

- the type of relationship between the agencies and the parents to date;
- the nature and range of topics to be discussed and your knowledge of relevant legislation and terminology;
- the way in which you will introduce yourself to the parents and explain your role;
- strategies for ensuring that everything is interpreted and the parents' voice is heard;
- the cultural issues that may arise in the course of the conversation and the strategies at your disposal to handle them;
- the issues of risk that are likely to be discussed.

For further guidance on preparing for multi-agency case conferences please see the materials on the Routledge Translation Studies Portal.

5.3 Interpreters and personal care

As mentioned earlier, the complex issues handled by social workers mean that interventions may not always end in a clear outcome for LLP service users, which can place social workers and interpreters under enormous emotional stress. In addition, the environment in which meetings take place can also be a source of stress. On home visits, for example, interpreters need to prepare themselves for a range of domestic environments, some of which may indicate high levels of neglect within the family.

In some cases social workers and interpreters confront situations of **professional dangerousness** (Knott and Scragg 2010) where family members engage in threatening behaviour (verbal and physical). Evidence suggests that this can lead to a flight response, as one early career social worker describes:

> that sense in which you are so preoccupied with your own survival that the safety and survival of the child becomes an afterthought, where just getting out of the house alive or relatively unscathed becomes the defining criteria of a good intervention.
>
> (Knott and Scragg 2010: 83)

In an interview with a social worker in Tipton (2012: 597), the social worker describes owing a duty of care to the interpreter in the event that physical violence occurred: 'I've certainly been in interviews where I've actually told the interpreter to sit slightly behind me, because if anybody's got to be thumped it has got to be me. I never have been thumped, but you know...' Although cases of physical violence are rare, interpreters need to discuss possible scenarios and courses of action with the social worker prior to the event, particularly if the meeting is in the limited proficiency speaker's home. Not all social workers will feel that they have a duty to protect the interpreter as in the interview above.

The freelance nature of much interpreting provision means that interpreters often have to find their own resources for building resilience and coping strategies. Encouraging local interpreter associations to hold Continuing Professional Development (CPD)-related events can be a cost-effective way to enhance development in this area (see resilience building in Chapter 3, Section 7).

▪ PERFORMANCE SKILLS

Activity 5: Coping with emotional stress

A social worker and interpreter are called to a mental health hospital located in England in the middle of the night after a young man was detained under Section 136 of the Mental Health Act.[3] The male was found wandering around a local railway station. Frustrated at being thrown off the train when he was unable to pay his fare, he had caused some criminal damage. He was slightly intoxicated due to overconsumption of alcohol; on being detained, he disclosed to the police in very broken English that he was homeless and wanted to kill himself. At the hospital he was deemed fit to be assessed, and the assessment concluded that his actions that evening were caused by behavioural issues and not mental health problems. He was then discharged from the hospital.

(Adapted with permission from Parris 2012: 195–6)

A   Knowing that this male has nowhere to go, what emotions do you think you would feel after the hospital assessment?

B   What opportunities are there for you in your local area to help you build strategies for dealing with the emotional burden such cases create?

6   Child protection and cross-cultural events

In this section we explore interpreter mediation in child protection cases, drawing on the case of Victoria Climbié whose death in 2000 placed interpreting services in the spotlight in relation to social work for the first time in Britain. Before discussing the case in question, it is important to understand that there are different definitions of abuse and neglect internationally and that regardless of definition, both can 'present in different ways' (Munro 2011; Munro and Manful 2012). The following categorizations serve as a basic guide, based on definitions in the UK context (HM Government 2015: 92–4):

Neglect: persistent failure to meet a child's basic and/or psychological needs; may involve failure to provide appropriate food, shelter, medicine, clothing, or protection from harm, and a lack of responsiveness to a child's emotional needs.

Physical abuse: physical harm to a child that can include hitting, burning or scalding, shaking, poisoning, drowning, or throwing or otherwise causing physical harm to a child.

Sexual abuse: forcing a child to take part in sexual activities, whether or not the child is aware of what is happening, or behave in sexually inappropriate ways, including watching or being involved in the production of sexual images.

Emotional abuse: persistent emotional ill treatment of a child that causes severe and lasting adverse effects on the child's emotional development; these can take the form of preventing a child's views from being heard or being ridiculed, inappropriate expectations, or preventing normal social interactions.

6.1 The Victoria Climbié case

The case of Victoria Climbié involved the torture, abuse and neglect of the child by her great-aunt, Marie-Therese Kouao, and her partner, Carl Manning, who were convicted of her murder on 12 January 2001. Originally from the Ivory Coast, Victoria was brought to France and then the UK by her father's aunt (Kouao), purportedly for educational reasons. The *Laming Report* into the death describes how in the last year of her life Victoria was 'living and sleeping in a bath in an unheated bathroom, bound hand and foot inside a bin bag, lying in her own urine and faeces'. When she died at the age of eight, the pathologist recorded 128 separate injuries to her body (Secretaries of State 2003: 2).

The report highlights instances in which professional social workers 'failed to appreciate how language could be manipulated in certain circumstances' (Chand 2005: 813) as well as instances of key personnel avoiding the family due to intimidating behaviour. The child's carers were described as 'routinely aggressive and menacing' (ibid.). Furthermore, two social workers and one police officer admitted that they did not want to visit the home because the child had been diagnosed with scabies and they were afraid of becoming infected (Knott and Scragg 2010: 88).

The possibility of language being manipulated came to light through evidence of the ways in which Victoria's great-aunt responded to interpreter mediation during questioning by police and Haringey social services, following suspicions that she was involved in the abuse. As Chand (2005) reports, even though an interpreter was present the aunt's command of English was generally good and she would often answer in English before the interpreter had the opportunity to do so. However, her English proficiency suddenly seemed to worsen 'whenever she was asked specific child protection questions' and she would turn 'to the interpreter for support' (Secretaries of State 2003: 152). The report also reveals information about the aunt's manipulation of communication in the hospital environment; she had convinced nurses of Victoria's competence in speaking English, which led to the following recommendation:

> When communication with a child is necessary for the purpose of safeguarding[4] and promoting that child's welfare, and the first language of that child is not English, an interpreter must be used. In cases where the use of an interpreter is dispensed with, the reasons for so doing must be noted in the child's notes/case file.
>
> (Secretaries of State 2003: 153)

The report underscores the problems of safeguarding, that is, protecting the welfare and well-being of vulnerable children who have limited proficiency in the language of the receiving country. At a broader level, the case also raises questions about the way in which services deal with children and the lack of priority given to ascertaining a child's wishes and feelings (Cleaver et al. 2009). In fact, the report makes a clear recommendation that children be interviewed alone when appropriate and in particular before any decision is taken to close a case file.

PERFORMANCE SKILLS

Activity 6: Self-evaluation

Imagine interpreting for the great-aunt in the interviews described above.

A With a partner discuss how you would have coped with the great-aunt's approach to you as the interpreter.

B Consider the way in which you would have presented yourself to those present and explained your role.

C Discuss whether, had you been asked to accompany a social worker on a home visit, you would have taken the assignment knowing the child had scabies.

Following the inquiry and report on Victoria's death, a number of subsequent reviews and policy developments shaped approaches to child protection in the British context, namely the Munro Review of Child Protection (Munro 2011) and the initiative *Working Together to Safeguard Children* (2013, revised 2015). Both the Munro Review and the *Working Together* initiatives draw attention to the importance of child-centred approaches and the need for early intervention, as opposed to reacting to a crisis at a later stage.

 PERFORMANCE SKILLS

Activity 7: Handling ethical issues in social care settings

The Victoria Climbié case draws attention to the possibility of adult carers manipulating a situation in order to conceal neglect and abuse. Interpreters can be caught up in such situations, as the following scenario suggests. Read the scenario and reflect on the points below.

Scenario

I During a home visit with a social worker about an eight-year-old child's recent absenteeism from school, the interpreter notices that while the social worker is engaged in writing notes the child's mother tries to adjust the child's clothing to conceal what appears to be a large bruise on the child's thigh, and realizes that the interpreter has seen the bruise. The conversation continues, and the mother emphasizes to the social worker how clever her daughter is and how they read together regularly while making a number of asides to the child that suggest a very different relationship.

A Research regulations in your area concerning the duty to disclose the issues raised in this scenario. With a partner discuss the point at which you think it would be appropriate to disclose the information to the primary service provider.

B Discuss your handling of the conversation between the mother and the child in this case.

II   A few weeks later, the child's school has contacted the social work department to report changes to behaviour, bruising and incontinence. The child is interviewed alone by the same social worker who did the home visit and you are assigned to interpret.

   A   Discuss the range of issues you think might arise in a conversation between the child and the social worker without the parent.
   B   Consider how you think the child might respond to you or to an interpreter s/he has never seen before.
   C   Consider the extent to which you think your previous experiences with this child might affect your approach to the interpretation and especially to encouraging the child to open up.

6.2 Child protection assessments

Interpreters play a vital role in the mechanisms of child protection and their involvement forms part of wider considerations of what constitutes culturally sensitive approaches to service delivery. For example, the use of interpreters is likely to be weighed against the practice of matching caseworker and service user background (linguistic and cultural), which has the advantage of bringing language and cultural competence directly to bear on trust-building processes that can facilitate engagement with families. This is a fairly widespread practice around the world (Sawrikar 2013). It is also considered to enhance the assessment of a child's well-being due to improved understanding of linguistic issues, especially in cases where words to describe sexual abuse might not exist or are rarely used (e.g. Owen and Farmer 1996).

   However, the impact of matching is still relatively underresearched, and a number of risks have been highlighted such as the possibility of overidentification between service provider and limited proficiency speaker that can lead to bias in the assessment process (see Chand 2003). At the same time, the use of interpreters in child protection assessments has raised important issues, not least the fact that it can complicate an already difficult situation particularly 'when combined with immaturity or special educational needs on the part of a family member' (Owen and Farmer 1996: 302). These authors also draw attention to the emergency nature of interpreting call-outs, which can lead to less-than-suitably prepared interpreters being sent to an assignment, a situation that continues today due to the lack of dedicated training available to interpreters in this domain.

   Interpreters encounter a range of child protection events involving family members and meetings with children in which family members might not be present. In both cases, despite assurances of impartiality and confidentiality, interpreters are often viewed by service users as a very intrusive and unwelcome presence; there is evidence of service users using strategies to converse with service providers in ways that bypass the need for an interpreter.

Owen and Farmer (1996), for example, cite the case of a female service user conversing with a service provider in a language in which she had limited competence (in this case Hindi). The fear that family matters will become known by the wider local community is often cited as a reason for both mistrust in interpreters and overconfidence that they will play down matters on the family's behalf, especially if the family in question knows the interpreter. The rapport-building process is therefore a focus for negotiation in the pre-meeting briefing between interpreters and service providers.

The apparent overrepresentation of families from ethnic minority backgrounds in child protection referrals (e.g. Osterling *et al.* 2008) has been the subject of research in recent decades. Some consider the impact of cultures in which physical discipline is more accepted as a possible reason for more frequent physical maltreatment (e.g. Mbagaya *et al.* 2013), but additional factors such as socioeconomic status are also considered (e.g. Alink *et al.* 2013). Although interpreters are not directly concerned with such matters, insight into some of the triggers for social work intervention can help them prepare for the emotional rigours of child protection work.

In regard to what interpreters can expect from interviews in child protection, the pioneering work of Fontes (2005, 2010) on cross-cultural communication in this type of interview provides an excellent point of reference. For example, Fontes (2010) categorizes child abuse interviews into key types: emergency investigations, investigations, ongoing interventions with families (e.g. where a child knows a social worker) and forensic interviews. Forensic interviews may take place at a police station and are likely to be audio or video recorded. Statements made during such interviews may be used later in court, which means that interpreters could be called to testify. Such interviews may involve the use of anatomically correct dolls and follow particular interview protocols, of which the National Institute of Child Health and Human Development (NICHD) protocol is a prominent example (see Lamb *et al.* 2007).

Fontes (2010) suggests that interpreters can expect a child to express a wide range of emotions in interviews and that it is common for there to be no mention of any abuse. If mention is made, accounts may be confused either because a child could be trying to protect an abuser or because there is confusion with regard to a specific event if abuse has occurred on multiple occasions. In common with other domains discussed in this guide (in particular in Chapter 3, Section 6), interpreters are advised not to try to make sense of or impose a false logic on what the child says in this type of interview. This can be difficult in situations in which an interpreter feels a need to try and protect the child and adopts strategies that hinder the interview process rather than help it.

Fontes (ibid.) stresses the need for interpreters to remain impassive on hearing details that might cause shock and feelings of disgust and anger; she echoes the guidance commonly given to interviewers in these settings. Interpreters also should not be surprised by the range of language a child might use in the course of interviews, even sexually explicit language that is more normally associated with adults; a child could even mimic sexual sounds when describing events, or resort to baby talk. Equally, if an interviewer remains expressionless on hearing certain details, interpreters should not respond negatively in the belief that the interviewer is lacking in compassion and overcompensate with their own behaviour since this risks distorting the relationship between the child and interviewer.

▲ COLLABORATIVE DIMENSIONS

Activity 8: Handling disclosure

A   During an interview with a child, the child implicates someone from your community that you have known for a long time and respect in their description of events. Discuss with a partner how you might respond to/ handle this information (during and after the interview)?

B   During an interview a child says things that remind you of a personal experience or an experience close to home. What sources of support might you be able to access to help you handle these emotions (after the interview)?

6.3 Fostering and adoption

The rise in unaccompanied minors in a number of countries around the world has placed significant demands on fostering services to meet statutory requirements for protecting individuals vulnerable to violence, abuse, neglect and exploitation. Services also provide support for the temporary and permanent removal of immigrant children as a result of neglect and abuse within the family, substance abuse, domestic violence, incarceration and parent mental health issues, among others. In the United States, for example, Lamb observes that

> Hispanic children represent a growing population of children removed from parental care and placed in foster care; they also represent an increasing proportion of children in foster care whose parents have had their parental rights terminated and who are legally free for adoption.
>
> (2008: 156)

Although the interpreter's involvement in the fostering process is likely to be limited to training and administrative events, and initial meetings between the foster carer and child, their contact with the child may extend to other institutional events as a result of physical and/or mental health problems. Interpreters are also called to work in the family court system in relation to matters such as visiting and parental rights.

Research on the placement of limited proficiency speaking children and young people engages with the problems of providing services that respond to the linguistic and cultural diversity of service users, including issues of cultural matching (i.e. recruiting sufficient foster carers that reflect the ethnic and racial diversity of a given area), and the involvement of interpreters in the training of foster carers and placement processes (see Brown *et al.* 2009; Capello 2006). Other research concerns the experiences of children in foster families and problems of adjustment. For example, some unaccompanied minors arrive in a new country context having already spent several years in a refugee camp. The experiences of survival and making life or death decisions while fleeing means that many find it difficult to adjust to parental authority in the foster family. In some cases this leads to a full breakdown of relations and a change of foster placement (Luster *et al.* 2009). Interpreters may therefore work with the same young person over several months as adjustments are made.

For many children the concept of fostering is completely new. The level of isolation experienced due to communication barriers can be considerable in the initial stages when feelings of separation and/or concern over the welfare and fate of distant family members can loom large:

> We didn't speak English, and had to get by with basic signing and pointing. It was very difficult for our carers to understand what we needed, and often those misunderstandings would only get resolved once we met up with social services and they provided an interpreter.
>
> (Be My Parent 2008)

Such infrequent contact with interpreters means that the child can come to view the interpreter as someone to talk to and not simply as a language mediator. However, the resources available to social workers should mitigate this, for example through activities and contact with other children from a similar language background in the local area. This is something that interpreters can discuss with service providers to limit any undue dependence.

Coping with language barriers is also a source of difficulty for foster carers. Although extensive training is provided in regard to matters of food, religion and so on the greatest challenges occur in delivering emotional support when there is a language barrier. The following personal account of a foster carer gives an example of an interpreter taking an interest in the case and sharing social contacts that supported the young person both culturally and linguistically, actively contributing as a **co-constructor** to the outcome of the interpreted events:

> She couldn't speak any English and cried for the entire first week she lived with me. I knew it was imperative to provide a patient and secure environment for her; I wanted her to feel safe, but I was very much out of my comfort zone. I couldn't communicate with her to tell her it would all be OK with her and I couldn't replace the family she was clamouring

for … there was a Vietnamese community near my home, and an interpreter put us in touch with a lovely family … eventually it was decided that she should move in with them.

(King 2011)

A study by Garcia *et al.* (2012) involving caseworkers in the US child welfare system highlights the often patchy nature of language support services in foster care. The study finds that interpreting services are provided for events like permanency hearings[5] in court but court documents are only available in English, which means that 'clients leave lacking clarity regarding what court-ordered services they are required to complete because they have no written documentation in Spanish to refer to' (2012: 1065). However, as noted by these authors, translation is not necessarily a solution due to differences in literacy levels. The quality and timeliness of interpreting services is also highlighted as problematic in the areas investigated in the study.

Adoption cases, by contrast, involve interpreters and translators in state-run and private services. For example, families involved in international adoption may hire interpreters[6] from commercial agencies, often in the country of the child's origin. In such cases written translation is a significant part of the process and includes notarized translations of documents such as birth certificates, letters of intent to adopt (sent to relevant embassies), medical reports and certificates of approval from the international adoption agency. Procedure and interpersonal contact, however, are often more emotionally challenging in regard to state services at the domestic level. For instance, interpreters may be involved in cases where an asylum seeker or refugee is putting up for adoption a child that was born as the result of being raped in a conflict zone, or in immigrant cases of adoption in which parental rights have been terminated.

7 Interpreting in the voluntary and non-profit sectors

Interpreting in public and community services has its roots in civil society and faith-based organizations as a response to myriad migrant flows over the twentieth century. In the past 30 years or so, mass migration and immigration has meant that the focus has shifted to the professionalization of interpreting and the supply of suitably accredited and trained interpreters to provide equality of access to statutory services. This change of focus has arguably led to assumptions that only non-professionals, who are for the most part untrained, operate in civil society and faith-based organizations. However, contrary to what might be expected, there has not been a polarization of provision between the sectors, with non-professionals in one and professionals in the other. Nevertheless, 'the co-existence of trained and untrained professional translators and interpreters has tended to be regarded … as a disruptive source of tension' (Pérez-González and Susam-Saraeva 2012: 151). Although disruptive, the frequency with which new language combinations emerge in some areas has led to a cycle of **natural interpreters** entering the field and practising alongside trained professionals, which looks set to continue.

The financial crisis that affected a large number of countries in the West in the early part of the new millennium, as Pérez-González and Susam-Saraeva (2012) observe, has seen renewed emphasis on the voluntary and non-profit sector in providing services for migrants. However, shifts in the organizational and ideological landscape of the sector (e.g. in the UK) that have led to increased professionalization call for a re-evaluation of how interpreting provision is understood. In some areas, interpreters are likely to find opportunities for remunerated work in the sector that require a certain level of training and qualification, opportunities that are often indicative of partnership work between the state and the voluntary sector. In such cases, issues of interpreter accountability and service user experience bring the quality of provision into sharp relief, which can lead to the reliance on untrained volunteers to diminish. By contrast in the United States, student language learners and non-professional interpreters are commonly used to provide social care interpreting (e.g. through student internship programmes), which suggests that across national contexts the sector is characterized by a mixed economy of language service provision.

Other developments of note in relation to structural shifts in the provision of interpreters include the emergence of refugee community organizations (RCOs) that draw on internal PSIT expertise and market it on a commercial basis in order to support organizations' wider activities in the community. These shifts raise interesting questions for both the statutory and non-profit and voluntary sectors and perceptions of professionalization and service quality.

As mentioned above, opportunities for interpreters also arise through faith-based organizations some of which have extensive involvement in social care and educational services for migrants, especially in the United States (see Chapter 7, Section 5). The sections that follow explore in more depth the sector and the nature of opportunities available for interpreters, paying attention to some of the role conflicts that can arise.

7.1 What is the non-profit sector?

The non-profit sector is a general term used to describe a range of organizations that support the delivery of health, housing, education and social care-related services. As indicated above, some of these services may be run in partnership with the state, whereas others operate independently. The sector encompasses organizations such as (officially registered) charities, charitable organizations, foundations, community organizations and social enterprises (commercial ventures aimed at generating funds that can be used for the public good). Non-governmental organizations (NGOs) are also associated with non-profit-making activities and may operate at a local, national or international level. The type of organization and its status are subject to the regulatory regimes in operation in each country.

Organizations in the sector vary in size from very small and informal groups to large organizations with very sizeable income streams. In smaller organizations individuals with multiple skill sets can provide a level of versatility and flexibility that supports the organization on several levels; however, such versatility comes with the risk that provision in some areas may be patchy at best with implications for service user experience, of which PSIT provision is a salient example. Depending on the legal status of the organization, income will be generated through private donations, grants, and income generated through activities. In operational terms, organizations often combine a small team of paid staff and unpaid volunteer support; interpreters are often recruited as part of the team of unpaid volunteers, although remunerated opportunities are increasingly available, as mentioned above.

 RESEARCH

Activity 9: Mapping the non-profit sector

A   Make a list of organizations in the non-profit, voluntary and charities sector in your area.

B   Identify the diversity of the service users and explore publicly available information about the organizations to see whether they

- require interpreter and translation services and, if they do,
- on what basis services are organized (remunerated, volunteer).

7.2 Activism and civic engagement

There are many different reasons why interpreters and translators might be attracted to working in the voluntary and non-profit sector in social care-related domains and beyond. Giving time freely to help others is a significant motivating factor, the rewards of which are satisfaction, even feelings of a 'warm glow' (Olohan 2012); indeed, former service users are often motivated to volunteer to support others who have had similar experiences, which is the case for many former asylum seekers who have become interpreters (Lai and Mulayim 2010). Motivation also includes individuals sharing an organization's mission, goals and values.

In recent years, research in translation and interpreting studies has documented and analysed the rise in activist approaches that are usually associated with individuals that are seeking social change, in some cases radical political change, and who give their skills to support gradual change over time (see Baker 2013). The role of the activist interpreter and translator is broader than most common understandings of role in institutional contexts, and is accompanied by the common assumption that the individual is involved in other aspects of an organization's activities, such as helping to decide which materials should be translated, helping to fundraise and facilitate meetings between interested parties, and promoting organizational aims and values in the wider society. The activist will therefore not be a neutral agent understood in the general sense of interpreter neutrality, but nevertheless may combine activist activity with other activities in commercial fields in which their boundaries and position are more in line with established professional interpreter profiles.

Examples of activist groups of interpreters include the Association of Volunteer Translators and Interpreters for Solidarity (known by the Spanish name ECOS), which was set up with the support of the University of Granada to provide interpreting to civil society organizations. However, because of concerns that its work would undermine the work of paid professional interpreters in the region, it later changed its remit to explicitly support non-governmental organizations and humanitarian organizations first and foremost. Babels is another interpreting organization with explicitly activist aims. Developed as a result of the European Social Forum, it provides interpreting services to support the work of the world social forum and is oriented toward conference-level meetings and modes of interpreting not typically covered in community and public service work. This group in particular challenges established paradigms of conference interpreter training and professional organization (see, for example, Boéri 2008; de Manuel Jerez 2010).

For those interpreters and translators who pursue less radical political aims, their choice to be involved in the non-profit sector falls more typically within a 'civic engagement' role. That is to say, they are likely to be less involved in wider aspects of organizational life and only support activities that relate to translation and interpreting in fairly narrowly defined terms. However, changes and cuts to services in a local area can lead to an interpreter's involvement in setting up community action groups, including in the area of language services provision, which suggests that an individual could move between different levels of activism and civic engagement, and hence roles, over the course of their involvement in the sector.

7.3 Professionalization and the voluntary sector

In some countries the non-profit sector has experienced significant change in recent decades as the role of the sector has evolved. For example, an important change in the UK concerns the increase in contracts between the government and the sector for the delivery of certain social care services, among others. A recent example in England is the partnership between the government and the Salvation Army to deliver services to support survivors of human trafficking. The contract approach has impacted the internal structures of organizations and led to increased professionalization of services and greater accountability, with some volunteers finding their informal support is no longer needed as roles across the organization have become more formalized and even remunerated in some cases (see Alcock et al. 2013).

These developments also concern dialogue interpreting provision; for instance, some interpreters who contact organizations to volunteer their time at no cost may have their offer rejected, not because their offer is not valued but because the organization needs to be able to rely on consistent service to meet what are often very complex service user needs. This draws attention to the fact that the sector offers variability in terms of opportunities, support and pay; like other workers, interpreters who work in the voluntary sector do not necessarily work on a pro bono basis, as illustrated in the case study below.

▲ COLLABORATIVE DIMENSIONS

Activity 10: Approaches to recruitment and training

You have been asked by the volunteer coordinator to help develop a recruitment and training policy for interpreters within a charitable organization.

A   Decide on the type of organization and the overall staffing profile, e.g. volunteer vs remunerated positions (look at the websites of different organizations for ideas, e.g. Caritas, International Committee of the Red Cross).
B   Write a sample job profile for a volunteer interpreter.
C   Devise an induction programme for new interpreters.
D   Consider the role of the volunteer coordinator in monitoring the work of interpreters, the resources they might need, and the range of activities that can support their work.

For further guidance on best practice in interpreter recruitment in the non-profit sector please see the materials on the Routledge Translation Studies Portal.

7.4 Case study: Freedom from Torture

This section concerns a case study of Freedom from Torture, an organization in the non-profit sector in the UK in which a substantial proportion of service users require interpreter mediation. In what follows the organization's approach to the training and use of interpreters is outlined, together with the organization's ethos of interpreter mediation. Note that the term *practitioner* is used to denote a staff member that provides therapeutic or other service to clients.

About the organization

Freedom from Torture was established in 1985, the year after the adoption of the UN Convention Against Torture in 1984, and was co-founded by Helen Bamber and five other founding members as the 'Medical Foundation for the Care Victims of Torture'. It has registered charity status in England and

Scotland. Its early work concerned the forensic medical documentation of the evidence of torture, but its scope soon broadened to include the provision of medical treatment, counselling and psychotherapy to survivors. Today the organization uses its experience to train others in the areas of judiciary, health, social services and education to be more aware of the needs of torture survivors. It supports torture survivors in speaking out about their situation to those in power, and to help break down negative attitudes toward those who seek refuge in the UK. It is the only human rights organization in the UK that uses the evidence of the torture survivors it treats to hold torturing states accountable internationally, such as its country reports on torture in Iran, Sri Lanka and the Democratic Republic of Congo.

Approach to interpreting: recruitment

In the very early days of the organization's operation, interpreters volunteered their services for free. However, it soon became apparent that the dialogue between interpreters and practitioners within the organization was a foundation for culturally sensitive therapeutic interventions, and that a reassuring environment in which service users feel safe was jointly established by practitioners and interpreters. As a result, interpreters were more formally integrated into the organization's structures and, since 1987, have been remunerated for their services. This serves to uphold several principles: first, that there is a professional commitment to the organization (for example, interpreters are required to take out professional indemnity insurance); second, that a level of responsibility and accountability is demonstrated, including a commitment to ongoing professional development.

The organization continues to receive a large number of offers from interpreters who wish to help and offer their time for free; however, the complexity of assignments and need for regular internal training and discussion means that the organization does not use unqualified interpreters or nonprofessional volunteers. Furthermore, in order to maintain commitment and retention levels among paid interpreters, it will not draw on volunteer services of qualified interpreters. Interpreters who work for the organization are encouraged to become involved in development activities and to support policy and advocacy work. To encourage such commitment, interpreters are paid to attend development and training events.

Neutrality and interpreting

Interpreters are recruited for their expressed commitment to human rights and are therefore not considered impartial outsiders. Intrinsic motivation is also present through the commitment to the organization's service users, through the desire to give back to others and a conviction that service users will benefit if they know someone shares their experiences to some extent. Interpreters' committed approach means that they are explicitly positioned as 'embedded' (i.e. an integral part of the organization), even if they are only involved infrequently in its work. For instance, on arriving for an assignment, interpreters are not required to wait in the service users' waiting area and instead are invited to mix with staff. The ability to see change and progress as a result of the organization's work and their interpreter mediation is an aspect that many interpreters report finding very rewarding and helps maintain their level of commitment to the organization. This contrasts with other types of domains in which interpreters often do not see the next stages in a service user's life or the outcomes of a service intervention.

The organization's work with torture survivors requires very high levels of interpersonal trust. The interpreter is viewed as a fundamental part of the trust-building process since their actions and presence are important to generating an atmosphere of safety, again showing that the usual protocols of interpreter neutrality are to a large extent adapted for the benefit of the service user. However, it is recognized that in some cases service users may be unsettled by the presence of an interpreter; for instance, the physical appearance of an interpreter might remind a service user of someone who did them great harm in the past, in which case the interpreter would be discharged from the case and a different interpreter brought in.

The organization makes strenuous efforts to ensure that the same interpreter is used over time, especially for therapeutic work. This is not necessarily considered an impairment to the interpreter's objectivity. In fact, the practitioners view the interpreter's objectivity as something that they need to pay close attention to and manage as part of the interaction with the service user's participation. In other words, the organization places emphasis on continuous dialogue during interpreter mediation – dialogue about the substance of the meeting (surviving torture) and about communication and feelings about the meetings themselves. As the service user's mood, state of mind and level of healing changes over time, the dynamics of the interaction between all parties will change as well. This means that in practice issues such as the interpreter's possible overidentification with the service user and the service user's attachment to the interpreter are subject to open (re-)negotiation and discussion.

Training

When the organization was initially established in 1985, there were very few interpreter training courses available and so training was largely acquired on the job. Over time, the importance of internal and external training provision has been recognized and incorporated into the organization's structures, particularly within its programmes dedicated to techniques of self-care that are particularly important to this type of high intensity and often harrowing work. Interpreters have thus been increasingly supported as the organization has evolved not only in relation to structures that support mental well-being, but also in relation to personal professional development that is designed to help both the interpreter and the practitioner in their joint work.

Since many interpreters are refugees that have had experiences similar to the service users, the organization has developed a particular philosophy of integration that encompasses the interpreters as much as the practitioners and service users. In practical terms this means efforts are made to prevent interpreters from feeling isolated within the organization, which can often happen in public service interpreting work due to its freelance nature. Since many interpreters have friends or family who have experienced torture or are themselves survivors, the organization seeks to avoid replicating feelings of isolation that were felt during the period of suffering and transit. The underlying principle is that interpreter well-being is crucial to quality service delivery to the client.

Reflection on the interpreter's work within the organization has led to a number of training-related initiatives designed to foster a clear sense of organizational identity. For example, the 'Language Day' event is held annually for all clinical practitioners and interpreters as a dedicated space for discussion of communication-related issues on different themes; examples include 'bonds of identification in therapy', 'language and power', 'cross-cultural communication in therapy', 'verbal and non-verbal expressions' and 'practitioner's perceptions of different service user groups'.

Language groups are also held for interpreters and bilingual practitioners as fora for sharing cultural and linguistic knowledge, and to discuss and devise strategies to address linguistically challenging and/or difficult issues that may occur in sessions with clients. The organization covers approximately 50 languages that include Turkish, Kurdish, Arabic and increasingly Amharic and Tigrinyan. Interpreters' meetings are held regularly throughout the year and serve as a venue for interpreters' presentations about issues relevant to the clients' particular geographical regions. This helps to outline cultural and linguistic traits that can further interpreters' knowledge about clients. It also encourages interpreters to research changes in the local context and in language (e.g. changes in relation to the human rights situation to facilitate understanding of the experiences of newly arrived service users). This space is also used for discussions of academic papers related to interpreting in therapy. It provides an opportunity to reflect on areas in which interpreters feel the need for adjustments; further training provides them with a sense of belonging in spite of their self-employed status and their work on an 'as required' basis.

Feedback from service users

In research that is unique in the UK, the organization conducted an internal evaluation of its interpreting services by eliciting the views of practitioners, interpreters and service users. The findings prompted the adoption of important substantive measures to further enhance the joint work between interpreters and practitioners, thus benefiting clients. Of particular importance to the service user's perspective is the way in which issues of gender are managed since this can affect the level of disclosure on the part of the service user. Service users are encouraged to inform staff if they do not feel comfortable with the interpreter's gender; this yields information not only on gender issues but also on the asymmetries that can arise in the triadic relation. For example, there are times when the educational levels of the service user are visibly higher than the interpreter's and must be managed by the practitioner and the interpreter; the management process is also often carried out in negotiations with the client.

▲ COLLABORATIVE DIMENSIONS

Activity 11: Navigating role

A   With a partner or group discuss the sort of risks you think could arise for interpreters who are former service users within the organization mentioned above.

B   Consider the possible impact that a difference in educational level could have on interpreted events, especially where the LLP service user is more educated than the interpreter. Discuss the range of actions open to the practitioner to mitigate the impact.

C   Discuss the extent to which the organization's approach to interpreter neutrality challenges your understanding of the interpreter's role.

D   Consider the impact of unpaid volunteer interpreting on the ethos of this organization and its goals.

8 Conclusion

Interpreting in social care-related settings possibly encompasses the widest range of settings discussed in this guide and as a result poses some of the greatest challenges in relation to professional development planning. In these settings, the unpredictability of the environment and the mood and response of limited proficiency speakers to challenging personal circumstances requires interpreters to build stamina and resilience and develop preparation strategies for handling both routine and extreme events.

Despite the lack of research in these settings and evidence of interpreter performance, insight from cases such as the death of Victoria Climbié help to support the development of domain-specific competencies, not least in the areas of **expectation management** and understanding of **risk**. Furthermore, increased commitment to promoting children's voices in situations of abuse and neglect identified in some geonational contexts shines a light on the importance of suitably prepared interpreters for cross-cultural events in these settings. Preparation extends to understanding the ethics of role and the responsibility of interpreters to view welfare protection as a shared responsibility, and the complex psycho-social and environmental pressures that may arise in this domain.

The changing face of the voluntary and non-profit sectors are opening up new opportunities for interpreters that in some cases also call for conceptualizations of interpreter neutrality to be revisited. The approach taken to interpreter mediation in organizations like Freedom from Torture provides useful starting points for reflection on the nature and range of development activity needed in social care settings and understanding the supporting role that organizations can play in helping interpreters both to provide setting-appropriate language services and maintain good levels of **psycho-social health.**

Notes

1 Casework is carried out by a type of social worker employed by a range of organizations to provide advocacy, information and other services to individuals, families and community groups.

2 Family group conferences have been adopted in child protection practice in a number of countries such as Australia, Ireland, Great Britain and the United States.

3 The scenario takes place in England. The phrase 'to be detained under the Mental Health Act' means that approved mental healthcare professionals have the power to admit a person to hospital (under a section of the 1983 Mental Health Act that applies in England and Wales (amended in 2007)) if they think necessary and provided they follow appropriate procedures. In other countries terms such as 'involuntary commitment', 'involuntary treatment and detention' and 'involuntary placement' are used but procedures and regulations will differ according to the legislation in force.

4 According to the Care Quality Commission in England, 'safeguarding' is a term that means to protect people's health, well-being and human rights.

5 A 'permanency hearing' is a term used in the United States of America and refers to a court hearing designed to review the status and determine a permanent plan for the placement of children who have been placed in out-of-home care, including foster care.

6 For example: www.mentalhelp.net/articles/issues-in-international-adoptions/ (accessed 21 May 2015).

References

Alcock, P., Butt, C. and Macmillan, R. (2013) *Unity in Diversity: what is the future for the third sector?* Third Sector Futures Dialogue 2012–2013, Birmingham: TSRC.

Alink, L.R.A., Euser, S., Ijzendoorn, M.H. and Bakermans-Kranenburg, M.J. (2013) 'Is Elevated Risk of Child Maltreatment in Immigrant Families Associated with Socioeconomic Status? Evidence from three sources', *International Journal of Psychology*, 48 (2): 117–27.

Allen, G. and Langford, D. (2008) *Effective Interviewing in Social Work and Social Care: a practical guide*, Basingstoke and New York: Palgrave Macmillan.

Baker, M. (2013) 'Translation as an Alternative Space for Political Action', *Social Movement Studies*, 12 (1): 23–47.

Be My Parent (2008) 'A Success Story'. Online. Available at: www.bemyparent.org.uk/features/a-success-story,249,AR.html (accessed 9 May 2015).

Ben-Ari, A. and Strier, R. (2010) 'Rethinking Cultural Competence: what can we learn from Levinas?' *British Journal of Social Work*, 40 (7): 2155–67.

Bloom, M., Fischer, J. and Orme, J.G. (1999) *Evaluating Practice: guidelines for the accountable professional*, 3rd edn, Boston: Allyn and Bacon.

Boéri, J. (2008) 'A Narrative Account of the Babels vs. Naumann Controversy: competing perspectives on activism in conference interpreting', *The Translator*, 14 (1): 21–50.

Brown, J.D., George, N., Sintzel, J. and St Arnault, D. (2009) 'Benefits of Cultural Matching in Foster Care', *Children and Youth Services Review*, 31 (9): 1019–24.

Bulcaen, C. and Blommaert, J. (1997) *Eindrapport VFIK project 307: begeleiding van migrantenvrouwen en -meisjes in centra voor residentieel welzijn*, Antwerp: International Pragmatics Association.

Burke, S. and Paxman, M. (2008) *Children and Young People from Non-English Speaking Backgrounds in Out-of-Home Care in NSW: a research report*, Ashfield: Centre for Parenting and Research.

Capello, D.C. (2006) 'Recruiting Hispanic Foster Parents: issues of culture, language and social policy', *Families in Society*, 87 (4): 529–35.

Chand, A. (2003) 'Race and the Laming Report on Victoria Climbié: lessons for inter-professional policy and practice', *Journal of Integrated Care*, 11 (4): 28–37.

Chand, A. (2005) 'Do you Speak English? Language barriers in child protection social work with minority ethnic families', *British Journal of Social Work*, 35 (6): 807–21.

Cleaver, H., Cawson, P., Gorin, S. and Walker, S. (eds) (2009) *Safeguarding Children: a shared responsibility*, Hoboken, NJ: Wiley.

Cox, P. (2011) 'Issues in Safeguarding Refugee and Asylum-seeking Children and Young People: research and practice', *Child Abuse Review*, 20 (5): 341–60.

D'Cruz, H., Gillingham, P. and Melendez, S. (2007) 'Reflexivity: a concept and its meanings for practitioners working with children and families', *Critical Social Work*, 8: 1.

De Manuel Jerez, J. (2010) 'From Ethics to Politics: towards a new generation of citizen interpreters', in J. Boéri and C. Maier (eds) *Translation/Interpreting and Social Activism*, Granada: ECOS, traductores e interprétes por la solidaridad.

Fontes, L.A. (2005) *Child Abuse and Culture: working with diverse families*, New York and London: The Guilford Press.

Fontes, L.A. (2010) 'Interviews for Suspected Child Maltreatment: tips for foreign language interpreters', Bridging Refugee Youth and Children's Services Wednesday Webinar Series. Online. Available at: https://usccb.adobeconnect.com/_a8334 22997/p70804945/?launcher=falseandfcsContent=trueandpbMode=normal (accessed 1 May 2015).

Garcia, A., Aisenberg, E. and Harachi, T. (2012) 'Pathways to Service Inequalities among Latinos in the Child Welfare System', *Children and Youth Services Review*, 34 (5): 1060–71.

Health and Care Professions Council (2012) *Standards of Conduct, Performance and Ethics*. Online. Available at: www.hcpc-uk.org/assets/documents/10003B6EStanda rdsofconduct,performanceandethics.pdf (accessed 9 May 2015).

HM Government (2015) *Working Together to Safeguard Children: a guide to inter-agency working to safeguard and promote the welfare of children*, London: The Stationery Office Department for Education.

Humphries, B. (2006) 'Supporting Asylum Seekers: practice and ethical issues for health and social welfare professionals', *Irish Journal of Applied Social Studies*, 7 (2): 76–86.

King, A. (2011) 'Fostering Asylum Seekers: their past is a foreign country', 20 December 2011, *The Independent*. Online. Available at: www.independent.co.uk/life-style/ health-and-families/features/fostering-asylum-seekers-their-past-is-a-foreign-country-6279382.html (accessed 9 May 2015).

Knott, C. and Scragg T. (eds) (2010) *Reflective Practice in Social Work*, 2nd edn, Exeter: Learning Matters.

LaFromboise, T.D. and Dixon, D.N. (1981) 'American Indian Perception: trustworthiness in a counseling interview', *Journal of Counseling Psychology*, 28 (2): 135–9.

Lai, M. and Mulayim, S. (2010) 'Training Refugees to become Interpreters for Refugees', *International Journal for Translation and Interpreting Research*, 2 (1): 48–60.

Lamb, K.A. (2008) 'Exploring Adoptive Motherhood: adoption-seeking among Hispanic and non-Hispanic white women', *Adoption Quarterly*, 11 (3): 155–75.

Lamb, M.E., Orbach, Y., Hershkowitz, I., Esplin, P.W. and Horowitz, D. (2007) 'Structured Forensic Interview Protocols Improve the Quality and Informativeness of Investigative Interviews with Children: a review of research using the NICHD investigative interviewing protocol', *Child Abuse and Neglect*, 31 (11–12): 1201–31.

Loxton, J., Shirran, A. and Hothersall, S.J. (2010) 'Risk', in S.J. Hothersall and M. Maas-Lowit (eds) *Need, Risk and Protection in Social Work Practice*, Exeter: Learning Matters.

Luster, T., Saltarelli, A.J., Rana, M., Qin, D.B., Bates, L., Burdick, K. and Baird, D. (2009) 'The Experiences of Sudanese Unaccompanied Minors in Foster Care', *Journal of Family Psychology*, 23 (3): 386–95.

Mbagaya, C., Oburu, P. and Bakermans-Kranenburg, M.J. (2013) 'Child Physical Abuse and Neglect in Kenya, Zambia and the Netherlands: a cross-cultural comparison of prevalence, psychopathological sequelae and mediation by PTSS', *International Journal of Psychology*, 48 (2): 95–107.

Miu, C.Y. (2008) 'Exploring Cultural Tensions in Cross-cultural Social Work Practice', *Social Work*, 53 (4): 317–28.

Munro, E. (1996) 'Avoidable and Unavoidable Mistakes in Child Protection Work', *British Journal of Social Work*, 26 (6): 793–808.

Munro, E. (2011) 'The Munro Review of Child Protection: Final Report. A child-centred system'. Online. Available at: www.gov.uk/government/uploads/system/uploads/attachment_data/file/175391/Munro-Review.pdf (accessed 20 February 2015).

Munro, E.R. and Manful, E. (2012) *Safeguarding Children: a comparison of England's data with that of Australia, Norway and the United States*, London: Department for Education.

National Association of Social Workers (2007) *Indicators for the Achievement of the NASW Standards for Cultural Competence in Social Work Practice*. Online. Available at: www.socialworkers.org/practice/standards/NASWCulturalStandardsIndicators 2006.pdf (accessed 9 May 2015).

Olohan, M. (2012) 'Volunteer Translation and Altruism in the Context of a Nineteenth Century Scientific Journal', *The Translator*, Special Issue: Non-professionals Translating and Interpreting, 18 (2): 193–215.

Osterling, K.L., D'andrade, A. and Austin, M.J. (2008) 'Understanding and Addressing Racial/ethnic Disproportionality in the Front End of the Child Welfare System', *Journal of Evidence-Based Social Work*, 5 (1–2): 9–30.

Owen, M. and Farmer, E. (1996) 'Child Protection in a Multi-racial Context', *Policy and Politics*, 24 (3): 299–313.

Parris, M. (2012) *An Introduction to Social Work Practice: a practical handbook*, Maidenhead: McGraw Hill, Open University Press.

Parton, N. and Kirk, S. (2009) 'The Nature and Purposes of Social Work', in I. Shaw, K. Briar-Lawson, J. Orme and R. Ruckdeschel (eds) *The Sage Handbook of Social Work Research*, London: Sage.

Pérez-González, L. and Susam-Saraeva, Ş. (eds) (2012) 'Introduction: Non-professionals Translating and Interpreting: participatory and engaged perspectives', *The Translator*, Special Issue: Non-professionals Translating and Interpreting: Participatory and Engaged Perspectives, 18 (2): 149–65.

Potocky-Tripodi, M. (2002) *Best Practices for Social Work with Refugees and Immigrants*, New York: Columbia University Press.

Robinson, L. (2007) *Cross-cultural Child Development for Social Workers: an introduction*, Basingstoke: Palgrave Macmillan.

Sawrikar, P. (2013) 'A Qualitative Study on the Pros and Cons of Ethnically Matching Culturally and Linguistically Diverse (CALD) Families and Child Protection Caseworkers', *Children and Youth Services Review*, 35 (2): 321–31.

Secretaries of State (Secretary of State for Health and Secretary of State for the Home Department) (2003) *The Victoria Climbié Inquiry: report of an inquiry by Lord Laming*, London: The Stationery Office.

Stalker, K. (2003) 'Managing Risk and Uncertainty in Social Work: a literature review', *Journal of Social Work*, 3 (2): 211–33.

Thoburn, J., Wilding, J. and Watson, J. (2000) *Family Support in Cases of Emotional Maltreatment and Neglect*, London: Stationery Office.

Tipton, R. (2012) 'A Socio-theoretical Account of Interpreter-mediated Activity with Specific Reference to the Social Service Context: reflection and reflexivity', Unpublished PhD thesis, University of Salford.

Tipton, R. (2014) 'Perceptions of the "Occupational Other": interpreters, social workers and intercultures', *British Journal of Social Work*, doi: 10.1093/bjsw/bcu136.

Trevithick, P. (2000) *Social Work Skills: a practice handbook*, Buckingham and Philadelphia: Open University Press.

van der Haar, M. (2007) *Ma(r)king Differences in Dutch Social Work: professional discourse and ways of relating to clients in context*, Amsterdam: Dutch University Press.

Wilkan, U. (2002) *Generous Betrayal: politics of culture in the new Europe*, Chicago, IL: University of Chicago Press.

Recommended reading

Fontes, L.A. (2009) *Interviewing Clients across Cultures: a practitioner's guide*, New York: The Guilford Press.

Kelly, E. and Bokhari, F. (eds) (2012) *Safeguarding Children from Abroad: refugee, asylum seeking and trafficked children in the UK*, London and Philadelphia: Jessica Kingsley Publishers.

7   Faith-related interpreting

We organized a procession starting from the cathedral and walking to a plaza in the city where, with the help of an interpreter, we announced the love of Christ. I was impressed by the zeal that the youth have for evangelization. I experienced again that, whenever I share the faith with others, the Lord deepens my own faith.[1]

(John Benson, World Youth Day, Rio de Janeiro 2014)

1 Introduction

Faith-related interpreting, also called *interpreting in religious settings* or *religious interpreting*, refers to oral translation provided during religious liturgies, ceremonies and prayer meetings, as well as interpreting for preachers and religious and lay missionaries, interpreting during pilgrimages and during other faith-related gatherings such as congresses, synods and religious orders' chapters.

The term *church interpreting*, according to Pöchhacker (2011) introduced by Brian Harris in his unpublished taxonomy of interpreting in 1997 and then readopted in recent research on non-professional interpreting (Pérez-González and Susam-Saraeva 2012), needs to be used carefully since it seems that its meaning has been narrowed down to interpreting inside a building/during a service for Christian congregations. However, interpreting services have been and continue also to be used in synagogues, for Islamic Hajjs to Mecca and in other non-Christian contexts. While approaches explored in this chapter can be applied across creeds and denominations, the primary focus is on interpreting in Christian settings.

The importance of the message to be conveyed and personal involvement seem to make faith-related interpreting different from other types of interpreting, but this is open to question. James states that:

Church interpreters, feeling intimidated, tend to be ostracized by and do not mingle with interpreters holding national credentials. However, that will not stop the church interpreters from doing what they do. The reason is that many, if not all, feel that what they do is in response to a 'calling' or a 'burden' meaning a divine responsibility toward their duty in service to God.

(1998: 16)

In this chapter, through discussing key concepts in faith-related interpreting, its subtypes, and the level of preparedness to work as an interpreter in this often-overlooked setting, we propose to answer the questions that James (1998) and Grindford (1998) raise in their respective overviews of religious interpreting in American Sign Language in *Views*, a monthly publication of the Registry of Interpreters for the Deaf in the United States:

* Are you interpreting in religious settings and churches and feel you cannot identify yourself as being involved in such areas?
* Do you consider yourself a church interpreter who wants to learn and is willing to learn, yet feels ostracized by the profession?
* Do religious interpreters tend to have a bad reputation among professionals within the interpreting community?
* Does one need to be a member of a denomination, sect or even congregation to do a credible interpreting job? If so, should s/he be paid then, or not?

As in the other chapters, practices that seem most appropriate for each subtype are outlined, and further readings are recommended at the end.

2 Faith-related interpreting: scope, nature and modes

Interpreting is considered to be one of the oldest professions in the world, and this particular subtype of oral translating for believers in different religions dates back centuries. In the book of Genesis, Joseph, as a high Egyptian officer, spoke to his brothers through an interpreter (Genesis 42: 23). The word used in Hebrew is *melitz*. Lewis (2004: 19) states that in

> one of the earliest translations from Hebrew text into Aramaic, the word *melitz* is rendered as *meturgeman.*... A *meturgeman* is a translator; the word is old, and goes back to Assyrian, where *ramu* means 'to speak', *rigmu* is 'a word' and the *taf'el* form indicates one who facilitates communication. This word *meturgeman*, also *turgeman*, passed from Aramaic to Hebrew, to Arabic, to Turkish, to Italian, to French, to English, and many other modern languages.

The Hebrew word *Targum* from the same root describes the earliest oral translations from Hebrew into Aramaic. By the first century BC, Aramaic had replaced Hebrew as the common language in the land of Israel. The Torah had to be made accessible to the congregation.

In the modern era, one of the primary fields in which interpreters worked was missions and the conquering of new territories, which were often parallel enterprises. Throughout the centuries, missionaries accompanied the expeditions of the European Kingdoms where interpreters, whether captured enemies, slaves, children of mixed marriages or officially appointed diplomatic representatives, were used as both brokers between religions and cross-culture communicators in an interchangeable manner (Chrobak 2012). For example, in addition to preaching the Gospel, many Jesuit priests became linguists, translators and interpreters. In the Ottoman Empire the *dragomans* were held in high respect since their office incorporated diplomatic as well as linguistic and confessional duties, and thus had an enormous impact on the Ottoman political and religious agenda. Later, interpreters used as cultural brokers and military scouts were also often partially used as interpreters for religious purposes.

 RESEARCH

Activity 1: Professional background

Look up the definition of *dragoman* and draw up a map of their tasks, then compare it to your understanding of the responsibilities of a religious interpreter based on your own experiences. You can also use the resource *Dragomans and 'Turkish Literature': The Making of a Field of Inquiry* by E. Natalie Rothman (2013).

In the twenty-first century, in the Catholic Church the Vatican City has its own team of interpreters that serves during the apostolic visits of the Pope and universal congresses of the Catholic religion, primarily International Eucharistic Congresses, Synods, World Family Encounters and so on. Religious congregations (e.g. Franciscans, Salesians, Verbum Dei Missionaries) usually designate the Italian language as the main language of their congregations, even though English is being used increasingly as the official language of some orders due to the growth of the vocations coming from Asian and African countries. However, for Chapters, congresses and formal gatherings, where Latin was used as the official language of the gathering until the end of the 1980s, members of the orders appoint multilingual members of their orders as interpreters.

Interpreting is used in all modes during World Youth Days, which were inaugurated by St John Paul II. Taizé, a monastic order based in an ecumenical prayer centre located close to Macon, France is one example of a religious setting in which volunteer interpreters translate during young people's sharing in small groups, as well as during the organization of the Taizé Youth Meetings that take place each year around the end of December or beginning of January in different cities across Europe (e.g. Strasbourg in 2013, Prague in 2014, Valencia in 2015).

In US Protestant churches a new revivalist and evangelization movement has been on the rise over the last three decades, primarily reaching out to

Russia, the countries of the former Soviet Union, several Asian countries and South America, mainly Brazil, where it has been viewed as proselytizing by the Catholic Church. Hild (2012) in her abstract of 'Interpreting the Prophetic: loyalty, authority and inspiration', for a paper presented at the 1st International Conference on Non-Professional Interpreting and Translation, notes that the

> establishment, growth and internationalization of the Christian revivalist churches has recently given rise to new liturgical practices, worship styles and teachings, fostered by active links between North American leadership centers and worldwide communities and religious groups. An important consequence of the continued and intensive growth of revivalist Christianity over the past 30 years is the emergence of new forms of bilingual interpreter-mediated intercultural liturgical communication.

Also, many Protestant communities in Germanic and Scandinavian countries have been reaching out to the new immigrants from post-Soviet bloc countries who, with the exception of Poles, come with little to no religious background and thus have a need for translation services within their host countries.

In the abstract of her oral presentation on 'Church Interpreting in Germany: making a case for a combination of conversation analysis and grounded theory in ethnographic fieldwork', Giannoutsou (2012) describes the situation in Germany:

> Church interpreting – i.e., oral mediation of the sermon into another language than the language used by the preacher – is a routine practice in the growing sector of Evangelical and Pentecostal/Charismatic churches in Germany and a powerful instrument of their global mission culture. Interestingly, little is known about the emerging Evangelical subculture in Germany and Evangelical practices of language mediation are, too, significantly under-researched in terms of their cultural, performative and linguistic characteristics. Research on the dynamic appearance of new groups in the German religious landscape necessitates an explorative approach and resists methodologies where empirical data just serves as a token to confirm or refute established assumptions about a particular group.

In many African countries, evangelical preachers use consecutive interpreters on a regular basis to reach out to the community in their native African languages and pidgin languages (Harris 2009c). In the Arabic-speaking world, Saudi Arabia has been noting the need for interpreters for pilgrims coming to Mecca and Medina according to Taibi (2014). Interest in religious tourism and activities in related fields such as the work of travel agencies, organization of accompanying exhibitions, and language services has been acknowledged by the Catholic Church as one of the elements of intercultural integration in Europe, and was discussed as such at the 2013 conference[2] organized in Cracow, a city considered the European capital of religious tourism.

3 Key concepts

Research on religious interpreting in Christian settings conducted during the first decade of the twenty-first century has demonstrated that interpreters' performance dimensions (see Chapter 1, Section 6), especially **involvement**, **visibility** and **co-construction** resurface as key issues in this domain. Involvement can be defined in relation to God and in relation to the preacher/presider and to the congregation. To a certain degree, this conceptualization may be drawing on an old Christian tradition that explains the symbolism of the cross, hence confirming that domain studies often borrow their conceptualizations and paradigms from the area they explore.

> Christian theology, in maintaining that the God who created and sustains the world is the same God who 'so loved the world that he gave his only-begotten Son, that whoever believes in him should not perish but have eternal life' (John 3:16), requires both perspectives, the **vertical** and the **horizontal**.
>
> (Preslar 2014, authors' emphasis)

Preslar (2014) explains that the glory of God as manifested in biblical history is most fundamental in that this precedes and is presupposed by specifically redemptive history, and focuses on the various stages of biblical history in a vertical relation to God, while the history of salvation is most fundamental in that it involves a deeper and more intimate relation of Creator to creation (culminating in the Incarnation and Passion) and the horizontal aspect of this same history, i.e. the various events or stages of biblical history are considered in relation to one another. Also, the vertical dimension of the cross is seen as a person's intimate relation with God manifested in one's response to His love and commitment to Him through prayer, through searching for and doing His will, worship and thanksgiving. The horizontal dimension refers to treating the neighbour as a brother, the close community and all of humanity as one family of the children of God, and involves forgiveness, service and efforts to build unity. Hence a similar up-down and right-left paradigm can be found in the work of an interpreter. This is evident in recommendations for characteristics of a good religious interpreter and how s/he should perform in various situations that are addressed in the following subsections.

We can therefore identify two **vertical** dimensions of interpreting, **God's call** and **co-creative power/co-creation** and two **horizontal** aspects, **co-performance** and **service/participation**. While rooted in the Christian symbol of the cross, this typology appears to reflect the involvement dimensions of faith-related performance that can be applied across various beliefs.

3.1 God's call

Interpreters work for God as well as the speaker, but primarily for God and then, as a result of their response to God, for the audience. One could also subsume under this heading the view that the interpreter has to be a Christian (or practising that particular religion) in order to have lived out the terms and then interpret them (Hokkanen 2012). Furthermore, in his book on interpreting in Christian settings Owen (2014) states that the implication is that a relationship to God must dominate every sphere of interpreting, whether in action, thought or emotion, and that interpreters must evaluate their personal attitude to identify and eliminate whatever is of higher priority than a focus on the Lord. Owen gives a detailed analysis of both Old and New Testament figures and offers practical advice for both sign and spoken language interpreters, presenting Ezra (Nehemiah 8:5–8) and Daniel (Daniel 5) as interpreters' models. Owen's views of the concept of the interpreter and her/his responsibilities come from a premise that includes exegesis as an integral part of the interpreter's role, which can be defined as the '**guardian of the message**', which can be viewed as parallel to the Jewish people considering themselves the guardians of Torah, God's law. Owen does not advocate for meaning changes, but to 'give the sense' ('gave the sense',[3] 'giving the meaning'[4] or 'interpreting it'[5] – שָׂכֶל וְשׂוֹם[6]) to the message as he himself interprets the Bible passage from Nehemiah (8:8). Another passage widely discussed by biblical scholars in relation to language interpretation as a divine gift is 1 Corinthians 14:27–28. Depending on the Christian tradition (Pentecostal, Catholic, Orthodox), this passage is understood as simply conveying the message or explaining a deeper meaning of what was expressed prophetically, sometimes even in the same language that the entire congregation speaks. Referring to that Scripture passage, Owen (2014: 115) adds:

> Because interpreting was listed within the spiritual gifts distributed to the Church at Corinth, we can surmise that either the regular interpreters had the Lord's help or a new breed of interpreters was selected by the Lord who were given a supernatural gift to interpret languages.

One of Owen's interpreting principles is illumination. He states that those who become church interpreters are eligible perhaps more by orientation of mind and heart than by qualifications, and continues, 'I may have insufficient confidence in my own intellect, but can be assured that God Himself will expedite my study to bring light to the words of Scripture'. He also proposes a code of ethics called 'Steps of Interpretation' developed from the Bible, and offers practical applications. In these practical applications, in addition to understanding the meaning of the source language, emulating the purpose of the source text, and cross-referencing different Bible target language versions to find the best equivalence, he reminds interpreters that the Bible itself exhorts the interpreter to have a particular attitude toward Scripture and summarizes it in a table (2014: 181).

Similarly, in the ethics and training manuals on working with interpreters on the website of Jim Harper's International Christian Interpreter Association,[7] there is a paragraph on the characteristics a good religious interpreter should have.

- Have a servant attitude and heart. You are providing a service that helps other people.
- [Be a]ble to be sensitive to the moving of the Holy Spirit and to the people you serve.
- [Be a]ble to transfer information without any personal reaction.
- [Be a]ble to convey the anointed message without hindrances:

The anointed message flows:

1   From the heart of God.
2   To the heart of the speaker.
3   Through the heart of the interpreter.
4   To the heart of the audience.

The association's Summary of Training states:

- Know what interpreting is and when you should be in an interpreting role.
- Always be prepared for an interpreting assignment. You are a professional.
- A good interpreter will hardly be noticed and will be in high demand.
- Are you just doing a job or has God called you into the ministry?
- Be led by and flow with the Holy Spirit while interpreting.
- You are an able minister, not of the letter that kills, but of the spirit that gives life (2 Cor. 3:5–6).

According to this association, the work of an interpreter is so intrinsic to the preaching of the Gospel that it is elevated to a ministry for which one can be anointed. This goes far beyond sharing the beliefs or being a member of a particular congregation.

3.2 Co-creative power

This power of co-creating through word, the illocutionary dimension as presented by Austin (1962), refers to the new quality being created due to the speech act, performed during the liturgical ceremonies, and to the pragmatic consequences of the act. It is the performative aspect of an utterance, the power of the word, which constitutes, produces and causes. It is most notable during the sacraments, e.g. baptism, marriage and also blessings and exorcisms.

3.3 Co-performance

Downie (2014a) emphasizes that almost from the beginning of the research on the interpreter's role in church settings, as seen in Rayman (2007), and Vigouroux (2010), there has been an awareness that the interpreter works in partnership with the speaker. Downie (2014a) for his part explores the topic of seeing the work of interpreting a sermon as a part of the sermon as a means to raising the status of church interpreting but also to opening up new avenues for homiletics. He advocates for a more proactive attitude of both the interpreter and the preacher in such situations stating that the interpreters may need to be encouraged to grow as co-preachers, and that the same kinds of training and support as are routinely available for preachers should be extended to them.

> Likewise, preachers could be encouraged to see and treat interpreters as partners in preaching, rather than as conduits through which the sermon gets mysteriously transferred into another language. Simplifying somewhat, this represents a paradigm shift from preaching *through* interpreters to preaching *with* interpreters.
>
> (Downie 2014a: 66, emphasis in original)

According to him, this is a fundamental challenge to traditional views of interpreting since it contradicts the idea of the interpreter as a neutral party, and instead gives them a responsibility similar to that of a source language speaker. In addition, performance often involves the interpreter being expected to agree with what the speaker is saying. This leads to interpreters sometimes making strategic omissions or shortening segments to avoid offence. However, Downie (2014a) adds that prescriptive researchers Musyoka and Karanja (2014) and Odhiambo *et al.* (2013) view them as errors and one, Adewuni (2010), even argues that such issues mean that professional interpreters should be used instead.

In her study on the simultaneous interpreting of a pastor's French sermon into English at a Congolese Pentecostal church in Cape Town, South Africa, Vigouroux (2010) suggests that 'a close examination of **participant roles** shows that although these may appear to be predetermined by the interpretee-interpreter format of the sermon, speaking roles are actually fluid and negotiated' (authors' emphasis). She submits that an important role of the church interpreter is to convey the pastor's inspiration from the Holy Spirit and reach out to the potential audience absent from the here and now of the service. The interpreter's high emotional engagement helps convey this inspiration prospectively to the audience and retroactively to the pastor himself. A good illustration of this concept is an excerpt from Harris's blog entry about a preaching interpretation between two local languages in Buea, Cameroon:

In front of the crowd a stage had been erected, and on it were just two men, the centre of rapt attention. I stopped to watch. Both men were Africans. Both were wearing black suits. There was not much difference between them of height or build, but one was younger. Both were carrying a black book in the right hand. Both were haranguing the crowd for a couple of minutes at time, alternately. They had similar voices. They made the same gestures. In fact they were speaking different languages, but I couldn't distinguish that. It was as if they were engaged in an impassioned mimicry of one another.... So far so good, but which was the speaker and which the interpreter? Either of them, by his strong voice, his intonation, his body language, appearance and dress, could have passed for preacher. They stood there side by side, neither showing deference. However, another question to my informant confirmed what I might have deduced: that the interpreter was the younger of the two. He, like his preacher model, put on a rousing performance that lasted for another half hour. 'Are all the church interpreters like this?' I asked my informant. 'Oh yes', she replied, 'How else could they inspire the congregation to turn to Jesus?'

(Harris 2009c)

3.4 Service

When analysing simultaneous interpreting offered by non-professional volunteer interpreters (see also Chapter 5, Section 4) in the Tampere Pentecostal Church, Finland, Hokkanen (2012) concludes that interpreting is understood within Pentecostalism as a service not only to God but also to its members. Similarly, Owen (2014) emphasizes that the aim of the church interpreter should always be the spiritual edification of the target language recipients. The concluding observations to his book discuss target recipient expectations, and highlight this concept of service to the other. This includes the reward and fulfilment of the interpreter because s/he answers the call and thus the mission is accomplished, the faithful have been edified, and there is a spiritual gain pouring out from the relation of the servant and the served:

It is among the best feelings in the world because interpreters working in the church cherish the message and want to share it with the congregation. After the meeting, notwithstanding how well interpreters assess their performance, a sense of achievement is often strongly felt, mixed with a relief in completion. Then, if the impact of Ezra's third stage, 'made clear to the understanding' is evident, there is mutual spiritual blessing.

(Owen 2014: 247–8)

RESEARCH

Activity 2: Interpreting or interpretation

Interpreter is also the term for an exegetist, one who analyses and explains religious meaning, who makes meaning more accessible. Following this tradition, Ezra is considered by some practitioners of religious interpreting as a model in the Bible, even though serving as a language interpreter was not his main or only role. Read the story of Ezra from the Bible (Nehemiah 8) and the explanation below. In Hebrew the name Ezra, עֶזְרָא, means 'help, helper, God helps'.

> This Ezra went up from Babylon – with the king's consent and commission. And he was a ready scribe in the law of Moses – He is called a scribe, as Buxtorf observes in his Tiberias, not from writing and describing, but from declaring and explicating those things that are contained in the Scripture. For, as סֵפֶר, sepher, signifies a book, so סוֹפֵר, sopher, signifies one skilful and learned in that book, an interpreter and teacher out of it. And, there being no book comparable to the book of the law, therefore Sopher became a name of great dignity, and signified one that taught God's law, and expounded it to his people. Thus, in the New Testament, the scribes were those who instructed the people in the law. It is said he was a ready scribe, because he was expert in the law, and understood it thoroughly, both in all things belonging to the priesthood, and to the civil power; in which he was so well versed, that he could give a ready account of any part of it. The Jews say, he collected and collated all the copies of the law, and published an accurate edition of it, with all the books that were given by divine inspiration, and so made up the canon of the Old Testament. Moses in Egypt, and Ezra in Babylon, were wonderfully fitted for eminent service in the church. This was the second time that Ezra came up from Babylon, for he came up at first with Zerubbabel, as we learn from Nehemiah 12:1, and probably returned to Babylon to persuade those who had stayed behind to come up to Jerusalem, and to obtain some further assistance from the king. According to the hand of the Lord his God upon him – God not only stirred up Ezra to this undertaking, but was so favourable to him as to incline the king to give a gracious answer to his petition.[8]

A   Do you think that a religious interpreter should only be a conduit, or would you rather follow Ezra's model? Do you think that you could be an involved interpreter in your own congregation or would your own understanding of your religion/beliefs influence your interpreting in that context?

B   Would it be easier or more difficult to interpret for a religious leader of a denomination that you do not belong to? How involved could you be if you were interpreting for a denomination that has beliefs/theology similar to your own religious convictions but is still considered erroneous?

C   After you write down your thoughts, try to discuss them with a peer interpreter of a different religion.

While these four involvement issues, God's call, co-creative power, co-
performance and service, seem to be the main concepts that affect the
outcome of an interpreted religious event, other aspects, such as motivation,
degree of theological knowledge, level of maturity in one's faith and interpreting experience in other settings, should also be taken into consideration.
These will vary depending on the type of religious interpreting. In Section 1
caution was advised as far as applying the term *church interpreting* to refer to
all religious language brokering activities, or as interchangeable with *religious
interpreting*. In the following sections, looking back at this activity that has
accompanied humanity for a thousand years and that in certain eras (e.g.
New World discoveries, evangelization of Asia) has been better documented
than any other community-oriented interpreting, four subtypes of faith-
related interpreting that occur in the twenty-first century are presented, thus
also demonstrating why 'church interpreting' as an umbrella term seems
insufficient, if not limiting and excluding.

4   Subtypes of interpreting in religious settings

Based on practices that appear most frequently in the twenty-first century
across the globe and across religions, various types of faith-related interpreting can be identified, depending on the context in which they occur and the
purpose they serve. With the intention that the following taxonomy can be
applied to different faiths and denominations, we propose four subtypes of
interpreting in religious settings depending on purpose/intended impact,
degree of canonical rigour, and location: **liturgical interpreting, missionary
interpreting, pilgrimage interpreting** and **interpreting for formation**. Each
subtype can include different modes of interpreting.

4.1 Liturgical interpreting

Liturgical interpreting refers to interpreting sermons, homilies and prayers
when the source language used in the liturgy differs from that of the congregation's majority language or when a minister/preacher from a different
country is visiting. This can be due to the linguistic inability of the leader or
to religious reasons, such as classical Arabic interpreted into dialects (Arabic
is the exclusively acceptable language of the Koran) or Hebrew into Aramaic
(providing community access to Sacred Scripture). It also includes interpreting during paraliturgical acts/ceremonies such as wedding, funerals, healing
services, prayer meetings or blessings. This type of interpreting is usually
conducted in short consecutive but not bilateral mode.

As mentioned in Section 2, the earliest recorded use of liturgical
interpreters was that of the *meturgeman* in the synagogues, according to

Kaufmann (2005), who analysed the rules and anecdotes related to the modalities of consecutive interpretation in public readings of the Hebraic Bible in the synagogue ritual. The *meturgeman*'s predecessors were: the *melits* (the one who speaks well, and 'in favour of') and the *balchane* (a language master and a polyglot). The *meturgeman* was expected to translate without looking at the words, hence that mode was close to the contemporary unilateral short consecutive form.

> As a translator, he [meturgeman] was required to follow accepted practices and a number of specific rules (though our knowledge of these principles from late antiquity is far from complete). For example, the meturgeman was not permitted to translate more than one verse at a time from the Pentateuch and not more than three from the Prophets.... Rabbi Judah ben Illai, a disciple of the influential Rabbi Akiba said, 'If one translates a verse literally, he is a liar, but if he adds to it, he is a blasphemer.... Hence the task of the meturgeman was by no means a simple one; it certainly involved much more than an explanation of the biblical text in the everyday language of the people, though the targumist no doubt had his intended audience in mind as he carried out his work'.
>
> (Young 1939: 729, cited in Harris 2009a)

Kaufmann (2005) indicates that a corpus of ancient rabbinic literature (the two Talmuds and the Midrach) gives an account of the existence of a well-defined professional, the *meturgeman*, the ad hoc or appointed interpreter of a rabbi, master or preacher in a tribunal or synagogue. Regardless of the heterogeneity of this corpus (several thousand pages) and the presence of some mythical elements, the translation historian can acquire a reasonably detailed idea of the way the function and practice of translation evolved over a period of more than a thousand years. Since in the Jewish tradition the *meturgeman* had to be selected and appointed, he can be considered a predecessor of a communal practice that has recently re-emerged and is introduced in areas of the world where incoming immigrants share the religion of the host country but the host country religions do not have linguistically capable leaders to minister to the newcomers.

In the United States in the twenty-first century, the flow of Hispanic immigrants and shortage of priests who are able to preach in Spanish has resulted in bilingual missalettes being provided and the celebration of Mass conducted bilingually, meaning that one reading is done in Spanish and the other in English. In addition, the presiding priest can switch between the two languages at his discretion during the Liturgy of the Eucharist but not for the homily. The priest is usually able to pray in a foreign language after having received some lessons in pronunciation due to the universality of prayers in the Catholic Church even if his knowledge of Spanish is limited. These practices have been introduced in order to accommodate newcomers and avoid splitting churches into monolingual subcommunities, sometimes for reasons of inclusion and communion, and sometimes due to the lack of priests who can offer Mass in the non-societal language. Some feel that bilingual services disturb the liturgical flow in such multilingual situations and it is more proper to have Masses in Latin, but these opinions are few. While bilingual celebration practices can consolidate the faithful of various ethnicities and testify to the universality of the Catholic Church, the explanatory and pedagogical purpose of preaching is eliminated. Several solutions have thus been pursued to deliver homilies in other languages, primarily Spanish:

a   The homily is translated prior to Mass and the English-speaking priest delivers it in Spanish after having received lessons in pronunciation and basic grammar.

b   A Spanish-speaking layperson reads the homily in Spanish, while the non-Spanish speaking priest celebrates the Mass in Spanish. This has been tried at certain parishes but does not meet theological approval.

c   The priest preaches in English and has consecutive interpreting provided, which would be a combination of short and long consecutive. This is the most encouraged mode of delivering the homily into Spanish. Ideally, the interpreter would be a church-approved minister, such as a deacon or a seminarian. Pope Francis used this option in 2015 when he put aside his prepared homily in English and decided to preach spontaneously in Spanish to the victims of the typhoon in Tacloban, the Philippines. His personal interpreter, Msgr. Mark Miles,[9] a priest himself, provided interpretation of the Pope's homily from Spanish into English (see Section 6).

Theologians are still debating which mode and form is most appropriate and at the same time practical. The issue of using a layperson to provide various types of language services during Mass has been addressed at length by Legionary of Christ Father Edward McNamara, professor of liturgy at the Regina Apostolorum University who does not believe that having a layperson read out a translation of a homily is a viable solution as it is likely to leave the impression that the layperson is actually giving the homily itself, a practice which has been repeatedly prohibited. He points out that a misunderstanding that a layperson is actually giving a homily could even be a source of scandal. Fr McNamara states that having the deacon read the text would avoid the problem of confusing ministerial roles but such a solution is still imperfect from the personal communicative point of view. A homily is more than just a text that is read; it is a personal communication in which the ordained minister explains God's word and exhorts the faithful to live in accordance with what they have heard. Hence Fr McNamara suggests that the best solution is always that the priest read his prepared text. Still, taking into consideration various circumstances Fr McNamara discusses other options:

Another, less perfect, but legitimate, solution would be to deliver the homily in English while someone else, either the deacon[10] or a layperson, either simultaneously translates the homily or reads a prepared text afterward.... If an immediate simultaneous translation is not feasible, but it is possible for someone to translate the text of the homily ahead of time, then I believe that the best solution is that the priest preach the homily in English and after each paragraph or principal point some other person read the translation, preferably using a different microphone.

(McNamara 2007)

Another model that seems to be the least intrusive liturgically concerns the Order of Mass being chosen in one language and the presider preaching in one language, while the participants are provided with a pre-translated homily in their own language. A variation of this solution consists of preacher code-switching throughout the homily that he is reading (parts of the homily are in different languages) while the participants follow the pre-translated text; speakers of all languages feel at least partially included in such situation. This solution has proven viable during celebrations in more intimate settings and when the participants speak more than one language other than the one chosen for the liturgy.

The need for interpreting is notable in many regions of Africa, where people of African native and tribal languages, in contrast to the many already Catholic immigrants from Spanish-speaking countries to the USA, often experience their first exposure to the Biblical message during these encounters. A study on consecutive interpreting during Pentecostal services from English into Kamba in Machakos town, Kenya by Odhiambo *et al.* (2013) demonstrates the ineffectiveness of consecutive mode. The article identifies a number of strategies that were unsuccessful and classifies them as reduction strategies, including filtering, skipping, incomplete sentences, message abandonment and approximation. In evaluating the strategies Odhiambo *et al.* conclude that in most cases the interpreters used reduction (unsuccessful) strategies for the sermons. In Musyoka and Karanja's study (2014) on consecutive interpreting from English into Kamba, also in a Pentecostal church in Machakos, Kenya, the following factors negatively impacted the interpreted sermons: problems originating from the input and the source language speaker such as lengthy utterances, use of technical terms, overlapping, elicitation of responses and speed of delivery. All the interpreters were untrained and thus several factors originated also from the interpreter's personal abilities and inabilities, such as educational level, professional qualifications and exposure to the language and religious discourse.

Still, many evangelical churches in Africa use short consecutive mode where the interpreter is of equal importance as the preacher, also called the **co-preacher** (Downie 2014a; Karlik 2010; Musyoka and Karanja 2014;

Odhiambo *et al.* 2013) (see Section 3.3). Here, even more than in other contexts, a liturgical interpreter needs to be highly aware of the profile of his users, not only in regard to the dialects but also to the level of familiarity with biblical language and concepts (see also *biblical interpreting* in Section 3.1).

In conclusion, short consecutive seems to be the preferred mode for the homily during Mass, and preaching in general, while for other prayer gatherings and liturgical activities the simultaneous mode is gaining popularity and the approval of the faithful themselves. Suppliers of simultaneous interpreting equipment have recognized this need and specifically target the religious setting in their advertisements. Enersound's white paper (2014) directed to church leaders in the United States offers 'a solution to the thousands of newcomers that do not speak the language of the sermon, yet want to seek out others who are of the same religion or creed, thanks to language interpretation ... equipment'. It states that by offering the immigrants simultaneous interpreting churches will provide them also with reassurance and comfort and will attract these groups to their religious services. Enersound's text emphasizes the fact that churches usually need to use volunteer interpreters (see Section 5) and that their equipment can easily address these most common arrangements:

> Most churches usually rely on volunteer interpreters from the community if they cannot afford to employ a professional one.... You can start small with a basic system for your existing foreign-speaking parishioners, and upgrade the system by getting additional receivers and headphones as this population grows. You can also increase the number of languages offered by purchasing additional transmitters and microphones, one per language interpreted.... Worship services can now be more fully integrated and accessible to all cultures and languages, helping newcomers to feel welcomed and included.
>
> (Enersound 2014)

 PERFORMANCE SKILLS

Activity 3: Domain-specific assignment preparation

Read the article 'The Joys and Challenges of Interpreting Jewish Prayers: it isn't about signs any more!' by Brunnlehrman (2000) that refers to ASL and Jewish liturgical ceremonies. The article can be accessed at: www2.palomar. edu/users/lmendoza/documents/Religious_Interpreting.pdf.

Highlight the parts with which you agree, the parts that surprise you and those with which you disagree based on your assumptions or experience in religious settings. Identify parts that you find relevant to the religion and language pairs in which you accept assignments. You can discuss this with a partner or use it as an individual exercise.

While not considered part of liturgical interpreting per se, another subtype of faith-related interpreting occurs during spiritual care encounters in hospitals, hospices and other care-giving institutions to the elderly, neglected or abandoned hence it should be mentioned here. It includes blessings, praying over or with the sick, anointment of the sick (in the Catholic Church). It may be considered a hybrid or border type of interpreting as it is situated in the medical setting but the focus of those services is to help the person be opened to receive the graces, edify them or offer spiritual counsel. Similarly, interpreting in paraliturgical or sacramental contexts (with the exclusion of the Sacrament of Reconciliation, i.e. individual confession, in the Catholic Church) can also be categorized under liturgical interpreting.

4.2 Missionary interpreting

Missionary interpreting occurs in the streets, during processions and evangelization events. It can be person-to-person interpreting or person-to-group interpreting. It can occur in a different country or for a different ethnic group in the same country. Since the emphasis is on proclaiming the message rather than establishing communication, it is also usually done in unilateral short consecutive mode unless a dialogue occurs. In most cases, missionary interpreting also requires the mode of escort interpreting since interpreters form part of a mission team and provide services in strictly religious but also social contexts, including food provision, transportation, medical care and contact with the local government.

Missionary interpreting can also happen in rural, remote, jungle or mountainous areas (e.g. Amazon region, Philippine mountains, Siberia) in which an interpreter will have no access to Internet-based terminology resources, and even the glossaries or dictionaries that s/he can carry may be limited. Missionary interpreting can present challenges similar to military interpreting in that **physical stamina** and **psychological preparation** matter significantly. While highly motivated and energized by the spiritual goals of her/his clients and by the possible outcomes of her/his work, especially when sharing the beliefs and objectives of the missionary work, an interpreter needs to even more firmly delineate boundaries in relation to needed sleep/rest, time to properly eat and drink, and time for solitude necessary to recover her/his cognitive abilities. Self-care should focus more on monitoring **the intensity and length of interpreting tasks** rather than being concerned with role confusion, emotional involvement and confidentiality. Many people in charge of Catholic missions have been trained on how to work with interpreters, often because they themselves have worked as interpreters in other situations or in the past. In other, mostly Protestant cases, the interpreter must request time to explain what his/her work involves to the entire mission team (if possible before the trip), agree on daily rules for the schedule, and ask that a team of one or two be created to act as her/his support group, advocate on her/his behalf with the primary users of interpreting services on both sides, and monitor her/his workload when in the field.

Missionary interpreting for different faiths is one of the best documented areas throughout history, particularly in relation to the spread of Christianity. This occurred even long before the Jesuits introduced their concept of acculturation, as can be seen in this document from the eleventh century, *Life of St Otto* (*Life from Prüfening*) cited by Rojszczak-Robińska (2010):

> Already during the time of the rule of the first Piasts, local language was used for catechization. Bolesław Krzywousty in his letter inviting St Otto from Bamberg to come as a missionary to the Pomerania region assures him: 'And also I, thy servant as is a son to the father, will cover all thy expenses and the expenses of thy travel companions and **language interpreters** and assisting priests and anything that may be needed I will provide, if only thou, dearest Father, art willing to come'. *The Life of St Otto* (*Life from Prüfening*) mentions that the bishop knew the Polish language when he undertook his missionary expedition to Pomerania.
>
> (2010: 79, authors' translation and emphasis)

An interesting point is to be noted here; remuneration of the interpreters is obvious and addressed in this excerpt describing missionary interpreters' work in the eleventh century; however, rates and payment arrangements remain a problematic and often ignored issue in the faith-related settings in the twenty-first century (see Section 5).

The Mormon religion is one of the heaviest users of missionaries to preach its beliefs. Categorized by some Christian denominations as a sectarian tradition, Mormons themselves consider themselves Christian. Mormon schools of translators and interpreters prepare well-trained missionaries because the Mormon youth are encouraged to consider an immersion two-year stay in a foreign country once they reach the age of 18.[11]

In non-Christian religions, emphasis on conveying the message during missionary endeavours is less predominant due to beliefs that acculturation means distortion of the sacred message and is actually sinful or even sacrilegious.

> In the case of Jews, Sikhs, and Muslims, religious rites conducted in the hostland language rather than the ethnic one are not considered by many to be 'authentic', because they constitute a departure from the religious norm. For Armenian, Jewish, and Sikh ethnonational identity, both religion and language are crucial; although fewer and fewer practice the religion in the homeland (where territorial-political identity often substitutes for religion), and fewer and fewer learn the language in diaspora, they are of continuing *symbolic* importance.
>
> (Safran 2008: 186, emphasis in the original)

In *Intermediaries, Interpreters, and Clerks: African employees in the making of colonial Africa* Lawrance et al. (2006) state that not only did all colonial administrators rely to some extent on African interpreters but also single European travellers – a missionary or a European military leader – were dependent to some extent on their interpreters. In his article on African employers in colonial Tanzania describing the governing practices of the British government in the 1960s, Eckert states:

> The British had to rely on a growing number of local staff members. Most of these locals were employed in auxiliary services; some of them, however, were put in charge of local affairs in distant places. And some of them, such as ubiquitous government interpreters working with European district officers, were even at the very center of things. Although they had no position of official authority, they had the power to influence things merely by their language skills.
>
> (2006: 249)

Several of those who later worked as civil workers and military liaisons in Africa began their mediation experiences in faith-related settings. Though born in England, Theophilus Shepstone was raised by Wesleyan missionary parents in a series of mission stations in the Xhosa-speaking areas east of the Cape's colonial frontier (McClendon 2006). Such background sometimes led to a mix of religious and political motivations that would move interpreters to undertake intermediary assignments to which the interpreter's personal agenda was frequently added. The early phase of colonial rule, from the era of conquest and the first generation of occupation through the 1920s, was a time when interpreters wielded enormous power. African intermediaries working closely with European colonial officials (or appearing to) could develop or carve out positions of considerable authority (Lawrance et al. 2006).

In the conclusion of *Re-'Interpreting' the Role of the Cultural Broker in the Conquest of La Florida, 1513–1600* (Luca 2000) we read about the multidimensional impact of interpreters' '**fusion actions**' on history, the spread of religions and the successful interactions between civilizations. Luca describes that relying on the interpreters who were abducted, alienated and forced to become informers, interpreters and mediators during the early stages of the conquest of Florida resulted for the most part in disasters. His analysis not only highlights the complexity of tasks that they were charged with but also brings to light the level of **shared power** (co-power) that those so-called 'go-betweens' possessed. He also states that, contrary to the lack of recognition they suffer from in the twenty-first century, during their time 'the central part played by these 'marginalized' men and women in shaping the destinies of not one, but several cultural traditions and histories' was obvious to the users who had no choice but to rely on their services:

The so-called 'central' and leading characters could not help but recognize the power these individuals wielded, and consequently went to great lengths to secure the services, allegiance, and loyalty of these culturally ambiguous individuals. The chronicles, relations, memoirs, and reports from the early contact period abound in references to anonymous 'interpreters' who, if standing in the shadows of more renowned historical figures, literally had the undivided attention of their ears.... The *adelantados, conquistadores*, and colonial promoters had no choice but to recognize that the loyalties, decisions, personal choices, and actions of these pivotal characters more profoundly affected the outcome of the early struggle for the domination of that land than has hitherto been acknowledged.

(Luca 2000)

Karlik's (2010) study on performance analyses the attitudes of participants and interpreters' approaches to their expectations in a group of Gambian churches where biblical discourse was rendered from English into Manjaku. The two most experienced interpreters who filled the role most frequently interpreted in a short consecutive mode during the bilingual Sunday morning services in the town church. Each of them also led regular monolingual midweek Bible study groups where they sight-interpreted the scriptural passage.

In the conclusion to her study, Karlik (2010) states that interpreters interpreted biblical discourse in a highly communicative and persuasive manner, accommodating audience expectations, and that they showed a strong sense of responsibility for conveying source text meanings faithfully. Their audiences expected this of them, though this was not always achieved with the same degree of success. Some suggestions are made for training at the level of fidelity. Following Hill (2007), who observes that the development of adequate key terms has significant benefits for local theology in African communities, Karlik indicates that this is something

which could be carried out with interpreters and mother-tongue preachers, with the help of Bible translation agencies, whether or not a written translation project is in view. In the short term this would greatly benefit the interpreters and the congregations who rely on them, and could also help in preparing a community for a shift in key term translations, which might come with an eventual carefully thought-out written text. Churches could also help their interpreters by including them in whatever training they offer (in whatever accessible language) to preachers, Sunday school teachers and other leaders, such as biblical history and exegesis, chronological Bible 'storying', and SL comprehension.

(Karlik 2010: 182)

Overall, missionary interpreting as described and documented throughout the centuries and as it continues today is a subtype in which the term 'interpreter' takes on a broader sense and linguistic mediation fuses intimately with both spiritual and cultural brokerage. This phenomenon could therefore be called **fusion interpreting**.

 RESEARCH

Activity 4: Fusion interpreting

Identify three to four interpreters in history that served primarily as brokers between communities of different beliefs. Read their biographies (see Recommended Reading) and draw a table in which you assign a percentage of their duties to each of their roles. Discuss this with a partner or colleague. Taking into consideration their historical circumstances, think about how their actions/assignments reflect today's confusion of role boundaries in religious interpreting and how they can be considered intercultural, interethnic or intersocietal mediators in addition to acting as interlinguistic and interreligious brokers.

Examples of figures to explore:

- Constantine Phalkon vel Costantin Gerachi (Thai-Malay-Greek-Italian-English-French-Portuguese);
- Father João Rodrigues 'Tçuzu' (Portuguese-Spanish-Japanese-Chinese);
- Wojciech Bobowski vel Ali Bej Ali Ufki (Polish-Turkish-German-Russian);
- Etienne de Lafond (French-Huron);
- Jan Tzatzoe (English-Dutch-Xhosa-Kaffer);
- Brother Daniel vel Shmei Oswald Rufeisen (Polish-German-Yiddish-Hebrew).

4.3 Pilgrimage interpreting

Pilgrimage interpreting, which is linguistic assistance to those travelling for religious motives, may appear similar to tourist interpreting. It would likely fall then under business interpreting, but it could also be considered as community interpreting. The mode is escort interpreting and while the interpreter happens to be the guide as well, interpreters are usually either members of the pilgrimage group or a linguistic specialist hired in addition to the pilgrimage guide/director.

Jewish heritage religious tours employ interpreters for their visits to the locations of German-Nazi concentration camps in the territory of Poland and sites of their ancestral patrimony such as Hassidic rabbis' tombs in Central-Eastern Europe. The character of these tours is partly ethnic and partly religious. These pilgrimage-type visits to places of tragedies for mourning, catharsis or guarding the collective memory are also called *thanatourism*, grief tourism or dark tourism.

Catholic pilgrimages focus on the Holy Land, the Vatican and Rome. They also include many Marian apparition sites, mainly in France (Lourdes,

La Salette, Paris) and Portugal (Fatima), places of the birth or work of popular saints in Italy (St Francis of Assisi or Padre Pio), Spain (Camino de Santiago) and recently Poland for visits to the Divine Mercy Shrine (a devotion started in the 1930s by Saint Faustina) and, after his canonization, significant places of John Paul II's life in the Cracow archdiocese.

In the Arabic-speaking world pilgrims are considered the third category of public service users who require translation and/or interpreting according to Taibi:

> In addition to migrant workers who have settled in Saudi Arabia either permanently or temporarily, the country receives millions of pilgrims throughout the year (*Umrah*: optional pilgrimage), especially in the last Hegira month (*Hajj*: compulsory pilgrimage). As the pilgrimage sites are concentrated in only two cities, *Makkah* (Mecca) and *Madinah* (Medina), and as the Hajj must be performed at a particular time of year, a temporary multilingual and multicultural community emerges in these Saudi cities every year. Statistics provided by the Ministry of Hajj show that the number of non-Saudi pilgrims was 1,732,924 in 2008 and 1,618,194 in 2009 (Saudi Ministry of Hajj 2009). They come from approximately 190 linguistically and culturally diverse countries.
>
> (2014: 58)

Several publications address religious pilgrimages in various geographical locations. While some researchers make a case for differentiating between pilgrims and tourists, the term 'religious tourism' has become widely accepted and has been studied with renewed interest in the last decade. Still, the importance of the linguistic broker in these contexts has not received adequate attention. In *Tourism, Religion and Pilgrimage in Jerusalem* by Cohen-Hattab and Shoval (2014) a tour manager, called *interpreter* or *dragoman* (see Activity 1 in this chapter), is only mentioned once in reference to groups travelling to Beirut in the nineteenth century, and the duties of the contemporary interpreter are not explored.

> These visitors were often helped by the local population, who translated the country's language for them, led them on its unfamiliar streets, and at times even provided armed protection from bandits on the roads. A new status quickly emerged: the 'tour manager', who took upon himself the provision of riding and pack animals; guaranteed lodgings, food, and a security escort; planned and executed tours; and explained throughout the journey. These people were called 'dragomans' in the European languages.
>
> (Cohen-Hattab and Shoval 2014: 35)

Recently Katic *et al.* (2014) in *Pilgrimage and Sacred Places in Southeast Europe: history, religious tourism and contemporary trends* and Maddrell *et al.* (2014) in *Christian Pilgrimage, Landscape and Heritage: journeying to the sacred* have provided a thorough overview of contemporary trends in Christian religious tourism in Europe. These two volumes focus on new or revived trends in the European religious pilgrimage movement in the last decades as related to commerce, the economy, landscape and heritage, but include no references to language brokerage in these situations. Even Delakorda Kawashima (2014), who discusses the role of a guide in Medjugorje, does not address her/his possible responsibilities as an interpreter.

In the twenty-first century one of the largest pilgrimage destinations in the world is Jasna Góra, a Marian Shrine in Częstochowa (Poland). Statistics provided by the Pauline fathers, the custodians of the Shrine, indicate that 3,600,000 pilgrims visited Jasna Góra in 2014 and that language brokering services in ten languages were provided in an **escort** mode by the guides to 94,978 persons from 78 countries with the five largest groups coming from Germany (26,457 people), Italy (17,314), USA (9,397), Spain (9,193) and France (7,011). Other pilgrim groups served by escort interpreters came from Portugal, Japan, Austria, Brazil, Hungary and Transylvania, Great Britain and Belarus.[12]

Based on the scarce information provided on the websites of the pilgrimage sites, escort interpreting seems to be the most frequent mode used at shrines or places of worship and devotional practices. However, for many of the liturgical activities, seminars and prayer meetings organized at several pre-eminent Catholic sites of pilgrimage, simultaneous interpreting with proper equipment has also been provided since the 1990s, e.g. Lourdes or Ars-sur-Formans (France).

Another of the major pilgrimage destinations in the twenty-first century, Medjugorje,[13] a Virgin Mary apparition site since 1981 in Bosnia-Herzegovina, offers services for simultaneous interpreting in eight languages – Spanish, English, French, Arabic, Croatian, Polish, Italian and German. For example, simultaneous interpreting in Polish, onsite and for streamed prayer meetings, has been offered continuously since March 2013. The Information Center for Medjugorje *Mir* states that a large number of Polish people from Poland and those living in other countries are benefiting from that service.

4.4 Interpreting for formation

Interpreting for formation, most common in the Catholic Church, refers to interpreting used in congresses, meetings and other religion-related gatherings such as international meetings for missionaries and ongoing formation for religious congregations. **Formation** is understood as a process of educating the whole person by means of the harmonious fusion of spiritual, doctrinal and practical elements and can include catechesis, priestly or religious preparation (initial and continuous) or charism-specific training for various communities of life.

For example:

> Franciscan formation is based upon a personal encounter with the Lord
> and begins with the call of God and the individual's decision to walk
> with Saint Francis in the footsteps of the poor and crucified Christ as His
> disciple under the action of the Holy Spirit. Franciscan formation is a
> continuous process of growth and conversion involving the whole of a
> person's life, called to develop his own particular human, Christian and
> Franciscan dimensions, radically living the Holy Gospel, in the spirit of
> prayer and devotion, in fraternity and minority.[14]

The mode used in this subtype is largely simultaneous, hence it will only be
signalled here since it would fall more under the category of conference
rather than dialogue interpreting. Simultaneous interpreting is more frequently provided during the Chapters of religious congregations in the
Catholic Church as well as during theological symposia and youth-oriented
events such as the already mentioned World Youth Day. Short consecutive,
escort or *chouchotage* are mostly used during formal or informal visits of
the superiors, small group discussions, task force meetings or evangelization
events.

As mentioned earlier, during the General Chapters of Catholic religious
orders Latin was the official language throughout history. Fr Sergiusz
Bałdyga, Vice-General Secretary for Formation and Studies and Vice-
Secretary of General Chapter 2015 of the Franciscan Order (Ordo Fratrum
Minorum)[15] indicates that since the introduction of simultaneous interpreting at the official gatherings in the late 1980s the dynamics of the interaction
have changed and both positive and negative effects of those linguistic
changes have been observed. The following languages are usually covered:
Italian, English, Spanish, French, German, Polish and Portuguese, in their
respective pairs. For example, the Franciscans used English, Italian and
Spanish as the official languages of their General Chapter 2015 and provided
simultaneous interpreting in these language pairs. Acceptance of three languages as official languages opens needs not only for more trained or semi-
trained simultaneous interpreters but also for consecutive and escort
interpreters. Managing teams of translators and interpreters, translations of
final documents into three official languages and the use of *verbalistas*[16] in
each of the official languages present additional challenges because it requires
a more multifaceted approach to the organization of interlingual communication within the Order during such crucial events. On the other hand, discussions are more inclusive and lively as interpreting allows interventions
from the members of the Chapter in their own language in a more precise
and elaborate way, when in the past only those who were fluent in Latin
would express their opinions or ask questions publicly. Working through
interpreters and with translators assures a broader and more thorough access
to the materials of the Chapter for all the members of the Order, but limited

direct interaction may affect fraternal relations and building of the community. All of the above discussed aspects are particularly important for orders and congregations who have provinces in various geonational contexts (e.g. see the Franciscans' website for a list of their provinces in all continents).[17]

An example of interpreting provided in the African context is the First Congress on the Divine Mercy in the Great Lakes Region organized by the Pallottine Fathers, that featured lectures by cardinals, bishops and priests both visiting from France and Poland as well as local representatives from Rwanda, Burundi and Uganda:

> Presentations were in English, French, Kinyarwanda and interpreted into other languages, including Swahili with the use of simultaneous equipment. Participants chose the language in which they wanted to listen to the presentations.[18]
>
> (Authors' translation)

The Conclave in the Catholic Church should be treated separately as it is a gathering of a particular nature. No one actually knows what language is spoken during the election proceedings because the cardinals meet in secret. The cardinals meet for two votes in the morning and then two more in the afternoon, with a break for lunch. They do have some contact with service staff at the special dormitory in which they stay throughout the conclave, but staff members are not permitted to speak to them. The official language of the Catholic Church is still Latin but the use of that language has been in decline ever since the Second Vatican Council of the early 1960s. There were communication problems among the cardinals even during that council. Cardinal Richard Cushing of Boston argued that he and others were being left out of the Latin proceedings, which, he said, were 'all Greek to me'. At his request, a simultaneous interpreting system was put in place.[19]

5 Professionals, trained volunteers, self-prepared: who interprets best in religious settings?

The need for faith-related interpreting services is beginning to rise and discussions on the status of those interpreting in congregations are becoming more frequent as well. Harris summarizes some opinions on ASL religious interpreters in the United States:

> Some churches do pay their interpreters, and some of the interpreters are professionals. In other churches, though there are professionals who might claim a fee, they donate their services. Some of their peers are against such donations: 'The profession of interpreting will never be recognized as a truly skilled profession if people offer their services for free'.
>
> (Harris 2009b)

It is fitting to emphasize that faith-related interpreting is not always pro bono work as commonly understood, and that voluntary work should be considered separately from a ministerial call to serve. Those interpreters who work as volunteers are provided room and board; transportation costs are also covered. In some cases interpreters are offered remuneration that may or may not be at the same level as regular interpreting rates in community settings.

In the Catholic Church trained volunteer interpreters working in social care (see Chapter 6) are used widely to provide services to immigrants and refugees regardless of their religion. For example in the US, they accompany clients to interpret during immigration interviews with US Citizenship and Immigration Services for naturalization; during social service-related appointments (i.e. enrolling in school or meetings with teachers, individual and family counselling appointments, health-related appointments or apply-ing for benefits such as social security and drivers licences); and assisting and interpreting during employment-related appointments. Catholic Charities (Caritas International) use interpreters, and many of their diocesan branches provide interpreter training for volunteers.[20]

Harris (2009d) provides another example of using trained or even self-trained volunteers in church interpreting. He describes his experience of giving a workshop on simultaneous interpreting to the Worldwide Church of God (now called Grace Communion International). The church already had non-professional interpreters working for their congregation who were 'bilingual members of the congregation itself who had volunteered for the task and then were, so to speak, "thrown in at the deep end"'. Harris' initial scepticism about the quality of interpreting seemed unfounded because of the models and mentors the bilingual members of the congregation had access to and due to their background knowledge of biblical phraseology and terminology. However, the level if competence and expertise are open to question.

Also, during the Taizé meetings mentioned in Section 1 volunteer inter-preters are often language students, linguistics or philology students, or stu-dents of translation and interpreting. They are either self-trained or they mutually prepare and support each other. These individuals could be con-sidered professionals in the pre-stages of their professional careers or as understood by some, because of the prefix *semi*, professionals-in-training. There are several definitions of semi-professional interpreting in the industry and in the literature which place emphasis on different aspects; some refer to the stage-trained nature of the practitioner, others to the working conditions, especially the low wages. The term **semi-professional interpreter** proposed in this guide intends to describe the semi-trained nature of the practitioner (see also Chapter 5, Section 3) and is suggested as more suitable for *non-professional interpreters*.

According to Fr Bałdyga, Vice-General Secretary for Formation and Studies of the Franciscan Order, OFM, a similar model that could be classified as a semi-professional interpreter concept can be found in several religious orders, for example the Franciscans. For their official gatherings, i.e. formative meetings, bilingual individuals are selected and tested. In most situations, bilingual or multilingual friars are identified and nominated by their co-friars from a particular language province and approved by their superiors to serve as interpreters in the General Curia in Rome, Italy. Having been tested either as simultaneous, consecutive or escort interpreters at regular but less important events organized by the General Curia, they are therefore selected, or not, for the Chapters and other more formal Order gatherings. They receive training from their more experienced peer interpreters during the pre-sessions where use of equipment and general strategies of interpreting are presented. Also in place are a regular feedback system and an ongoing education of users, e.g. guidelines for speakers on how to work with interpreters are provided by the moderators. Other models used by various congregations, for example the Sisters of the Sorrowful Mother, include employing on a regular basis professional interpreters who have been educated about charism, spirituality and the mission of a particular congregation. Fr Bałdyga also states that the most qualified and experienced internal interpreters are shared among congregations as they are already well versed in theological and biblical concepts and terminology.[21]

Hokkanen (2012) provides an interesting and thorough comparative analysis of volunteering versus service, and non-professional versus professional interpreting in relation to church interpreters. She supports the need to coin a separate term to describe the concept of non-trained and non-professional but well-prepared interpreters working in churches (possibly **semi-professional interpreters**), and argues that 'interpreting is understood within the church itself as **serving** rather than volunteering' (2012: 299, emphasis in original). She also explores the idea of ministry as an activity that is not only established, long-term and organized but also 'stems from the heart of that servant'. As opposed to volunteering, it is rooted in God's love and the love of God and His commandment to love one another, and not in a type of altruism without God that is tainted by some hope of personal gain. As an illustration, she provides the image of Christ washing the feet of the Apostles at the Last Supper. This confirms an earlier point (see Section 3.4) that those in the congregations equipped with some language talent and feeling that they are being called or prompted to serve as intermediaries are enouraged to search for a certain commission to the **ministry of interpreting**, or even an anointment.

Along the same lines, Downie (2014a) advocates for a mutually beneficial relationship between the so-called non-professional church interpreters and professional interpreters that could expand horizons of professional language brokers in terms of involvement, self-monitoring and co-construction of the event. This is also a promising area for future research projects on faith-related interpreting.

Perhaps this is a case where the *professionals* can learn from the *naturals*. In church interpreting, there is no way to pretend that interpreting can or should make itself invisible. There is an admission by everyone involved that a church service with interpreting is completely different to one without it. Rather than trying to erase this difference, many churches seem to want to celebrate it and use interpreting to the full. I have personally visited a church where interpreting is given pride of place in the constitution and is seen as a core activity.

(Downie 2014b)

Central to the debate on the religious interpreter's preparation appears to be a question of who would have the most appropriate profile to interpret successfully in religious contexts, which parallels the ongoing debate over who translates sacred texts best: the scholar or the devout. Whether a member of the congregation/community of that particular religion who is partially trained in interpreting strategies provides a better quality service than a language brokerage specialist of a different creed is a matter to be explored further. Is it only affinity with the faith, or is there a rhetoric to biblical speech one can learn, strategies to pace the speaker so the rhythms are not broken and other determining variables that are situated beyond the obvious terminological and conceptual issues? Fr Bałdyga states that in his experience professional or semi-trained interpreters can become quite quickly well versed in theological and Order-specific concepts and phraseology, as this depends on their motivation, commitment and open-mindness, thus being able to provide better interpreting services in faith-related settings. By contrast, those who are less fluent in their working languages, whether they be members of the Order or people familiar with theological concepts and even Order-specific spirituality, tend to perform less satisfactorily as religious interpreters. Hence, in terms of selection criteria for interpreters, Fr Bałdyga ranks core and developmental competencies higher than domain-specific ones (see Introduction, Section 3), emphasizing in particular competencies such as awareness of sources of bias and limits of competence, attention to personal care and responding to pressure and change. Developing domain-specific competencies, according to Fr Bałdyga, can be addressed, for example, during setting-specific pre-session training.

In addition to the complex question of who is better prepared to interpret, a less-prepared member of the congregation or a lay language professional, the issue of remuneration remains one of the most problematic and sensitive topics in religious settings. Even though high quality of interpreting and a high level of commitment are expected in faith-related interpreting, perceptions of the interpreter's job as a response to God's call, service, volunteering, etc., as discussed in earlier sections of this chapter, affect the appropriate treatment and appreciation of interpreters at different levels. Church leaders tend to undermine or disregard the need to properly reward interpreters' work. Several congregations and religious orders offer room and board, and even a small stipend to the members of their congregations that work as interpreters but other than that it is rarely appreciated and remunerated properly. One of the approaches worth mentioning is a model followed by the Congregation of Missionaries of the Precious Blood of Our Lord Jesus Christ (CPPS) which, when hiring interpreters, mostly semi-professional interpreters, either lay or from other religious congregations, offers them financial compensation. Rates are slightly lower than those accepted by professionally educated interpreting practitioners but still constitute fair pay for language brokerage services performed.

6 Case study: Pope Francis' homily at the Holy Mass in Tacloban, Philippines[22]

The interpretation of Pope Francis' homily in January of 2015 in the Philippines presents several aspects that are typical of religious interpreting. It is a case of liturgical interpreting provided at the highest church level: interpretation of a homily delivered by the Holy Father and interpreted by his personal interpreter who works for the Holy See.

Two previous Roman Catholic pontiffs of the twenty-first century were plurilingual. John Paul II, who was proficient in seven languages and had a passive knowledge of several others, delivered homilies in the language of the faithful of the country he would visit or who attended religious celebrations in Rome. Benedict XVI also was fluent in five languages, and for other languages he had his speeches transliterated phonetically so that he could address the faithful in their native language as well.

The pontificate of Francis offers researchers a unique opportunity to study interlingual communication in the setting of faith-related interpreting, both in regard to interpreting (when Spanish is a source language) and code-switching between various Romance languages. Francis is fully proficient in Spanish and Italian and while he has a passive knowledge of German, French, English and basic Portuguese (as well as Latin and Greek). For languages other than Italian and Spanish he sometimes chooses to use interpreters or has a person who is proficient in a particular language read his message that had been previously translated into that language. He also often opts to express himself in Spanish when he knows he can be understood, as for example, when reading the homily during the World Youth Day in Rio de Janeiro, he delivered his homily in Portuguese but he switched several times to his native Spanish when adding improvised comments, feeling more comfortable with speaking spontaneously in Spanish and knowing that the Brazilian audience would understand him. His spontaneous utterances in Spanish require the intervention of an interpreter who may be informed about the Pope's intention only a few moments before the celebration begins, as occurred in the Philippines, a case study analysed in the following pages.

Tacloban is a city in the Visayas where the typhoon Haiyan (Yolanda) caused catastrophic destruction in 2012. According to UN officials, about

11 million people were affected: over 6,300 people died, nearly 2,900 were injured and 1,061 were left missing.[23] The interpreted homily that the Holy Father gave at the Mass celebrated with over 80,000 faithful at that city's airport in February of 2015 is not only a classical example of the liturgical subtype but also contains several characteristics of the other three faith-related interpreting subtypes as discussed in Section 4. The aspects that are relevant to religious interpreting in the interpreted encounter that took place during the Mass that Pope Francis celebrated in Tacloban are:

a   location: the outdoors and its element – wind, rain;
b   mode: short consecutive, unilateral, one-to-many;
c   physical proximity: distant stage similar to conference interpreting set-tings rather than community; use of microphone and sound system to deliver the speech to a large gathering;
d   scriptural references and theological content;
e   spiritual guidance and counsel;
f   highly personal aspect: emotions, trauma, crisis;
g   interpretation into the major societal language which is English, while the languages of that region are mostly the Visayas languages: Hili-gaynon (or Ilonggo), Cebuano, Waray, Aklanon; Tagalog is rarely used in that region; the religious ceremonies are primarily held in English throughout the entire country of the Philippines.

The following excerpts were selected to illustrate strategies applied by the Pope's interpreter – omissions, additions, expansions, reductions, para-phrasing, equivalence, terminological choice:

•   appropriate/good – that did not affect the meaning;
•   those that were not as good but acceptable – without affecting the meaning too severely;
•   those, very few instances, where the meaning was changed and affected.

Possible explanations for the interpreter's choices are also provided, when justifiable, in order to encourage reflection.
     Legend for the analysis:

POPE FRANCIS: SL speech
     Translation into English in italics (provided only when the meaning was affected)
INTERPRETER: TL speech
                 Analysis: Parts of the speech in both SL and TL that differ and are analysed have been underlined.

The analysis of the entire homily can be found on the Routledge Translation Studies Portal.

The Pope begins with an introductory remark in English where he tells the assembly that he would like to put aside his prepared homily and asks the faithful for permission to switch into Spanish and use Msgr Miles as his consecutive interpreter, whom he calls 'translator'.

POPE FRANCIS: If you allow me ... I prefer ... today ... speak in Spanish. I have a translator, a good translator. May ... I do that? (applause) May I? Thank you very much.

Then the interpretation of the homily begins.

POPE FRANCIS: En la primera lectura ... escuchamos ... que se dice ... que tenemos un gran sacerdote ... que es ... capaz de ... (Pope does not read the scripture in Spanish)
    In the first Reading ... we hear ... that it is said ... that we have a high priest who is capable.
INTERPRETER: We have, we have, we have a high priest who is capable of sympathizing with our weaknesses. But one who is similarly been tested in every way, yet without sin.
    Omission of the first part of the sentence: In the first Reading ... we hear ... that it is said
    Part starting with: ... sympathizing with ... is read directly from the Scripture in English
POPE FRANCIS: Jesús es como nosotros.
INTERPRETER: Jesus is like us....
POPE FRANCIS: Pero para ser más igual a nosotros
INTERPRETER: But to be more like us
POPE FRANCIS: se vistió, asumió nuestros pecados.
    He took upon himself, he assumed our sins.
INTERPRETER: He assumed our condition and our sin.
    Paraphrasing: our condition instead of took on himself – acceptable; for clarification.
POPE FRANCIS: Y Jesús ... va delante nosotros siempre,
INTERPRETER: And Jesus always goes before us.
POPE FRANCIS: y cuando nosotros pasamos por alguna cruz,
    and when we pass by a cross
INTERPRETER: and when we pass and experience a cross,
    Expansion: Good strategy; for clarification
POPE FRANCIS: Él ya pasó primero.
INTERPRETER: He passed there before us,
POPE FRANCIS: es porque tenemos la seguridad ... de que no nos vamos a frustrar en la fe
    it is because we have the certainty that we will not feel frustrated in our faith

INTERPRETER: it is because we have the security of knowing that we're not going to weaken in our faith

    Meaning change: slight hence acceptable

POPE FRANCIS: porque Jesús pasó primero.

    because Jesus passed there first.

INTERPRETER: because Jesus has been there before us.

    Equivalence: good strategy

POPE FRANCIS: En su Pasión él asumió todos nuestros dolores

INTERPRETER: In His Passion he assumed all our pain

POPE FRANCIS: y cuando – permítanme esta confidencia

    and when – permit me this confidence

INTERPRETER: I'd like to tell you something close to my heart (…)

    Paraphrasing: good strategy …

POPE FRANCIS: Estoy para decirles … que Jesús es el Señor.

INTERPRETER: I've come to tell you that Jesus is Lord….

POPE FRANCIS: que Jesús no defrauda.

INTERPRETER: and He never lets us down. (applause)

    Addition: <u>never</u> – for emphasis

POPE FRANCIS: Padre, me puede decir uno de ustedes,

    Father, one of you might say to me,

INTERPRETER: Father, you might say to me

    Reduction: <u>one of you might say</u> changed into <u>you might say</u> – acceptable

POPE FRANCIS: a mi me defraudó … porque perdí mi casa, perdí mi familia, perdí lo que tenía, [INTERPRETER: I was…] estoy enfermo.

    Jesus let me down … because I lost my house, I lost my family, I lost what I had, I am sick.

INTERPRETER: I was let down because I've lost so many things, my house, my livelihood, I have illness.

    Addition: <u>so many things</u> – acceptable as the introduction of the list coming next

    Terminology choice: <u>family</u> into <u>livelihood</u> – incorrect (…)

POPE FRANCIS: Pero lo miro ahí clavado

    But I look at him nailed there

INTERPRETER: But Jesus there … nailed to the cross

    Reduction: acceptable

POPE FRANCIS: y desde ahí no nos defrauda.

INTERPRETER: and from there, He does not let us down. (applause) …

POPE FRANCIS: Tantos de ustedes … han perdido parte de la familia.

INTERPRETER: Some of you have lost part of your families.

    Paraphrasing: <u>so many of you</u> changed into <u>some of you</u>; acceptable but the meaning has been affected

POPE FRANCIS: Los acompaño … con mi corazón en silencio.

INTERPRETER: And I walk with you all with my silent heart (…)

POPE FRANCIS: y él nos comprende porque pasó por todas las pruebas [INTERPRETER: He understands us] que nos sobrevienen a nosotros.

> *...that we experience...*

INTERPRETER: He understands us because He underwent all the trials that we, that you have experienced.

> Expansion and modulation (tense change): <u>that we, that you have experienced</u> instead of <u>... that we experience ...</u> acceptable; for emphasis

POPE FRANCIS: Y junto a él en la cruz estaba la madre.

> *And beside Him on the cross was His mother.*

INTERPRETER: And beside the cross, was his mother.

> Reduction: acceptable

POPE FRANCIS: Nosotros somos como ese chico que está ahí abajo,

INTERPRETER: We are like this little child ... just there,

POPE FRANCIS: que en los momentos ... de dolor, de pena; en los momentos que no entendemos nada, en los momentos que queremos rebelarnos,

> *In the moments of pain, of sorrow; in the moments that we do not understand anything, in the moments that we want to rebel,*

INTERPRETER: In the moments where we have so much pain, where we no longer understand anything,

> Reduction: one synonym <u>of sorrow</u> – good strategy
> Omission: <u>in the moments we want to rebel</u> – incorrect

POPE FRANCIS: solamente nos viene estirar la mano [INTERPRETER: All...] y agarrarnos de su pollera

> *all we can do is reach out a hand and grab hold of her skirt*

INTERPRETER: all we can do is grab hold of her hand firmly ...

> Omission: the interpreter collapses 'extend our hand and grab her skirt' into 'grab hold of her hand'

POPE FRANCIS: Es quizás la única palabra que puede expresar lo que sentimos en los momentos oscuros: ¡madre!, ¡mamá!.

> *It is perhaps the only word that can express what we feel in the dark momentos 'mother, mum!'*

INTERPRETER: It is perhaps the only word we can say in such difficult times 'mother, mum'.

> Terminology change: <u>dark</u> into <u>such difficult</u> – acceptable

POPE FRANCIS: Hagamos juntos un momento de silencio,

INTERPRETER: Let us together hold a moment of silence,

> Equivalence: good strategy

POPE FRANCIS: miremos al Señor,

> *let us look to the Lord,*

INTERPRETER: Let us look to the Christ on the cross,

> Terminology choice: <u>Lord</u> changed into <u>Christ</u> – incorrect
> Addition: <u>on the cross</u> – acceptable

POPE FRANCIS: él puede comprendernos ... porque pasó por todas las cosas.
He can understand us ... because He went through everything.

INTERPRETER: He understands us because He endured everything.

Equivalence: <u>went through</u> changed into <u>endured</u> – acceptable; for emphasis, but a better choice would probably be: 'He passed through all the same things'.

POPE FRANCIS: Y miremos a nuestra Madre,

INTERPRETER: Let us look to our Mother,

POPE FRANCIS: y como el chico que está abajo agarrémonos de la pollera,
and like the little child that is below, let us grab hold of her skirt

INTERPRETER: and like that little child let us grab hold of her mantle,

Terminological choice: 'pollera' is 'skirt'; the Peninsular Spanish differs from the Argentinian Spanish but it is acceptable as the meaning was equivalent

POPE FRANCIS: y con el corazón digámosle 'madre'.
and with your heart, let us say to her 'mother'.

INTERPRETER: and with a true heart say 'mother'.

Expansion: <u>heart</u> changed into <u>true heart</u> – acceptable; meaning reinforced

POPE FRANCIS: No estamos solos ... tenemos una Madre ... tenemos a Jesús [INTERPRETER: Let us...] nuestro hermano mayor.
We are not alone. We have a Mother ... we have in Jesus an older brother.

INTERPRETER: Let us know that we have a Mother Mary and a ... senior brother, a great brother, Jesus.

Omission: <u>We are not alone.</u>

Expansion: <u>Mother</u> particularized into <u>Mother Mary</u>; for cultural reasons

Paraphrasing: mayor is <u>older</u>, and the interpreter's first choice was <u>senior brother</u>, he wondered whether the speaker meant <u>great</u>, hence the addition; probably uncertainty of the intended meaning: ...

POPE FRANCIS: Esto es ... lo único que me sale decirles. Perdónenme si no tengo otras palabras.
This is the only thing that comes to me to say to you. Forgive me if I do not have any other words.

INTERPRETER: This is what comes from my heart and forgive me if I have no other words to express this.

Omission and paraphrasing: '<u>this is the only thing that comes to me</u>' changed into 'that is <u>what comes from my heart</u>' – unnecessary but acceptable; emotional reinforcement

POPE FRANCIS: Pero tengan la seguridad ... de que Jesús no defrauda.
But rest assured that Jesus does not let you down.

INTERPRETER: But please know that Jesus never lets you down.

Paraphrasing: '<u>rest assured</u>' changed into '<u>know</u>' and '<u>please</u>' added; message softened ...

POPE FRANCIS: Y como hermanos caminemos.
                And as brothers, let us walk.
INTERPRETER: And walk together as brothers and sisters in the Lord, forward.
               Expansion: brothers changed into brothers and sisters; for cul-
               tural reasons
               Addition: in the Lord and forward; for emphasis

The following activities focus on the meaning changes and their impact on the users. Was the meaning changed and how much?

 COLLABORATIVE DIMENSIONS

Activity 5: Speaker, interpreter and delivery structure

The interpretation analysed above presents some shortcomings; however, they are minor as far as meaning changes. Please read again the excerpts above and reflect on whether you would recommend any strategy improvements for the following:

A   In a few instances, the interpreter started his delivery too early; however, he did correct himself in most of those situations.
B   Interpreting longer parts of the source speech that would include 10–14 units of meaning instead of 5–7 might seem more efficient. This, however, can also depend on the preference of the speaker and the capacity of working memory of the interpreter. What is your view on the length of interpreted segments in this particular setting?
C   Was the intended purpose of the source speech maintained with this pace and segmentation? Did the interpretation cause the same reaction in the audience that the source speech would as well (e.g. applause)?

 PERFORMANCE SKILLS

Activity 6: False equivalences versus literal translation

A common mistake observed in religious interpreting is when interpreters use interchangeably Lord, Jesus, Christ or Lord, God, Father. It is important to choose the same name (in this case *Señor* should be *Lord*, not *Christ*); only in very few situations it may be better not to choose it. Do you think the interpreter's choice in the extract above was intentional and justifiable or was it just an error? Identify situations when the faith tradition in a particular language uses the other name as an established practice that is allowed in that particular contextual usage.

With regard to this last activity, the seriousness of using the incorrect equivalences for religious titles and names will depend on the subtype of faith-related interpreting. The names of God should be translated very rigorously as each one has very specific theological connotations and the preacher may choose it having that specific attribute in mind. At the other extreme, during pilgrimage interpreting, due to the immediacy and immersion factor of escort interpreting, the opposite can be noted as literal translation of names and titles occur frequently. For example, during the visits to sacred places, the titles of the Virgin Mary are transferred from one ethnic religious tradition to another even within the same denomination; in these cases interpreters often use literal translation while adaptation strategies (equivalence) should be applied. For example in Polish the most common title of the Virgin Mary, especially in reference to her Shrines, is Mother of God and not Our Lady; hence it sounds unfitting to hear, for example, in Polish *Nasza Pani Fatimska* from Portuguese *Nossa Senhora de Fátima* (Our Lady of Fatima) instead of *Matka Boska Fatimska* (Mother of God of Fatima). Similar incorrect renderings will, however, have a less significant negative effect on the target message during pilgrimages than in liturgical or missionary interpreting, as the receivers of the interpretation in those contexts will make adjustments without major distortion to the source message.

 PERFORMANCE SKILLS

Activity 7: Discourse preparation

Look up the most recent speech on the Internet by the Pope from his Wednesday audiences in St Peter's Square. Gloss it and prepare it as if you were to interpret it consecutively to your local congregation or a group of friends who are non-believers. Pay particular attention to scriptural, theological and cultural references.

7 Conclusion

Religious or faith-related interpreting is characterized by a wide variety of modes and contexts, ranging from escort, short consecutive and simultaneous, and from field interpreting, to conference interpreting, to media interpreting. Similarly, hired professional interpreters or partially trained interpreters who have background knowledge in theology, liturgy, beliefs and practices of a particular denomination but limited training in interpreting strategies and techniques work side by side with natural interpreters or non-professional interpreters. One of the commonly found approaches is an umbrella arrangement in which a professional interpreter or a more experienced non-professional interpreter acts as a chief interpreter and manages a team of volunteers who have received brief training or in many cases only a set of instructions. However, due to the importance of the impact of the message, ad hoc interpreters or unprepared interpreters are rarely used.

Another typical feature is a combination of extracontextual factors that influence the interpreter's involvement and boundaries of responsibilities: small group sharing, solemn official celebrations, family events with lifelong or eternal consequences, social work, travel and mobility, and crisis situations including persecution and religious wars. Flexibility and the ability to maintain emotional distance as a provider of language services are frequently challenged. We propose calling people who perform all these tasks in mixed contexts **fusion interpreters**.

Throughout history we have seen the significant impact of interconfessional mediators on the consequences of contact between civilizations, empires, tribes, ethnicities, nations and countries around the world. In light of new developments in Western countries in Europe and North America and in the Southern hemisphere that bring the need for religious interpreters in various spiritual traditions, one may wonder if a similar power to affect those coming to the receiving countries and searching for better opportunities as well as spiritual meaning is not within the hands of those linguistic brokers, especially in the case of liturgical intermediaries whose task appears similar to that of missionary interpreters in the past. This time, however, it is occurring in their receiving countries, or for interpreters who are second-generation heritage speakers serving newcomers in their homelands rather than in remote foreign lands.

The religious interpreter is thus highly involved, or expected to be highly involved, but at the same time needs to remain adaptable and flexible in her/his role, ready to become a fusion interpreter at any time. Faith-related interpreting can also be described as intrinsically close to a person's identity, worldviews and beliefs that influence her/his involvement in providing this type of interpreting, even if not always entirely shared with the users of interpreting services in a particular spiritual context. The most adequate conclusion, and consequently the recommendation, for this particular setting is a **semi-professional interpreter** approach. This includes maintaining professional integrity in terms of background knowledge and glossary preparation, and meaning rendering that is attentive to possible omissions and additions, but also carries within itself an additional inner motivation to serve the purpose of the communicative encounter that reaches farther than the material world. It is a motivation accompanied and reinforced by awareness that religious interpreting, unlike all other subtypes of interpreting, can have consequences that extend beyond this earthly life.

Notes

1 http://cathstan.org/Content/News/Archdiocese/Article/World-Youth-Day-helps-seminarian-reaffirm-his-vocational-call/2/27/5805. An excerpt from an article by a user of interpreting services during the World Youth Day in Rio de Janeiro, 2014 (accessed 5 May 2015).
2 http://franciszkanska3.pl/Miedzynarodowa-konferencja-o-turystyce-religijnej,a, 21861 (accessed 2 May 2015).

3 King James Version (KJV).

4 New International Version (NIV).

5 New American Bible, Revised Edition (NABRE).

6 Source text in Hebrew.

7 After the disbanding of the Soviet Union, the countries of Eastern Europe and Russia were finally opened to the Word of God. As foreign missionaries hastened to bring the Gospel to multitudes of thirsty hearts, the need for qualified Christian interpreters increased. In 1994 the International Christian Interpreter Association was established by Rev. Jim Harper to help supply trained interpreters to the mission field.

8 http://biblehub.com/commentaries/ezra/7–6.htm (accessed 5 May 2015).

9 A native of Gibraltar, Msgr Mark Miles works in the English Section of the Secretariat of State in the Vatican. He currently serves as the official translator of the Holy See. Reports have it that he is 'an excellent singer', has a degree in music and is a 'keen cyclist'. www.gmanetwork.com/news/popefrancis/story/410396/translator-msgr-mark-miles-helps-bring-pope-s-message-to-the-world (accessed 10 April 2015).

10 Since the deacon may also give the homily, it would probably be better that the pastor entrust him with this task until he acquires a sufficient dominion of the language.

11 www.mormon.org/missionaries (accessed 5 May 2015).

12 www.jasnagora.com/news.php?ID=9071 (accessed 5 May 2015).

13 In 2015 the number of consecrated communions distributed during Masses in Medjugorje exceeded 1,800,000 and the total number of priests who concelebrated the Holy Masses was 37,498. In 2011 the total number of consecrated communions exceeded two million for the first time, and a total of 41,094 priests concelebrated the Holy Masses. www.medjugorje.org/stats.htm (accessed 5 May 2015).

14 *Ratio Formationis Franciscanae*, The Order of Friars Minor, General Secretariat for Formation and Studies, ROME 2003, Introduction # 1 and 2.

15 Interview with Fr Sergiusz Bałdyga, OFM, PhD, Vice-General Secretary for Formation and Studies of the Franciscan Order, on 10 June 2015.

16 *Verbalista* is a transcriptionist taking minutes during the official meetings of religious orders in the Catholic Church.

17 www.ofm.org/ofm/?page_id=408andlang=en (accessed 10 May 2015).

18 www.pallotyni.org/prowincja.wa/prowincje-regie/89-regia-swietej-rodziny-rwanda-kongo-dem/431-rwanda-pierwszy-kongres-o-miosierdziu-boym-w-rejonie-wielkich-jezior.html (accessed 10 May 2015).

19 www.slate.com/articles/news_and_politics/explainer/2005/04/is_the_conclave_held_in_latin.html/ (accessed 5 May 2015).

20 Boston: www.ccab.org/cis; Louisville: http://cclou.org/programs-services/interpreter-translation-services/training-for-interpreters/; New Orleans: www.ccano.org/–uncategorized/volunteer-interpreter-training-opportunity/ (accessed 5 May 2015).

21 Interview with Fr Sergiusz Bałdyga, OFM, PhD, Vice-General Secretary for Formation and Studies of the Franciscan Order, on 10 June 2015.

22 See the video of the homily at www.rappler.com/specials/pope-francis-ph/81106-full-text-pope-francis-homily-tacloban (accessed 20 April 2015).

23 www.gov.ph/crisis-response/updates-typhoon-yolanda/casualties/ (accessed 20 April 2015); Haiyan is also the strongest storm recorded at landfall, and the strongest typhoon ever recorded in terms of one-minute sustained wind speed.

References

Adewuni, S. (2010) 'Evaluation of Interpretation during Congregational Services and Public Religious Retreats in South-west Nigeria', *Babel*, 56 (2): 129–38.

Austin, J.L. (1962) *How to Do Things with Words*, The William James Lectures delivered at Harvard University in 1955, 1962 (eds J.O. Urmson and M. Sbisà), Oxford: Clarendon Press.

Brunnlehrman, N. (2000) 'The Joys and Challenges of Interpreting Jewish Prayers. It isn't about signs any more!', *Views; Registry of Interpreters for the Deaf, Inc.*, 17 (1): 5–6.

Chrobak, M. (2012) *Między światami. Tłumacz ustny oraz komunikacja międzykulturowa w literaturze odkrycia i konkwisty Ameryki*, Kraków: Wydawnictwo Uniwersytetu Jagiellońskiego.

Cohen-Hattab, K. and Shoval, N. (2014) *Tourism, Religion and Pilgrimage in Jerusalem*, Hoboken, NJ: Taylor & Francis.

Delakorda Kawashima, T. (2014) 'Current Trends in Behavious of Visitors to Medjugorje Pilgimage Centre: pilgirms and tourists as metaphors', in M. Katic, T. Klarin and M. McDonald (eds) *Pilgrimage and Sacred Places in Southeast Europe: history, religious tourism and contemporary trends*, Zurich, Berlin: LIT Verlag.

Downie, J. (2014a) 'Toward a Homiletic of Sermon Interpreting', *Journal of the Evengelical Homiletics Society*, 14 (2): 62–9.

Downie, J. (2014b) 'Church Interpreting and The Philosopher's Stone'. Online. Available at: http://unprofessionaltranslation.blogspot.com/2014/06/church-interpreting-and-philosophers.html (accessed 7 May 2015).

Eckert, A. (2006) 'Cultural Commuters: African employees in late colonial Tanzania', in B.N. Lawrance, E.L. Osborn and R.L. Roberts (eds) *Intermediaries, Interpreters, and Clerks: African employees in the making of colonial Africa*, Madison, WI: University of Wisconsin Press.

Enersound (2014) 'Helping Newcomers Break the Language Barrier: the importance of simultaneous translation in houses of worship'. Online. Available at: http://enersound.com/helping-newcomers-break-the-language-barrier-the-importance-of-simultaneous-translation-in-houses-of-worship/.

Giannotsou, M. (2012) 'Church Interpreting in Germany: making a case for a combination of conversation analysis and grounded theory in ethnographic fieldwork'. Second ISA Forum of Sociology 2012. Online. Available at: www.researchgate.net/publication/268093805.

Grindford, R. (1998) 'Interpreting in Religious Settings', *Views; Registry of Interpreters for the Deaf, Inc.*, 15 (3): 12–14.

Harris, B. (2009a) Church Interpreters 1: antiquity. Unprofessional Translation website. Online. Available at: http://unprofessionaltranslation.blogspot.com/2009/07/church-interpreters-1.html (accessed 7 May 2015).

Harris, B. (2009b) Church Interpreters 2: from divine inspiration to professionalisation. Unprofessional Translation website. Online. Available at: http://unprofessional translation.blogspot.com/2009/08/church-interpreting-2-from-divine.html.

Harris, B. (2009c) Church Interpreters 3: West Africa. Unprofessional Translation website. Online. Available at: http://unprofessionaltranslation.blogspot.com/2009/08/church-interpreters-3-africa.html.

Harris, B. (2009d) Church Interpreters 4: simultaneous. Unprofessional Translation website. Online: Available at: http://unprofessionaltranslation.blogspot.com/2009/08/chrch-interpreters-4-simultaneous.html.

Hild, A. (2012) 'Interpreting the Prophetic: loyalty, authority and inspiration', Paper presented at the 1st International Conference on Non-Professional Interpreting and Translation, University of Bologna at Forli.

Hill, H. (2007) 'The Effects of Using Local and Non-Local Terms in Mother-Tongue Scripture', *Missiology: An International Review*, 35 (4): 383–96.

Hokkanen, S. (2012) 'Simultaneous Church Interpreting as Service', *The Translator* Special Issue: Non-professionals Translating and Interpreting: Participatory and Engaged Perspectives, 18 (2): 291–309.

James, R. (1998) 'Me, A Religious Interpreter? No Way!', *Views; Registry of Interpreters for the Deaf, Inc.*, 15 (3): 15–17.

Karlik, J. (2010) 'Interpreter-mediated Scriptures: expectation and performance', *Interpreting: International Journal of Research and Practice in Interpreting*, 12 (2): 160–85.

Katic, M., Klarin, T. and McDonald, M. (eds) (2014) *Pilgrimage and Sacred Places in Southeast Europe: history, religious tourism and contemporary trends*, Zürich, Berlin: LIT Verlag.

Kaufmann, F. (2005) 'Contribution à l'histoire de l'interprétation consécutive: le metourguemane dans les synagogues de l'Antiquité', *Meta*, 50 (3): 972–86.

Lawrance, B.N., Osborn, E.L. and Roberts, R.L. (eds) (2006) *Intermediaries, Interpreters, and Clerks: African employees in the making of colonial Africa*, Madison, WI: University of Wisconsin Press.

Lewis, B. (2004) *From Babel to Dragomans: interpreting the Middle East*, New York: Oxford University Press.

Luca, F.X. (2000) 'Re-"Interpreting" the Role of the Cultural Broker in the Conquest of La Florida, 1513-1600', the Jay I. Kislak Foundation, Miami Lakes, FL. Online. Available at: www.fiu.edu/~history/kislakprize/KISLAKFIXEDFIN.htm (accessed 2 April 2015).

Maddrell, A., della Dora, V., Scafi, A. and Walton, H. (2014) *Christian Pilgrimage, Landscape and Heritage: journeying to the sacred*, Hoboken, NJ: Taylor & Francis.

McClendon, T. (2006) 'Interpretation and Interpolation: Shepstone as native interpreter', in B.N. Lawrance, E.L. Osborn and R.L. Roberts (eds) *Intermediaries, Interpreters, and Clerks: African employees in the making of colonial Africa*, Madison, WI: University of Wisconsin Press.

McNamara, F.E. (2007) Spanish Homilies Read by a Layman. *A ZENIT DAILY DISPATCH*. Online. Available at: www.ewtn.com/library/Liturgy/zlitur187.htm.

Musyoka, E.N. and Karanja, P.N. (2014) 'Problems of Interpreting as a Means of Communication: a study on interpretation of Kamba to English Pentecostal church sermon in Machakos Town, Kenya', *International Journal of Humanities and Social Science*, 4 (5): 196–207.

Odhiambo, K., Musyoka, E.N. and Matu, P.M. (2013) 'The Impact of Consecutive Interpreting on Church Sermons: a study of English to Kamba interpretation in Machakos Town, Kenya', *International Journal of Academic Research in Business and Social Sciences*, 3 (8): 189–204.

Owen, A. (2014) *'One among a Thousand': interpreting in Christian settings*, London: The Wakeman Trust.

Pérez-González, L. and Susam-Saraeva, Ş. (eds) (2012) 'Introduction: Non-professionals Translating and Interpreting: participatory and engaged perspectives', *The*

Translator, Special Issue: Non-professionals Translating and Interpreting: Participatory and Engaged Perspectives, 18 (2): 149–65.

Pöchhacker, F. (2011) 'NT and CI in IS: taxonomies and tensions in interpreting studies', in M.J.B. Mayor and M.A.J. Ivars (eds) *Interpreting Naturally: a tribute to Brian Harris*, Bern: Peter Lang.

Preslar, A. (2014) 'Dispensationalism and Covenant Theology: a Catholic perspective on a debated point'. Online. Available at: www.calledtocommunion.com/2014/06/dispensationalism-and-covenant-theology-a-catholic-perspective-on-a-debated-point/ (accessed 15 April 2015).

Rayman, J. (2007) 'Visions of Equality: translating power in a deaf sermonette', *The Sign Language Translator and Interpreter*, 1 (1): 73–114.

Rojszczak-Robińska, D. (2010) 'Język a Kościół (propozycja rozdziału podręcznika do nauczania treści historycznojęzykowych na studiach I stopnia)', *Kwartalnik Językoznawczy* (2).

Rosenberg, A.S. (1997) *Jewish Liturgy as a Spiritual System*, Northvale, NJ and London: Jason Aronson Inc.

Safran, W. (2008) 'Language, Ethnicity and Religion: a complex and persistent linkage', *Nations and Nationalism*, 14 (1): 171–90.

Taibi, M. (2014) 'Community Interpreting and Translation in the Arab World', *Babel*, 60 (1): 52–69.

Vigouroux, C.B. (2010) 'Double-mouthed Discourse: interpreting, framing, and participant roles', *Journal of Sociolinguistics*, 14 (3): 341–69.

Recommended reading

Cooper, M. (1994) *Rodrigues the Interpreter: an early Jesuit in Japan and China*, New York and Tokyo: Weatherhill.

Federici, F.M. and Tessicini, D. (eds) (2014) *Translators, Interpreters, and Cultural Negotiators: mediating and communicating power from the Middle Ages to the modern era*, New York: Palgrave Macmillan.

Lawrance, B.N., Osborn, E.L. and Roberts, R.L. (eds) (2006) *Intermediaries, Interpreters, and Clerks: African employees in the making of colonial Africa*, Madison, WI: University of Wisconsin Press.

Lewine, R.S. (2010) *A Living Man from Africa: Jan Tzatzoe, Xhosa chief and missionary, and the making of nineteenth-century South Africa*, New Haven, CT: Yale University Press.

Owen, A. (2014) *'One among a Thousand': interpreting in Christian settings*, London: The Wakeman Trust.

Rothman, N.E. (2013) 'Dragomans and "Turkish Literature": the making of a field of inquiry', *Oriente Moderno*, 93: 390–421.

Stephens, H. (2009) *For the Love of Siam: the story of King Narai and Constantine Phaulkon*, Gaberville, CA: Wolfenden Publishing.

Tec, N. (2008) *In the Lion's Den: the life of Oswald Rufeisen*, New York: Oxford University Press.

Yates, L. (2006) *Interpreting at Church: a paradigm for sign language interpreters*, BookSurge Publishing.

Concluding remarks

Dear Interpreter Colleague,

As stated in the introduction, our aim for this guide is to help interpreter practitioners navigate their way through what is rapidly becoming a very expansive discipline of dialogue interpreting by illuminating current practices in what can be termed more traditional domains, as well as providing insight into new areas in which the needs are only beginning to be identified and understood.

Chesterman's (2005) concept of 'emancipatory translation' quoted at the beginning of the guide inspired us to expand the field to a more inclusive discussion on education and professional advancement in dialogue interpreting, that in addition to linguistic and cultural dimensions would also include socioinstitutional contexts specific to each domain in which dialogue interpreting takes place. The idea of emancipatory interpreting therefore foregrounds the importance of norms while recognizing the need for practitioners to make informed judgments founded on advanced, research-based knowledge of domain-specific structures, protocols and language use applied to their own professional experiences. We do not intend to challenge the existing norms or promote the establishment of new ones, but rather call for a greater interest in and reflection on actual methods, standards of practice and perceptions of dialogue interpreters' work. Our guide encourages the idea of applying this approach through enhanced self-critique founded on structured reflection on different performance dimensions in contextualized interpreted events.

The emphasis on co-power, shared responsibility and incremental intervention particularly situates this guide in the emancipatory interpreting paradigm. We have broadened the debate to emerging areas of practice in ways that take account of the myriad issues concerning the practicalities of organizing timely, risk-aware and culturally informed interpreting services on a scale that could not have been imagined a few decades ago. Consequently, we have developed concepts of semiprofessional and fusion interpreting in relation to domains in interpreting studies that have received very little attention to date, namely education and faith. We realize that to some extent these concepts challenge certain discourses about professional interpreting, particularly those that promote professionalization as an all-or-nothing process with little awareness of the realities of organizing linguistic and cultural services in situations where need is acute, less structured or traditionally less recognized.

Aware of both the complexity and the multifaceted nature of interpreted events, and of the growing body of solid research that is rapidly advancing the field of dialogue interpreting studies, we chose to not multiply additional theories and conceptualizations. Instead, we decided to compile, organize and streamline approaches to the organization of linguistic and cultural services that are sensitive to the demographic, institutional and organizational realities of the local context, especially in situations where more conventional interpreting services cannot be promptly engaged.

While we have tried to include the most common settings for public services and communities across various geonational contexts, we realize that dialogue interpreting also covers interpreting in conflict zones, military field interpreting, media interpreting, and sports and tourism interpreting. Educational resources for these and other emerging subtypes of intersocietal and interpersonal mediation will likely appear in the near future, thus complementing this work on dialogue interpreting practice.

Our holistic approach to professional development is supported by a belief in the potential for an increased intraprofessional and interprofessional collaboration. We are not suggesting that these are new ideas; however, we are drawing attention to the lack of available structured guidance on how collaboration can be achieved and attempt to address this need.

We hope that the CPD paradigm and the structure proposed for our activities (research, performance skills and collaborative dimensions) will continue to help you organize your personal search for problem-solving in your current interpreting practice, and also in new interpreting contexts that you intend to explore.

Wishing you all the best in your professional interpreting endeavours,

Rebecca Tipton and Olgierda Furmanek

Appendix 1: Chapter 2

Activity 7: Interviewing techniques in practice

Phases of the PEACE interview model based on available guidance from the College of Policing, UK.

- **Planning and preparation**
  This phase includes setting up the interview, preparing a plan which takes account of the time a suspect has been in custody, the points necessary to prove the potential offence(s) under investigation and any points that may be a defence for committing the offence, exhibits to be introduced, material that suggests the suspect may have committed the offence and a contingency plan for what to do if interviewees are uncooperative. It also includes rapport-building phases.
- **Engagement and explanation**
  This concerns the early phases of the interview during which the interviewing officer will set out the reasons for the interview, the objectives and expectations (e.g. whether notes will be taken).
- **Account**
  This phase concerns the substantive part of the interview in which an account is taken and developed, followed by clarification of facts and possible challenges to the account.
- **Closure**
  This phase concerns the end of the interview, which is planned to prevent it from ending abruptly, and usually involves a summary of points and scope for the interviewee to ask questions. It also usually includes an explanation of what will happen next.
- **Evaluation**
  After the interview, the account is evaluated to see whether any further action is needed and to explore the way(s) in which it fits with the wider investigation. It also includes reflection on the investigation process and the interviewer's performance.

Appendix 2: Chapter 4

Activity 1: Guidelines for providers and patients (Answer Key)

- Speak clearly, and at a reasonable pace and volume.
- Speak directly to the party offering you the service; do not use phrases like 'tell him' or 'ask her'.
- Do not speak for a long period without pausing.
- Avoid discussion with the interpreter that will leave the other party out.
- Do not interrupt the interpreter; allow the interpreter to finish her/his statement.
- Give any written material you have to the interpreter.
- Give the interpreter some background information.
- Be aware of the setting of your meeting and the possibility of disruptive noises.
- Allow extra time for the meeting.
- Inform the interpreter in advance of the use of any audiovisual aids.
- Allow the interpreter to ask open-ended questions to clarify.
- Do not be offended if an interpreter asks you to clarify or restate a part of your statement.
- Do not attempt to bias the interpreter or make the interpreter the mediator.
- Keep in mind that the interpreter is just a facilitator; do not unload your emotions on her/him.

Appendix 3: Chapter 4

Activity 6: Role boundaries: co-workers' perspectives

Job Title: Medical Interpreter
Job Summary:
Adheres to all Medical Center and departmental policies and protocols. Performs job duties assigned in accordance with Standards of Practice and Code of Ethics for medical interpreters. Provides face-to-face, over the phone, and videoconference interpreter services for Hispanic/Latino patients and Medical Center personnel in a wide range of settings. Networks with Medical Center personnel and the local community to best meet their needs for interpreter services. Ensures that all contact with patients, the public, and Medical Center personnel is carried out in a friendly, courteous, helpful, and considerate manner. Conducts interpersonal relationships in a manner designed to project a positive and caring image of the department and Medical Center. Works well with others in the department to promote a harmonious work environment.

Education/Experience:
Two year degree required; BA or BS degree preferred. Demonstrated knowledge of medical terminology and basic human anatomy/physiology. High verbal proficiency in English and Spanish required. Work experience in providing Spanish interpreter services, preferably in a hospital environment.

Skills and Qualifications:
Strong linguistic skills:

- understands variety of regional accents and linguistic styles and registers;
- selects appropriate interpreting mode for each situation (i.e. consecutive, simultaneous or sight translation);
- interprets with highest degree of accuracy and completeness;
- self-corrects, understands own linguistic limitations, seeks clarification and accepts correction;

- picks up cues from encounter participants regarding level of understanding and/or need for clarification;
- strong writing skills.

Strong cultural awareness competencies:

- understands language as an expression of culture, recognizes the underlying assumptions of each party about medicine, the encounter, the illness etc.; uses this understanding to empower patient and provider to understand each other better;
- avoids generalizations and stereotyping by recognizing that cultural patterns are generalized abstractions;
- uses culturally appropriate behavior and is able to choose the appropriate time to clarify or interject respecting the goals of the encounter;
- is aware of own personal values, beliefs and cultural characteristics which may be a source of conflict or discomfort in certain situations, is able to acknowledge these and/or to withdraw from encounters when these may interfere with successful interpretation.

Strong interpreting skills:

- introduces him/herself to patient and provider;
- recognizes the complexity of the clinical encounter and added factor of linguistic barrier;
- adequately manages the flow of communication to preserve accuracy and completeness, and to assess and address potential areas of discomfort for patient (age, gender of interpreter, no previous experience with interpreters);
- encourages direct communication between provider and patient;
- maintains professional distance and integrity;
- remains calm and impartial during conflicts between patient and provider.

Ethical competency:

- understands and abides by Medical Center policies on patient confidentiality, informed consent, non-discrimination and by interpreters' code of ethics.

Interpersonal and customer service skills.
Organizational skills.

Primary Accountabilities:
1   Adheres to the general hospital standards to promote a cooperative work environment by utilizing communication skills, interpersonal relationships and team building.

- Following hospital policies and procedures.
- Following departmental policies and procedures.

- Contributing to the overall quality of services.
- Assuming responsibility for keeping informed about changes in policies and procedures.

2   Provides interpreter services for Hispanic/Latino patients.

- Accurately and thoroughly interpreting a wide range of information for Hispanic/Latino patients and Medical Center personnel.
- Responding to calls in a timely manner.
- Effectively prioritizing requests.
- Efficiently completing assignments.
- Culture brokering between Hispanic/Latino patients and Medical Center personnel.
- Consistently adhering to interpreter-specific protocols.

3   Promotes "caring" image of the Medical Center.

- Smiling, giving appropriate eye contact, respectfully addressing patients.
- Introducing yourself and your role and greeting the patient and provider; asking and anticipating patient, family, and/or staff needs; responding to patients, family, and/or staff queries or request rapidly or identifying someone who can; exiting the encounter courteously.

Job Title: Pediatric Critical Care Navigator
Job Summary:
The Pediatric Critical Care Navigator provides assistance and support to patients and families by facilitating communications with medical/nursing staff regarding patient/family needs. The Navigator utilizes appropriate service referrals addressing patient/family needs.

Education/Experience:
High School graduate or equivalent, Bachelors degree in sociology, psychology, or other human relations discipline preferred, Hospital experience desired, Personal parent experience in Pediatric Critical Care, Bilingual preference for fluency in Spanish.

Skills and Qualifications:
Requires problem solving, decision making and critical thinking. Must be able to work in a self-directed environment, with ability to work with and lead teams. Demonstrates ability to work in fast paced environment with multiple interruptions. Bilingual preference with fluency in Spanish desirable. Expertise in MS Office and ability to efficiently and frequently prepare program reports required.

Primary Accountabilities:

Ensures quality patient care by adhering to the policies of WFBMC, involving patients and their families in identifying their needs, creating a plan to meet those needs, and effectively communicating the plan across the continuum of care. Identifies barriers to efficient and effective management of patient care and seeks strategies to remove them.

Implements outreach efforts to establish and maintain positive working relationships with key community agencies, serves as community liaison and educator in underserved communities.

Collects and maintains up to date and accurate program data and documentation according to program standards. Delivers reports which demonstrates outcomes and performance improvement activities; adheres to established productivity benchmarks.

Demonstrates ability to function in a professional practice model through active participation in shared governance and acceptance of personal responsibility for professional growth. Demonstrates responsibility for personal development by participating in continuing education offerings. Seeks new opportunities for self-improvement. Seeks and applies constructive feedback to improve performance.

Provides age/developmentally appropriate patient care in accordance with Age-Specific guidelines for the specific age groups served.

Appendix 4: Chapter 5

Activity 11: Comparing interpreting and translating competencies for users

Similarities and differences between the ten most important translator and interpreter competences according to Kermis (2008: 42).

Note: Kermis uses *competence* as referred to authors' concept of *competency* (see Glossary).

↓ *Competences*		*Professionals →* *Translators*	*Interpreters*
1	Linguistic Competence	✓	✓
2	Comprehension Competence	✓	✓
3	Production Competence	✓	✓
4	Subject Area Competence	✓	✓
5	Cultural Competence	✓	✓
6	Translational Competence	✓	–
7	Instrumental Competence	✓	–
8	Attitudinal Competence	✓	–
9	Communicative Competence	✓	–
10	Assessment Competence	✓	–
11	General Knowledge	–	✓
12	Memory Skills	–	✓
13	Public Speaking	–	✓
14	Moral Competence	–	✓
15	Stress Tolerance	–	✓

Common competences for translators and interpreters

- Linguistic Competence
- Comprehension Competence
- Production Competence

- Subject Area Competence
- Cultural Competence

Specific competences for translators

- Translational Competence
- Instrumental Competence
- Attitudinal Competence
- Communicative Competence
- Assessment Competence

Specific competences for interpreters

- General Knowledge
- Memory Skills
- Public Speaking
- Moral Competence
- Stress Tolerance

Glossary

Ad hoc interpreting interpreting activity performed in some contexts by untrained interpreters (also known as *natural* and *non-professional interpreting*), and, in others, performed by professional interpreters on an infrequent basis.

Alignment approach to continuing professional development that promotes coherence between the aims and *intended learning outcomes* of an activity, the type of activity and materials used.

Co-construction action by an interpreter that manifests her/his commitment to and interest in the outcome of an interpreted event and contributes to the achievement of outcomes.

Community of Practice network or group of individuals who share an interest in a particular subject or activity and who demonstrate a commitment to maintaining a community through learning with and from others.

Compassion fatigue condition characterized by growing indifference toward the difficulties and/or suffering of others due to over-focusing on the needs (physical/emotional) of others and lack of self-care.

Competence ability of a person to do a job and successfully organize competencies in a performance.

Competency aspect of interpreter practice that is subject to specific learning and quality assessment processes.

Co-participant person that is present during interaction but does not consciously exercise power over it.

Co-power conscious or subconscious force that shapes the outcome of an interpreted event.

Coordination action taken by an interpreter during interaction to support communicative flow and regulate turn taking where appropriate through linguistic and extra-linguistic means.

Country of origin country that is a starting point of a migrant's journey to another country or her/his country of birth.

Cultural humility awareness of cultural difference and a commitment to self-reflection and self-critique in intercultural working especially in the human services.

Domain field of occupational and/or intellectual activity.

Dominant language language characterized by its high social status and political power also known as societal language.

Formation process of educating the whole person by means of the harmonious fusion of spiritual, doctrinal and practical elements; can include catechesis, priestly or religious preparation, or charism-specific training for various communities of life.

Fusion interpreting interpreting activity in situations in which the interpreter adopts a multirole function, e.g. interpreter/tour guide.

Horizontal learning approach in which a learner constructs a relevant body of knowledge based on her/his needs and interests with or without the support of peers/experts.

Host country end destination country for migrants, usually for a limited period; sometimes used interchangeably with *receiving country.*

Intended Learning Outcomes series of statements made in relation to an activity that set out what an individual should be able to do having completed it.

Interaction time actual amount of time needed for an interpreted event.

Interpreter practitioner professional interpreter.

Interpreting event gathering of individuals for which interpreter mediation is required.

Intervention time amount of time taken up by interpreted utterances in an event.

Involvement interpersonal intervention and latitude for action of the interpreter, e.g. negotiation of meaning.

Language services linguistic and cultural services provided to support limited language proficient service users, also known as *language brokerage.*

Lifeworld public and private spheres in which an individual operates in social life.

Mode way in which interpreting is carried out.

Natural interpreting interpreting activity undertaken by untrained bilinguals, also known as *non-professional,* or *ad hoc interpreting.*

Neutrality impartial mindset and attitude enacted by participants in interpreted events in support of the principle of fair communication in institutional and organizational interaction.

Non-dominant language language characterized by its lower social status and power in a given geonational context, sometimes known as a *minority language.*

Non-professional interpreting interpreting activity carried out by individuals who have not undertaken or had the opportunity to undertake a dedicated interpreter education programme but who offer interpreting services on the open market also known as *ad hoc* or *natural interpreting.*

Non-societal language language usually used in the home that differs to the language used by wider society in that geonational context.

Peer interpreting interpreting activity carried out by partially trained or natural interpreters, e.g. student interpreters.

Power   capacity and/or ability of a participant to influence topic choice, interactional parameters, time and outcomes of an event.

Primary/principal interlocutor   main interested party in an interpreted event.

Receiving country   country to which individuals migrate or immigrate, and sometimes used interchangeably with host country.

Reflective practice   approach to professional development through which interpreters review their performance in a structured manner and apply outcomes to the planning and execution of future assignments.

Role-space   multidimensional axes along which interpreter performance in different modes and settings can be articulated and evaluated.

Self-reflexivity   individual's ability to be critically aware of her/his social and cultural position in events, level of cultural sensitivity and the limits of her/his domain-specific knowledge when making decisions during interpreted events.

Semi-professional interpreting   interpreting activity carried out by partially trained bilinguals, usually in domains or geonational contexts with limited professional interpreter services.

Setting   specific location or contextualized type of gathering in a particular domain or subdomain.

Shared responsibility   planned interaction between interpreters and primary service providers to negotiate interactional parameters and achieve intended outcomes.

Societal language   standard variety of a language that is used by the majority of the population in a given geonational context, sometimes also known as the *dominant language*.

Subdomain   subfield of occupational and/or intellectual activity.

Transparency   value-based practice of openly communicated decision making about what is and is not being interpreted during the interpreted event.

Users/Service users   individuals and/or institutions that require interpreter mediation.

Utterance   stretch of speech that may take the form of a full sentence or a partially formulated sentence.

Vertical learning   approach in which knowledge is typically transmitted from teacher to student.

Visibility   physical/virtual presence of an interpreter in an event and/or the interpreter's active articulation of her/his presence in an event through linguistic or extra-linguistic means.

Volunteer interpreting   interpreting activity usually carried out on a pro bono basis by professional/non-professional, trained/untrained interpreters, also known as *civic* or *spontaneous interpreting*.

Working Languages   languages that an interpreter works from and into in dialogue interpreting, and in which s/he has achieved a very high level of proficiency/has native or near-native command; sometimes categorized as A, B, C languages.

Index